CLIMBING THE WORLD'S 14 HIGHEST MOUNTAINS

THE HISTORY OF THE 8,000-METER PEAKS

RICHARD SALE & JOHN CLEARE

THE
MOUNTAINEERS

Published by
The Mountaineers
1001 SW Klickitat Way, Suite 201
Seattle, WA 98134

Library of Congress Cataloging-in-Publication Data
A catalog record for this book is available at the Library of Congress

ISBN 0-89886-727-4 (North America)

Designed by Liz Brown
Colour origination by Saxon Photolitho, Norwich
Printed and bound by The Bath Press

contents

Foreword

As a boy I was a drain on the resources of my local library, reading every book they had or that I could persuade them to find or buy on climbing. There were few books on the European Alps, even fewer on British climbing. Most were on the Himalaya – Kamet, Nanda Devi, Mason's *Abode of Snow*. And there were the accounts of the first ascents of the highest mountains on Earth. But despite my love of the hills and enthusiasm for climbing I was a climber of relatively modest accomplishment. Not good enough for the sponsored teams to the high peaks and, when they became available, not rich enough to join the commercial trips, I could afford only to go to the Himalaya to gaze at the great peaks and dream. When, finally, I did acquire some personal sponsorship for an expedition to an 8,000m peak I had a nightmare trip, illness preventing me from discovering if I had the potential to join the 8,000m club.

There will be some who will question the right of anyone who does not list the ascent on an 8,000m peak in his list of climbing achievements to write a history of the first 50 years of climbing on them. But that is flawed logic which would see books on art written only by artists, those on sport only by players. Books on climbing by climbers can bring an immediacy that cannot be matched by non-practitioners. But they can also bring a subjectivity which can mask much that is worthwhile. I bring, I hope, enough climbing knowledge to understand the climbs and the objectivity of one who is a step back from the real heat. I also bring a love of high hills. I hope that is enough.

Richard Sale

Above Everest from the south, with the south-west face rising from the Western Cwm *Main picture* Gasherbrum I *Far Right* Summit day on Everest's south-east ridge. In the background, to the right of the climber, is Makalu

In 1793, just months after the execution of Louis XVI and with the Reign of Terror about to start, the French Revolutionary Council appointed the scientist Joseph Lagrange, Italian-born but of French ancestry, to head a commission charged with the creation of a new system of weights and measures. The system was destined, as the Council had hoped, to gain world-wide acceptance.

The commission decided that its unit of length should be one ten-millionth of the length of the quadrant from the equator to the north pole which passed through Dunkirk, France's most northerly town, a unit which had been first proposed a century earlier by Gabriel Mouton. As the surveyors of the Great Trigonometric Survey in India during the next century were to discover, measuring the length of a quadrant was not easy.

Having obtained an approximate value the commission abandoned its plan and adopted instead a length (equal to that of the approximate value) defined by two marks scratched on a bar of platinum-iridium alloy held in Paris. This length was called a metre (the French for 'measure', deriving from the Greek metron – measure), a unit which has now received world-wide acceptance in the scientific community and acceptance in many countries, with the notable exceptions of Britain and the USA.

Half a century after the definition of the metre the world's highest mountains were discovered in the Himalaya and Karakoram ranges. Conversion of the imperial measurements of the British survey's heights of these peaks into the metric system showed that of the vast numbers of huge peaks that form the 2,400km (1,500 mile) Himalayan ranges just 14 were more than 8,000m (26,240ft) high. This book concerns itself with those 14.

On the scale of difficulty of climbing on lower peaks – say those of the European Alps where climbing as a sport is usually said to have developed – the easiest routes to the summits of the 8,000ers are at the lower end, certainly no more difficult than routes which were being climbed in the late 19th century

or the early years of the 20th century. The problem of climbing the great peaks was altitude, which fatigued the climber, making clumsiness and errors of judgement more likely and forcing him or her to spend longer on the climb. The longer a climb takes the more vulnerable the climber is to changes in weather, the risk of avalanches and the effects of the cold. At sea level a fit man can climb 300m (1,000ft) up a hillside of reasonable steepness in 30 minutes or so. Most of the 8,000ers rise 3,000–3,500m (10,000–11,500ft) above the base camps used by climbers. Applying the same ascent rule suggests a climb of 5–6 hours. While no one would be foolish enough to suggest that such an ascent time is possible (though the fastest times, on the 'easiest' routes are now making the conversion much less outrageous than it would have seemed even 20 years ago) it is interesting to compare this ascent time with the time allocated for an ascent of Cho Oyu, one of the 'easiest' 8,000ers, on a commercial climb – about 40 days. The difference is the slowing effect of altitude with its attendant need for a series of camps, each of which must be stocked, and the period of acclimatisation of the climbers.

Before climbing began as a sport, humans had climbed above 5,350m (17,500ft) for religious and trade purposes and,

Ed Webster jumarring up the 'Fourth Cauliflower Tower' on Everest's Kangshung Face

Summit day on a commercial expedition to Everest's south-east ridge

general conclusion. As more than one climber has noted, at great altitudes everything can go well – and you can still die. When the actual environment of the climber is considered – probably dehydrated, certainly mildly (at least) malnourished and exhausted – it is no surprise that deaths occur, these factors adding to the effects of anoxia. Newspapers, ever anxious for a sensational headline to boost sales, have referred to heights above 8,000m as the 'Death Zone'. While it is easy, not to say worthwhile, to sneer at such easy copy, the papers have it about right, though it might be argued that it is an error to pick 8,000m rather than 7,500m or 7,000m. The only difference is in the speed of corpse-creation and the scarcity of 8,000m peaks.

probably, for hunting, but there were no permanent settlements above that height. Above 5,350m there is insufficient oxygen in the air (about 50 per cent of that at sea level, though the actual situation for the climber is made worse by the fact that the diffusion process of oxygen from the air into the blood is less efficient when the oxygen partial pressure is reduced) to maintain life indefinitely. By the time a man reaches 6,000m (20,000ft) deterioration of bodily functions has begun. As altitude increases further this deterioration accelerates. Acclimatisation seeks to reduce the effect of the decrease in available oxygen by increasing the number of red blood cells. At sea level the average number of red cells is about 5 million per 1 cc (0.6 cubic in) of blood. Proper acclimatisation to 5,350m might raise this to about 6 million per cc (compared to 7 million per cc plus for a person born and raised at a comparable altitude). Above that height further acclimatisation is not possible: the body's capability, in terms of adjusting to the lack of oxygen, has reached a limit.

At altitudes above 7,000m (23,000ft), and particularly beyond 8,000m (26,247ft), the survival time for a human being reduces dramatically. As always, there is a spread of abilities between individual climbers, but in general, a well-acclimatised climber placed at 8,000m in warm conditions with an adequate supply of food and drink will die in a few days. At the summit of Everest this survival time reduces to a very few days. In 1999 the Sherpa Babu Chire spent almost 24 hours on the summit of Everest without supplementary (ie. bottled) oxygen. Though impressive (if somewhat bizarre), this feat in no way negates the

Since climbing above 8,000m is, therefore, to look death in the face it begs the question of why anyone should want to. Faced with this question many choose to trot out the tired response attributed (probably incorrectly, but that's another story) to George Leigh Mallory who, when asked why he wanted to climb Everest, on which he was killed in 1924, replied 'because it's there'. The phrase has been used so often it has acquired near mythical status, its apparent profundity able to put an end to further discussion. But strip away the quasi-philosophical gloss from this mantra and the phrase is irritatingly banal, the sort of comment you might expect from someone caught vandalising a bus shelter. Mountains are there for everyone, but not everyone chooses to climb them or even cares whether they are climbed or not. The same is true of any human endeavour. To answer the question 'Why?' probably takes more understanding of the human psyche than we will ever possess. Jerzy Kukuczka, the second man to climb all 14 8,000ers, stated – 'There is no answer … to the endless question about the point of expeditions to the Himalayan giants. I never found a need to explain this. I went to the mountains and climbed them. That is all.'

Yet despite the illogicality of the activity (Lionel Terray, one of the finest climbers France has ever produced, entitled his autobiography *Les Conquérants de l'Inutile – Conquistadors of the Useless*) and the dangers – both of high altitude and the objective dangers of climbing in the Himalaya (poor weather, avalanches) there has never been any shortage of those willing to try. These aspirants ensured that the history of 8,000m

Makalu from the First Step on Everest's north-east ridge

climbing was a retracing of that of climbing in the European Alps, but on a much compressed timescale. On the great peaks the era of first ascents took a decade (1950–1960: Shisha Pangma was not climbed until 1964 but there seems little doubt that had it been in Nepal or Pakistan rather than closed Tibet its first ascent would have been much earlier). The face era – in the Himalaya it is the south rather than the north faces which usually command the climber's interest – also took about ten years, but did not start until 1970, in part because of access difficulties to the peaks. By the 1980s climbers were already talking of 'last great problems' and shifting their interest to much steeper faces on lower peaks. The third stage, what had been disparagingly termed 'easy day for a lady' in the Alps, had arrived by the late 1980s (a good case could be made for an even earlier date) with commercial expeditions leading clients to the summits, clients who might have limited, even no, experience.

Many of the climbing elite, and a good few others, decried the advent of commercialism, but it was inevitable for two reasons. The first was economic: the great peaks lie in the territories of China, Nepal and Pakistan, very poor countries by western standards. Given the desire of these countries for hard currency any idea for increasing the number of climbers (and therefore income as each climber pays a peak fee) was bound to be greeted with enthusiasm and encouraged. This situation causes loud lamenting occasionally from individuals and organisations in the wealthier countries. Much of this lamenting smacks of elitism and should be listened to with scepticism: climbing is a sport with a huge potential for egotism, and self-importance and elitism are symbiotic. Some of the lamenting is plainly naïve, an expectation that the great peaks are too noble to be sullied with commercialism, but if Everest was in one of the world's developed countries is there anyone who seriously believes it would not have been exploited in a similar, or even more hard-nosed, way? But there are good reasons why some of the protestations should be listened to with care. A case

Nearing the summit on Makalu

probably more crowded than Everest's summit ridge and on more days in a year – yet no credible voice is raised in complaint (though it is, of course, true that guiding does not – nor ever has by virtue of the relatively small numbers involved in its earliest period – involve the cultural and environmental problems in the European Alps that it does in, say, Nepal).

could be made for maintaining that in the Alps of the 19th century affluent British climbers were exploiting a poorer native population in a way that echoed the imperialism of British foreign policy. Calling this racially based pseudo-slavery would probably be stretching the point, but there are some who would go that far in describing the current western approach to climbing the great peaks. The effect of large numbers of rich Westerners on poor Himalayan and Karakoram communities has been significant, both in terms of cultural upheaval and environmental damage. The government ministers of the countries involved enjoy the dollar-earning potential of expeditions, but are not directly affected by the havoc wrought by them.

The second reason for the inevitability of commercial climbing has to do with climbers themselves. The climbing scene has its own magazines, each crammed with advertisements. None of these offer paid employment to climbers. Although climbing is the profession of some individuals it is not a profession *per se*. Many climbers who wish to do their own climbs on the 8,000m peaks – which can demand large expenditure in both time and equipment – or just want to reach the top of them must become guides, just as they do in the Alps. On a good summer's day in the Alps the Matterhorn's Hörnli Ridge will be crowded with guided climbers –

Within the ranks of those climbers who did not join the commercial expeditions – and there are few who have not taken this option at least occasionally – the competition for the limited available sponsorship has always been high. The era of national sponsorship of expeditions to the great peaks did not last long, though the sponsorship of single nation teams by national corporations continues: indeed, it remains a significant way of raising funds for major projects for certain high-profile climbers. For individuals such sponsorship has always been haphazard, the likelihood of being included in such a team being dependent on factors outside the control of most climbers. And though such expeditions allowed individuals to raise their own profiles, the publicity (and therefore potential for future sponsorship) was diluted if sizeable teams were involved. This was especially the case in climbing as most of the publicity went to the team leader and the climbers who reached the summit. In that sense

Commercial expedition on Gasherbrum I

climbing differed from most other team sports: in large expeditions team success was invested in individuals and it was their names, not that of the team, that won the plaudits. Half the world has heard of Hillary and Tenzing: how many of those people could name two other team members? It is surprising that there were not more problems on large expeditions than there appear to have been, especially as one frequent effect of high altitude is to make people fractious: Frank Smythe noted that happy teams in the Himalaya were 'as much of a miracle as a happy marriage' and that was before the advent of full-time climbers (though it is worth recalling that Smythe had a reputation as a difficult man at the best of times).

Publicity was important, at least for some climbers, because a high media profile guaranteed success in the book lists, on the lecture circuit or with sponsors willing to cover the costs of travel and equipment. There were those who treated the idea with disdain, but played the media

Langtang Himal from Pungpa Ri during an unsuccessful attempt on Shisha Pangma in 1987

game anyway: often those who dismissed the suggestion of sponsorship by an equipment manufacturer could afford to because of their book sales or lecture income. But to sell more books or encourage a larger audience more audacious climbs were required. Out of this arose, in parallel with the growth of commercial expeditions, the 'race' to climb all 14 of the 8,000ers; the record fast ascents; the ascents of several 8,000ers in a season; and the soloing of the peaks, occasionally by new hard routes.

The challenge to complete all 14 peaks is, in many ways, the most interesting of these because it, too, is in part dependent on history. Had the metre been a little longer then there would be fewer peaks above the magic figure and the climbing of all of them would have been a simpler task. Had there been just two, or three, or four many climbers would have climbed them all and in relatively short periods, and the completion may not have raised many eyebrows. Had the metre been a little shorter

Looking west from Shisha Pangma towards the peaks around Manaslu

there would have been more peaks. Had there been 30 or 40 then it is doubtful whether anyone would have felt the need to climb them all (or been able to). Fourteen peaks is almost exactly the right number. To climb them all takes a very special commitment over a long period of time.

Reinhold Messner was the first climber to reach the top of all 14 8,000ers. He claims the idea of climbing them all grew over time rather than being his objective from an early stage and it is certainly the case that his early climbs seemed to be intent on pushing at the borders of the possible on the great peaks rather than peak-bagging: Nanga Parbat's Rupal Face, Gasherbrum I in pure alpine style with Peter Habeler, Everest without bottled oxygen (again with Habeler), Nanga Parbat and then Everest solo. His late rush to complete the climbs even allowed further advances – the Gasherbrum I and II traverse, a new route on Annapurna by a small team – though mostly he climbed the original routes (always, it must be said, without supplementary oxygen and usually in lightweight expeditions). It took Messner 16 years to complete the 14, starting with Nanga Parbat in 1970 and finishing with Lhotse in 1986. A year later Jerzy Kukuczka became the second man to complete the 14. It had taken him eight years and on 12 of the peaks he had completed either a new route or the first winter ascent. The only exceptions were Dhaulagiri (Kukuczka completed the first 'official' winter ascent, but the summit had been reached in winter three years before by a team which had started climbing before the official winter season) and Lhotse, his first 8,000er in 1979. Ironically, during an attempt at a new route on Lhotse in 1989 he was killed just short of the summit. The third to complete the 14 was the Swiss Erhard Loretan, but by then the quest had become a clear competition. Frenchman Benôit Chamoux was on Kangchenjunga, Loretan's 14th peak, at the same time and was also seeking to be the third to complete the set. Many have said that the race between them caused (or, at least, contributed) to Chamoux's death on the mountain. There was a French media team at Kangchenjunga's base ready to relay news of Chamoux's ascent (had he made it) to the world. Chamoux might have followed Loretan to the top, as he would have done had he survived, but he would have been first to broadcast the news: the climbing world would have known the truth, but in today's world the first with the news is the first, inconvenient facts rarely being allowed to get in the way of a good story. By the time the truth had emerged the news would have moved on.

The climbing world would also have questioned the validity of Chamoux's claims as he had not reached the true summit of Shisha Pangma but a slightly lower subsidiary summit. This was a problem that was to resurface later and continues to create correspondence in climbing journals. Fausto De Stefani admitted not reaching the summit of Lhotse when he became the sixth 'all-14' climber, but just how close he came is disputed. Was it just a few metres, as he claimed, or was it 150m (500ft)? How close is close – when is a summit not a summit? As the millennium draws to a close there is a queue forming to be next to complete the set, but question marks hang above many – did they reach Cho Oyu's summit or just the edge of the summit plateau? Broad Peak's top or the fore-summit? Shisha

Shisha Pangma from the Pang La, Tibet

Pangma's top or a subsidiary point on the long summit edge?

To the non-climbing world those allegations may seem trivial, but to a sponsor-led and, therefore, media-concerned (if not obsessed) sport they are vital. The issue is even more stark when solo ascents are considered. Messner provided a panorama of shots on Nanga Parbat's summit and himself plus Chinese tripod on Everest, but later soloists, because of poor visibility, lack of time or lack of media savvy have not. Climbing is no more immune to fraud than other activities involving ambitious human beings and has its share of known deceptions (the claimed first ascent of Denali (McKinley) for instance) and claims which are still debated – Maestri's first climb on Cerro Torre as an example. As a consequence it is perhaps no surprise that some of the more outrageous claims are treated with caution. But occasionally these outrageous

Lhotse (left), the South Col and Everest from Makalu

claims are true. Several Sherpas doubted Habeler and Messner's bottled oxygen-free ascent of Everest, particularly in the time they claimed, and there might have been doubters of Messner's solo climb too without the summit shots. Sometimes the doubts raised are legitimate, but, it seems, some claims are doubted for more than technical reasons – did the Sherpas resent not having made the first bottled gas-free ascent of Everest because it usurped their position of physical pre-eminence in high altitude climbing? Can we be sure that none of the doubts over Tomo Cesen's claimed solo ascent of Lhotse's south face in 1990 were untouched by envy or the problems it raised for future sponsorship, the 'last great problem' having been solved?

By coincidence the fiftieth anniversary of the ascent of Annapurna coincides with the end of the millennium (more or less: remarkably it lies almost exactly half-way between the popular millennial end – 31 December 1999 – and the pedantically correct one – 31 December 2000). In The White Spider, his book on the history of the Eiger's north wall, Heinrich Harrer chose, as an arbitrary endpoint for updating the story, the 50th ascent. He had a point: in the early years of the wall's history it was possible for most climbers to list the names of the ascentionists, they were the famous names of the sport. But then, inevitably, progress means a general increase in standards: the list of ascents grows longer, the rate of ascents increases and the names of the ascentionists become

and most of the names are virtually unknown. There might be arguments about K2, perhaps even about Annapurna, but it could be said with justification that the sun has now come out for all the great peaks.

As the second millennium ends it is reasonable to ask what the third one will bring. It would be easy to fall into the trap of assuming that equipment will not improve, that one-piece down suits, lightweight step-in crampons on plastic boots, ice axes which weigh almost nothing and all the rest is as advanced as it can ever be. They doubtless thought the same on Annapurna in 1950. Equipment will improve, it always does. Personal fitness will too and, because they are climbing on the shoulders of their predecessors, the confidence of climbers will also increase. The supremely fit Messner took 2½ days to solo Everest from the north: it has now been done in a day. Conditions might have been easier, but they cannot explain all of the near 300 per cent improvement. So, ascent times will come down. Many will join of the 'all-14' club. Climbs of several, probably all, of the 14 will be completed in 12 months, in a calendar year, in less than a year. Someone will climb Everest a dozen times, two dozen times. The Everest horseshoe – Nuptse, Lhotse, Everest – will be climbed. Other last great problems will be identified and quickly dispatched.

Climbers will strive. They will succeed. They will die.
And the peaks will be indifferent to it all.
Nothing changes.

less well-known. As Don Whillans, the great British climber said of the rock climbs he and partner Joe Brown had put up, climbs which had such an aura of invincibility that at first few even attempted them – 'everyone will be doing them when the sun comes out'.

The sun came out for the Eiger's north wall. Then it came out for Everest: in 1975 there had been about 50 ascents and the names of the climbers were famous ones. Twenty-five years later there have been 1,200 ascents

Makalu from Base Camp. To the left is the south face, with the south-east ridge to the right of the summit

discovery

Sir George Everest

In Sanskrit, the language of the ancient civilisations of the Indus and the Ganges, the language of the Vedas, the Upanishads and the Bhagavad Gita, the vast mountains which separated the plain of the Ganges from the Tibetan Plateau were the Hima alaya, the abode of snow.

Though obviously known to the earliest nomads and settlers of Tibet and northern India, the Himalaya was unknown to Europe until the expedition of Alexander the Great reached the Hindu Kush. Later, trade between the countries of the eastern Mediterranean and Asia doubtless brought news of the great peaks further east, but the barbarian invasions from the 3rd century AD cut the old silk route and brought trade and communication to a virtual standstill. Not for another 700 years would trade links be re-established. Marco Polo made his

journeys in 1271 and 1295, but only in the 16th century does the Himalaya appear on a map of European provenance, drawn by a Spanish Jesuit who visited Hindustan.

In the mid-18th century both the British and French established trading centres on the east coast of India and sought to expand their spheres of influences over the sub-continent. Though their interests were nominally commercial – the British were represented by the East India Company rather than the Crown, but the difference was technical rather than real – both countries were seeking eastern empires. This led, inevitably, to conflict and the British won a decisive battle at Plassey in 1757. After the battle Britain controlled Bengal, extending its control to the whole eastern coast of India by 1805 and to the entire sub-continent by about 1815.

Although limited trade can be carried out along learned routes, real commerce requires maps. Government also needs maps, particularly as taxation is often based on landholdings. Maps have been in existence since the civilisations of Babylon and Egypt, and regular surveys have probably been carried out over the same period, even if, as with the Domesday Book of post-invasion Norman Britain, they were based on ad hoc measurements of area such as the land which could be ploughed by an ox-team in one day. After the battle of Plassey the commander of the victorious army, Robert Clive, was appointed Governor of the new British holding of Bengal and created Baron Clive of Plassey. One of Clive's first acts was to appoint Capt. James Rennell to survey his governorate. Rennell's survey took him north to the borders of Bhutan. There, within sight of the Himalaya he was stopped by the descendants of the Mongols who still hold that kingdom. Rennell surveyed an area of 3,800km^2 (1,500 sq. miles) and published, in 1783, a Map of Hindoostan, though the representation of the unsurveyed Himalaya was based on early travellers' maps.

Rennell's work was continued by later surveyors, but they headed south towards Madras. Then, in 1800, William Lambton, who had been captured – as an Ensign in the Infantry – at Yorktown in 1781, before serving under Col Arthur Wellesley (later to be the Duke of Wellington) in India, proposed a survey of the whole sub-continent. Lambton called the work the Great Trigonometrical Survey (it was known as the GTS for short) and ordered the construction of a half-ton theodolite almost 1m (3ft) across which was christened the Great Theodolite. Lambton also proposed the measurement of a Great Meridional Arc, a survey of the 78° line of longitude.

Lambton was a man of vision and one whose use of the word 'great' as an adjective implies that he was also perfectly aware of the status of his vision. The GTS would survey a country almost 30 times the size of Britain to the same accuracy as the Ordnance Survey of 1791. The measurement of the Great Meridional Arc would allow a calculation of the extent to which the Earth deviated, if it did at all, from a perfect sphere. The 78° meridian was the longest on accessible land, stretching for 2,500km (over 1,500 miles) from east of Cape Comorin, at India's southern tip, to the Himalaya. Lambton began work in 1802. For his survey he used a network of triangles, a thorough, but slow

technique. In 1818 Lambton took on a new chief assistant, Lt George Everest whose contribution to the work was to be fundamental when he became Superintendent of the GTS in January 1823. At that time Everest succeeded Lambton, who was at work until the end, dying during the working day at the age of 70.

But before considering the work of Everest, it is worth noting that although accepted heights of Himalayan peaks were not available until after the new Superintendent's death, measurements were being made much earlier. Sketch maps showing the routes through the difficult country around the India-Nepal border, and into Nepal, had been made by British army officers from the late 1760s, though it was not until 1804 that Charles Crawford, the commander of the military escort which accompanied the first British Resident to the Nepalese king's court in Kathmandu, suggested that the peaks of the Nepal Himalaya (or the Indian Caucasus as he called them) could be among the highest in the world, perhaps even higher

A survey team during the early surveying of the Himalaya

than the Andes of South America. In 1808 Lt WS Webb set out to explore the upper reaches of the Ganges. On his return journey he could see some of the high peaks noted by Crawford and took sightings of them from survey stations on the plain. Back at his base Webb calculated the height of one particular peak – Dhawala Gira – and was astonished by his results. Crawford's suggestion that these peaks were among the world's highest was much less than the truth – they were the actual highest. In 1809 Webb returned to validate his measurements: there was no doubt, and he published the result, Dhawala Gira (which we would spell Dhaulagiri) was 26,862ft high. This height, 8,190m, is only 23m (75ft) higher than the currently accepted figure of 8,167m, an indication of the accuracy of Webb's survey. But rather than marvelling at this colossal height, the geographers of Europe scoffed at this crazy army man who could not do even the simplest calculations. For them Chimborazo in the Ecuadorean Andes was the world's highest mountain and would officially remain so for many years. One interesting exception to this official line was the publication, in 1842, of an article which gave the comparative heights of the world's tallest peaks. Chimboraco [sic] is listed as 21,464ft, but four peaks in the Himalaya are also given. Dhawala Gira in Thibet [sic] is 26,462ft. The height is curious as it does not agree with Webb's, but is identical with that shown on an engraving of 1817 of unknown provenance. There are also two illustrations published between 1817 and 1842 which show 'Dhawala Gira' but give differing heights. Equally interesting is the fact that measured from the geocentre (the centre of mass of the earth, that is the point about which it rotates) Chimborazo is actually the furthest summit. The earth's rotation causes it to flatten at the poles: Everest is 28° north, while Chimborazo is on the equator (more or less). Despite being 2,600m (8,530ft) lower than Everest it is actually 2,200m (7,220ft) further from the geocentre.

The limited, tentative journeys into Nepal of Crawford and others were the last for over 140 years. By 1814 the East India Company had finally had enough of raids on its trading routes and centres and began the two-year Nepalese War. This ended with a re-defining of Nepal's western border, bringing the Kumaun Himalaya (the mountains around Nanda Devi) into India, but closing the Nepalese borders to foreigners. Surveys to the highest peaks would, for the present, have to be carried out from India.

George Everest was born on 4 July 1790, probably at Gwernvale, a beautiful house (now a hotel, and extended in less splendid style) near Crickhowell, a small town nestling beside the River Usk and below the Black Mountains of southern Wales, where his father, Tristram, was a solicitor.

George was the third child of six of Tristram (who also had an office in Greenwich) and Lucetta Mary, née Smith. In view of the now common pronunciation of the name of the world's highest mountain as Ever-est, it is interesting to note that George would have been appalled. Throughout his life he followed his family's preferred pronunciation of Eve-rest.

George became a Gentleman Cadet at 14 and joined the Royal Military Academy, Woolwich soon after. He left Woolwich in November 1805 and the following year, just seven days after his 16th birthday, he arrived in India having been gazetted as a Lieutenant in the Bengal Artillery. Little is known of his early military career, but he was certainly engaged in survey work by 1811 when he was temporarily stationed on Java. He became Lambton's chief assistant in 1818 and took over as Superintendent of the GTS in 1823. He was made Surveyor General of India in 1830. He retired from both posts in 1843. In 1846 he married 23 year old Emma Wing and fathered six children between 1849 and 1859. George was knighted in 1861 and died on 1 December 1866. He is buried in the churchyard of St Andrew's Church, Hove on England's south coast. Sir George had only two grandchildren, both born to his eldest son: neither had children of their own, the Everest line dying out in 1935.

In his capacity as senior surveyor in India Everest replaced Lambton's system with a gridiron of triangular chains, speeding the work on the meridian, and improved the design of theodolites with a consequent improvement in the precision of the survey. Everest completed the measurement of the Great Meridional Arc in 1841, but had not progressed the survey of the country to the borders of Nepal before his retirement. In the years that followed, the 'North-Eastern Himalaya' and 'North-Western' series of triangulations completed the task. In 1849, during surveys from the Ganges plain around Bihar observations were made of a previously unsurveyed peak in forbidden Nepal. On a numbering system that started to the east of Darjeeling, with Kangchenjunga's southern and main summits being Peaks VIII and IX, and Makalu Peak XIII, this newly surveyed mountain was Peak XV. The computations of the height of the peak were begun in 1852, but not until 1856 did Andrew Waugh, who had succeeded Everest as Surveyor General, feel justified in publishing the calculated height and the fact that Peak XV was probably the highest mountain in the world.

It is usually said that not until 1865, after an exhaustive search for a local name for Peak XV, was it given the name Everest, but in fact the name was in use from the first time the peak's height and probable status were published. In March 1856 Andrew Waugh wrote to Maj Thuillier, the Deputy

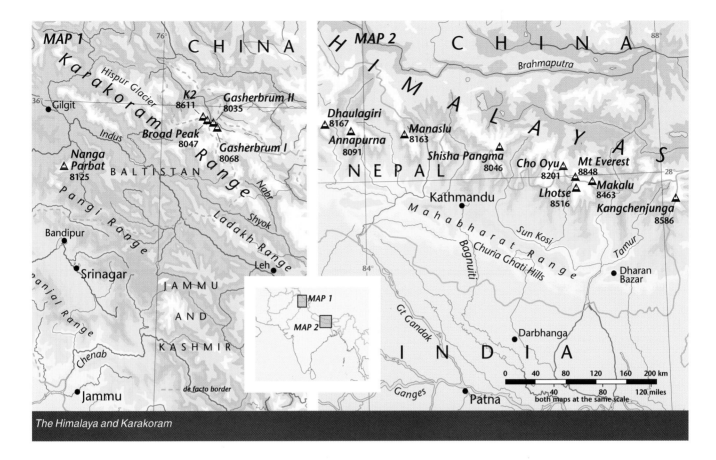

MAP 1
CHINA
Karakoram Range
Hispur Glacier
K2 8611
Gasherbrum II 8035
Broad Peak 8047
Gasherbrum I 8068
Nanga Parbat 8125
Gilgit
Indus
BALTISTAN
Nabr
Shyok
Ladakh Range
Pangi Range
Bandipur
Srinagar
Leh
JAMMU
AND
KASHMIR
Chenab
Jammu
de facto border

The Himalaya and Karakoram

Surveyor-General, in Calcutta (and later, as Gen. Sir Henry Thuillier, to succeed Waugh as Surveyor General) – 'I was taught by my respected chief and predecessor, Col. George Everest, to assign to every geographical object its true local or national appellation … But here we have a mountain, most probably the highest in the world, without any local name that we can discover, whose native appellation, if it has any, will not very likely be ascertained before we are allowed to penetrate Nepal, and to approach very close to this stupendous mass. In the meantime, the privilege, as well as the duty, devolves on me to assign to this lofty pinnacle … a name whereby it may be known among geographers, and become a household word … In testimony of my affectionate respect for a revered chief – in conformity with what I believe to be the wish of all the members of the scientific department over which I have the honour to preside – and to perpetuate the memory of that illustrious master of accurate geographical research – I have determined to name this noble peak … Mont Everest'. The height was given as 29,002ft (8,842m).

Later this height was increased to 29,028ft (8,848m), which is the currently accepted altitude. In 1999 a Boston Museum of Science GPS system attached to Bishop's Ledge, the outcrop just below the summit – and so-called because it is visible in the famous shot of Lute Jerstad taken by Barry Bishop

during the American 1963 expedition – suggested a height of no more than 8,830m (28,970ft): just a few days later the National Geographic Society, co-sponsors of the experiment, announced that the correct height was actually 8,850m (29,035ft).

Thuillier used Waugh's letter to formally announce the findings of the world's highest mountain in August 1856 at a meeting of the Asiatic Society of Bengal. Apart from the use of the French 'mont' (used either to denote a single peak rather than a massif or an affectation by the alpine-travelling British – and dropped in 1857 in favour of Mount, which has itself now been dropped altogether) the name of the world's highest mountain had been fixed. In August 1856 in a letter to the Asiatic Society following Thuillier's announcement, Brian Hodgson, a former political resident of Kathmandu, and then resident of Darjeeling, claimed the peak was actually called Devadhunga or Bhairathan. As a result of this letter, in early 1857 Waugh set up a committee to investigate the peak's name. This concluded that Devadhunga (meaning God's Seat) was applied to many places and that there was no evidence to support Bhairathan. This was fortunate as in January 1857 an official letter from the Secretary of State for India (written in reply to one from Waugh in July 1856) accepted the name Everest.

early climbs

The Diamir Face of Nanga Parbat. Mummery attempted the face up the prominent ribs

The 'discovery' of the highest mountain in the world coincided with the beginning of the 'Golden Age' of climbing in the European Alps.

Mont Blanc had been climbed in 1786, and though other peaks had also been ascended (Piz Bernina and the Jungfrau for instance) it was not until the arrival of the British in the mid-19th century that there was any real impetus for the climbing of the remaining 4,000m (13,123ft) peaks. The highest summit of Monte Rosa was climbed in 1855 – by five Britons, one of whom, Charles Hudson, was to die in the Matterhorn's first ascent tragedy, and three guides – and in the following ten years virtually all the remaining 4,000m peaks were climbed, culminating in the ascent of the Matterhorn by Whymper, Croz

and their team in 1865. The pace of exploration increased during the ten years, something approaching 100 peaks being climbed between 1863 and 1865. The equipment of these early pioneers was rudimentary. A type of crampon had been produced soon after the ascent of Mont Blanc, but was infrequently used, most climbers relying on nailed boots and steps cut into steep snow or ice. The steps were cut with a long handled ice axe, many still with the blade set hatchet-like rather than today's design. Rope was made from hemp which was heavy when wet and hawser-like when frozen. Rope handling was rudimentary with few real belays and little belay technique: the rope's value was more comfort than reality, a slip by one member often resulting in the whole team falling. Clothing was little more than old street clothes, heavy tweed coats and trousers, a hat or cap pulled down tight over the head. A sustained period of bad weather would have been extremely serious to these early climbers and it says much for their endurance, speed over (albeit straightforward) mixed terrain and good weather forecasting that so few accidents occurred: even with modern equipment these earliest routes can still trouble, even kill, the unwary or unlucky.

After the Golden Age climbing changed. The ascent of Mont Blanc had been for scientific (and later aesthetic) as much as adventurous reasons. In the Golden Age the sport had been the preserve of gentlemen – clergymen, noblemen and the leisured merchant class – climbing with local guides. Whymper had been different, a humble engraver motivated by a more modern approach. After the Matterhorn the use of guides by pioneers declined and any pretext of science/exploration was dropped: the climbing now was solely for the sport. The change was personified by Albert Mummery, a British climber who, after a long period climbing with the Swiss guide Alexander Burgener, began to climb hard routes

The first team to attempt K2 – Wesseley, Eckenstein, Jacot-Guillarmod, Crowley, Pfannl and Knowles

simply for the joy of it rather than as a means to reach a particular summit. The Mummery era, the last 20 years of the 19th century, also saw improvements in technique. Abseiling was first used in about 1879 and in the Eastern Alps pitons began to be used to supplement natural belays on the compact rock walls of the Tyrol and Dolomites. Mummery was also an early pioneer of climbing on ranges outside the Alps. Unsurprisingly, the aim of the early explorations was to repeat the development of the Alps – first the tops had to be reached by the easiest route available, only then would climbers turn to harder variations.

After Mummery the improvement in

techniques and equipment accelerated. In the early years of the 20th century Oscar Eckenstein manufactured lightweight crampons which could be carried on a rucsac and short-handled ice axes, while in the Eastern Alps pitons with an eye (rather than a ring through which the rope could be threaded) and

Mallory and Norton at about 8,200m (26,900ft), the highest point reached during the 1922 expedition

karabiners were invented. With these inventions climbers could more easily climb mixed, and steeper, ground, and could protect themselves with running belays, allowing standards to be pushed forward. Rock climbing standards were further improved with the invention of lightweight boots with felt soles and advanced rope techniques such as the tension traverse.

The 1914–18 War brought developments to a halt. When the conflict ended the order in the Alps changed. The Britain

Vittorio Sella's photograph of the west face of K2 taken in 1909 during the Duke of the Abruzzi's expedition

which gave birth to the early pioneers was in decline and losing its confidence. Though its climbers were still in the forefront of Himalayan exploration – India (and dreams of empire) would still be British for another 25 years – in the Alps they had lost their position of pre-eminence. Now the nations which possessed the mountains produced the climbers, Armand Charlet from France, Hans Lauper from Switzerland, Emilio Comici from Italy, Willo Welzenbach from Germany. In the wake of the advances by these new

'modern' era. It is almost a reflex action to smile and shake the head at the Victorian mountaineer's clothing and equipment, yet there is really very little difference between it and that worn and carried by the Schmid brothers who first climbed the Matterhorn's north wall. Fifty years on again, the modern climber, encased in man-made fabrics that are light, warm, wind and waterproof and virtually indestructible, and carrying equipment of new alloys of superior strength and design, seems to inhabit a completely different world. Yet the inherent challenge of climbing remains the same, the advances in equipment and technique being mirrored by equal advances in the standard of the climbs completed by the best. On the first ascent of the Eiger's north face Heinrich Harrer did not have crampons (though this was by design rather than through lack of availability: it is not a decision today's climbers would contemplate) while Fritz Kasparek had 10-points, though Andreas Heckmair and Ludwig Vörg had sets of the new 12-points. None of the four had boots shod with Vibram (Vitale Bramani's revolutionary sole – named after him – did not appear until 1939) or were clad in clothes that shed water. Instead their jackets became sodden wet and then

Edward Norton approaching the Great (Norton)Couloir at about 8,500m (28,000ft) in 1924, probably the highest point reached, and the highest photograph taken, for almost 30 years

pioneers the great faces of the Alps were attempted; the 'six great north faces' of the Matterhorn, Cima Grande di Lavaredo, Petit Dru, Piz Badile, Grandes Jorasses and Eiger were all climbed in the 1930s. It is illuminating to compare the photographs of the Alpine pioneers of Mummery's era with those of 50 years later – the 1930s, the period of north face climbing – and then with those from a half century later, the

Members of the 1921 Everest reconnaissance expedition – Woolaston, Howard-Bury, Heron and Raeburn (back row), Mallory, Wheeler, Bullock, Morshead (front row)

cold when water from the upper face drenched them. Yet for all that the photographs of the four seem to place them in an era as remote as that of Mummery their achievement was considerable, the face retaining a reputation as the ultimate Alpine test piece for half a century and still being no easy day. When, not so many years ago, after a lecture in Britain Heckmair was asked how he had managed the climb with an old-fashioned ice axe, one without the modern inclined pick he famously responded that whether one climbed the Eiger or not did not depend on the droop of your ice pick.

The Sikkim side of Kangchenjunga, seen from the forepeak of Siniolchu. The expeditions of the 1930s attempted the north-east spur (facing the photographer) a route not finally climbed until 1977

Early Climbs in the Himalaya

Note: Explorations and early climbs on the 8,000m (26,247ft) peaks are detailed in the chapters on each peak. Below they are cross-referenced only.

The history of the early exploration of the Himalaya is studded with occasional claims to have reached a higher point or summit than any previous human. The recent discovery of the frozen corpses of children close to the summit of Llullaillaco, a 6,723m (22,057ft) mountain in northern Argentina renders most such claims redundant. The three children are believed to have been human sacrifices by the Inca priesthood, killed perhaps 500 years ago. It is likely that this was as high as men reached in South America, the Andes rarely rising above the

6,000m (19,700ft) contour. On the north (Tibetan) side of the Himalaya the summer snow line can be as high as 6,500m (21,300ft) and though vegetation at such a height is scarce, yaks and snow leopards have been reported from 6,100m (20,000ft) and the Tibetan gazelle (or goa) at over 5,500m (18,000ft). It is likely that man reached equivalent heights in search of game, perhaps even higher when exploring trade routes, but did not live at such heights: Gorak Shep, well-known to Everest trekkers because of the superb view of the Everest massif from nearby Kala Pattar, is at

The ridge camp at about 6,000m (19,750ft) during one of the early German attempts on Kangchenjunga's north-east spur

Mallory and Irvine about to leave the North Col camp for their final assault in 1924

Nanga Parbat seen over the Fairy Meadow

choose one peak rather than another, or choose to press on to the summit when a lower shoulder would be adequate for his purposes? One of the most striking examples of a figure reconnoitring this grey area was William Johnson who, though a member of the GTS, seems to have climbed as much for the thrill as to place triangulation stations. In 1865 on an unsanctioned journey into China's Kunlun Shan (a journey which led to his resignation from the GTS) he claimed to have climbed a 7,284m (23,898ft) peak. More recent surveys give the peak's height as 6,710m (22,014ft) and some, both at the time and today, question Johnson's claim, though it is beyond doubt that Johnson did achieve such altitudes elsewhere.

It is now generally agreed that the first pure climber to visit the Himalaya was WW Graham in the spring of 1883. At that time Bhutan and Nepal were off limits, Sikkim vaguely hostile

5,190m (17,000ft). The early surveyors in the Indian Himalaya climbed several dozen peaks over 6,100m (20,000ft) and several over 6,400m (21,000ft). There is also a famous incident from 1862, when a khalasi (an Indian assistant of the survey staff) reached a summit to the north of the Spiti River in Himachal Pradesh claimed to be over 7,000m (22,950ft) high. The man's name is not recorded, but the peak's name is given as Shilla. More recent surveys have fixed its height at 6,111m (20,049ft), sadly dismantling a myth it would have been nicer to maintain. As an aside here, a delightful insight into the methods of the India survey is gained by asking just how such khalasis checked the heights of their stations. Triangulation used theodolites from fixed platforms – and many of these were dotted around the northern India highlands – but such instruments were too expensive to be handed out to everyone (and, probably, were most definitely not entrusted by British members of the survey to local helpers). Instead the helpers were given thermometers, no less fragile perhaps, but a great deal cheaper, and told to boil water, measuring the boiling point allowing a measure of the local air pressure and, therefore, height.

Exactly when climbers, rather than explorers or map makers, came to the Himalaya is a matter of opinion – when does an explorer become a climber? Why does a map maker

Uli Wieland making trail towards the Moor's Head with the ridge to the Silver Saddle beyond during the 1934 German expedition to Nanga Parbat

and the Karakoram both remote and politically sensitive, the borders of Russia, Afghanistan and British Indian having still to be defined. Of the Himalaya only Himachal Pradesh and northern Uttar Pradesh (Garhwal and Kumaun) were easily and safely accessible. It is therefore surprising that Graham, accompanied by his Swiss guide Joseph Imboden, chose to go to Sikkim. The pair explored the southern approaches to Kangchenjunga, but then Imboden fell ill and had to return to Switzerland. Graham next employed two Swiss guides. Emil Boss and Ulrich Kauffmann and headed for Garhwal. The trio arrived in July and completed two climbs which, if true, were astonishing. Graham claims to have reached 6,900m (over 22,600ft) on Dunagiri (7,070m/

Kamet, seen from a peak on the ridge between the East Kamet Glacier and Banke Plateau

23,196ft and not climbed until 1929), then climbed Changabang (6,864m/22,520ft) the peak whose fierce granite spire dominates the Ramani Glacier. The ascent of Changabang is now given no credence: indeed, it was being questioned within 15 years of Graham's trip. The accepted first ascent of Changabang did not take place until 1974 when the peak was climbed by an Anglo-Indian team. The claimed height on Dunagiri is also disputed: many believe it likely he got no higher than 6,100m (20,000ft) on a subsidiary ridge.

After his Garhwal climb Graham returned to Sikkim with Boss and claimed to have climbed Kabru (7,349m/24,111ft) to the south of Kangchenjunga. If true Graham and Boss would have been the first men known to have gone above 24,000ft (7,315m), but that ascent is also discounted by most authorities who believe that Graham actually climbed a peak about 1,220m (4,000ft) lower. It is not thought that Graham was a liar, his explorations being well documented. More likely his obvious inability to tell north from south and east from west, and to make assumptions about what he was looking at which owed more to wishful thinking than geography, meant he was genuinely mistaken about which mountain he was actually on. It would be a few more years yet before man definitely passed the 24,000ft contour.

In the 1880s FE Younghusband, a young British army officer stationed at Meerut met (at Dharmsala, now famous as the home of the Dalai Lama, the exiled Tibetan spiritual leader) men who had accompanied RB Shaw, Younghusband's uncle, the first Englishman to cross the Himalaya. Perhaps fired by this meeting, Younghusband explored the Indus Valley and what is now Afghanistan, and then joined an expedition to Manchuria. Returning from Peking (now Beijing) he became the first European to cross the Gobi Desert. In expeditions in 1887 and 1889 he explored the Karakoram, crossing the Muztagh Pass, a feat which still arouses the admiration of climbers. Then, in 1890 he explored the Pamirs meeting a Cossack patrol under Col. Yonoff who told him he was trespassing on soil that Russia had annexed. Yonoff escorted Younghusband south and expelled him from 'Russian' territory. This was the era of the 'Great Game' when the empires of Britain and Russia were expanding their influence in the Asian heartland. The incident caused a political storm and led to the defining of the borders of Britain, Russia and China. The British secured the Karakoram, Russia the Pamirs, and to ensure that the two great powers did not share a border, that being seen as a potential source of conflict, a long finger of Afghanistan was poked out between the two, reaching the border of China, a geographical oddity which still remains. Defining the borders meant the Karakoram could now be safely explored.

Following Younghusband's trips to the Karakoram, Conway took his influential expedition to the Baltoro, naming Broad Peak and Hidden Peak (the early name for Gasherbrum I) and Concordia, but from a point of view of climbing the next significant expedition was that of Mummery, Collie and Hastings, together with Bruce and two Gurkhas, to Nanga Parbat in 1895, a trip which ended in the what can probably be claimed as the first deaths of climbers in the Himalaya. The loss of Mummery was also a significant blow both to the British, and the world climbing scene, as he was arguably the most competent and experienced climber of the period.

Holdsworth on the summit of Kamet, pipe still firmly clenched between his teeth

Two years after Mummery's disappearance on Nanga Parbat Matthias Zurbriggen, who had been with Conway in the Baltoro in 1892, climbed Aconcagua in Argentina. Zurbriggen, who had been employed as a guide by the Briton Edward Fitzgerald, soloed the last section of the mountain, reaching the top on 14 January. The climb was repeated soon after by other members of the expedition. Aconcagua, at 6,960m (22,835ft) was probably the highest summit to have been reached at that time.

It was ten years before this peak height was surpassed, Dr Tom Longstaff and the Brocherel brothers Henri and Alexis – or Enrico and Alessio, as they were French guides from Italian Courmayeur – reaching the summit of Trisul, a 7,120m (23,360ft) peak close to Nanda Devi on 12 June 1907. It had been Longstaff's intention to climb Nanda Devi after Trisul but

Shipton on the summit of Kamet

he was unable to find a reasonable route before he ran out of supplies. After restocking the expedition headed north-west, away from Nanda Devi: it was now nearing the end of June and Longstaff preferred Kamet to Nanda Devi as it was further from the approaching monsoon and so offered a better chance of good weather. But that year's monsoon was severe and its effects reached the Garhwal, forcing the expedition to retreat.

In 1909 the Duke of the Abruzzi's expedition to the Baltoro reached a height of 7,500m (24,600ft) on Chogolisa, an altitude record which was to stand until the Everest expedition of the 1920s, though there were to be further increases in the height record for summits. The first was as a by-product of the 1930 International Expedition to Kangchenjunga led by the Swiss geologist Gunther Dyhrenfurth. The attempt on the big peak was abandoned after the death of a Sherpa, but the team stayed on in the area to climb a number of 6,000m and 7,000m peaks. One of the latter, Jonsong, 7,420m (24,343ft), was the highest and was climbed by six members of the team together with two Sherpas in early June 1930.

The new height record was to last just a year. Following Longstaff's initial look at Kamet the peak was attempted several times in the years before the 1914–18 War. In 1913 Charles Meade, who had already tried the peak in previous years, reached Meade's Col (between Kamet and Abi Gamin) with the French guide Pierre Blanc. The pair had found the route to the summit, but bad weather and the fact that they had not fully acclimatised stopped them from going further. After the war there was a further attempt to climb the peak in 1920 after which it was left alone until 1931. That year a team under Frank Smythe, and including the young Eric Shipton, reached the top by way of Meade's Col. The summit was reached by five of the six expedition members, together with two Sherpas, climbing as two teams on 21 and 23 June 1931. The climb not only established a peak height record – Kamet is 7,756m (25,446ft) – but the book of the expedition was a model of its kind, establishing a template which was to be used for the next 50 years. It included a list of sponsors – a list which was to expand and so form a significant part of later books – which noted not only the assistance of the steamship company which took the expedition to India, the food and film companies, but

Nanda Devi in early morning light, seen from Changabang. The north face is in sun, with the north ridge dividing light from shade

1936 a British-American team co-led by Graham Brown and Charles Houston climbed the mountain, Tilman and Noel Odell (the last man to see Mallory and Irvine alive) reaching the summit on 29 August 1936.

The ascent of Nanda Devi was memorable for reasons other than it being the highest peak climbed until 1950. The small well-knit team was a model for the democratic groups which would operate in the Himalaya after the era of the first ascents: the team even declined, at first, to release the names of the summiteers. The expedition book, by Tilman, is, arguably, the finest of its kind ever produced, Tilman's laconic style and elegant wit making it a joy to read. The climb also represented the last days of Empire: Tilman notes that when he and Odell reached the summit 'I believe we so far forgot ourselves as to shake hands on it'. Although something of this gentlemanly behaviour can be detected in the 1950s, particularly on the 1953 Everest expedition, it had disappeared by the time of the summit rushes and overt competitiveness of the late and post-8,000m era.

the Gramophone Co Ltd of Calcutta who supplied a gramophone and records. This delightful touch, totally of its time, but a forerunner of today's CD and cassette players (and radios and satellite phones), is complemented by an equally dated (but equally delightful) aspect of the book's photographs. On the pre-climb group shot Holdsworth (who, as with the other team members, is never referred to by, or even given, his Christian name throughout the book) is shown with a pipe clenched between his teeth. The pipe is still there in the shot of Holdsworth at the summit.

The peak height was to be raised once more before the 1939–45 War halted further exploration of the Himalaya. Nanda Devi was, at 7,816m (25,643ft), the highest peak in the British Empire and had inspired climbers since Longstaff had photographed it in 1905. It is a magnificent, beautiful mountain, but one as well protected as the legend of its name would suggest. Nanda was the daughter of the king of Kumaun (part of Garhwal). She was very beautiful and much desired, and a stronger king demanded her as his wife. Nanda's father refused, but was defeated in battle by her suitor. Nanda fled to a mountain sanctuary, taking refuge on its highest peak. Nanda Devi means Princess, or Goddess, Nanda, and other peaks of the sanctuary are named for the legend – Trisul, for example, means 'trident', the weapon threatening the suitor king.

Nanda Devi's sanctuary, an almost continuous circle of peaks (including Changabang) and huge mountain walls prevented access to the peak for many years. Then, in 1934, Eric Shipton and Bill Tilman, together with three Sherpas, forced a way through the gorge of the Rishi Ganga, reaching the inner sanctuary and identifying a route to the summit. In

A climber at about 7,000m (23,000ft) during the successful 1936 expedition to Nanda Devi

'Do you think it is worth it?'

annapurna 8,047m

LOUIS LACHENAL TO
MAURICE HERZOG
on the summit climb during
the first ascent of Annapurna

annapurna

The 1939–45 War brought an end to Himalayan climbing, the major nations participating in the exploration and climbs of the 1930s being those most actively involved in the conflict. In the immediate post-war years exhausted nations recuperated, but it was not long before man's restlessness overcame the austerity and relative disorganisation.

The demands of war meant that British influence in Tibet waned between 1939 and 1945. Then, in 1947 the Dalai Lama's horoscope prophesied that Tibet would be threatened by foreigners and the country closed its borders to all outsiders. Before the British had a chance to re-assert their influence – they were, technically, still the guarantors of Tibetan autonomy – or the Tibetans had calculated that the advantages of outside friends in limiting the colonial ambitions of its vast neighbour outweighed the horoscope's predictions, the Chinese invaded, closing access to the northern side of Everest and other great peaks for decades. In the face of such a formidable opponent the British quietly forgot their obligations.

With Tibet closed interest might have shifted to the western end of the Himalaya, but the great peaks of the Karakoram were also off-limits as the newly established nations of India and Pakistan quarrelled over border lines. Then, in 1948 the formerly closed, secretive nation of Nepal, concerned over the longer term intentions of China and wanting to acquire powerful friends, tentatively opened its borders, firstly to a group of American ornithologists, then to a team of Swiss climbers who, under René Dittert, explored the north-east of the country. In 1949 the French Fédération Française de la Montagne began negotiations with the Nepalese government for permission to climb one of the great peaks that stood wholly within Nepal.

France was in an excellent position to mount a determined attempt, many of the leading climbers of the late 1940s/early 1950s being French, a situation due, in large part, to the unfortunate circumstances of the war. Although some French men escaped German-occupied France to form the Free French battalions, most were trapped in the country. Military service was abolished, but the French civilian authorities introduced Les Chantiers de la Jeunesse, an organisation aimed at giving idle young men something to do, with a view to promoting the ideas of honest toil and citizenship, fearful that otherwise the fabric of the nation would rot away. A parallel organisation, Jeunesse et Montagne, was set up in mountain areas. Here officers from the French armed services helped civilian instructors to train young men in skiing and mountaineering. The JM, as it was known, helped maintain the officer corps' fitness and expertise while teaching mountaincraft to a generation of climbing enthusiasts. Lionel Terray, arguably the greatest alpinist of the immediate post-war era, was a product of the JM and notes the rigours of the training and the later work the trainees did in helping the maquis liberate the French Alps. Terray records one day when, carrying 20kg (44lb) packs, his troop climbed almost 3,000m (nearly 9,000ft) and descended almost the same height with little food. The JM training and partisan battles took place in both summer and winter, giving the French an almost unrivalled understanding of snow conditions and of climbing and survival techniques in the harshest conditions. When the war ended France had a group of young men capable of repeating the great alpine climbs of the Germans, Austrians and Italians and of pushing standards even higher. Gaston

Annapurna I (the main summit) from Poon Hill

Annapurna's northern flank is seen over the Annapurna North Glacier. Annapurna East rises on the left skyline

ANNAPURNA: ASCENT ROUTES

Above South Face
1 *British (1970)*
2 *Japanese (1981)*
3 *Polish (1981) to Central Summit*
4 *Spanish (1981) to Central Summit*

Below North Face
A *East Summit*
B *Main Summit*
1 *French (1950)*
2 *Dutch (1977)*
3 *Polish (1996)*
4 *East Ridge (skyline from left), Loretan and Joos (1984) over East and Central (hidden in cloud) Summits to Main Summit*

Left West Face
1 *Messner/Kammerlander (1985)*

Maurice Herzog on the summit of Annapurna

The 2,700m/9,000ft south face of Annapurna I rears over the secluded Annapurna Sanctuary at the head of Modi Khola

Rébuffat made the second ascents of the Walker Spur and the north face of the Piz Badile, as well as early ascents of the other great north faces. Louis Lachenal and Lionel Terray made the second ascent of the Eiger's north wall and reduced the fastest time on the Piz Badile's face from 19 hours to 7½ hours, a tribute to their astonishing fitness as well as their climbing abilities. These men were to form the core of the French 1950 Himalayan expedition.

Name

Annapurna was Peak XXXIX of the Indian survey, its local name being a combination of two Sanskrit words whose literal meaning is 'filled with food'. However, the name also contains the root of another name for Durga, the Hindu Divine Mother, consort of Lord Shiva, and, as Maurice Herzog was told during his expedition, is more correctly translated as 'Goddess of the Harvests', ie. the Divine Mother Provider.

Exploration and First Ascent

When the French arrived in the spring of 1950 their permission was for an attempt on either Dhaulagiri or Annapurna, but before they could set foot on either they needed to explore approaches to the peaks. Maps from the Indian survey existed, but these were soon shown to be highly inaccurate, while aerial photographs taken by the Swiss Foundation for Alpine Exploration in 1949, though intriguing, were from too low an altitude to be of great value. The French arrived in Nepal on 5 April 1950, but it was not until 23 May that Herzog decided to attempt to climb Annapurna, much of the intervening period being filled with attempts to reach the base of either of the 8,000ers. Attempts to reach Dhaulagiri from the east and north provided only views of the mountain which suggested that it would be a formidable undertaking (indeed, Lionel Terray questioned whether it would ever be climbed) while the first attempt to reach Annapurna failed to find the mountains at all: it seems hardly credible that an 8,000m peak could be lost, but so poor were the maps that the French were actually in the wrong valley.

The climbing team which turned to Annapurna was Jean Couzy, Louis Lachenal, Gaston Rébuffat, Marcel Schatz and

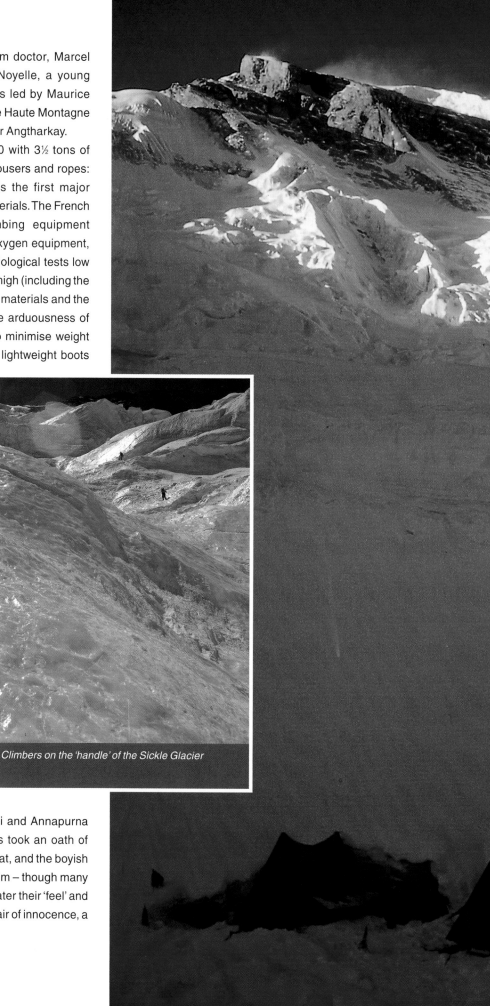

Lionel Terray. Jacques Oudot was the team doctor, Marcel Ichac the photographer and Francis de Noyelle, a young diplomat, the liaison officer. The team was led by Maurice Herzog, General Secretary of the Groupe de Haute Montagne and supported by eight Sherpas under sirdar Angtharkay.

The team left Paris on 30 March 1950 with 3½ tons of equipment, including nylon anoraks, overtrousers and ropes: spin-off from the 1939–45 War made this the first major expedition to be equipped with synthetic materials. The French had down jackets and lightweight climbing equipment (crampons etc.). They also had improved oxygen equipment, though this was actually only used for physiological tests low on the mountain, none of the climbers going high (including the summit pair) using it. Though the use of new materials and the lightest equipment was a recognition of the arduousness of climbing on the great peaks, the attempt to minimise weight was to have disastrous consequences: the lightweight boots meant that all the climbers suffered from cold feet and the summit climbers were frostbitten.

Maurice Herzog's account of the expedition is one of the greatest mountaineering books of all time, a multi-faceted diamond of a book. With it the reader can feel compassion, marvel at heroism, grimace at horror. It is epic tale, grand tragedy, a perfection of schadenfreude. The early chapters on Nepal (and, to a lesser extent, India) before the tourist invasions of later years are fascinating: the acetylene lamps lighting the customs office in Old Delhi; the old Nepalese seeing white men for the first time and eyeing them suspiciously while the children crowded around bug-eyed with curiosity; caravans of joyful Tibetan traders arriving from a country which would soon change for ever, replacing joy with sorrow.

Climbers on the 'handle' of the Sickle Glacier

Herzog's description of the exploration of the approaches to Dhaulagiri and Annapurna are equally fascinating. The team members took an oath of allegiance to the leader before departure. That, and the boyish nature of the dialogue Herzog quotes verbatim – though many of the exchanges must have been invented later their 'feel' and context are presumably real – conjure up an air of innocence, a

Annapurna from the west. The north-west face, first climbed by Kammerlander and Messner, lies furthest from the photographer

group of naive, young men on a great adventure: it is no surprise when members ride in and out of camp on horseback. The much more recent publication of the unabridged version of Louis Lachenal's diaries (the earlier version of them had been edited by Herzog's brother and Lucien Davies, who omitted sections which did not reflect Maurice's view of the expedition) and those of Gaston Rébuffat (quoted in a biography of him) suggest that things were not quite as idyllic as Herzog makes them seem. But whatever the case, the innocence was soon to be lost.

After spending many weeks exploring Herzog finally decided that Annapurna's north face offered the best chance of success (a decision perhaps aided by a conversation with a Buddhist lama who visited the team's camp and told them that 'Dhaulagiri is not propitious to you ... give up and turn your thoughts towards the other side ... towards Muktinath' – the town near Annapurna).

The French first attempted the north-west ridge (the Cauliflower Ridge as they called it), but soon realised that even if they could climb it there was no chance of the Sherpas being able to carry loads up it. They therefore abandoned it in favour of the north face, choosing a route across the relatively easy-angled face to the foot of the Sickle, a prominent snow-field/glacier (named for the shape of its icewall edge) descending from the summit. The route to the Sickle, at the base of which Camp V was established on 2 June, took only ten days from Camp I, an exploration camp of the North Annapurna Glacier. That is an astonishingly quick time for so big and unknown a mountain, made even more remarkable when the weather the French experienced is recalled. Though they had a run of fine mornings, the afternoons invariably brought thick snow which required the routes between camps to be broken almost daily. The snow also brought the threat of avalanches. Annapurna's north face is now known to be avalanche prone, the weight of new snow in 1950 (30–50cm/12–20in fell most afternoons) adding to the ever present risk. But, of course, time was valuable – the monsoon was due to arrive on 5 June.

On the northern flank the great serac wall of The Sickle hangs over Camp II of the 1970 Expedition

Herzog's account notes that those Sherpas with pre-war experience said the climbing on Annapurna was much harder. He notes too the inexperience of the Sherpas in ice climbing and their resulting disinclination to take a lead in developing the route. How things change, today's Sherpas often being more experienced and skilled than their clients. Herzog's account also displays the lack of understanding of the best method of acclimatisation. The strongest climbers pushed ahead until they were exhausted, then descended for rest, a strategy now discarded in favour of a phased gain in altitude. The consequence was that on 2 June it was Herzog and Lachenal who occupied Camp V, not Lachenal and Terray as had been expected. Herzog offered Angtharkay the chance of continuing to the summit on 3 June, but he declined as his feet were frozen and descended.

Herzog and Lachenal had no sleep on the night of 2 June, being kept awake by the wind – which threatened to blow the tent down – and the build up of snow on the fabric. In the morning they were so worn out they failed to make any drinks. Dehydration is now recognised as a major contributor to frostbite, blood thickening due to the increase in red cell numbers being aggravated by a thinning of plasma. The pair were also taking a mix of pills prescribed by the team doctor. These included Maxiton which suppresses feeling of fatigue, in part by creating a sense of euphoria. Herzog's book shows that he enjoyed every aspect of the early expedition – the thrill of being in the Himalaya and being with some of the world's best climbers – but his occasional unbounded joy was as nothing to the almost permanent sense of euphoria on the summit climb. While Lachenal stopped periodically to massage his frozen feet, Herzog climbed in a world seemingly remote from reality. Eventually Lachenal asked Herzog what he would do if he (Lachenal) descended. Herzog said he would continue alone and so Lachenal agreed to accompany him. Herzog's book implies that the pair were climbing for the glory of France, but Lachenal's unabridged diaries show he did not share this view. He felt that if Herzog continued alone he would not return – 'this summit climb was not a matter of national prestige. It was une affaire de cordée.' Une affaire de cordée, a matter of the rope, the obligation one man on a rope has for the man on the other

end – the more so, perhaps, as Lachenal was a far more experienced climber and a professional guide, while Herzog was an 'amateur'. Elsewhere Lachenal states that for him Annapurna was no more important than any other mountain and that he did not owe his feet to the youth of France. When the pair reached the summit at about 2pm Herzog was utterly overjoyed, almost oblivious to Lachenal's insistence that they go down immediately. Lachenal clearly sensed how close to the limit they were.

On the summit photo most often published a snow slope rises beyond the triumphant Herzog, a fact which led some to

Gerry Owens makes the last stride to the summit during the second ascent. A few days later Dougal Haston and Don Whillans stood on the left-hand hump after climbing the south face

question (and still to question) whether the true summit had been reached. Herzog dismissed the objections by saying that there was a cornice at the summit and that the angle the photograph had been taken at gave a distorted view of it. With the snow fall and winds of the days before the top was reached, it is hardly surprising that a significant cornice had formed and when all the shots of Herzog are examined it is definitely the case that as Lachenal changed his position, the apparent snow slope beyond Herzog diminishes. Given Herzog's strange mental state it is easy to see why doubters distrust his insistence, but those who knew Lachenal point to the fact that his diary states simply that they had reached the summit and that he would not have said so had it not been the case. On later climbs there has been a less distinct cornice, or no cornice at all: subsequent photos show that the summit, the highest bump on a ridge which is the culmination of the mountain's south face, can be a narrow point on which two or three people can stand.

In Herzog's account of the descent from the summit he is pursuing Lachenal who, fearful of frostbite, has descended at speed. Herzog recalls losing his gloves when he opened his rucsac, though he does not know why he opened it or why he did not use his spare socks as makeshift gloves. Clearly he was still euphoric. He claims to have followed Lachenal until mist enveloped them both. However, Lachenal's version is that Herzog was in front and that, unable to catch his team leader, he was constantly shouting and pointing to his hands in an attempt to draw Herzog's attention to his lack of gloves. Lachenal being behind Herzog would also explain why Herzog arrived at Camp V first, with Lachenal's cry for help after his fall being heard by Herzog, and by Terray and Rébuffat who had come up to the camp to meet them. Lachenal fell on relatively easy ground and was brought back to the camp by Terray though he was by now frantic to get down so that Oudot could attend to his frozen feet.

Herzog's frozen hands were probably already beyond saving, but his and Lachenal's feet might have been saved if 4 June had been fine. Terray and Rébuffat treated them in the then-approved method of lashing the bare, frozen flesh with knotted rope. Today it is recognised that body warmth is the best treatment, the whipping technique having been relegated to dubious massage parlours. After a night of poor sleep and pain – with the summit pair having their first liquid for some 24 hours – the four climbers started out for Camp IV in a snowstorm. All day they tried to reach the camp, failing because of poor visibility and deep snow. The night spent in a fortuitously-found crevasse – Lachenal fell into it – was fearful

Climbers pause for rest during the second ascent in 1970

Gerry Owens just below the summit furing the second ascent

and probably caused the permanent damage to the summit pair's feet. The four climbers were buried by an avalanche the following morning and had the monsoon arrived on time would almost certainly have died, but 5 June was fine. Terray and Rébuffat were snow-blinded, having spent much of the previous day without goggles trying to peer through the storm. Lachenal, seeing the chance of salvation slipping away shouted towards Camp IV – and was heard at Camp II 1,260m (4,100ft) below. The distraught occupants of II – many hours climbing away – were relieved to see a search party from IV arrive soon after: the crevasse had been only 200m (650ft) from the camp.

Herzog's account of the retreat from the mountain is harrowing. He had given up hope in the crevasse and asked to be allowed to die, and was then caught in an avalanche on the treacherous lower face, he and two Sherpas being carried down 150m (500ft) and saved from death by a miraculous snagging of the rope. The rest of the descent and the march out from the mountain through the monsoon, with pauses for excruciating injections and, eventually, the casual amputation of Herzog's fingers and toes and Lachenal's toes, is as gripping an evocation of horror as could be imagined. Herzog spares nothing, of himself or the situation: he overhears Oudot fearing that gas gangrene would kill him in appalling fashion; the sweeping away of black amputated digits with a twig broom; and the fact that red-bellied flies lay eggs on his open stumps, the doctor allowing maggots to hatch so they would consume the dead flesh, cleaning the wound. In Paris 225g (½lb) of maggots were extracted from his mutilated extremities.

Herzog's account of the climb is factual rather than lyrical, yet his style allows the beauty of the mountains to shine through. His inclusion of team conversations, warts and all, set a standard followed, usually much less successfully, by later writers. His final sentence, after thoughts on an expedition which almost killed him and which maimed both summit climbers, that 'there are other Annapurnas in the lives of men' is as profound an explanation for man's exploratory zeal as could be written.

Later Ascents

The returning French were greeted by a nation hysterical with joy and pride, its self-worth restored, its prestige renewed. For the team members the Annapurna experience was more traumatic, and only two would answer the call when four years later, the French returned to the high peaks.

Climbing fixed ropes above Camp V during the British south face climb in 1970

After Annapurna the 'Golden Age' of 8,000m peak climbing occupied the world's leading climbers for a decade. Political difficulties then made travel to Nepal impossible for several years. By the time travel problems eased again in the late 1960s a new generation of climbers, some barely of school age when Annapurna was climbed, had arrived. The French ascent of Jannu in 1962 had pointed the way to a new era of climbing on lower, but technically difficult, peaks, though the impetus had still been the first ascent. Next came the German attempts at Nanga Parbat's Rupal face which they tried several times during the 1960s. Another early indication of the new outlook came on Annapurna in 1969 when a German expedition failed in an ambitious project to climb the 7.5km (4½ mile) ridge from Glacier Dome to main summit. Then, in 1970 a British expedition arrived on the south side of the mountain to attempt the vast south face. This expedition, together with the German Rupal face climbs, heralded a new era in Himalayan climbing, a deliberate attempt at a difficult line to a previously climbed summit. Development in the Himalaya was thus taking the same path as in the Alps, but with the timescales hugely compressed. Ironically, at the same time a British-Nepalese Army expedition was on the north side of the

mountain, repeating the French line, but using oxygen. Simultaneously, therefore, the old (some would argue retrograde) and new styles were at work, separated by a vast mountain of snow and ice and an equally large difference in attitude.

From its base Annapurna's south face rises almost 3,000m (about 9,500ft), making it twice the height of the north wall of the Eiger – but the base of the wall is 1,000m (3,300ft) higher than the Eiger's summit. From the start of the major difficulties the face has an angle of 55°, about the same as the ice-fields and Ramp on the Eiger. The comparison with sections on the Eiger are a feature of the expedition book by Chris Bonington, the team leader, who had completed the British ascent of the north wall's 1938 route with Ian Clough, another team member. The other climbers were Martin Boysen, Mick Burke, Nick Escourt, Dougal Haston, Mike Thompson and Don Whillans – as strong a team as had been assembled at that time in the Himalaya – together with the American Tom Frost. The latter was included for sponsorship reasons, his presence helping to sell the climb in the US. Such overt commercialism was another new feature in the Himalaya. The team was completed by Dave

Annapurna from the west, showing the peak's well-defined rock strata

north side of the mountain was. Taking turns, the pair climbed to the narrow summit bump, the tracks of Henry Day and Gerry Owens – who had made the second ascent of Annapurna on 20 May – being just discernible. Two days later Burke and Frost attempted to repeat the climb, Burke getting no higher than Camp VI, Frost continuing alone to about 7,700m (just over 25,000ft).

After the attempt by Burke and Frost, Bonington ordered the team to clear the mountain, aware that with the monsoon due, with regular avalanches on the face and falling stones threatening to injure climbers and cut the fixed ropes, the climbers' luck might be running out. Ironically it was during this final phase that an ice tower collapsed, killing Ian Clough. But despite this tragedy the expedition had been a major success, the first 'modern' climb of an 8,000er. It was a business success too, Bonington's astute commercial sense preparing the way for later expeditions of his own and others.

There were further deaths on the mountain in 1973. Having failed on the north-east buttress a Japanese team transferred their interest to the original route. On this two teams climbed to within 150m (500ft) of the top before being forced to retreat by high winds and exhaustion. During the descent four Japanese and a Sherpa were killed by an avalanche. Later in the year an Italian team failed on the north-west ridge, two members being killed by an avalanche during the descent.

In 1974 a Spanish team climbed Annapurna East, the 8,012m (26,280ft) point that represents the eastern end of the long, summit ridge, by a route to the east of the French route, continuing up the north ridge, but an attempt on the main summit via the south-east ridge in 1975 by an Austrian team failed when their Sherpas went home, claiming that their clothing, food and equipment was inadequate. The Austrians continued, but abandoned the attempt when one team member was killed by an avalanche. The Spanish route was followed again in 1980 when a German team used it to gain the upper north face which they climbed to the central summit.

The fourth ascent of the main peak came in 1977 when a Dutch team, celebrating the 75th anniversary of the Royal Dutch Alpine Club (an organisation which sounds as unlikely as the Saharan Canoe Club, but one which has produced some notable climbers), completed the first post-monsoon climb. The Dutch route, to the left of the French route, along what is now termed the Dutch Rib, had the advantage of being less prone

Lambert as doctor and Kelvin Kent as Base Camp Manager. The team's equipment was much improved over that of the French, with warmer clothing, lighter climbing gear (though problems with crampons coming off are a recurrent theme of the ascent – step-in crampons would help in later years, as would droop pick ice axes) and better tents. One other detail should not be overlooked: as Bonington noted, the French had first to find their mountain, whereas his team didn't even need a map to find the face.

The climb (up the face's left buttress) was straightforward to Camp III at 6,100m (just over 20,100ft) but then a narrow ice ridge, which had to be turned on the left, required seven days of hard climbing. Further up a 300m (1,000ft) rock band was overcome with climbing which was equally difficult. Towards the end of May, with deteriorating weather perhaps predicating the early arrival of the monsoon, Dougal Haston and Don Whillans occupied Camp VI at 7,300m (about 24,000ft). The intention had been to establish another camp 300m (1,000ft) higher, but with exhaustion affecting virtually the entire team and, consequently, limited food and equipment reaching the lead climbers, the pair left the camp on 27 May on what, in retrospect, was a make or break bid for the summit. Climbing ropes they had fixed earlier – the last of the 4.5km (almost 3 miles or 15,000ft) of rope which had been fixed on the face to aid load carrying – then climbing unroped they reached the summit ridge just 10m (33ft) below the summit. Haston was surprised, after many weeks on the face, at just how flat the

to avalanches and, therefore, the preferred option for later parties on the north side of the peak. The summiteers used oxygen.

1978 brought a notable success when a team of American women (but including one British woman in a mirror-image of the 1970 south face team) repeated the Dutch route, claiming several firsts. The team, led by Arlene Blum, needed to raise US $80,000 to finance the climb. Of this three-quarters was realised by the sale of T-shirts bearing the legend 'A Woman's Place is On Top ... Annapurna'. Blum wanted to employ Sherpanis rather than Sherpas for the climb, but discovered that they were only interested in helping with the cooking and laundry, a somewhat chastening position in view of the overtly feminist aims of the expedition. In the event the team was supported by Sherpas – hardly a body blow to the feminist ideal as the woman did the lead climbing and the use of Sherpas has never been seen as diminishing the achievements of male teams. The expedition was post-monsoon and used oxygen, claiming the first female ascent when Irene Miller and Vera Komarkova, together with two Sherpas reached the summit. Sadly a second summit attempt failed, with Alison Chadwick-Onyszkiewicz, the British team member, and Vera Watson being killed.

A French team followed the original route in 1979 but during an attempted ski descent Yves Morin skied into the loose end of a fixed rope and was killed. There was further

Dougal Haston on the fixed ropes between Camps V and VI during the 1970 British south face expedition

success on the Dutch route in 1980, then significant climbs in 1981, a Polish team climbing a new route on the south face to the right of the British route, with climbing of a similar standard to that of the north face of the Matterhorn. The route led directly to the middle top (Annapurna Central) of the summit ridge (at 8,051m/26,538ft). The summit climbers, Maciej Berbeka and Boguslav Probulski reached the top in a severe storm and did not continue to the main summit. That was reached by two members of a Japanese team which completed a hard route, post-monsoon, on the south face between the British and Polish routes (the central buttress). A Japanese climber died in a second summit attempt. Meanwhile, on the north-west ridge four climbers (two French and two Sherpas) died attempting a new route.

In 1982 the south face was again the centre of attraction, a three-man team attempting an alpine style ascent of a route to the right of the Polish route. The climb was abandoned when the Briton Alex McIntyre was killed by stonefall. The route was climbed (to the middle summit) in alpine style in 1984 by the Spaniards Nil Bohigas and Enric Lucas. That year also saw the ascent of the east ridge by a six-man team under Frank Tschirky. The summit pair of Erhard Loretan and Norbert Joos. In just three days they climbed the ridge from close to Glacier Dome to the east summit, continuing over the middle and main summits and descending the north face. Also in 1984 a Korean team claimed to have climbed the peak in winter. This claim was denied by their Sherpas and also by a French team on the mountain at the same time. The French stated that the Korean claim was not consistent with French observations, nor with the state of the mountain which was dangerous due to heavy snow fall. General opinion now suggests that the Koreans stopped about two hours short of the summit.

Late in 1985 the Japanese failed in a winter attempt on the British south face route (a Bulgarian team having no more success on the Polish route in early 1986), but 1985 was most notable for the first ascent of the north-west face by Reinhold Messner and Hans Kammerlander, Messner claiming his eleventh of the 14 8,000ers. The vast concave north-west face was one of the last unclimbed faces on the great peaks and proved difficult, requiring Messner's small team to set up two fixed camps, with two bivouacs above that. The final climb was into the teeth of gale-force winds, the summit ridge testing both climbers. In his account of the climb Messner claims it was only Kammerlander's drive that kept the pair going and only his presence that allowed Messner to believe in his own survival. During the descent the pair had to contend with new snow and were glad of the assistance of other members of the team, Reinhard Patscheider and Reinhard Schiestl. During the night

Ian Clough on fixed ropes during the 1970 British south face expedition

only Patscheider's constant clearing of fresh snow from the tent prevented the exhausted pair from suffocating. A few days later Patscheider, Schiestl and Swami Prem Darshano (the fifth member of the team) attempted to repeat the climb, but were forced back by deep snow. During the descent Patscheider survived a 400m (1,300ft) fall.

Maurice Herzog returned to the north side base camp with a French expedition in 1986. The emotional return did not ensure success, the French failing on the north ridge, though an Italian team followed Herzog's original route in just six days (base to summit and return). The first winter ascent of Annapurna was finally made in 1987 by a small Polish team, Jerzy Kukuczka (climbing his thirteenth 8,000er) and Artur Hajzer following the French route to reach the top on 3 February. Kukuczka, a man seemingly immune to cold and suffering, referred to the climb as 'cold hell' as, being on the northern side of the peak, the climbers did not see the sun after leaving base camp, climbing in a perpetual shade on ice so

The summit of Annapurna (the second ascent)

hard crampons barely bit into it. In the post-monsoon period of the same year a Spanish team completed the first alpine-style ascent of the French route, while in December the Japanese completed the first winter ascent of the south face following the British route (with some minor variations). Two of the four summiteers were killed during the descent.

In 1988 Annapurna came of age with its twenty-first ascent. That year also saw the second ascent of the north-west face by a Czech/Italian team. The following year Reinhard Patscheider returned to solo the face, finding that his luck, both good and bad, had not changed. Retreating by paraglider after an avalanche had destroyed his camp he crash-landed and dislocated a shoulder. On his next attempt a piton pulled and he fell 15m (50ft), escaping with an injured back. He retreated, vowing to return. In 1991 a semi-solo ascent was made up the British south face route by Gabriel Denamur of a Belgian/Polish team. Denamur certainly made the top – his tracks were later followed to the summit by Kryzysztof Wielicki. Wielicki saw Denamur's tracks heading down the north side of the peak, but he was not seen by expeditions on that side. Denamur's climb followed a disputed solo by the Italian Giancarlo Gazzola who,

climbing illegally (ie. without a permit), claimed a solo ascent during the post-monsoon period.

During the 1990s Annapurna's south face continued to exercise a fascination for those seeking very hard climbing at altitude. Post-monsoon in 1992 the French climbers Pierre Beghin and Jean-Christophe Lafaille attempted a new line to the right of the British route. Climbing in part at night for better snow conditions the pair reached 7,500m (24,600ft) before deciding to retreat. During the descent Beghin fixed an abseil from a Friend, saving a piton for lower down. The Friend pulled and Beghin fell to his death, leaving Lafaille to downclimb solo over extremely difficult terrain. He reached a bivouac at about 7,000m (23,000ft) and continued down, now using tent pegs as pitons and a 20m (70ft) 6mm rope. Nearing an early camp at 6,500m (21,300ft) a stonefall broke Lafaille's right arm. As he is right-handed his position was now serious. He shouted to Slovenian climbers on the British route, but was not heard and so was forced to put a makeshift splint on his arm and to abseil down the face using his good arm and his teeth. He eventually reached the base of the wall and walked to the Slovene base camp from where he was helicoptered to Kathmandu. In 1996 Lafaille returned to the face, attempting to solo the British route. He failed due to deep snow, but claimed 'It's a very nice route, not very dangerous – an interesting route'.

In 1993 Annapurna and Dhaulagiri became the first peaks climbed by the 'Chinese Tibetan Expedition to 14 Mountains of 8,000m of the World' whose aim is to put a Tibetan (hopefully, but not necessarily, the same one) on all 14 summits by 2002. Post-monsoon in 1994 the south face was again the main attraction, a South Korean team climbing the British route, but an attempt at a new route to the right by Catherine Destivelle and Eric Decamp failing. The pair than attempted to follow the Korean ropes but gave up at 7,700m (25,250ft).

Later ascents have filled in some of the 'missing' firsts on the peak. In April 1995 the Slovenians Andrej and Davorin Karnicar climbed the French route on the north side, reaching the top at 8.25am. After a stay of about an hour they descended by ski, reaching base camp at 6pm. In spring 1996 the French climber André Georges soloed the French route, the first confirmed solo. Just eleven days earlier Georges had soloed Dhaulagiri. Post monsoon in 1996 a Polish-Ukrainian team made the first ascent of the north-west ridge, reaching it by following the early stages of the original route. The ridge required the fixing of 2km (1¼miles) of rope. The summit was reached on 20 October by the Pole Andrzej Marciniak and the Ukrainian Vladyslav Terzyul.

It seemed as though the mountain, renowned for its avalanches and notorious for the deaths during early climbs, had, in the face of modern equipment, techniques and levels of fitness, been tamed. But in the Himalaya that never happens. On Christmas Day 1997 Anatoli Boukreev, one of the world's finest high-altitude climbers, famous for his involvement in the 1996 Everest tragedy, was killed together with Dimitri Sobolev when they were avalanched from the south face of Fang, having chosen to climb the main summit via the south-west ridge. Simone Moro, who was climbing with the pair, was carried 800m (2,600ft) down the face, landing only 50m (160ft) from the team's first camp, his hands badly injured, his clothes torn, all his equipment except his crampons lost. He re-equipped himself, climbed 1,500m (almost 5,000ft) down the face to base camp from where he was helicoptered out after the team's Nepalese cook had walked through the night to raise the alarm.

Two years later, on 29 April 1999 the Spaniard Juan Oiarzábal climbed Annapurna to complete the set of all 14 8,000ers, a quest which had taken him 14 years. The immediate question following his climb was whether he had become the sixth or seventh man to complete the set, given the problem of Fausto di Stefani's ascent of Lhotse. The general feeling in the climbing world seems now to favour the Spaniard being sixth. Finding the French route too dangerous, Oiarzábal's team, funded by Spanish TV, followed the Spanish 1974 East Summit route, then the German 1980 Central Summit route, before climbing the Sickle to the main summit. On the descent the Sherpa Kami Dorje, who had just completed his second ascent of Annapurna, and a female Korean climber fell to their deaths.

At the time of writing there have been fewer ascents of Annapurna than on any other of the 8,000ers. The peak has a fierce reputation, second only to K2 in terms of the ratio of summiteers dying on the descent to successful climbs. It is also the 8,000er with the highest ratio of deaths to successful ascents: for every two climbers who reach the summit one climber dies. These statistics explain why there has been no genuinely commercial expedition to the peak so far: the avalanche-prone north face and the difficult south and north-west faces are likely to ensure that there will be no change to this during the early years of the new millennium, the first 8,000er to have been climbed remaining an elusive, committing summit.

The west face of Annapurna from Kalopani. The main summit (Annapurna I) is to the left, with Fang on the right

Many climbers approach Everest with a do ir die attitude. Some of them do, some of them die, and some of them do both.

ANON

everest 8,848m

Everest

Everest was Peak XV of the Indian Survey, named by Surveyor-General Sir Andrew Waugh for his predecessor. Waugh had noted that no local name seemed to exist for the peak – though the search for one had not, at that stage, stretched as far as Nepal and Tibet, both closed to foreigners.

By the time a name could be sought 'Everest' had become a fixture among British mountaineers. As the British were the only nation to approach/attempt the peak in the years prior to the 1939–45 War the name was internationalised by the 1950s when the Swiss and French sought permission for attempts from Nepal.

In later years the search for a local name began again. The most likely candidate is Chomolungma, of which there are several spelling options. This was the name used by the Tibetan authorities in the official document for the 1921 British expedition and was used by team members when talking to locals. The name, meaning 'Mother Goddess of the Country' (with country used in its local sense), seems to have been applied to the Everest massif, ie. including Lhotse, Nuptse and other, smaller, peaks, rather than the main peak itself. Though the name was discovered in Tibet, it seems to have been used in the Khumbu region of Nepal too – no great surprise in view of the trading links across the Himalaya. Interestingly, though, in his autobiography when Tenzing notes the name he claims he was told by his mother that it meant 'the mountain so high that no bird can fly over it' which, if true, suggests a remarkably economical use of syllables. After the Chinese invasion of Tibet, Nepal nervous that the Chinese might attempt to annexe the peak, sought its own local name and came up with Sagarmatha meaning 'Sky Mother' or 'Mother of the Universe' in the Sherpa language. This name has now been applied to a National Park covering the Khumbu region. The Chinese responded to this by producing their own – Qomolangma (sometimes Qomolangma Feng), what might be termed a Sino-local version – claimed to be based on a Tibetan legend of five goddesses (qomo) of whom the most beautiful, the one with a face of emerald green, was Qomo Langsangma or Qomo Langma.

Though there are many who would like to see Chomolungma adapted as the peak's official name, Everest has now been accepted by custom and practice and is very unlikely to be supplanted.

Exploration

Although there had been suggestions about expeditions to reach (and climb) Everest in the years before the 1914–18 War, they had all fallen through for one reason or another, and not until 1921 was an expedition approved. It was led by Charles Howard-Bury and included George Leigh Mallory whose name has become associated with the mountain in a way rivalled only by those of Hillary and Tenzing. The expedition was purely reconnaissance, exploring the north, north-west and eastern sides of the peak. Mallory saw the Khumbu icefall and named the west (now, usually,

The summit pyramid from the Second Step

The mountains of the Everest horseshoe, Everest (left), Lhotse (centre) and Nuptse (right)

High on the north face. This shot is from much the same position as that of Norton on the 1924 expedition (see Early Climbs)

western) cwm beyond it – and dismissed as unlikely the possibility of a route going through it and ascending via the col between Everest and the 'south peak' (Lhotse). The expedition also saw the east (Kangshung) face, dismissing it out of hand and climbed to the Chang La, which they renamed the North Col. Mallory, Wheeler and Bullock reached the Col, and Mallory was prepared to push on, believing that in the time available to them they could explore another 600m (2,000ft), but the wind forced him to reconsider. Nevertheless, the team had seen enough to prove that a route to the summit via the North Col and north ridge was feasible. It had been a successful trip, though marred by the death of Alexander Kellas, arguably the most experienced Himalayan climber of the time, whose heart failed

EVEREST: ASCENT ROUTES

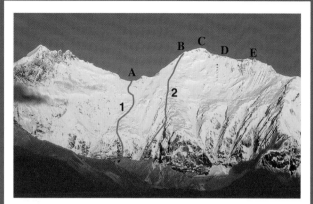

Above East Face
A *South Col*
B *South Summit*
C *Main Summit*
D *North Ridge*
E *Pinnacles*
1 *UK/US 1988*
2 *US 1983*

Above North Face
A *Great or Northern Couloir (in shadowed area), first climbed by the Australians 1984*
1 *Hornbein Couloir, Japanese (1980)*
2 *North Ridge route, Chinese (1960). The face below the ridge has been climbed*
using many variants of the classic route
3 *West Ridge, partial ascent by the Americans via Hornbein Couloir (1963); complete ascent by the Yugoslavians (1979)*

Above From West
A *North (NE) Ridge*
B *Great Couloir*
C *Hornbein Couloir*
D *Summit*
E *South Summit*
F *South Col*
G *Western Cwm*
H *West Ridge*
1 *SE Ridge, first ascent/standard route (1953)*
2 *SW Pillar, Russians (1982)*
3 *SW Face, British (1975)*
4 *South Pillar, Polish (1980)*

due to exhaustion after a prolonged bout of dysentery.

The British returned in 1922, this time led by General Charles Granville Bruce, a giant of a man with a character to match and an enviable knowledge of the Himalaya. Learning from the 1921 trip, the expedition had better food and boots, but the rest of their equipment was much the same – the heavy woollen trousers and jackets which had been used in the Alps for years, though the Australian-born George Finch had a duvet jacket of his own design. Finch was also responsible for the expedition's oxygen equipment, though few of the climbers had any faith in oxygen, and even less in the equipment. The team reached the North Col in mid-May and from it set a number of height records. During the first attempt Mallory, Morshead, Norton and Somervell moved up to a point higher than men had previously reached – and camped there. Next day, Mallory, Norton and Somervell passed the 8,000m (26,240ft) contour for the first time, eventually reaching about 8,200m (about 26,900ft). The trio did not use oxygen, but the second attempt, by Finch and Geoffrey Bruce (the leader's nephew), did. They reached 8,320m (27,300ft), a world record and one especially significant for Geoffrey Bruce: it was his first climb. Later, during a third attempt in early June, with the monsoon already arrived, four climbers and thirteen Sherpas climbed back towards the North Col. The deep fresh snow avalanched and seven Sherpas were killed.

The British returned in 1924, again under General Bruce, though a bout of malaria on the approach march caused him to leave the expedition: Edward Norton took over the leadership. Equipment was much as it had been in 1922, the lesson of Finch's duvet jacket not having been learnt. It is instructive to look at just what the climbers were wearing. For the first summit attempt in 1924 Norton lists his clothing – 'Personally I wore a

The Chinese ladder on the Second Step. Note the snow build up in the crack to the left of the ladder

The Western Cwm from the air showing Everest's south-west face (left), the South Col and Lhotse (ahead), Makalu (beyond), and Nuptse (right)

thick woollen vest and drawers, a thick flannel shirt and two sweaters under a lightish knickerbocker suit of windproof gaberdine the knickers of which were lined with light flannel, a pair of soft elastic Kashmir putties and a pair of boots of felt, bound and soled with leather and lightly nailed with the usual Alpine nails. Over all I wore a very light pyjama suit of Messrs Burberry's 'Shackleton' windproof gaberdine. On my hands I wore a pair of long fingerless woollen mits inside a similar pair made of gaberdine; though when step-cutting necessitated a sensitive hold on the axe-haft. I sometimes substituted a pair of silk mits for the inner woollen pair. On my head I wore a fur-lined leather motor-cycling helmet, and my eyes and nose were protected by a pair of goggles of Crooke's glass, which were sewn into a leather mask that came well over the nose and covered any part of my face which was not naturally protected by my beard. A huge woollen muffler completed my costume.' When Mallory's body was found in 1999 he was wearing

Climbing the Khumbu Icefall to reach the Western Cwm

In the Western Cwm a Sherpa team traverse below Nuptse. To the left is Everest, with Lhotse and the South Col ahead

seven, eight or nine (it was difficult to be exact) layers of clothing, clearly a similar 'costume'. The American climbers noted that Mallory's clothing was equivalent to about two layers of modern fleece – much less than they were wearing. As they pointed out, the clothing was adequate, but left virtually no margin for bad weather or being benighted: Mallory and his comrades were not only skilled climbers, but very brave men.

Norton planned for summit attempts in mid-May, fearful of an early arrival of the monsoon, but a severe and prolonged storm disrupted his plans and it was not until 4 June that the first attempt, by Howard Somervell and Norton himself was made. The pair, neither using bottled oxygen, climbed the rocks of the Yellow Band then moved on to the north face, climbing below the north-east ridge to avoid the First and Second Steps, the latter of which was thought to be a formidable obstacle. Somervell had been troubled with high altitude cough, his throat injured by the thin, cold, dry air, and gave up, Norton continuing across the obvious couloir (the Great – or, occasionally, Norton – Couloir) towards ground which, he believed would offer him easy access to the summit pyramid. But the terrain became more difficult and, at 1pm, realising he did not have the time to reach the summit and return safely, he stopped. He had reached 8,570m (about 28,100ft) a height record which would not be broken, with certainty, for almost 30 years and one that would remain unbroken for 54 years for a climber without bottled oxygen. On the descent Somervell's cough grew worse, one coughing fit dislodging the mucous membrane of his larynx which threatened to choke him. Only by pressing his chest violently did he manage to cough up the obstruction, freeing his windpipe.

The second summit attempt was made on 8 June by George Mallory and Andrew (Sandy) Irvine, the youngest and least experienced member of the team. Much has been made of Mallory's choice of companion: his stated reason was Irvine's familiarity with the oxygen equipment the pair would use – but Noel Odell was just as familiar and a more experienced climber. Numerous possible explanations for Mallory's choice have been put forward over the years, many seeing a homoerotic reason, though there is no evidence to

A mountaineering icon: Tenzing photographed by Hillary on the summit of Everest

support the claim of Mallory's homosexuality: he was married with a son (though this, in itself, is not, of course, evidence). The most likely explanation seems to be the obvious, banal one – Mallory had become friendly with Irvine, liked his company and was impressed by his fitness and understanding of the delicate oxygen equipment they would be taking. It is true that by the time of the attempt, Odell was probably the best acclimatised and fittest member of the team – but Mallory's choice of Irvine was made on 22 April, not in June. Whatever the reason, it was Mallory and Irvine who occupied Camp VI on 7 June. Sometime on the morning of 8 June they left the camp and climbed into legend.

The known facts of the climb are limited: at 12.50pm Odell, climbing up to Camp VI and having reached about 7,960m (26,100ft), saw, through a break in the clouds, the two climbers on the north-east ridge. Where exactly he saw them would stoke the fires of speculation. Later, at about 2pm when Odell was in Camp VI, a storm broke, lasting for about two hours. When it cleared the mountain was bathed in sunshine, but Odell saw no sign of the summit pair anywhere above him. They did not return to Camp VI and the expedition returned to Britain. In 1933, an ice axe believed to have belonged to Irvine was found below the crest of the ridge near the First Step, lying on shallow-angled slabs.

The discovery of the axe was followed by 60 years of speculation about whether the pair had reached the summit. Then, in 1975 during a Chinese expedition Wang Hongbao claimed to have found an 'English dead', a body with old-fashioned clothing and a wound on its face at about 8,200m (26,900ft), directly below the point where the axe was found. Unfortunately Wang's story was not made public until 1979 when he told a Japanese climber during a subsequent Sino-Japanese expedition. The next day, before further details could be obtained, Wang was killed in an avalanche. In May 1999 George Mallory's body was found on the north face. It, too, was below the point at which the ice axe was found, but the fact that the body was face down, solid frozen into the rocks and was undisturbed has lead to speculation that the body Wang saw was that of Irvine. The pair were clearly descending together – Mallory still had a climbing rope attached to his waist – and there had clearly been an accident: Mallory had broken his lower right leg during a fall – he was several hundred feet below the ice axe – dying of shock and exposure.

The finding of the body was claimed by some to solve the mystery – but it does no such thing. The possible success or probable failure of the Mallory/Irvine attempt still largely rests on Odell's sighting. He first claimed to have seen the pair just below the final pyramid (that is, at least at the Second Step, possibly even higher). If that is so, they could have reached the summit and fallen on their descent. Mallory's snow goggles were in his pocket which might imply a descent in darkness, consistent with a late afternoon arrival at the top. Against this are the difficulties of the Second Step, that no anchor was found at the top of it (implying no abseil, while others who have climbed the step say it would be difficult to downclimb – but Hans Kammerlander skied around the bottom of the Step, so there is a way of bypassing it, and the fact that Odell saw no sign of the pair during the rest of a perfect day.

Odell later changed his mind, believing his sighting was much lower, perhaps at, or just above, the First Step. In that case it is likely the pair were caught by the storm en route to the Second Step and retreated, falling during the height of the

Climbers on the final ridge above the Hillary Step; South Summit in the foreground

storm (with Mallory, perhaps, having removed his goggles because of poor visibility). If that is the case then when Odell saw the mountain again the pair would have only just fallen. Though the likelihood is that the pair failed to reach the top, until Irvine's body is discovered (re-discovered ?) and the film in his camera (if it is found and the film is still processable) unlocks the secret, the real story will remain a mystery.

The next British attempt did not take place for nine years, the Tibetans having taken exception to aspects of the early British expeditions: in 1921 Dr Heron, a geologist with the team, dug into the plateau for samples, convincing the locals he was releasing demons from the earth. Then, in 1924 John Neil filmed one Tibetan delousing another and killing the offending creatures between his teeth. The Tibetans saw this as implying they ate lice and were outraged.

When diplomacy finally smoothed the way, Hugh Ruttledge led an expedition in 1933. It discovered the Irvine ice axe and during two attempts Wyn Harris and Wager, and Frank Smythe climbing alone reached about the same point as Norton had in 1924. During the years that followed, before the 1939–45 War put an end to further attempts, the British came back three more times but never bettered the height record. The 1935 trip, led by Eric Shipton, was notable for including a 19 year old Sherpa on his first expedition. His name was Tenzing.

In 1934 an eccentric Briton, Maurice Wilson, attempted the North Col route solo, dying at about 6,400m (21,000ft), and there were two further solo bids after the war. In 1947 the Canadian Earl Denman, accompanied by Tenzing and another Sherpa, failed to reach the North Col and in 1950 the Dane Klaus Larsen retreated from the North Col. Then, in October 1950 the Chinese invaded Tibet and all foreign expeditions to the northern side of the mountain stopped for 30 years.

Interest in the world's highest mountain did not stop however. The Nepalese opened their borders and in 1950, with the French on Annapurna, Charles Houston, Bill Tilman and others approached the Khumbu icefall, though they did not see into the Western Cwm. In 1951 an expedition under Eric Shipton (including Michael Ward, Tom Bourdillon and Ed Hillary) climbed to a point on Pumori from where they could see that a route existed by way of the Western Cwm, the South Col and south-east ridge. Later they climbed the icefall to the entrance to the Cwm. Though they were shaken by the dangers of the fall and by the risk of load carrying up it, they concluded that the southern route was climbable.

Back in London the British Himalayan Committee appointed Shipton leader of a planned 1952 expedition only to discover, to their astonishment, that the Nepalese had granted

The Hillary Step. The climber is Israeli Doron Erel

permission to the Swiss. The British therefore approached the Swiss making them an offer which amounted, in effect, to allowing them to send a group of climbers on a British expedition. The Swiss declined, hardly surprisingly. The British therefore decided that the Swiss could try pre-monsoon and that they would try post-monsoon. But the Nepalese said no. The British were being required to learn, and quickly, that in the post-war world a glorious past was no passport to a dependable future.

The Swiss pre-monsoon expedition under Ed Wyss-Dunant was exploratory as well as a real attempt: no one had come this way before. Considering that, and the appalling weather which plagued them, they made remarkable progress. They found the Lhotse Face steeper than expected (about the same as Mont Blanc's Brenva Face), and chose to climb the Geneva Spur, a rib of rock on its left edge, which led to the South Col. In screaming winds and perishing cold three Swiss, Tenzing and three other Sherpas camped on the Col. The next day the three Sherpas descended while Lambert, Tenzing, Flory and Aubert continued up the south-east ridge. At about 8,380m (27,500ft) a tent was pitched. Here Raymond Lambert and Tenzing stayed while Flory and Aubert retreated to the Col. The following day, despite using oxygen Lambert and Tenzing managed only some 200m (650ft) up the ridge in five hours of climbing. Their attempt had ended, but their estimated height of about 8,600m (28,200ft) was probably a little higher than that reached on the north side. A second attempt got no higher than the South Col.

The Swiss returned post-monsoon, aware that the British had permission for 1953 and the French for 1954. This time

they were led by Gabriel Chevalley who, with Lambert, was the only survivor from the pre-monsoon team. Tenzing went again, but now as a member of the climbing team rather than just Sherpa sirdar. The expedition was dogged by ill-health and a Sherpa, Mingma Dorje, died after being hit by falling ice on the Lhotse Face. The delays these problems caused meant that by the time the South Col was reached winter had come. A token few metres of the south-east ridge were climbed and then the team retreated.

First Ascent

Just as the Swiss had been in the summer of 1952, the British were aware that 1953 might be their last chance for success. Not only had the French been given permission for 1954, but the Swiss had been granted another go in 1955. What they

Don Whillans leaving Camp IV during the attempt on the south-west face in 1971

needed, therefore, was a determined, decisive leader and Eric Shipton, for all his experience and abilities, was a cautious man and one not over-fond of large expeditions. On Cho Oyu in 1952 Shipton had demonstrated all his undoubted abilities as an explorer but, equally, all his failings as a single-minded leader. The British Himalayan Committee therefore appointed John Hunt, an army officer with an impressive Alpine and Himalayan record who had narrowly failed to make the 1936 Everest expedition, as leader.

Hunt's team was a large one and included several who had been with Shipton on Cho Oyu in 1952. It comprised George Band, Tom Bourdillon, Charles Evans, Alf Gregory, Edmund Hillary, George Lowe, Wilfred Noyce, Griffith Pugh (expedition physiologist), Michael Ward (expedition doctor: Evans was

The Khumbu Icefall pours out of the Western Cwm

also a surgeon), Michael Westmacott and Charles Wylie. James Morris of The Times went to write dispatches for the paper and Tom Stobart was there to make a film of the attempt: Alf Gregory, an expert photographer was an 'official' stills photographer. Tenzing was invited to join the climbing team as well as being sirdar of the Sherpas.

Hunt's planning for the expedition was meticulous, his military background clearly evident. The British public offered advice, too, much of it eccentric, some downright bizarre. One idea involved the use of a mortar to fire oxygen cylinders from the Western Cwm to the South Col, obviating the need for tiring load carrying. This even seems to have been considered seriously for a while and the expedition did indeed take a two-inch mortar, intending to fire it at avalanche-prone slopes. In

the event is was not used, but led to a remark which firmly sets the expedition in place and time. On hearing that a newspaper had reported that the 'assault' on the mountain would start with a bombardment by the mortar George Band wondered if, at the same time, Spitfires would circle the South Col. In an age of cruise missiles the remark dates the expedition more than any photograph of climbers not clad in the now-obligatory one-piece down suit.

The expedition established a series of closely spaced camps between the base of the Icefall and that of the Lhotse face. Hunt then outlined his plan for the summit attempts. The expedition had two types of oxygen equipment, the 'open-circuit' in which bottled oxygen is mixed with the surrounding air, enhancing the climber's oxygen supply and the 'closed-circuit', which used a soda-lime canister to extract oxygen from the carbon-dioxide exhaled by the climber and recycled it, topped up with bottled oxygen. The advantage of the latter is that a richer supply of oxygen is produced, allowing the user to climb faster. The drawback is that the user is cut off from the outside world, a claustrophobic situation and one which, if the system fails, causes a much sharper decrease in oxygen supply than users of the open-circuit system experience. The closed circuit system is also much more complex, making problems more likely. As a consequence the open-circuit is now used exclusively by those climbers who choose to use bottled gas at all.

Hunt decided that the first attempt on the peak would be by Bourdillon and Evans using closed-circuit equipment from the South Col, the second by Hillary and Tenzing using open-circuit systems and starting from a camp high on the south-east ridge.

The make-up of the first party was understandable: Bourdillon was the expedition's oxygen equipment expert, and, as a scientist, had helped develop the closed-circuit system; Evans had been his climbing partner during the early stages of the expedition. But why were they to start from the South Col when their chances of success were clearly higher if they started from higher up? Hunt's stated view is that the faster climb rate of users of the closed-circuit system would overcome the problem of a lower start, but it is likely that other unstated factors also played a part. Establishing a camp above the South Col was extremely difficult, supplying it twice might prove impossible. It therefore made sense to supply it once, and man it with the pair who had the best chance of success. Hunt seems to have mistrusted the closed-circuit system, and so probably felt that Hillary and Tenzing stood more chance of reaching the top. If Bourdillon and Evans did succeed – excellent, but even

The east or 'Kangshung' faces of Everest (right) and Lhotse reflected in a pond on the Kharta Glacier

their failure was likely to provide information valuable to the second team. It is probably overstating it to suggest that Hunt's military background was evident again – using the first wave of troops to clear the minefield, one way or another, and the so provide the second wave with an easier passage – but there have been some since who have used it.

The choice of Hillary and Tenzing was less controversial. The pair had gelled well, matching each other for speed and drive. Before Hunt's arrival at Base Camp, Hillary had pushed the route through the Icefall to the Cwm, and the pair had proved far faster than any other team on the mountain. In his latest published look back over an eventful life Hillary states that the partnership was not entirely fortuitous. Realising that Hunt was unlikely to chose a pair of New Zealanders for the summit attempt (and George Lowe was his usual climbing partner) Hillary had deliberately distanced himself from Lowe: it is an admission of startling honesty and one at apparent odds with the idea of Hillary being a lucky innocent. The fact that Hillary was a New Zealander and that Tenzing was Nepalese (or Indian – he was given passports by both nations after the climb) and the only Sherpa who had any desire to reach the summit, has also been used to suggest that Hunt had other motives for his choice – Empire man and local man, a very British choice. There is certainly some evidence to suggest Tenzing was indeed seen as a symbol of the Sherpas in the quest for success on Everest.

Hunt made his announcement of 7 May, but 10 days later it looked premature – the South Col was still an elusive target and the expedition's timetable was going wrong. Not until 21 May was the Col reached, though the pace of the climb then accelerated. On 26 May Bourdillon and Evans set out from the Col at 7am, with Hunt and the Sherpa Da Namgyal following to establish Camp IX on the ridge. Though Bourdillon and Evans made good progress at first, problems with Evans' oxygen set and poor snow conditions slowed them as they got higher. Not until 1am did they reach the South Summit. Reaching it was an achievement, the highest point reached to date, but on Everest it was only a point on the journey. For 30 minutes the pair discussed their options. They had enough oxygen for another two or three hours climbing which, they estimated, should get them to the top. Would they survive a bottled gas-free descent? What if Evans' faulty set failed going up the final ridge? Should Bourdillon go on alone? Finally, they turned to descend.

After the expedition Tom Bourdillon is said to have regretted the decision (or, at least, his own decision) not to continue. Down on the Col the Sherpas, seeing the pair on the South Summit had cheered loudly, believing it to be the true summit. Tenzing, by contrast, was less ecstatic – the sight of

the pair disappearing from view, probably on their way to the true top, meant his own dreams were dashed and he felt the loss keenly.

On their return Bourdillon and Evans were utterly exhausted. The next day the weather was bad, but so poor was

Approaching the summit, climbers toil up the final few rope lengths of the south-east ridge

Bourdillon's condition that he had to be taken down despite it. On 28 May Hillary and Tenzing, supported by Lowe and Ang Nyima moved up to Camp IX. On 29 May Hillary and Tenzing started up at 6.30am, quickly reaching the poor snow below the South Summit which had troubled the first pair. Hillary tackled it head on (Bourdillon and Evans had skirted it on poor rock to the left) and was soon frightened by its condition. He pressed on, knowing a slip would be fatal for them both and knowing the slope could avalanche, but knowing, too, that this was Everest and his only chance of the top. By 9am they had overcome the

comfortably. After the congratulations, Hillary took summit shots of Tenzing and then peered down the north side for a sign of Mallory and Irvine. This he mentions in his account, but does not say what he later confided in Ruttledge, that he believed that the last 275m (900ft) of the north ridge looked unclimbable. The pair then ate a bar of Kendal mint cake and started down. At the South Col they were met by George Lowe, Hillary's countryman. Hillary gave him the great news – 'Well', he said 'we knocked the bastard off'.

The north face from the head of the Rongbuk Glacier, with the west ridge on the right and the North Col on the left

slope and reached the South Summit. The final ridge looked hard, but went straightforwardly, the only difficulty being the now-famous Hillary Step. Hillary's later description of the step caused Tenzing deep offence. Hillary first said that after he had climbed the step he was 'gasping like a fish'. In the official expedition book he transferred the (much elaborated) metaphor to Tenzing and implied he had all but hauled the Sherpa up. Tenzing was very offended by both suggestions (and also thought the step was only a third or so the height claimed by Hillary). Hillary omitted fish references from his autobiography, Tenzing mentioned them verbatim in his.

The pair then continued over easier ground to the summit. The discovery of Mallory's body in 1999 led to interviews with Hillary during which, several newspapers claimed, he finally admitted who had been the first to reach the top. Since Tenzing had already admitted this in his ghosted autobiography several decades before, this 'new' information seemed surprisingly dated. Below the summit the pair paused. Hillary was concerned that the apparent top might be a cornice overhanging the stupendous east face and so made Tenzing take a belay while he continuously probed his way up to a table-sized summit on which half-a-dozen men could stand

Later Ascents

The news of the climbing of Everest reached Britain by way of a coded message in time for *The Times* to announce it on 2 June, the day Queen Elizabeth II was crowned. The French, who had 'booked' the mountain for 1954 abandoned their plan, but the Swiss, due to return, in 1955 merely slipped a year and went for the double, not only repeating the South Col route twice but making the first ascent of Lhotse. Thereafter, there was a steady stream of expeditions to the peak, a stream that grew to something more akin to a river once cheaper travel, better equipment, familiarity and the increased number of experienced Sherpas and climbers allowed mere mortals (wealthy mere mortals that is) to realise their ambitions. To date the mountain has had over 1,000 ascents by more than 800 climbers, some climbers chalking up multiple ascents: the Sherpa Ang Rita was the first to have climbed Everest ten times, all without bottled gas (though there are persistent rumours that he sometimes used bottled gas for sleeping before his summit climbs, rumours he denies) – he retired from high altitude climbing in 1999 saying he was 'sick and tired and old enough to retire' at 51, the same year that his record of ten ascents was equalled (by Apa Sherpa) and several Sherpas were threatening to break it. Several Sherpas have completed five or more ascents of the peak, and in May 1999 the American Pete Athans made his sixth ascent, a record (at present) for a non-Sherpa.

Everest has also given rise to a plethora of books, perhaps more than for all other mountains combined. Such a library makes a detailed account of the numerous climbs here superfluous, and below only the key ascents are noted.

In 1960 the Chinese claimed to have climbed the north side of the mountain, following the classic 'Mallory' line over the First and Second Steps. The Second Step proved to be very difficult, taking several hours to climb and requiring the leader to take off his boots in order to climb on the shoulders of a team-mate without inflicting too much damage to him. Three of the four climbers then continued to the summit, climbing through the night to arrive in the early hours of 25 May. On top they claimed to have left a bust of Mao. The rest of the world viewed the claim with scepticism – climbing barefoot? reaching the summit at night? – but later evidence, of the bootless climber's frost-bitten feet (he was never able to climb again) and a photograph almost certainly taken above the Second Step suggest that Wang Fuzhou (often written Wang Fu-Chou in the west), Qu Yinhua (Chu Yin-hua) and the Tibetan Gongbu (Gonpa) probably did make the first ascent of the north/north-east ridge (the Mallory route) in 1960. In 1975 the Chinese repeated the climb and installed a ladder at the crucial section of the Second Step. Only Chinese climbers had therefore climbed the step before 1999 when the American Conrad Anker ignored the ladder to test the grade of the climb: the lack of Chinese climbers in the West, and vice versa did not allow the time taken on the step by the Chinese (amounting to many hours on the first ascent) to be translated into a formal grade. Anker thought it is about 5.8 (British 4c/HVS, French 5, Australian 16), but rightly noted that sea-level 5.8 and 5.8 at 8,580m (over 28,150ft) were quite different propositions. Anker's climb suggests that Mallory and Irvine did not climb the step, and certainly not in the five minutes Odell saw them take over a rock step on the ridge (though Anker took only a few minutes over the climb), but as the climbing is almost certainly affected by the extent of snow banking it is impossible to be certain. If the snow was banked high enough the rock climbing required would be much reduced.

On the Kangshung Face during the first ascent of the Anglo-American route

In 1963 an American team not only put four men on top along the original route, but followed a shoulder of the mountain from the Western Cwm to the west ridge which they followed to the summit. At one point the summiteers, Tom Hornbein and Willy Unsoeld were forced on to the north face, following a prominent snow gully now known as the Hornbein Couloir. Hornbein and Unsoeld descended the original route, making a traverse of the peak. The Indians climbed the mountain in 1965, after which Nepal closed its borders for three years. When the next expedition arrived, the Japanese in 1969, they were assessing the chances of climbing the south-west face. The Japanese tried, and abandoned, the face in 1970 and 1973 (though placing men on the summit along the classic route on both occasions: the 1973 climb was the first post-monsoon ascent), and the face also repulsed an international team in 1971, an Anglo-German team in spring 1972 and a British attempt in autumn 1972. The first two expeditions were notable for their attempts at cross-nation co-operation, attempts foiled by poor weather, poor planning, personal ambition and, it must be said, a degree of cross-nation antagonism.

Approaching the South Col, with the south-east ridge and the South Summit beyond

Everest's first female ascent came in 1975 when the Japanese Junko Tabei summitted: just eleven days later the Tibetan woman Panduo (Phantog) summitted on a second Chinese ascent of the north ridge. The main event of 1975 was, however, the ascent of the south-west face by a British team under Chris Bonington. The team, many of whom had been on the Annapurna South Face expedition, climbed the rock band, the face's main obstacle, on its left side (all other attempts had sought a route on the right), then traversed to the South Summit, following the classic route from there to the top. Dougal Haston and Doug Scott reached the summit, followed by Peter Boardman and Sherpa Pertemba, and, in all likelihood, Mick Burke who disappeared near the top, probably breaking through a cornice during his lone descent in a storm. The first pair, Haston and Scott, survived a bivouac without bottled oxygen in a snowhole dug at the South Summit when benighted during their descent.

In 1978 the Italian (Tyrolean) Reinhold Messner and the Austrian Peter Habeler became the first men to climb Everest without bottled oxygen. The pair were attached to an Austrian expedition and when a solo attempt by Messner (after Habeler had gone down with food poisoning) was cut short by a storm which almost killed him, Habeler had second thoughts about the project. He asked to join the Austrian team officially but was turned down. Furious at the refusal he rejoined Messner and the pair climbed to the South Col. From there they followed the classic route, utilising the steps of Austrians who had summitted five days earlier. They reached the South Summit in 6½ hours, the summit an hour later. Habeler descended to the South Col, in part glissading and at one point falling, in one hour. Messner took only a few minutes longer. The times astonished the world, especially the Sherpa community who doubted whether anyone could outperform them at altitude. But Messner and Habeler were very fit and very fast, a fact they had already proved on Gasherbrum I and, in Messner's case, would prove again. Everest was Messner's fourth 8,000er.

The following year a Yugoslavian team climbed the West Ridge from the Lho La, four members (Nejc Zaplotnik, Andrej Stremfelj, Stane Belak and Stipe Bozik) and the Sherpa Ang Phu reaching the top. Ang Phu was killed on the descent. Then, on 17 February 1980, the Poles Leszek Cichy and Kryzysztof Wielicki, using bottled oxygen, completed the first winter ascent of the peak, following the classic line. 1980 also saw the first non-Chinese ascent of the north side of Everest, the Japanese Yasuo Kato soloing the Mallory line from the top camp when his companion stopped, while two of his countrymen followed a direct line up the north face and Hornbein Couloir to the summit. At the same time a Polish team climbed the South Pillar (which flanks the south-west face, leading directly to the South Summit). One of the two who reached the summit on 19 May 1980 was Jerzy Kukuczka, climbing his second 8,000er: the other climber was Andrzej Czok. The two Poles used bottled oxygen as far as the South Summit, continuing to the summit without bottled gas when their supply ran out. During the 1980 monsoon Reinhold Messner returned to the mountain, climbing a route on the north face solo. Although the last stage of the mountain had been soloed before (by Burke on the south side and Kato on the north) those climbers had been with full teams and each had started out with a colleague. Messner was completely alone on the mountain (in itself a situation unlikely ever to be repeated) making his achievement an astonishing exercise in both ability and control. He camped above the North Col on his first night, than traversed the north face (the Mallory route was deep in snow) to a camp at 8,200m (26,900ft). The next day he continued below the ridge, then climbed up to the summit, reaching it at 3pm. He regained his camp that night and descended to the East Rongbuk Glacier the next day. The climb remains one of the great achievements of mountaineering.

In 1982 a Russian team climbed a pillar at the left edge of the south-west face, a very hard route, probably the hardest line to the highest summit: eleven climbers reached the top. In the winter of 1982/83 a French attempt on the west ridge failed, but a Belgian climber who disappeared on 7 January 1983 turned up in Kathmandu on 14 January. He had slipped down the Tibetan side of the Lho La and walked out via the Rongbuk glacier (being

Litter on the South Col. Beyond is the south-east ridge leading up to the South Summit

The tiny figure of a climber on the Rongbuk Glacier (bottom right) is dwarfed by Everest's north face. The right skyline is the west ridge, the left skyline is the classic north-side route

mistaken for a yeti in a Tibetan village en route), a remarkable escape. Later in 1983 an American team made the first ascent of the east face via the central pillar direct to the South Summit, six members reaching the summit, a very under-rated climb on a formidable face. In 1984 the Australians Tim McCartney-Snape and Greg Mortimer climbed the Great (Norton) Couloir up the north face. Later McCartney-Snape returned to the mountain: he walked in from the shore of the Bay of Bengal and climbed to the summit, the first 'full' ascent. An even more 'full' ascent occurred in 1996 when Göran Kropp cycled to Nepal from his Swedish home, climbed the peak without bottled oxygen and cycled home again.

In December 1987, the Sherpa Ang Rita became the first person to summit Everest in winter without bottled oxygen when he summitted as part of a South Korean expedition. It was his fourth ascent of the peak. In the spring season of the following year the peak was traversed by a Chinese/Japanese/Nepalese team, climbers on the Mallory and original routes meeting at the summit and some descending each way so that the traverse was completed in both directions. The same spring Stephen Venables reached the top via a new route on the east face (to the South Col, continuing along the classic route) he had made with two American colleagues. In the post-monsoon period of 1988 the Frenchman Marc Batard soloed the classic route from Base Camp to summit in 22½ hours (following a trail made by previous climbers) and the New Zealander Lydia Bradey made the first female ascent without bottled oxygen, though her ascent has been questioned by some experts, based on timings from others on the final climb on the same day. (The first

Climbers approach the South Summit at about 8,500m (28,000ft) on the south-east ridge. Beyond lies the frontier peak of Shartse (7,444m/24,423ft) with Makalu standing in the distance

undisputed female, bottled oxygen-free ascent was made in 1995 by the Briton Alison Hargreaves following the Mallory route on the Tibetan side.) Also in 1988 a four-man Czech team completed an alpine-style, bottled oxygen-free ascent of the south-west face (British route). Only one man reached the summit, though at least three made the South Summit. Tragically all four died during the descent. 1988 also saw the fastest descent of the peak, Frenchman Jean-Marc Boivin parapenting from the summit to Camp II (at 6,700m/22,000ft) in just eleven minutes.

By 1990 the first commercial expeditions were climbing the mountain (the actual first commercial climb was in 1985 when American Dick Bass was guided to the top by David Breashers) the rate of successful ascents accelerating. Some variants to existing routes were climbed and there were still significant achievements. In 1993 the Japanese climbed the south-west face in winter, but Fernando Garrido failed at 7,750m (25,400ft) in an attempt at a winter solo. The Japanese fixed 3.6km (2¼miles) of rope in temperatures as low as minus 36°C and six men reached the top in three pairs between 18 and 22 December.

In 1995 a Japanese expedition completed the full north-east ridge. This, the 'pinnacle ridge', had been attempted several times and had cost the lives of the British climbers Peter Boardman and Joe Tasker. It had been climbed as far as the junction with the north ridge in 1986 by Briton Harry Taylor and New Zealander Russell Brice, but bad weather prevented them from continuing to the top. Also in 1995, the Sherpa Babu Chhire (or Tshering) made two ascents of the Mallory route separated by just 12 days as part of a commercial expedition. Between Babu's two ascents the Italian (Tyrolean) Reinhard Patscheider climbed the same route from the base of the North Col to the summit in 21 hours. More poignantly, on the same day as Patscheider's ascent George Mallory, grandson of the British Everest pioneer, completed the route on which his grandfather had disappeared 51 years before. In 1996 Patscheider's time on the classic north face route was reduced to 16¾ hours by another Tyrolean, Hans Kammerlander. Kammerlander intended a ski descent of the Great Couloir, but finding it too icy skied his ascent route instead, finding a way around the base of the Second Step. As the wind had stripped much of the snow from the north face he was forced to downclimb short sections, but could claim a nearly-ski descent.

Dougal Haston on the summit, photographed by Doug Scott after the first ascent of the south-west face

The north face from the Rongbuk Glacier

But just as ascents of Everest were appearing to have become routine – not since 1993 has there been a year without a successful ascent – with tens of climbers reaching the summit on the same day, just how fragile a man's existence is at the summit was illustrated when a sudden storm on 10 May 1996 caught the members of two commercial expeditions on the way down from the summit killing several, including the two expedition leaders Rob Hall and Scott Fischer, and maiming another through frostbite. It was a cruel reminder that 8,000m peaks are not to be taken for granted, but only a comma in the Everest story. On 16 October 1998 the Sherpa Kaji climbed the southern original route in 20 hours 24 minutes, his fifth ascent. He would have been quicker but lost an hour on the Lhotse face due to high winds and another hour near the South Summit waiting for a rope to be fixed by his assisting party of Sherpas. He also rested for 30 minutes. It was an impressive achievement, though Japanese climbers on the peak at the same time have raised doubts over whether he actually summitted. Another, more curious, time record was established in 1999 when Sherpa Babu Chhire (or Tshering) camped on the summit, remaining there for 21½ hours. He arrived at 9am on 6 May with two other Sherpas and stayed until 7.30am on the 7 May, returning to a hero's welcome on the South Col. A fortnight later Apa Sherpa completed his tenth ascent (all with bottled oxygen) from the north side. On that same day Sergio Martini finally climbed Everest and would have joined the 'all-14' club but for the disputed ascent of Lhotse with partner Fausto de Stefani.

Everest has now been climbed about 1,200 times, but such is its draw that many of these have been multiple ascents: fewer than 900 climbers have their names on the summit roll. It has been climbed by 60 year olds and a 17 year old, and in 1998 had its first ascent by a disabled climber, Welsh-born, but US-naturalised, Tom Whittaker who had lost a foot in car crash. He was accompanied to top by Jeff Rhoads and Sherpa Tashi Tshering. On his first try he had to retreat, the other two reaching the top. A week later Whittaker tried again and made it. His co-climbers thus reached the top twice in seven days.

It might be assumed that as the fiftieth anniversary of the first ascent approaches the Everest story has few remaining chapters to write, but that is a rash suggestion to make. The draw of the world's highest mountain will remain and its records will always be broken.

nanga parbat 8,125m

"I could no longer stand upright; I was but the wreck of a human being. So I crawled slowly forward on all fours, drawing imperceptibly nearer to that rocky spur, towards which I was struggling with such grim doubts."

HERMANN BUHL on the final steps to the summit

nanga parbat

Nanga Parbat is the most westerly of the 8,000m peaks standing in massive isolation about 125km (80 miles) north of the Kashmiri capital of Srinigar. Though geographically close to the Karakoram peaks it is actually the western bastion of the Greater Himalaya, overlooking the Indus River which forms the range's western border.

Though geographically close to the Karakoram peaks it is actually the western bastion of the Greater Himalaya, overlooking the Indus river which forms the range's western border. In the winter of 1840/41 an earthquake caused a huge rock slide from the northern Nanga Parbat massif blocking the Indus valley and creating a vast lake stretching almost to Gilgit over 60km (40 miles) away. The natural dam eventually broke in the summer of 1841, the resultant tidal wave causing massive damage and loss of life. It is said that a Sikh army camped in the lower valley was completely annihilated.

The mountain's name derives from the Sanskrit Nanga Parvata, 'naked mountain', probably from its isolation. The Kashmiri name Diamir, meaning King of Mountains, has been popularly overtaken by the Sanskrit version, though it is applied to the peak's western flank. Many believe the peak to be the most beautiful of all the great peaks which would make Diamir a fitting name, though the longer version does seem more appropriate, its lyricism reflecting the mountain's magnificent presence, if not its brutal history.

Exploration

The peak was probably first seen, by western eyes, by the British explorer and artist GT Vigne who explored Kashmir in 1835, seeing the 'stupendous peak' from a pass to the north of Srinigar. It was visited by the three Germans brothers Von Schlagintweit in 1856, then by the doctor/missionary Dr Arthur Neve in 1887. Neve was probably the first westerner to see the peak's Rupal flank, the tallest mountain wall in the world. Over the next few years the peak was sketched and photographed several more times, the very fact of its isolation from other major peaks meaning that its base was relatively easy to

The Mazeno Ridge, one of the last great problems on Nanga Parbat

The Diamir Face of Nanga Parbat from the Diamir Valley

approach on all sides. It is likely that the photographs of EF Knight, taken in 1891, and Conway's view of the peak from near Gilgit before his Baltoro expedition, were among the reasons for the interest in the peak shown by three of Britain's finest alpinists in 1895.

Albert Mummery was, arguably, the best climber of the time. Born in 1855, he was a very unlikely mountaineer, being slightly hunchbacked because of a spinal birth defect and very short-sighted. But firstly in the company of the guide Alexander Burgener (with whom he did the first ascent of the Zmutt ridge on the Matterhorn) and then climbing guideless (notably on the Grépon) he established a reputation for bold, difficult ascents. In 1895, together with Geoffrey Hastings and J Norman Collie, Mummery went to Nanga Parbat intending to explore it thoroughly and, if possible, to climb it.

The Britons first looked at the gigantic Rupal Face which they thought unclimbable, then crossed the Mazeno Pass to look at the Diamir Face which looked much more promising. The three were now joined by the young Major Charles Bruce who, as General Bruce, was later to lead expeditions to Everest, and two of his Gurkhas, Ragobir and Goman Singh, though Bruce soon left the expedition, mumps and the impending end of his leave forcing his withdrawal.

Though Mummery's enthusiasm for the climbing was high throughout the trip, the expedition record makes it clear that the Britons had little understanding of what they were involved in (at least at first – Collie later commented ruefully on the difference in scale of Himalayan and alpine peaks). The party often ran low on food – rarely a problem in the European Alps with their studding of farms and villages – and Mummery firmly believed that a single day was all that was needed to reach the summit from a height of about 6,100m (20,000ft). With Hastings off getting supplies Mummery, together with Collie,

NANGA PARBAT: ASCENT ROUTES

Above North-east Face
1 *First ascent, Buhl (1953)*
2 *Japanese 1995*

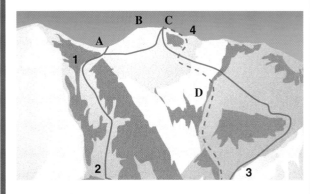

Above Rupal Face
1 *German 'Schell Route' (1976)*
2 *German/Italian (1970)*
3 *Polish/Mexican (1985)*

Above Diamir Face
A *Bazhin Gap*
B *Shoulder*
C *Main Summit*
D *Mummery Ribs*
1 *Germans (1962) climbed to Bazhin Gap and followed Buhl (1953) line to summit. Now climbers traverse below the summit*
pyramid and take a direct line to the summit
2 *German (1962) 'Kinshofer Route'*
3 *Messner solo (1978); dotted line is descent route*
4 *'Schell Route' follows upper part of this ridge (see above)*

The Rakhiot flank of Nanga Parbat

of about 6,100m (20,000ft) they were forced to turn back when Ragobir, who appears only to have eaten when told to, fell ill.

Abandoning the Diamir Face Mummery next decided to explore the northern side of the peak. Unimpressed by Hastings' and Collie's idea of taking the long route around the north-west ridge, Mummery and the two Gurkhas set off to cross the Diama Pass. On the far side of the ridge Hastings and Collie waited in vain: Mummery, Ragobir and Goman Singh probably died in an avalanche on the Diamir side of the pass.

Not until 1930 did climbers consider returning to Nanga Parbat, and again it was one of the foremost alpinists of the time who had the dream. Wilhelm (Willo) Welzenbach was born in Munich in 1900, taking an engineering degree at the city's university and working as an architect for Munich City Council. He was a good rock climber, but is famous as an innovative ice climber, inventing the ice piton and pushing the use of 10-point crampons and step-cutting to their limits on steep ice: not until

the two Gurkhas and a local hunter called Lor Khan, attacked what is now called the Mummery Rib, a complex of rock spurs leading up the Diamir Face towards the main summit. After an initial retreat Mummery tried again accompanied only by Ragobir. At a height

Hermann Buhl looks across to the final ridge

Buhl's classic shot from the summit, looking back down his ascent route

the arrival of front-point crampons and short ice axes were ice climbing standards advanced. Welzenbach used his improved techniques to climb north faces in the eastern Alps (and, later, the western Alps) which had been thought unclimbable. His ascents of the north faces of the Gross Weissbachhorn, the Grands Charmoz and some Bernese Oberland faces were the hardest climbs of the late 1920s/early 1930s. But some of the climbs were not only hard but risky, the faces swept by avalanches or stones, and climbers of the old school thought them completely unjustified. Welzenbach, the leader of the new developments, climbed mostly with others from Munich, the 'Munich School' producing climbers who went on to climb some of the great north faces including the Matterhorn and the

Eiger. Their apparent 'death or glory' attitude to climbing appealed to Germany's new rulers, the Nazi party enjoying the reflected glory of handsome, blond youths risking death to bring famous victories back to the Fatherland, a fact which only served to increase the polarisation between the old and new schools. Today it is clear that the Bavarians were just advancing the standards of the sport, as is inevitable, but at the time the movement was seen to have more sinister overtones. Doubtless some of the young German climbers were not opposed to the fame their exploits brought – but that is equally true today.

There is no evidence that Welzenbach's desire to extend his climbing horizons beyond the Alps were motivated by anything other than an interest in the next challenge. In 1928 Munich School climbers went to the Caucasus and the Pamirs and in 1929 Paul Bauer led an expedition to Kangchenjunga. Illness stopped Welzenbach from going to the Pamirs, business commitments from joining Bauer. In 1930 he applied for permission to go to Nanga Parbat, but though the British were willing for him to go, the Germans were not, giving state backing to another Kangchenjunga attempt. When that failed Welzenbach tried again for Nanga Parbat in 1931 – but Bauer, with whom Welzenbach had fallen out, convinced the authorities to back him on Kangchenjunga again. This they did, though when the expedition failed they gave Welzenbach their blessing for 1932. But that year Munich City Council refused Welzenbach's request for leave and so it was his partner on the Grands Charmoz, Willy Merkl, who led the expedition.

Merkl's expedition, which included an American, Rand Herron, Fritz Wiessner, who was later to become a naturalised American and was almost to climb K2 in 1939, and the Austrian Peter Aschenbrenner, included no climbers who had been with Bauer (a clear indication of the needle between Welzenbach and Bauer) and no one who spoke the local language. Because of possible problems with a difficult local tribe, the Germans were required to approach from the south, having to cross numerous high and heavily snowed-up passes to reach their preferred, north-east face. From its base, and a marvellously pastoral camp site Merkl named the Marchenwiese, Fairy Meadow – all climbs on Nanga Parbat start low and, consequently, in pleasant surroundings: as Jerzy Kukuczka put it, it is the only mountain on which you climb through all the seasons, from real summer to -40° – the team forged a long route up the face of the Rakhiot Peak, aiming to cross the Silver Saddle and Silver Plateau to reach the peak's northern ridge. The weather, and sheer inexperience, stopped them at Camp VII, placed on the east ridge beyond the Rakhiot Peak at about 7,000m (23,000ft). As a reconnaissance the expedition had

The mountain from the Rupal Valley

been a success, but a shadow was cast over it during the return: stopping over at Cairo Rand Herron climbed the Pyramids at Giza. Descending from the second at a run he tripped, fell and was killed.

In 1934 the Germans returned, now with the full backing of the Nazi regime which ensured that the best of equipment and Sherpas were available. Welzenbach went too, but the leader was, again, Willy Merkl despite the misgivings of many who had been in the 1932 team. Steady progress was made along the route pioneered in 1932 until one of the climbers, Alfred Drexel, died quite suddenly, probably of pulmonary oedema. The retreat to the Fairy Meadow which followed cost the expedition 17 days, a loss that was to cost it victory and create a tragedy.

The route was eventually pushed out again, crossing the face of the Rakhiot Peak to reach the east ridge and a rock pillar the Germans called the Mohrenkopf (literally the Moor's Head, but actually named for a chocolate-covered cream cake popular in Germany at the time). From there the ridge dipped 120m (400ft) then rose to the Silver Saddle. The Germans placed Camp VII beyond the dip and from it on 6 July five climbers and eleven Sherpas climbed upwards.

The Austrians Aschenbrenner and Erwin Schneider broke trail, reaching the Saddle at 10.30am. They waited until noon when the others arrived, then started across the wide, flat Silver Plateau towards the summit. At around 2pm they arrived below the Subsidiary Summit, at a height of about 7,830m (25,700ft). They were only about 300m (1,000ft) below the summit, but still over 1½ km (more than a mile) horizontally from it. They found a good campsite, but when the three Germans and the Sherpas did not arrive Schneider went back to see what the delay was. After another 1½ hours Aschenbrenner trudged after him. Merkl, Welzenbach and Uli Wieland had stopped at the Saddle, deciding to camp there despite Schneider's attempts to persuade them across the plateau. It seemed a trivial point, however, as the team thought it certain that the following they would all make it to the top.

The expedition was now dangerously extended. There were 16 men at Camp VIII, but no one between them and Camp IV over 1,500m (5,000ft) below and some 4km (2½ miles) away horizontally. Worse still, bad weather at Camp IV – quite unlike the sunshine on the plateau – prevented supplies being carried higher. Had the weather stayed fine those details might not have mattered, but on the night of 6 July a fierce storm broke. Nanga Parbat, as with the Karakoram peaks, is sufficiently far west to avoid the monsoon which makes summer climbing in Nepal dangerous, but occasionally storms from severe monsoons do creep as far as the Punjab Himalaya and the Karakoram.

The storm of early July 1934 lasted many days. By the morning of the 8 July the 16 men on the plateau were in a poor state. Poles had snapped, semi-collapsing their tents, allowing in blown snow which soaked and froze them. With daylight came the decision to retreat despite the continuing storm: it was a stark choice – stay and die, descend and probably die. Aschenbrenner and Schneider, still the fittest, set off to break trail with three Sherpas, but an early fall by one Sherpa lost the Austrians' sleeping bags. Knowing there were spares only at Camp V the Austrians unroped from the Sherpas and ploughed down through the storm. At 7pm the pair collapsed, exhausted into Camp IV. They assumed the others, following their trail, would soon follow.

The other three Germans and the remaining Sherpas, exhausted by the storm, the lack of food and drink, and affected by the altitude, did not even make Camp VII on 8 July, spending

On the 'Kinshofer Wall', Diamir Face

Approaching the 'Kinshofer Wall' on the Kinshofer Route, Diamir Face

a night in the open. During it one Sherpa died. The next day the remaining climbers descended, but Wieland died just metres from the camp. Over the next five days a tragedy of increasing agony was played out on the ridge. Welzenbach died in Camp VII, Merkl some time on 14 or 15 July near the Moor's Head. Of the Sherpas, five more died, a second at the bivouac above Camp VII, three between Camps V and IV and one, Gaylay, who chose to stay with Merkl.

Looking into the Diamir Valley from the summit at dusk

On the expedition's return Aschenbrenner and Schneider were ordered before a 'Court of Honour' of Munich climbers and declared to be 'without honour' for having abandoned the three Sherpas (and, implicitly, the Germans). Given the desperate fight for life on the mountain the decision, taken in warmth and comfort, was harsh, though the circumstances of the Austrian decision to unrope from the Sherpas is still debated.

The tragedy was a blow to the pride of nationalist German, one which they immediately sought to rectify. Paul Bauer was given state aid to found the Deutsche Himalaja-Stiftung (German Himalayan Foundation) but it was not until 1936 that he was able to raise a team. But rather than Nanga Parbat Bauer went to Sikkim: his claimed reason was that '1934 had destroyed everything and we had to begin again', but was there a remnant of the old animosity with Welzenbach in the decision?

In 1936 Angerer, Hinterstoisser, Kurz and Rainer died in a drawn-out tragedy on the public stage of the Eiger's North Wall, glorious deaths, perhaps, but a further blow to nationalist pride. There could be no further delay in the demand to 'vindicate (1934's) tragic blow' on Nanga Parbat: in 1937 the Germans returned to the mountain though, significantly, under the leadership of Karl Wein (who had been on the 1936 Sikkim expedition) not Paul Bauer.

Following the line of the 1934 route the Germans established Camp IV, an Advanced Base Camp, beneath the Rakhiot Peak. On 14 July it was occupied by seven Germans and nine Sherpas. The Germans represented the entire climbing team, only the team doctor and a cartographer being left lower on the mountain. Just after midnight a serac broke high on the ridge above the camp causing an avalanche which overwhelmed the camp. All sixteen men were buried beneath tons of ice, dying instantly.

Now Paul Bauer had no choice and he led the fourth German expedition in 1938. An interesting sidelight on the extent to which Germany felt it owned Nanga Parbat, having paid for it in blood (eleven Germans, together with 15 Sherpas now lay dead on its flanks – as well as Mummery and his two Gurkhas) is revealed by the response to a suggestion by the British climbers Smythe and Shipton that they might try the peak: they received many outraged letters from Germans claiming that it was improper for Britons to attempt Germany's mountain. Bauer's team followed the 'standard' route, discovering the bodies of Merkl and Gaylay near the Mohrenkopf (Merkl's body had on it a poignant note from Welzenbach asking for aid), but were defeated by bad weather before the Silver Saddle was reached.

In 1939, with war clouds gathering over Europe, the Germans returned, this time with a four-men reconnaissance team to see if the long, avalanche-swept route past the Rakhiot Peak was actually the best line. The four men explored the Diamir Face – finding remains of Mummery's 1895 attempt – and decided that a route existed there. They sent a letter of their findings back to Germany and preparations were made for an attempt on the Diamir Face in 1940. But war intervened: back in British India the four Germans were interred. The escape of one of the four, Heinrich Harrer (who had been one of the first team to climb the Eiger's North Wall), into Tibet, formed the basis of his book Seven Years in Tibet, recently the basis of a successful film. Unfortunately for Harrer the film re-opened the question of the links between the Nazi party and the German climbers of the later 1930s and, in particular, his own position on National Socialism.

First Ascent

In November 1950 three young Britons (Crace, Marsh and Thornley), together with four Sherpas, including Tenzing, approached Nanga Parbat. They were poorly equipped for winter climbing, more intent on an adventure than a real

On the south-east pillar of the Rupal Face

attempt at the peak. Against the advice of Tenzing and the other Sherpas the three Britons climbed along the Rakhiot Glacier. Marsh soon retreated suffering from frostbite, but the other two continued. On 1 December they were seen at about 5,500m (18,000ft), but after a snow storm no trace of them was seen again.

Two years later the Germans, recovered from the devastation of the 1939–45 War, were considering a return to 'their' mountain. There was, however, no unanimity of purpose between the German Himalayan and Alpine Clubs, and, eventually, a physician of limited climbing experience decided to mount his own expedition. Dr Karl-Maria Herrligkoffer was the step-brother of Willy Merkl and, as a youth of 17 in 1934, had hero-worshipped his older brother. He was determined that his expedition would climb Nanga Parbat as a memorial to Merkl. The unknown Herrligkoffer's single mindedness and confrontational style led to serious dissent in Germany, much of the climbing establishment and, due to their influence, the press being against his expedition. Despite this he assembled a strong team. Peter Aschenbrenner, veteran of the 1932 and 1934 expeditions, was the climbing leader, Herrligkoffer's lack of experience preventing him from going much beyond base camp, and with him were Fritz Aumann, Albert Bitterling, Hermann Buhl, Hans Ertl (who was also the expedition photographer), Walter Frauenberger, Otto Kempter, Hermann Köllensperger and Kuno Rainer, a mix of Austrians and Germans. Of these the best known was Buhl, who could perhaps be best described as the German-speaking rival of great French post-war climbers – Lachenal, Rébuffat and Terray. He had completed an early ascent of the Eiger's north wall in a large team – created when appalling weather forced an amalgamation of three separate ropes – with Rébuffat. Buhl specialised in solo and winter climbs, climbs which required amazing resolve and self-control, these climbs including the first solo of the Watzmann's east face which he completed in winter and at night. He was also phenomenally quick, completing an early, and solo (the first solo), ascent of the Piz Badile's north face in less than half the best time to date. Kuno Rainer, another Tyrolean, was Buhl's partner on many of his best climbs, including the fourth ascent of the Dru's north face, an early ascent of the Walker spur on the Grandes Jorasses and the first winter ascent of the Marmolada's south-west face.

Perhaps in deference to his step-brother Herrligkoffer chose the 1930s route rather than the Diamir Face, but progress in establishing camps was slow because of the lack of Sherpas. Herrligkoffer's explanation for this was that the half-dozen who had been hired were not allowed into Pakistan, but Buhl's account of the climb suggests that because they were not met at the border they were turned away. The Germans therefore used Hunza porters, finding them less willing to carry heavy loads across steep ice, a fact which slowed the build up. The weather, too, was poor, but on 30 June it changed, the first half of July being almost perfect. On 30 June Buhl, Ertl, Frauenberger and Kempter were in Camp III at 6,150m (20,180ft) below the Rakhiot Peak preparing to push towards the Silver Saddle for a summit attempt. The expected summit pair had been Buhl and Rainer, but Rainer had developed phlebitis and Kempter was to be Buhl's partner. Herrligkoffer's official account of the expedition notes nothing of interest on that day, but the four at Camp III are adamant that they received repeated demands by radio to return to base camp. The reasons were vague – the monsoon was expected (yet the weather was now glorious), everyone needed to rest (yet

Climbing fluted ice on the south-east pillar

On the Mazeno Ridge

An aerial view of the Rakhiot face with the Diamir flank on the right hand side

In the Great Couloir on the south-east pillar, Rupal Face

progress had been so slow any further delay would result in almost certain defeat), Aschenbrenner was leaving the expedition early and the team should assemble to say goodbye. The four at Camp III refused to descend, and after a long period Herrligkoffer eventually relented.

The four now returned to Camp IV and pushed on to place Camp V just beyond the Mohrenkopf. There, on the night of 2 July Buhl and Kempter slept ready for an attempt on the summit the following day. With hindsight it is easy to see that Camp V was too low. Set at about 6,900m (22,640ft), it was over 1,200m (about 4,000ft) below the summit, and with the descent into the Bazhin Gap closer to 1,400m (4,600ft) below. It was also over 6km (nearly 4 miles) away horizontally. The reasons for not putting another camp on the Silver Saddle are not clear. It is probable that the four climbers at Camp III, the only part of the expedition now operating, just did not have the resources to do so, but it is also possible that the experience of Aschenbrenner and Schneider in 1934, reaching the base of the Subsidiary Summit by noon and believing themselves only an hour or so from the top played a part. In reality, the final climb to the main

summit took Buhl ten hours and involved the hardest climbing on the final day.

Unable to sleep Buhl dressed at 1am and left the tent at 2.30am, intending to break trail so that Kempter, who followed about 30 minutes later, could easily catch him. Climbing without bottled oxygen Buhl reached the Silver Saddle at 7am and began to cross the plateau beyond in heat that was 'merciless, parching my body'. He left his rucsac on the plateau, convinced he would return to it by nightfall, taking only what he could carry in his pockets. As he climbed towards the Subsidiary Summit (which he did not reach, traversing some 40m/130ft – below it) he saw that Kempter had given up. Buhl reached the Bazhin Gap at 2pm absolutely exhausted and racked by hunger and thirst.

At the Gap Buhl took Pervitin, a stimulant developed by the Luftwaffe to combat exhaustion in air-crews, and began the climb to the Shoulder, the last hump of the ridge before the main summit. The climbing was now hard, with steep, iced and loose rock, dangerous cornices and an uninviting drop down the Rupal Face to the side. Buhl had thought the climb from the Bazhin Gap would take about an hour: it took five. Not until 7pm did he reach the summit – he had been climbing for 16½ hours. Buhl stayed on the summit – a raised dome on which several climbers could gather – for 30 minutes. He took some photos, then with the light fading fast, he started to descend.

Buhl had left his ice axe, with a Pakistani flag attached, on the summit. Soon after starting the descent he lost a strap from his left crampon. With one crampon and two ski sticks his progress slowed – he had hoped to reach the Bazhin Gap before darkness fell, but was forced to bivouac standing on a ledge, holding the ski sticks in one hand and a small hold with the other. Utterly exhausted he dozed occasionally,

High on the south-east pillar, Rupal Face

miraculously maintaining his balance when he did. Equally amazingly the night was calm, so that although the temperature plunged he was not wind chilled. He hoped to continue by moonlight, but his stance was in moon shadow and he was forced to wait until dawn. The day was beautiful, the sun warming him – but then roasting his dehydrated body.

On the final descent to the Bazhin Gap and the climb towards the Subsidiary Summit and Silver Plateau, Buhl's emaciated condition led him to hallucinate. He had conversations (two-way conversations) with an imagined colleague and distinctly heard voices calling him. When he recovered his rucsac his mouth was so dry he could not swallow glucose tablets and was forced to eat snow. On the plateau realising that night was approaching and knowing he was unlikely to survive a second bivouac he took more Pervitin – he had also taken Padutin, an anti-frostbite drug – and with its help reached the Silver Saddle. It was 5.30pm. The sight of the tent and other expedition members now buoyed him as he descended to the camp. He reached it at 7pm 40½ hours after leaving. His first words were 'Yesterday was the finest day of my life'. It was no understatement, Buhl's climb ranking among the greatest feats in the history of mountaineering.

When Buhl came in to view on the Silver Saddle Walter Frauenberger was fixing a memorial tablet to Merkl, Welzenbach and Wieland on the Mohrenkopf. The question which immediately comes to mind was why none of the climbers at Camp V went out to look for Buhl on the Silver Plateau at any time on 4 July. Rainer had waited on the Silver Saddle for most of 3 July, not returning to camp until 7pm. He was too exhausted to go up again on 4 July, but what of the other two? There was a plan, apparently, to go up to the plateau with oxygen equipment on 5 July if Buhl had not returned. The lack of oxygen to administer to the possibly exhausted Buhl is cited as the reason for there being no rescue attempt on 4 July, but to have waited until the 5th would have meant looking for a man who had spent over 48 hours alone and ill-equipped above 7,800m (25,600ft). But whatever view is taken today, so many years after the event, it is clear that Burl had no hard feelings about Frauenberger and Ertl. His own account of the climb records the three becoming firm friends and meeting on 3 July 1954 to celebrate the anniversary of the climb.

Events surrounding the retreat from the mountain led to bitter wrangling back in Germany. Herrligkoffer claims that on Buhl's return to Base Camp there were celebrations (the official expedition includes a photograph of clearly-staged cheering), but Buhl recalls only a cool, joyless reception. Herrligkoffer claims that treatment of Buhl's frostbite would have been pointless as the damage was already too far advanced. Buhl states that the expedition's medical supplies had already left base camp en route for Germany when he arrived and notes that 'there was no Dr Oudot among my team-mates', a bitter comparison to the treatment of Lachenal and Herzog after Annapurna's first ascent. Buhl's feelings were obviously even more bitter, but he had by then learned, as others would later, that Herrligkoffer was both litigious and tenacious when crossed. In the event Buhl lost the ends of two toes on his right foot, an injury was caused him pain for the rest of his climbing life.

Rakhiot Peak from the south-east pillar

Later Ascents

In 1961 Karl-Maria Herrligkoffer organised another team and returned to Nanga Parbat to look at the Diamir Face. Taking a line between Mummery's Rib and the suggested route of the 1938 reconnaissance his team hoped to reach the Bazhin Gap from where they would follow Buhl's route to the summit. Bad weather forced a retreat from a height of about 7,100m (23,300ft), but Herrligkoffer returned the following year. A summit attempt by a team of five climbers on 22 June was reduced to a team of three – Toni Kinshofer and Anderl Mannhardt (who had been on the first winter ascent of the Eiger's north wall) and Siegi Löw – when two stopped as a result of exhaustion. In poor weather the three took seven hours to climb to the summit from the Bazhin Gap (Buhl had taken five hours) reaching the summit at 5pm. At the top they found the small cairn Hermann Buhl had constructed in 1953. The three bivouaced only 70m (230ft) below the summit – all being frostbitten in the extreme cold – and continued their descent, unroped the following day. Löw had taken a heavy dose of Pervitin and, badly affected by frostbite and the drug, fell on the descent to the Gap. He died of his injuries. Kinshofer (who waited with Löw until he died and spent two nights bivouaced above the last camp with no sleeping bag or tent) and Mannhardt climbed down, but each suffered subsequent amputations due to frostbite.

After success on the Diamir Face Herrligkoffer turned his attention to the Rupal Face, the highest mountain wall in the world. With sections almost as steep as the south face of Annapurna, though not as sustained as that face, the Rupal was a formidable challenge. The Germans reconnoitred the route in June 1963 Toni Kinshofer, recovered from frostbite injuries, favouring a line along the face's left edge (later climbed by a team under Hanns Schell), but others feeling a direct line was feasible. It was the later line that was attempted by the first full expedition in January 1964. To attempt a new route on a long, steep face in winter was highly ambitious, but Herrligkoffer's reasons were not pioneering – he had an Antarctic trip planned for the autumn of 1964 and so could not go in the summer. Before the Germans had set foot on the face Herrligkoffer had named various features, attaching Wieland's name to those at the base, Welzenbach's to the central features and Merkl's to those at the top. In 1964 the team barely climbed beyond 'Wieland' before difficulties with their Pakistani liaison officer caused their permit to be cancelled.

Political problems prevented Herrligkoffer returning to the Rupal Face until 1968 when he brought a team built around three of the four Germans who had completed the John Harlin Route on the Eiger's north wall. The team reached the foot of the 'Merkl'

A phoenix cloud formation over a cloud sea obscuring the sun, seen from high on the south-east pillar

Herrligkoffer came back again in 1970. Only one of the 1964 team came with him, but he still had a strong team, including the young Italian Tyrol climber Reinhold Messner. In 1968 Messner had made the first solo ascents of the Philipp-Flamm route on the Civetta and the Les Droites north face, and had a reputation as a brilliant and fast climber. The team also included Reinhold's brother Günther. For six weeks the team fixed route up the face, finally establishing a camp (Camp V) at 7,350m (24,100ft) at the foot of the Merkl Gully. There was no radio at Camp V, but it had been agreed earlier that Base Camp would fire a flare on the evening of 26 June to tell V's occupants (the Messner brothers and Gerhard Baur) what the weather forecast was for the 27th. A red flare meant bad weather, a blue one good. With the weather apparently set fair Camp V was surprised to see a red flare. The events which followed the flare ended – as so many of Herrligkoffer's trips – in the German courts with ugly accusations on all sides. The facts are that Reinhold Messner left Camp V early on 27 June climbing solo, followed later by Günther Messner and Baur who were to fix ropes in the Merkl Gully. The rope fixing went badly and Baur, troubled by an altitude cough, returned to camp. Günther

section of the face – at about 7,100m (23,300ft) – at which point Günther Strobel sustained a badly broken leg. Strobel's rescue from the face brought antagonisms between the climbers and Herrligkoffer to the surface and the expedition broke up.

On the Mazeno Ridge

climbed off to catch his brother which, using his trail, he managed. The two continued to the summit reaching it at about 5pm. Reinhold states his brother was now suffering from altitude sickness and hallucinating, and was incapable of soloing back down the difficult ascent route. The pair therefore retreated along the south-west (Mazeno) ridge, bivouacing in a hollow (the Merkl Gap) below the mountain's south shoulder.

Early on 28 June Felix Kuen and Peter Scholz started up from Camp V. At around 6am they heard shouts – apparently calls for help – as did Gerd Mändl in the camp below. At about 10am they reached a point 80m (250ft) or so from the ridge and had a shouted conversation with Reinhold Messner. Messner claims that during this conversation he asked for a rope, as Günther could not descend without one, and told Kuen and Scholz to climb across to him as the route from him to the summit was easier than the face. Kuen and Scholz claim Reinhold did not ask for a rope, denied calling for help and said that all was well. The pair say they did not see Günther Messner and that at the end of the conversation Reinhold bent down to pick up something which was clearly heavy: they assumed this was a rucsac. But neither of the Messner brothers had taken a rucsac.

Kuen and Scholz continued to the summit, bivouacing near the south shoulder on their descent. On returning to Camp V

they discovered that the Messner brothers had not arrived. In fact the Messners had descended the easier-angled Diamir Face, bivouacing on 28 June and descending again the next day. Reinhold was climbing faster than Günther and at some time on 29 June Günther disappeared, presumably killed by an avalanche. Reinhold spent 30 June searching for his brother, then continued alone, rejoining the surprised expedition with the help of the Pakistani army. Messner subsequently lost six toes and several finger joints to frostbite.

Back in Germany Messner made a number of accusations against Herrligkoffer, chiefly over the red and blue flares, which resulted in court cases which found in the expedition leader's favour. There was also an unpleasant accusation that what Messner had stooped to pick up at the end of his conversation with Kuen and Scholz was his brother. This he

Kinshofer Route, Diamir Face

Late evening shot towards the Mazeno Ridge from close to the summit on the Kinshofer Route

vehemently denied. The court cases silenced the parties (at least in public) but have not resolved the issues raised by the incidents of 26–28 June. Why was a red flare fired? The leader claimed that all the 'blue' flares were actually red by accident – how could this be? and how was it known without firing them? What were the cries (of help) heard early on 28 June? What exactly was said during the exchange between Reinhold Messner and Kuen and Scholz? Why did Reinhold not simply climb back on to the south shoulder to meet the other two and

so obtain help for his brother? What, if anything, did Reinhold bend to pick up? It is unlikely now that a satisfactory answer will ever be obtained to these questions, and to speculate runs the risk of court proceedings. The only undebated matters from the expedition are that the first ascent of the Rupal Face and the first traverse of an 8,000m peak were achieved, and that Reinhold Messner put his foot on the first rung of a remarkable ladder. Sadly, the aftermath of the climb completely overshadowed its achievement. Though less difficult than the

British Annapurna south face route completed just a few weeks before (in subsequent years it has been the Annapurna face rather than the Rupal which has attracted the top climbers), the ascent of the Rupal face was a significant milestone in the history of climbing on the great peaks.

In 1971 a Czechoslovakian team repeated the Buhl route (having failed in their first attempt in 1969) placing two members on top. This is the only repeat to date of the long line of the first ascent and makes Nanga Parbat one of only two 8,000ers on which the usually favoured route is not the line of the first ascent: the other is Gasherbrum I (though here the reason for the change is very different). The Czechs also made the first ascent of the Subsidiary Summit which Buhl had traversed below. Herrligkoffer returned in 1975 to try three separate routes with one team. The climbers made most progress on the south/south-west ridge (at the left edge of the Rupal Face), but failed at 7,550m (24,7756ft). The route was climbed the following year by a team of four (Hanns Schell, as leader, with Siegi Gimpel, Robert Schauer and Hilmar Sturm) which placed three camps on the ridge before being forced to retreat by a storm. On their return they discovered Camp III to be under 2m (6½ft) of fresh snow. They placed a fourth camp at 7,450m (24,450ft) and started from it early on 9 August. They bivouaced at 7,700m (25,300ft) that night and at 8,020m (26,300ft) on the 10th. On 11 August they reached the summit after an hour's climb and descended to Camp IV. Though Schell was now very ill, probably from a minor pulmonary embolism, the four safely reached their base camp. The team had made limited use of porters (only on one section low on the mountain to gain time lost on the walk-in) and had achieved a near-alpine ascent of a new route, a superb achievement, but one which was to be eclipsed within two years.

In 1977 two Americans were killed during an attempt on the Diamir Face and a Polish expedition failed to repeat the Schell route (often called the Kinshofer route as Toni Kinshofer was the first to point out its feasibility, a fact which causes confusion as the 'standard' line on the Diamir Face is also usually called the Kinshofer). Then in 1978 Reinhold Messner returned to the mountain. In 1971 Messner had searched the base of the Diamir face for signs of his brother and had come again in 1973, attempting to solo the face: he retreated from a point about one-third of the way up. Now he was determined to complete the climb. Setting out from a bivouac at the foot of the wall be climbed a new route on its right side, bivouacing at 6,400m (21,000ft) and again at 7,400m (24,300ft). From this second bivouac he climbed directly to the summit rather than taking the ridge from the Merkl Gap (and therefore avoiding the point where he bivouaced with his brother). He reached the summit at 4pm on 9 August, then returned to his top bivouac (just a few weeks after his ascent an Austrian team climbed the left side of the face, finding the tin Messner had left at the summit). On the following day avalanches following an earthquake destroyed his ascent route, forcing him to descend the Mummery Rib: Messner had completed the seventh ascent of the peak, having already completed the third, the climb establishing him as probably the finest high-altitude mountaineer in the world. Indeed, a strong case could be argued for Messner being one of the greatest, all the major innovations on 8,000m peaks being his – first true alpine ascent (of Gasherbrum I), first solo ascent from base camp (here on Nanga Parbat), first ascent of Everest without bottled oxygen, first solo of Everest (also without bottled gas) and first man to climb all 14 8,000m peaks. It is a phenomenal record: one is forced to wonder to what extent the achievements were initiated by the trauma of his brother's death in 1970.

Sunset at Camp II on the Kinshofer Route, Diamir Face

Left-hand side of the Diamir Face. The Kinshofer Route threads a way through the cliff line

Also in August 1978 a six-man Austrian team climbed the Kinshofer route on the Diamir Face, five of the six reaching the summit. (Though usually called the Kinshofer, the now standard line deviates from that of Kinshofer, Löw and Mannhardt, crossing the upper face directly to the summit rather than climbing to the Bazhin Gap.) There were then no further successful climbs until 1981 when an Italian team climbed a variant of the Kinshofer route (on the Diamir Face) and a Dutch team climbed a variant of the Schell route. The four Dutch climbers, Ger Friele, Bas Gresnigt, Ronald Naar and Gerard van Strang, reached the south-west (Mazeno) ridge and decided to cross the Diamir Face to reach the top. They bivouaced on the ridge at 7,516m (24,660ft) on 3 August, but the next day three of them (Gresnigt descending exhausted) progressed by only 35m (115ft) on the face, taking the wrong line several times. They bivouaced again at 7,550m (24,775ft). Friele was now too sick to continue, the other two continuing to 7,800m (25,600ft) where van Strang was forced to abandon. Naar continued alone to the top. After the climb Friele lost two joints from each of his fingers.

In 1982 Herrligkoffer returned, intent on climbing the south-east pillar, to the right of the German Rupal face route.

Seen in profile on photographs from the Buhl route this line is steep, averaging 65°–70°, but has the advantage of being relatively avalanche free. In May 1982 a strong team under Yannick Seigneur had attempted the line, but had abandoned it after a porter had slipped to his death off a fixed rope and Seigneur had been caught in an avalanche – ironically in view of the line's supposed safety – and was lucky to escape with broken ribs and a cracked pelvis. The team had reached about 7,100m (23,300ft). Herrligkoffer's team arrived in July and by mid-August had established Camp V at 7,500m (24,600ft). From it, on 16 August, four climbers set out, climbing the near-vertical pillar. Three retreated, but the Swiss Ueli Bühler continued alone. He bivouaced without equipment and at noon on 17 August reached the South Summit (8,042m/26,385ft), but was unable to continue to the main summit and retreated to Camp V. His companions abandoned a summit attempt to bring him down – a journey he was lucky to survive. Bühler later lost the last joint of several fingers and half his toes to frostbite. In 1985 a predominately Polish team completed the route, the main summit being reached by Jerzy Kukuczka and Carlos Carsolio (each on their way to completing the 14 8,000ers) together with Zygmunt Heinrich and Slavomir Lobodzinski, the summit climb involving two days without food or water. During this expedition the climbers found that one of their lower camps had been blown away by the blast from a vast avalanche falling over 1km (over ½ mile) away and at one point, during a violent storm, Kukuczka noticed sparks jumping between the piton he was belayed to and the rock. There can be few better motives for getting away from a place, but he was forced to stay attached for 30 long minutes.

In October 1984 Tsuneo Hasegawa, having been part of a Japanese expedition which failed on the Schell route in the summer, returned to attempt the first winter and first solo ascents. He chose the Rupal Face for this audacious plan, but was forced to abandon. The summer of 1984 saw Liliane and Maurice Barrard on the summit. They were part of a porter-less four person team on the Diamir Face and achieved the first French, first female and first married couple ascents. Any married couple ascent might be thought of as a likely unique achievement, but Nanga Parbat has been climbed several more times by couples. A year after Liliane Barrard's ascent three Poles from an all-woman expedition repeated the climb.

1988 saw the German Sigi Hupfauer complete his seventh ascent of an 8,000er by way of the now standard Diamir Face route. It was an ascent notable for the cold, the wind and a dramatic descent in worsening weather, but Hupfauer's account is dismissive of these 'minor' problems, noting, in a laconic, but clearly hurt way, that 'we had difficult relations with

The Rupal face of Nanga Parbat

the Pakistani authorities. We also found the Chilas people deceitful.'

In 1992 the Britons Mark Miller and Jon Tinker led a semi-commercial team attempting a new route. The aim was to climb the Rakhiot Peak from the east, than to follow the Buhl route to the summit. The attempt was abandoned low on the mountain due to huge snowfalls. Later that year the French pair Eric Monier and Monique Loos failed in a winter attempt on the Schell route. 1992 also saw the first of several attempts on the Mazeno Ridge by British climber Doug Scott. The ridge is about 15km (9 miles) long from the Mazeno Pass, the longest ridge to any 8,000er. It had been attempted in 1979 by a French team who spent 30 days in bad weather on it before retreating. Scott's team (British and Russian climbers with Sherpa support) used the Schell route to place supplies above 7,000m (23,000ft), but during that period several climbers were injured by rock falls. The remaining members then climbed from the Pass, reaching Pt6,970 (22,280ft) just less than half-way along the ridge. Scott tried again in 1993 with Wojciech Kurtyka and Richard Cowper. Though they climbed the Mazeno Spire (a probable first ascent) they were less successful on the ridge than in '92. An avalanche carried Scott almost 400m (1,200ft) down the mountain – he was lucky to escape with a damaged ankle – and the climb was abandoned. Another attempt in 1995 (by Scott, Kurtyka, Rick Allen and Andrew Lock, though Scott was ill and forced to retire) reached 7,000m (23,000ft) about two-thirds of the way along the ridge. Kurtyka and Erhard Loretan tried again in 1997, failing at about one-third distance.

A Japanese team opened a new route on the north side of the mountain in 1995, taking a direct route to the Silver Saddle where they placed a camp at 7,350m (24,100ft). The first summit attempt was abandoned due to the cold and one climber's chest pains, but a second attempt was made on 23 July. Starting at 3am after a night breathing bottled oxygen, Yukio Yabe, Takeshi Akiyama and Hiroshi Saito followed Buhl's route to the top, reaching it at 5pm. They left the summit after an hour, but failed to reach the Bazhin Gap before nightfall, bivouacing at 7,700m (25,250ft). They finally reached the Silver Saddle camp on 24 August 39 hours after leaving it. The climb was yet another demonstration of the phenomenal performance of Hermann Buhl. A year later Krzysztof Wielicki soloed the Diamir Face (Kinshofer line) to become the fifth 'all-14' climber at the age of 46. Wielicki arrived in base camp after completing an ascent of K2, but found that he was too late to join his prospective team as they had already left. He therefore decided to solo the mountain, a climb delayed by 24 hours by an abscess which erupted on his face. He spent the time high on the mountain in a tent he fortuitously found left from an earlier expedition, suffering hallucinations from an antibiotic he took to combat the abscess. He eventually reached the top on 1 September 1996. Wielicki's record of ascents included the first winter ascents of Everest in 1980, Kangchenjunga (1986) and Lhotse (part solo, 1988), first solo of Broad Peak in 1984, new routes on Manaslu (1984), Dhaulagiri (1990 – the new route on the east face reached the original route and Wielicki did not continue tot he summit having already sumitted along the original) and Shisha Pangma (solo, 1993). Only on Everest during the first winter ascent did Wielicki use bottled oxygen.

Attempts to claim the first winter ascent in late 1996 and early 1997 again failed. In February 1997 two Poles reached a point just 250m (800ft) from the top, but retreated with severe frostbite. Their expedition subsequently notched up an unwanted first – first helicopter rescue from the Diamir base camp. In February 1998 another Polish team returned, determined to complete Nanga Parbat's first winter ascent. After battling winds up to 140km/h (90mph) the team were forced to abandon the climb when one member fell and broke a leg. There has been no winter ascent of Nanga Parbat to date and the long Mazeno Ridge remains one of the great peaks' outstanding problems.

To date there have been around 170 ascents of Nanga Parbat, but the mountain's position means that summit climbers usually have to contend with extreme cold. This slows progress and a large number of summiteers have been forced to bivouac on the way down. With its high number of fatal accidents – more climbers have died on the peak than on any 8,000er apart from Everest which, of course, has had a great deal more traffic – Nanga Parbat has long had a reputation as a killer mountain. But the accidents of the 1930s have distorted the statistics which suggest that Nanga Parbat is second only to Annapurna in the ratio of deaths to successful ascent. Now a summiteer is as likely to survive a descent from Nanga Parbat as from any other 8,000er apart from the 'dangerous five' peaks – K2, Annapurna, Makalu, Kangchenjunga and Everest. Despite this comforting fact Nanga Parbat remains a very serious undertaking, climbers drawn by the romance of its name and history sustaining a higher-than-average number of frostbite injuries. Even with improvements in equipment the intense cold on Nanga Parbat and the usually long summit days are likely to ensure that this grim statistic remains true.

Looking north-east towards the Rakhiot Peak from the south-east pillar

K2 8,611m

"It was one of those sights which impress a man forever, and produce a permanent effect upon the mind, a lasting sense of the greatness and grandeur of Nature's work, which he can never lose or forget."

FRANCIS YOUNGHUSBAND
on seeing K2 from the north

K2

In 1856 Capt. TG Montgomerie, a British army survey officer working in what is now northern Pakistan but was then British India, surveyed a number of peaks in the Baltoro region of the Karakoram from a distance of about 200km. (125 miles). He catalogued the peaks he surveyed by number, giving each the prefix 'K', for Karakoram.

n 1861, the area was explored and resurveyed by parties under Col. HH Godwin-Austen. They discovered that the second peak of Montgomerie's list, K2, was actually the highest in the area. Godwin-Austen's men produced the first map of the area and also described the route to the peak. Later, when it was discovered that K2 was the second highest mountain in the world, the British tried to name it Mount Godwin-Austen, a name which can still be found in very old books on the Karakoram or climbing. The Indian authorities were very much against this naming of peaks for prominent members of the ruling classes and objected strongly. Indeed, the Indian protests over the use of such commemorative names were sufficient to prevent their use on any mountain except the world's highest. Godwin-Austen had a much better claim to be recognised in the name of K2 than Sir George

Everest had with the highest peak, but the protests were heeded and the name quietly dropped. Later, when the official numbering of Karakoram peaks was undertaken the decision was made to renumber them so as to conform to current convention (from east to west, as in the Himalaya). K2 became K13, a name used in an official publication of 1879. But by then the older designation had become so ingrained that the new one soon disappeared. In view of the reputation that the peak has gathered it is perhaps a good thing that the superstitious number 13 did not find favour.

A later search for a local name for the peak revealed that there was none. Latterly the Pakistan authorities have attempted to rename the peak using names 'discovered' among local peoples, but these have all failed. Dapsang gained some credence and is occasionally still heard, but it seems to

Camp II on the Abruzzi Spur. Masherbrum dominates the south-western skyline

derive from a plateau some distance from the peak and is unknown to the Hunzas. Mount Akbar was also tried, the name meaning Great Mountain, but seemed to have nationalistic overtones and was ignored. Pakistan also tried to impose Lamba Pahar, a Kashmiri name, also meaning Great Mountain, but that had the disadvantages of being clearly (and overtly) tied up with the border dispute with India over Kashmir and also of being completely unknown to the Kashmiris, the latter fact being deemed positive proof of its unsuitability. In Baltistan the name Chogori (which also means Great Mountain) does appear to have been applied to the peak and would probably have been accepted had not the peak been known as K2 for decades before Chogori came to light. Chogori is a very beautiful name (and is probably the basis for a Chinese attempt to rename the peak Mount Qogir, an attempt which has, thankful, failed), but the clipped and impersonal nature of K2 seems just so appropriate for a mountain with a reputation for difficulty and danger which exceeds that of any other 8,000m peak.

Exploration

In 1892 the base of the peak was reached for the first time by the British mountaineer Martin Conway. Conway explored the Baltoro, naming Concordia (either after Konkordiaplatz, a junction on Switzerland's Aletsch Glacier, or the Place de la Concorde in Paris – though the former seems more likely there is evidence to suggest the latter: it is, for instance, quoted in Desio's book on the first ascent) and discovering the Godwin-Austen and Vigne Glaciers. Conway also named Broad Peak and Hidden Peak (Gasherbrum I). Conway's team made an attempt on a peak he called Golden Throne (Baltoro Kangri) reaching a subsidiary summit. Although Conway's expedition did little actual climbing, in terms of exploration it was a major success. Conway also logged the effects of altitude on pulse rate and general health, the effects of different diets and the behaviour and value of equipment, all of which were very important for later expeditions. Ten years after Conway's trip a small team of British and Austrian climbers and a Swiss doctor under Oscar Eckenstein arrived to climb K2. Alfred Mummery had attempted Nanga Parbat in 1895, but as yet no one had any idea of the difficulties of attempting 8,000m peaks. Eckenstein had been with Conway during the early stages of his trip, but had left after a disagreement, possibly over differing views of the aims of the expedition (climbing or exploration), but more likely over personal matters, Eckenstein being a radical, Conway an establishment man. Eckenstein clearly believed that the peak was just a bigger version of those in the Alps, but the two Austrian climbers, Heinrich Pfannl and V Wessely, who

North Face
1 NE Ridge. Lower section followed by Americans (1978) before traverse of East Face to Abruzzi Spur

2 Japanese (1982)
3 Japanese (1990)
4 Beghin/Profit (1991), approach from NW Ridge

South and West Faces
A Bottleneck
B Shoulder
1 West Ridge/West Face Japanese (1981); variation Japanese (1997)
2 SSW Ridge Polish (1986)

3 Kukuczka/Pietrowski (1986)
4 SSE Spur Basques (1994); but lower section earlier by International team (1983) and Cesen (1986)
5 Abruzzi Spur (and ESE Ridge) Italians (1953); the classic route

were among the best in Europe, seem to rapidly have come to the conclusion that K2 was too big a mountain for the small team to attempt. They suggested abandoning the attempt in favour of climbing Skyang Kangri. Had they done this they might well have succeeded, establishing a summit record that would have lasted for decades – Skyang Kangri is 7,545m (24,750ft) – and completing one of the great feats of mountaineering. But despite their warnings Eckenstein doggedly refused to deflect from his objective, with the result that the team did not get higher than 6,600m (21,650ft) and then had to retreat hastily when Pfannl contracted pulmonary oedema. That he survived was due to the presence of the Swiss

Climbing House's Chimney on the Abruzzi Spur

under the leadership of the Duke of Spoleto was for scientific and exploratory purposes and made no attempt to climb the peak. One member of the team was the geologist Ardito Desio.

Today, almost a century after these early struggles on the peak and half-a-century after the first ascent – the idea of K2 being an Italian mountain seems ludicrous, but at the time the national pride engendered by the expeditions and in anticipation of success was very real. British influence over Tibet meant that all of the early attempts on Everest were by British teams. By the time Nepal opened its borders in the early 1950s Everest was established as a British mountain and the issuing of a permit to the Swiss in 1952 was met by a mixture of outrage and fear: Britons had died on Everest – what right had these newcomers to attempt our mountain? By the same logic the Germans 'owned' Nanga Parbat, a peak on whose flank eleven Germans (together with 15 locals) lay buried. The Italians were therefore aggrieved to discover that an American expedition had set out for K2 in the early summer of 1938. (There had been further exploration in 1937 when a small British team under Eric Shipton visited the Shaksgam Valley and photographed the northern flank of K2.) Mussolini's ill-considered invasion of Ethiopia had ended, though the invasion of Albania must have been at the planning stage, but despite these distractions it is strange that an expedition to K2, Italy's mountain, did not fire the nationalistic imagination of Il Duce.

Dr Jacot-Guillarmod who recognised the symptoms – the European Alps being high enough for some climbers to contract the condition on rapid ascents – and to evacuate him to lower ground. The expedition was also notable for including Edward Alexander (Alesteir) Crowley, the self-proclaimed Great Beast 666 etc, whose abilities as a climber have been completely overshadowed by those as a self-publicist, though they actually seem to have been far greater than his abilities to conjure up the Devil.

Gary Ball abseiling down House's Chimney

In 1909 K2 was attempted by an Italian team led by the Duke of the Abruzzi who correctly identified the south-east ridge – now often referred to as the Abruzzi Ridge or Spur – as the most straightforward way to the summit. The Duke's team included Vittorio Sella, arguably the greatest mountain photographer of all time whose shots still inspire new generations of climbers. Ironically in view of this, the most famous photograph taken by the expedition – of K2 from Windy Gap (Skyang La) to the north-east – was actually taken by Abruzzi himself, though it is frequently credited to Sella. Abruzzi's team did not get high – only to about 6,000m (19,700ft) – but they established, in their own eyes at least, the Italian 'ownership' of the peak, a fact reinforced by another Italian expedition which arrived in the area in 1929. This trip,

The Americans, under Charles Houston solved the problems set by the lower section of the Abruzzi Ridge, Bill House climbing the chimney which now bears his name, probably the hardest single pitch climbed at that time in the Karakoram or Himalaya. The Americans set seven camps along the ridge and from the top one Houston and Paul Petzoldt climbed up to the Shoulder. There the exhausted Houston stopped, Petzoldt continuing up to about 7,925m (26,000ft). The summit looked so close, but Petzoldt could go no further.

The following year, while Europe was distracted by the prelude to war, the Americans tried again, this time with a team led by the German-born, American-naturalised Fritz Wiessner. Wiessner was a brilliant rock climber, but his team was not in the same league and included a deputy with limited experience and one member, Dudley Wolfe, who was apparently taken because he was rich enough to buy his way on to the trip despite having no experience at all. With Wiessner lead climbing virtually the whole time and taking Wolfe with him (the young man's ambition seemingly over-riding Wiessner's mountain judgement) the team established eight camps, Camp VIII being just below a prominent change of angle on the ridge, a feature now known as the Shoulder. Here Wolfe was finally forced to stop, overcome by exhaustion, but Wiessner and Sherpa Pasang Dawa Lama continued, placing another camp at about 8,000m (26,247ft). From it they set out for the top, but Wiessner, being a rock climber, chose to tackle the headwall above the Shoulder rather than the now-used route (the Bottleneck Couloir). The pair reached about 8,370m (27,450ft) with just a one more short section of difficult climbing before they would reach easy ground. Wiessner wanted to push on but Pasang Dawa Lama refused to move. Some have suggested he was afraid of the mountain gods who would kill them if (as was inevitable) they reached the summit or were descending when night fell. Others have suggested the Sherpa showed good sense, realising the two would either not survive a night out or, if they did, the difficult descent of the headwall. Wiessner reluctantly retreated planning to try again the following day. On the descent the pair's crampons were dislodged from Pasang's rucsac. After a rest day (it is now known that there is really no such thing above 8,000m, physical

deterioration outweighing any perceived benefit) they did go up again, this time trying the Bottleneck Couloir, but without crampons the step cutting was too arduous and they were forced to retreat.

Wiessner now planned to go down to Camp VIII to collect crampons, supplies and someone to replace the exhausted Pasang Dawa Lama, but on arriving he found that no one had arrived to resupply the camp or help Dudley Wolfe. He was therefore forced to continue down taking Wolfe as far as Camp VII. On the way an accident resulted in the loss of Wolfe's sleeping bag, leaving the three men with just one between them, Wiessner having left his at Camp VIII. After a grim night Wolfe was too exhausted to descend so Wiessner and Pasang continued alone. To their horror they found the mountain had been stripped – on whose orders would be the subject of debate for years. Wiessner and Pasang spent another bagless night at Camp II and continued to Base Camp. Wiessner nor any of the Americans were fit to attempt a rescue of Dudley Wolfe, but four Sherpas set out. They reached him at Camp VII, finding him in a dreadful state: he had not even had the strength to leave the tent to relieve himself and had had nothing to eat or drink for some time. The Sherpas tried to get him down to Camp VI but he did not have the energy. Forced to retreat, three of the Sherpas – Pasang Kikuli, Pasang Kitar and Phinsoo – set out from Camp VI again the following day. Neither they nor Dudley Wolfe were seen again. K2 had exacted its first blood sacrifice.

Back in America an attempt was made to blame Wiessner

On the Bottleneck traverse

for the tragedy, something made easier by the fact that he was German born. History has largely vindicated him, the American Alpine Club, from which he had resigned in protest at his treatment, eventually making him an Honorary Member. Wiessner may not have been a good team leader and seems to

Compagnoni and Lacedelli on the summit after the first ascent

have had a definite blindspot over Wolfe's abilities, but the unsavoury nature of some of the attacks on his character are a slur on the name of mountaineering.

War prevented either the Americans, who now also saw K2 as their mountain, or the Italians from attempting the peak for several years. In 1953 permission was given for the Americans to try again, the Italians being given a permit for 1954. Realising that this might be their last chance the Americans prepared a strong team of eight under the leadership of Charles Houston, but a ten day storm destroyed all hope of success and put the men – all eight caught in a camp just below the Shoulder – in jeopardy. Art Gilkey developed thrombosis and when the weather finally cleared could not climb down. The others therefore lowered him in a stretcher, a remarkable feat. But during a traverse of an icy section of mountain to the site of an earlier camp one man slipped, dragging away his rope-mate and knocking another rope of two off. The four falling men became entangled with the ropes from Gilkey's stretcher, to which another climber was attached, and six men were suddenly falling. Pete Schoening, later to be in the first team to climb Gasherbrum I, stopped all six plummeting to their deaths. The accident exhausted the men, and Gilkey's stretcher was fixed with pitons while the others retreated to the

camp. While erecting the tents they could hear Gilkey's muffled shouts from across the slope, shouts they assumed were of encouragement. When they returned for him the slope had been swept bare by an avalanche: Gilkey could have been shouting in warning, a desperate thought that could make strong men weep.

The Americans had not been allowed to bring Sherpas into Pakistan making it necessary to carry all their own loads. They had reached the Shoulder and then also safely evacuated themselves down one of the most dangerous mountains in the world in appalling conditions. True, Art Gilkey had died, but to mountaineers everywhere the expedition had been outstanding.

First Ascent

The Italians returned to K2 in 1954 and,

Early morning sun catches K2, as seen from Concordia

K2 from Concordia. The classic view from the junction of the Baltoro and Godwin-Austen Glaciers, with Broad Peak to the right and Marble Peak to the left

knowing that the Americans too would come back to a mountain knew they had to succeed. The expedition was jointly sponsored by the Italian National Council for Research, a scientific body, and the Italian Alpine Club and had a dual purpose: not only was K2 to be climbed but a whole series of geographic, geological and natural history studies were to be carried out. The National Council, backed by funds from the government, were the major sponsors and their man, Prof Ardito Desio (who had been with Spoleto in 1929) was to be overall leader. The Italian Alpine Club suggested Ricardo Cassin, Italy's greatest climber, as head of the climbing team. When the two men went on a reconnaissance in 1953 the difference not only in funding but in perceived class was obvious. Desio travelled around Pakistan by air, Cassin by drawn-out, exhausting train journeys: Desio went to the posh receptions, Cassin did not. Back in Italy Desio engineered Cassin's resignation from the expedition. Later, to add to this injustice, Cassin was declared unfit for the rigours of the trip by the Desio-headed expedition committee, a dubious decision which left him understandably bitter.

With a free-hand Desio now organised a series of medical tests and a training camp to whittle down the list of 23 candidates to a final team. This comprised Enrico Abram, Ugo Angelino, Walter Bonatti, Achille Compagnoni, Cirillo Floreanini, Pino Gallotti, Lino Lacedelli, Mario Puchoz, Ubaldo Rey, Gino Soldà and Sergio Viotto. Dr Guido Pagani was the team doctor and there were four scientists – Paolo Graziosi, Antonio Marussi, Bruno Zanettin and Francesco Lombardi – as

well as Mario Fantin who was to make a film of the climb. The Pakistani 'observer' was Ata Ullah and there was a team of ten high-altitude Hunza porters. Desio also published a plan for the expedition. In part this was excellent, referring to the need for correct acclimatisation and the need to minimise time spent above 7,500m (24,600ft), but also included the suggestion that all members 'should conform to a diet and a hygiene regime calculated to maintain them in a state of maximum physical efficiency. This is an obligation which devolves on all ... the indisposition of one or more members ... due to over-eating or drinking may jeopardise the whole undertaking.' The 57 year old Desio clearly believed the young climbers needed to be treated as schoolboys. Desio also issued a four-phase plan for the climb which amounted to no more than reach mountain;

Marble Peak from Concordia, K2 is on the right

climb up, establishing camps; gain summit; go home. While undeniably correct the plan was wholly unhelpful. Desio added timings to the phases and, not surprisingly, they all turned out to be wrong.

On the walk-in, during a bout of horse-play between Bonatti and Lacedelli, two of the youngest team members, Bonatti rolled down a slope and was concussed and badly bruised. Anxious that the headmasterly Desio did not know about the incident Bonatti spent several days in his tent with 'stomach trouble', a fact which might have influenced team selection later on. The Italians made good progress on the Abruzzi Ridge assisted, in part, by a detailed route description from Charles Houston who also told them about camp sites and what food the Italians might find there, a typically generous gesture by the American: an interesting detail of this information was the quantity of marmalade the Americans had left behind. The Italians used a winch to haul loads low on the mountain and another for the same purpose on House's Chimney (Compagnoni being less impressed by its difficulty than later climbers have been), but progress was halted when Mario Puchoz died. His sudden death was put down to pneumonia, but was almost certainly oedema. In the expedition book Desio notes his death 'after a very brief agony'. After bringing the body down for burial climbing began again, but was now slowed by bad weather. Desio, whose age and lack of experience kept him low on the mountain, had sent regular, numbered message of exhortation to the climbers, many of them couched in eyebrow-raising tones of nationalistic fervour. Now he sent another pointing out the 'moral responsibility' of the climbers to succeed and noting that success would lead them to be hailed throughout the world 'as champions of your race' and that 'your fame will endure throughout your lives and long after you are dead'. He added 'even if you never achieve anything else of note you will be able to say that you have not lived in vain'.

Despite Desio's plan, the bad weather meant that when Camp VIII was established (at 7,820m/25,650ft – at the edge of the Shoulder) it was already late July and the Italians were in a poor position to mount a summit bid. They had decided to use bottled oxygen from their top camp (Camp IX) but minimum supplies only had reached Camp VII. Only six climbers were still capable of going high and now Bonatti, arguably the strongest, went down with a real stomach upset. Desio had put Compagnoni, the second-oldest team member and the one the leader seemed to find the most agreeable, in charge of the

Rob Hall on a fixed rope below House's Chimney

K2

summit bid: it is likely that this latest Bonatti illness, together with the (non-existent) earlier one coloured Compagnoni's view of his suitability for the final team, but whatever the reason Compagnoni chose Lacedelli to accompany him to the top. However, to make a summit bid a superhuman effort was required from the others. While the summit pair climbed up to establish Camp IX Bonatti and the others descended from VIII to VII to collect the oxygen and other supplies and carry them all the way to IX, clearly a plan of last resort. What happened next became the subject of arguments for years and even reached the law courts.

Having brought the oxygen sets to Camp VIII only Bonatti and the Hunza Mahdi had the energy to continue. But it was now mid-afternoon. Bonatti claimed Compagnoni had agreed to re-site Camp IX 100m (330ft) lower to help those carrying the sets, Compagnoni states the intention was to place it as high as possible. As a result night had fallen before Bonatti and Mahdi reached the camp. Bonatti claims that his cries for help were ignored, the only interest the summit pair had during a

On the Bottleneck section of the first ascent route

shouted conversation being whether the oxygen had been brought up. Compagnoni claims that the two were told to dump the oxygen and return to Camp VIII when it became clear that they could not reach Camp IX. Unable to downclimb in the dark Bonatti and Mahdi were forced to spend a night in the open at 8,000m (26,247ft). Bonatti survived unscathed, but Mahdi, whose boots were inferior, subsequently lost both toes and fingers to his frostbite injuries.

On 30 July Compagnoni and Lacedelli had first to climb down to retrieve the oxygen sets (which supports Bonatti's views that the camp should have been lower), then set out for the summit. The snow in the Bottleneck Couloir was rotten, so

Joe Tasker on the west ridge, with Masherbrum in the background

Sunrise over the Gasherbrum peaks and Broad Peak from the Abruzzi Spur

they climbed the rocks to the left (but not as far left as Wiessner in 1939), Compagnoni taking a short fall. They then traversed below a band of ice cliffs. Their oxygen ran out, but they continued upwards still carrying the sets (which weighed over 20kg – 45lbs), eventually reaching the summit of the most beautiful, most difficult 8,000m peak on earth at 6pm. It had been a fine, committing climb and one which had taken a heavy

toil on Compagnoni particularly: on the descent to Camp VIII he fell three times, the last a 16m (50ft) fall he was lucky to survive uninjured. The next day, on the descent from Camp VIII he fell again, sliding 200m (650ft) down the mountain and stopping in a snow drift on the edge of oblivion.

When the expedition book was published Bonatti was appalled at the way his and Mahdi's bivouac was downplayed. He

Bonatti successfully sued a newspaper which claimed his manoeuvring on the mountain was in order to reach the summit first, a clearly ludicrous suggestion, though there is little doubt that he felt cheated of the summit. He claims that Compagnoni suggested that, as the strongest, he might replace either himself or Lacedelli, and almost certainly wanted to reach Camp IX so that might happen. But after the bivouac survival came before ambition. That Bonatti felt cheated is evident from the fact that in 1955 he tried to raise sponsorship for a solo repeat of the climb, planning to carry a 25kg rucsac and to spend one week on the route using equipment left behind in 1954. His attempt to raise the money failed, but it is interesting to speculate what might have happened had he returned to K2. After K2 Bonatti became the greatest alpinist of the day with a string of remarkable climbs which showed not only great ability but a phenomenal willpower. Perhaps he might have succeeded on K2 in which case the whole history of climbing on the great peaks would have been rewritten. As it was, Bonatti only returned once to the high peaks, making the first ascent of Gasherbrum IV on an Italian expedition in 1958.

Later Ascents

As with the other 8,000ers, after the first ascent K2 was left alone for many years, though in the case of the Karakoram peaks this had less to do with lack of interest than lack of access. Border tensions between Pakistan and India over Kashmir and border discussions between Pakistan and China persuaded the Pakistani authorities to close the area. The tensions have continued, sometimes easing but, at the time writing, increasing, while the discussions resulted in the northern side of K2 becoming Chinese territory, two of the mountain's ridges defining the border between the two countries, a summiteer having a foot in each.

Not until 1975 was permission for a major expedition given (though in 1960 a German-American expedition reached about 7,250m/23,800ft on the first ascent route). The 1975 expedition was American, led by Jim Whittaker, the first American to reach Everest's summit, and attempted a new route on the north-west ridge. But tensions between factions in the team mirrored, on a smaller scale, those over Kashmir and the climb was abandoned at 6,700m (22,000ft). The various disputes were aired in Galen Rowell's book In the Throne Room of the Mountain Gods. By covering issues which other expedition books had ignored or brushed aside, the book, was a complete contrast to those which preceded it and set a trend for many which followed. Also in 1975 a strong Polish team (19 climbers, seemingly a large number until it is remembered that poverty meant the Poles did not employ high-altitude porters,

wrote his own version and tried for years to secure an apology from the Italian Alpine Club. When he got one, on the 40th anniversary of the climb, Compagnoni, by then 80 years old, was incensed, though no one was inclined to listen to him as he had lost the respect of his team mates by suing the Club for a share of the film profits on the grounds that he had lost several fingers to frostbite which, he claimed, was caused by filming at the summit.

carrying their own loads) attempted to climb the north-east ridge, the one Eckenstein's team had looked at in 1902. The Poles fixed rope up the ridge and eventually established Camp VI at around 8,000m (26,250ft). Using oxygen above the camp Cichy and Holnicki failed at 8,250m (27,000ft) in the summit bid, while the next day Chrobak and Wróz reached 8,400m (27,550ft). Their oxygen then ran out and reluctantly they retreated. Illness in the team prevented any further attempt.

While the Poles were on the north-east ridge a Japanese team was reconnoitring the Abruzzi ridge prior to a full-scale attempt in 1977. The 1977 expedition was vast, 50 Japanese and 1,500 porters: given these resources it is no surprise the expedition succeeded. On 8 August Shoji Nakamura, Tsuneo Shigehiro and Takayoshi Takatsuka made the second ascent of K2 following the Italian line. The following day three more Japanese and the Pakistani Ashraf Aman repeated the climb.

The following year Pakistan gave permission to two expeditions, but gave a British team led by Chris Bonington first choice of route and first go. The British tried the west ridge, but had reached only about 6,700m (22,000ft) when Nick Estcourt was swept away by an avalanche and killed. The attempt was then abandoned. The second team, of Americans again under Jim Whittaker, had also wanted to attempt the west ridge, but were forced to try the north-east ridge instead. Some of the 1975 team returned and again factions formed. One comprised those climbers who believed they could and should reach the top, the other those who the first group thought couldn't and shouldn't. The factions were nicknamed A and B and when one member of the 'shouldn't' team was naive enough to ask a 'should' man what A and B meant he was told 'Best and Asshole', a comment unlikely to guarantee maximum harmony and co-operation. Despite this the Americans made steady progress up the 1976 Polish line. But with a camp established below the final, difficult headwall, Whittaker realised he had neither the time nor an adequate supply line to finish the climb. Lou Reichardt and Jim Wickwire therefore traversed the east face to the Shoulder above the Abruzzi Ridge and continued along the original route to the top, reaching it late on 6 September. The pair carried oxygen equipment but intended to

Camp I on the Abruzzi Ridge with the Godwin-Austen Glacier already far below

K2 from the Baltoro Glacier. The Abruzzi Ridge is to the right

use it high on the climb. When he tried to use it Reichardt found his equipment was faulty. He continued without it, becoming the first man to climb K2 without supplementary gas. Wickwire stayed for 40 minutes on the summit and consequently was overtaken by night on the descent and forced to bivouac. He was found by Rick Ridgeway and John Roskelley, but had survived well enough to descend unaided as they continued to the top. Neither of the second pair used supplementary oxygen.

In 1979 Reinhold Messner led a team of six to attempt the south-south-west ridge (which he dubbed the 'Magic

Broad Peak (left) and K2 from Gasherbrum I

Line'), but rapidly concluded it was too dangerous for the team's porters and probably too much for such a small party. To the disgust of several members (notably Renato Casarotto) Messner therefore transferred to the original route, reaching the summit with Michl Dacher. It was Messner's fifth 8,000er. After Messner's team withdrew from the south-south-west ridge a large French team (including Pierre Beghin and Yannick Seigneur) attempted it, reaching a height of 8,400m (27,550ft) before bad weather forced a retreat. During the expedition Jean-Marc Boivin set a world record for hang gliders by using one to descend from Camp IV, at 7,600m (24,900ft), to Base Camp. The following year a four-man British team (Peter Boardman, Dick Renshaw, Doug Scott and Joe Tasker) returned to the west ridge, but at about 7,000m (23,000ft) time pressures and internal disputes led to Scott leaving the team and the other three attempting an alpine-style ascent of the original route. At 8,100m (26,600ft), poised for a summit bid, their camp was destroyed by avalanches: they were lucky to survive these and the nightmare descent which followed.

Early in the 1981 season the Pakistani permit system allowed a four man Franco-German team to try the south face – the team, led by Yannick Seigneur reached 7,400m (24,300ft) – before a large Japanese team arrived to attempt the west ridge. The Japanese followed the 1980 British line, continuing along the ridge to reach about 8,200m (26,900ft). From there they followed a snow band across the west face to the top of the south-west ridge. The route, which was fixed with 5,500m

(almost 3 1/2 miles) of rope, had taken 52 days to climb. On 6 August Eiho Otani, Matsushi Yamashita and Nazir Sabir climbed the fixed ropes to the south-west ridge and started for the summit. The three climbers had helped fix the last ropes on 5 August using bottled oxygen, but now, at 8,300m (27,250ft), dumped their sets in the face of extremely difficult climbing where the flow of gas did not compensate for the weight of the equipment. By 6pm they had climbed to about 8,470m (27,750ft) where they decided to bivouac without any equipment or food, using a candle to warm a hastily dug snow hole. Next morning, 7 August, they climbed another 100m (328ft) to arrive at the end of the difficulties, just 50m (160ft) from the top. Here Otani and Yamashita radioed the team leader and were told to descend as they were too tired to continue. Sabir, a Hunza high-altitude porter who had become a leading mountaineer and was ambitious to climb K2, was appalled. After 45 minutes of sometimes heated argument the leader eventually agreed they could continue. Yamashita was by now too exhausted to continue, but Otani and Sabir climbed on, reaching the top an hour later. Despite a nightmare descent the three, tired and badly dehydrated, reached base camp safely.

Another Japanese expedition attempted K2 in 1982, choosing to attempt the north ridge on the Chinese side of the mountain, having reconnoitred the route the previous year. The approach was epic, the last place camels (!) could reach being 15km (10 miles) from the peak. The absence of a local

Avalanche on the south face, seen from Base Camp

The Japanese north ridge route was repeated in 1983 by an Italian team, their climb being the only success of the year, though an international team led by Doug Scott climbed the south-south-east spur (to the left of the Abruzzi Spur) to within a few metres of the Shoulder. There were no successes in 1984, and 1985's eleven summiteers all climbed the original route: one of the eleven died descending. Then came 1986 a year about which much (some objectionable, some probably actionable) has been written. The facts are that nine expeditions were given permission for K2, many of them for the original route, and some of the others transferring to that route when their intended climb proved too difficult. Two Americans Alan Pennington and John Smolich were killed by an avalanche on 21 June, but two days later six people reached the top. Wanda Rutkiewicz made the first female ascent followed shortly after by Liliane Barrard making the second. Liliane climbed with her husband Maurice, but the pair were killed during their descent. On 5 July eight more climbers summitted, all along the original route, these including Benôit Chamoux who climbed the route in 23 hours, and Josef Rakoncaj, climbing K2 for the second time. To date he is the only climber to have sumitted more than once. Given the reputation of the mountain it is likely that those who do achieve multiple ascents will remain a select band.

On 8 July Jerzy Kukuczka and Tadeusz Piotrowski summitted having completed an astonishing climb on the south face. The two Poles had been members of Dr Karl-Maria Herrligkoffer's international expedition, the other members of which (apart from the German Toni Freudig) had decided the face was too hard and too dangerous and had gone off to climb the original route, two Swiss members summitting on 5 July. It was this expedition which prompted Kukuczka's famous comparison of western and Polish expeditions, claiming they were similar to their cars: the western vehicle is better on good roads, but the old Polish model keeps going when the road gets rough. Most of those who have quoted the remark see it as a

population meant the Japanese had two teams, one of high altitude climbers, the other of support climbers who ferried loads to the mountain. The lead climbers followed the 45° north ridge, setting camps and fixing ropes, but deviated from the ridge towards the summit, climbing an obvious snow field to the left. High on the peak they met a Polish team which was attempting the north-west ridge from Pakistan, but had been forced into China by the difficulties of their route. The encounter led to a high-level protest by the Chinese: the Poles failed to reach the top which is, perhaps, just as well. The Japanese did summit, Naoé Sakashita, Yukihiro Yanagisawa and Hiroshi Yoshino reaching the top on 14 August with four more Japanese following them the next day. All the Japanese climbed solo and without bottled oxygen. All seven were forced to bivouac on their descent and sadly Yanagisawa, after a bivouac without a down jacket or sleeping bag, fell and was killed.

The Gasherbrum peaks and Broad Peak from high on the Abruzzi Spur

A few days after the Poles completed their climb the Italian Renato Casarotto fell into a crevasse and died while descending from an attempted solo of the 'Magic Line'. The number of deaths on the peak had risen from 12 to 18, but 1986 was not over yet. A few weeks later a group of climbers gathered in a camp (Camp IV) on the Shoulder. On 1 August three Austrians, Willy Bauer, Alfred Imitzer and Hannes Wieser arrived at the camp and on 2 August they made a summit bid, being forced to retreat from 8,400m (27,600ft). On return to the camp they met three Koreans (Chang Bong-Wan, Chang Byong-Ho, and Kim Chang-Sun), Austrian Kurt Diemberger and Briton Julie Tullis (from an Italian expedition), Alan Rouse (sole remaining member of an expedition he had led) and a Polish woman, Dobroslawa Wolf, known as Mrówka (Ant), from a team that was attempting to climb the south-south-west ridge (Magic Line). The ten climbers shared three tents which should have accommodated just seven. On 3 August the three Koreans climbed to the summit, two returning to Camp IV, one being forced to bivouac at the Bottleneck. The others at Camp IV decided to rest, a dubious decision since it is known that above 8,000m (26,247ft) rest cannot compensate for the body's deterioration. To make matters worse the nine at Camp IV (one Korean bivouacing higher) were joined by two other climbers.

On 3 August the Poles Przemyslaw Piasecki and Wojciech Wróz and the Czech Peter Bozik had completed the Magic Line, an under-rated climb whose completion was overshadowed by the subsequent tragedy. Wróz fell to his

comment on expeditions in general, but Kukuczka actually meant it as applying to the climbers not the organisation, being scathing of prima donna western climbers who retreat at the first sign of danger, extreme difficulties or bad weather. It is a very controversial view, which may explain why it has been so frequently mis-assigned, but the fact that most of the very hard climbs at high altitude are now accomplished by teams from ex-eastern bloc countries would seem to support it. Of the western nations, only Japan consistently produces climbers which operate at the highest levels of difficulty rather than making very fast ascents of explored lines. There are exceptions, of course (and it must be said that most of the pioneering climbs on the peaks were completed by western climbers), but these are notable chiefly because of their scarcity.

With Freudig's help the Poles climbed the face to just below a serac barrier that had frightened off previous expeditions and their own team-mates. Then, without Freudig they established an equipment dump at 7,000m (23,000ft). After a ten-day delay due to bad weather Kukuczka and Piotrowski returned to the face. It took two days to reach their dump, two more to reach the final headwall. On this they also spent two days, on the first of which Kukuczka, in the lead, climbed only 30m (100ft) of what he later described as the hardest climbing he had ever done at altitude. At their bivouac the Poles dropped their last gas cylinder, but used a candle to melt a mug of water. The next day they summitted and descended towards the shoulder, but were forced to bivouac again. Now, in appalling weather and badly dehydrated they continued to descend towards the camps on the original route, but Piotrowski lost his crampons and immediately slipped off the mountain. Kukuczka made it down safely: K2 had been his eleventh 8,000er and the one which took him closest to the limit.

The Chinese (north) side of K2

Nick Escourt leads two other team mebers on the west ridge during the 1978 British expedition

Battling through deep snow on the west ridge

death as the three descended the original route, but the surviving pair made a total of eleven in Camp IV which had been overcrowded with 10. On 4 August the two Poles and the three Koreans descended, while Bauer, Imitzer, Diemberger, Tullis, Rouse and Wolf (Mrówka) went for the summit. Wieser, who was not strong enough for another summit bid, declined to descend with the Poles, preferring to wait for his team-mates. Of the six, all but Mrówka summitted, but Diemberger and Tullis, who were lucky to survive a long fall on the descent, were forced to bivouac above Camp IV. A storm now trapped the seven climbers at Camp IV for five days during which time Julie Tullis died. On 10 August, knowing that further delay would be fatal, five climbers set out to descend during a break in the weather: the delirious Rouse was left at Camp IV. On the descent Imitzer and Wieser stopped and died close to Camp IV, Mrówka on the fixed ropes lower down. Only the frostbitten Bauer and Diemberger made it to Base Camp. The accusations and counter-accusations over this tragedy rumble on. (For Diemberger's account see *K2 – The Endless Knot*.)

If the Polish ascent of the Magic Line was overshadowed by the tragedy so too was the claimed solo ascent by Tomo Cesen of the south-south-east spur. Cesen climbed the route to the Shoulder, reaching it on 4 August, but did not attempt to reach either the summit or Camp IV before descending the Abruzzi Spur. The climb was controversial because Cesen claimed a new route, though virtually (actually?) all of it had been climbed by Scott's team in 1983, and many doubted his claim. His unseen descent of the original route was possible

(no one was moving on it that day) and supported his story (why claim decent of a well-known route, risking possible non-sightings by other climbers, when he could claim a descent of his deserted ascent route?), but though Cesen's claim is now accepted by many it is still classed as dubious by some.

During the next four years there were no further ascents of K2, but there were many failures. A Swiss-Polish team failed on the west face, two teams failed on the east face and a Polish team failed in a winter attempt of the original route. Then in 1990 a Japanese team climbed a new route on the north side while a four man Australian-American team put three men on the summit along the 1982 Japanese north ridge route, a fine effort. The next year Pierre Beghin and Christophe Profit completed the Polish north-west ridge/north-west face/north ridge route in an epic 40-day climb. The pair reached the summit as night fell on 15 August, the flash bulbs of their ritual photos being seen by trekkers at Concordia.

1992 and 1993 were more successful years, seven climbers following the original route to the top in 92, 14 in 93. The total to the top in 1993 was 16, the Briton Jonathan Pratt and American Dan Mazur following the Japanese west ridge route in an epic climb: the summit climb and descent took 32 hours from their top camp. In 1994 a Basque team completed the south-south-east spur route to the top, but they used fixed ropes on a route which Scott and, probably, Cesen, climbed without. There were successes on the original route and the north ridge too, but tragedy struck three Ukrainians on the original. Two weeks after their summit bid the remains of one were found below the Bottleneck and the other two were found dead in a bivouac at 8,400m (27,600ft). It is assumed that they were on their way down – bivouacs on the way to the summit are rare – but did they reach the top?

There was further tragedy in 1995. After successful climbs

in July, six climbers summitted late on 13 August, their ascents confirmed by radio. As they descended a vicious wind strafed the peak and, it is assumed, blew the Spaniards Javier Escartin, Javier Olivar and Lorenzo Ortiz, the Briton Alison Hargreaves, the American Rob Slater and the Canadian Bruce Grant to their deaths. The same year a German commercial expedition failed to climb the north ridge.

In 1996 Japanese climber Masafumi Todaka sooled the original route (though there were several teams on the line at the same time and on the summit on the same day) after he had failed to solo the 1986 Kukuczka/Piotrowski route and a Japanese team repeated of the 1994 Basque route on the south-south-east spur, twelve Japanese reaching the top after fixing 4km (2½ miles) of rope. The Japanese reached the summit in two groups of six on 12 and 14 August, a team of four Chileans who had also climbed the route summitting on 13 August. The Japanese were back in 1997, this time fixing 3km (2 miles) of rope in completing a variant to the west face route.

Seven Japanese and four Sherpas – using oxygen above 7,500m (24,600ft) for reasons of safety – reached the summit. It was the first time Sherpas had climbed in the Karakoram since 1939 and were only allowed into Pakistan because they were added to the Japanese permit as climbers. It was also to be the last climb of the century. In 1998 and 1999 K2 repulsed everyone who had made the long trip along the Baltoro, though there was a significant attempt by Hans Kammerlander in 1999. He reached about 8,400m (27,000) on the Basque route with the intention of skiing down from the summit. He vowed to return.

By the end of the century the number of successful summiteers on K2 was approaching 200, a remarkable number for so difficult and dangerous a mountain, one which illustrates the unique fascination of this beautiful peak. But the statistics go on to show that the chances of being killed on the descent from the summit are about 1 in 7, a frighteningly high ratio, but one which is unlikely to dissuade future climbers.

The summit of K2 looking north east

cho oyu 8,201m

"In the red glow of the setting sun I reached the summit. Doing so I experienced a wonderful feeling, as one step took me into another world. The steep walls and the knife-edged ridges vanished, it was as if I had stepped out of a dark and dangerous canyon onto a plateau bathed in purple light.

JERZY KUKUCZKA

cho oyu

Despite its vast bulk – it is the sixth highest mountain in the world – the British India Survey did not at first assign Cho Oyu a peak number. Though it was eventually assigned T45 (later changed to M1) it must have originally seemed a minor peak among the giants that spread across the Nepalese horizon from Makalu to Dhaulagiri.

The name is now invariably stated to mean 'Goddess of Turquoise', the peak glowing turquoise when seen from Tibet in the light of an afternoon sun (and, as any visitor to Tibet soon realises, turquoise is a favourite stone of the Tibetans). As goddess is chomo in Tibetan, and turquoise is yu, the contraction of chomo yu to Cho Oyu seems conclusive, but it is worth noting that this derivation is by no means certain. A lama at Namche Bazar told Herbert Tichy that the name meant 'Mighty Head' and Heinrich Harrer claimed that the real name was cho-i-u meaning 'god's head'. Harrer's suggestion is interesting because many early books have the peak's name as Cho Uyo which would be a good phonetic approximation of the three Tibetan syllables. Harrer's name is also close to the alternative Tibetan translation of the name as 'bald god'. In Tibetan legend Cho Oyu, the bald god, has his back turned to Chomolungma, the mother goddess, because she refused to marry him.

Exploration

Prior to 1921 little notice was taken of the mountain even though it had certainly been observed many times. In that year Howard-Bury's Everest reconnaissance, heading south from Tingri, reached the Nangpa La, to the west of the peak and obtained several good photographs of it from both the west and

Above Cho Oyu from the Tibetan plateau near Tingri. *Right* Camp II on the classic route

Above From West
A Point 7570
1 First ascent/'classic' route (1954)
2 SW Ridge, first climbed (in part) by the Polish (1986), but in its entirety by an

international team (1993)
Below From North
1 Yugoslavians (1988)
2 Kotov/Pierson (1997)
3 Spanish (1996)

Above From South 1 Poles (winter 1985)
2 East Ridge (skyline to right of summit), Soviets (1991)
Below South-west Face
A Summit **B** Gyabrag Lho Glacier

C Point 7570 **1** First ascent (1954)
2 SW ridge, Polish (1986), international team (1993) **3** Yamanoi solo (1994)
4 Kurtyka/Loretan/Troillet (1990)

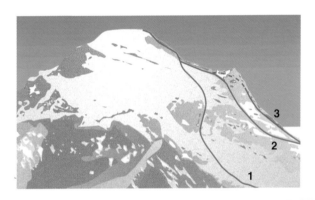

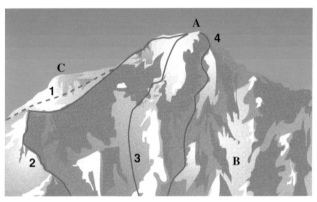

the north-west. It was also photographed on the Houston Everest flight of 1933. However with access through Nepal denied it was not until 1951 that the approaches to the mountain were explored. The main objective of the 1951 British reconnaissance under Eric Shipton was an exploration of the Nepalese side of Everest as a prelude to an assumed British expedition in 1952. Shipton's team included several who were to take part in the 1953 British Expedition – including Edmund Hillary. The team tried, but failed, to reach the Nup La to the east of Cho Oyu, but from close to it saw no easy route from that side.

In 1952 Shipton returned with a stronger team intent on continuing the exploration of Cho Oyu (the Swiss being on Everest) and, if possible, climbing it. The main purpose of the expedition, however, was to test oxygen, equipment

Pasang Dawa Lama on the summit after the first ascent

and personnel for the 1953 Everest attempt. This time the Nup La was climbed, but the view of Cho Oyu reinforced the opinion formed in 1951. The expedition then went to the west side of the peak, climbing the Nangpa La. From here it was clear that a route existed from the north-west. But on that side of the mountain lay an undefined border between Nepal and Tibet. The Chinese were now occupying Tibet and, rumour had it, were already just a short distance to the north. If his team were discovered by Chinese soldiers in an area that might form part of a border dispute Shipton was fearful that the Nepalese might react by cancelling the British 1953 permit for Everest. By contrast Hillary was of the view that as the climbers would at all times be above 5,700m (18,700ft) there was no possibility of detection. In the end Hillary and George Lowe (who was also on Everest in 1953) made an attempt, reaching a height of about 6,800m (22,400ft) where they were stopped by an ice fall. Realising that to overcome this, and to fix it with ropes so that Sherpas could carry loads through it, would take greater resources than they had at their disposal, they retreated.

First Ascent

Herbert Tichy was born in 1912 and studied geology at

Early morning sun illuminates the southern flanks of Cho Oyu, seen over Gokyo Tsho beside the Ngozumpa Glacier

Cho Oyu from the north on the Tibetan plateau

university, completing his doctorate at Vienna with a thesis on Himalayan geology, with practical work carried out in Tibet in 1936. During the winter of 1953/54 he went on a private expedition to western Nepal accompanied by the Sherpas Pasang Dawa Lama (who had almost climbed K2 with Wiessner in 1939), Adjiba and Gyalsen. The four climbed several 6,100m peaks (20,000ft) and discussed the possibility of climbing something bigger. On his return to Austria in January 1954 Tichy applied for permission to attempt Cho Oyu and this was granted in April. With two friends, Sepp Jochler, a

brilliant climber who had accompanied Hermann Buhl on the Eiger's north wall, and Helmut Heuberger, a geographer from the University of Innsbruck, Tichy returned to Nepal in late August. The three-man, nominally leaderless, team were accompanied by seven Sherpas – Tichy's three west Nepal companions plus four others – with Pasang Dawa Lama as sirdar. The team carried two oxygen cylinders for emergency use and limited medical equipment: though Tichy and Heuberger were Dr Tichy and Dr Heuberger, neither was a medic. In his book of the expedition Tichy notes the advice given to him by a surgeon before the trip on the use of a scalpel for the amputation of severely frost-bitten fingers or toes – 'press hard and then make as clean a cut as possible'.

Though he was an oil geologist, Tichy had worked for a short time as a journalist and despite his self-deprecating view of his literary abilities his expedition book is a marvellous read, a fairy-tale of a story. While later books have tended to concentrate on the drudgery of approach marches Tichy found the walk-in a joy. Indeed, the climb is the middle, almost incidental, section of a book that explores eastern Nepal. There are profound insights – the difference between porters and Sherpas is that the former live longer, the latter more proudly – and unexpected hilarity – the team bought a sheep which they walked (dog-like on a lead, the Sherpas vying with each other for the privilege of holding its rope and everyone looking for good grass patches for it to feed on) for several days before it changed from companion to evening meal.

As with Shipton, Tichy was concerned about trespassing into Tibet from the Nangpa La, but took the view that discovery was unlikely. From a Base Camp at about 5,500m (18,000ft) the team rapidly climbed up to the ice cliffs which had stopped

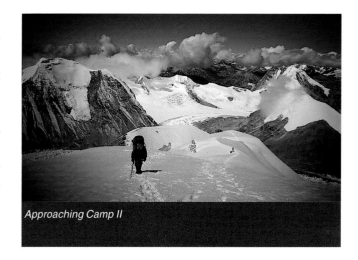
Approaching Camp II

Camp II below the classic route on Cho Oyu

Hillary and Lowe, Tichy doing much of the work as Jochler was slow in acclimatising and Heuberger seems content to have played a supporting role. To Tichy's amazement he, Pasang and Adjiba climbed through the ice fall in an hour. Deciding that a fixed rope was necessary the trio tried to fix long wooden pegs at the top of the fall, but found the snow beneath the ice too rotten to hold them. The problem was solved by the three urinating on the pegs, the cold rapidly creating a solid, and presumably yellow, anchor. The next day Tichy and five Sherpas climbed up and established a camp (Camp IV) at about 6,930m (22,750ft). Here Tichy and three of the Sherpas stayed, intending to make a summit bid the following day.

The following morning it was cloudless but bitingly cold, with a fierce wind threatening to sweep tents and climbers from the mountains. The four climbers dressed and left the tents which were immediately blown flat by the wind. The Sherpas were convinced they would all die, Pasang repeating this view over and over. Then, as the wind threatened to blow one tent away, Tichy flung himself across it burying his hands in the snow as an anchor. He was gloveless and within seconds his fingers were frozen. He thrust his hands between the thighs of Pasang and Adjiba, but the pain was so bad he could barely think rationally. Fortunately the accident galvanised the Sherpas who packed the tents and began an epic descent. Tichy was lowered down the ice cliffs and the team successfully reached Camp III where Sepp Jochler, now fully fit, met them. The team retreated to Base Camp, sending Pasang off to Namche Bazar for supplies.

As they rested at base two figures were seen approaching. Tichy nervously assumed that they were Chinese soldiers, but it was Mde Claude Kogan and another member of a Swiss team, led by Raymond Lambert, that the Austrians had met in Kathmandu. The Swiss had intended to climb Gauri Sankar, but finding it too hard they had decided to climb Cho Oyu instead. Tichy was appalled and pointed out that he, not they, had the permit for the mountain. During discussions that became increasingly acrimonious the Swiss refused to back down and the Austrians refused to join forces. Sepp Jochler was particularly adamant over the latter: they had come as a small team to climb the peak and he preferred failure to compromise. Tichy suggested that the Austrians be allowed one attempt before the Swiss tried, but Lambert declined: it was late autumn, winter's storm would start soon, delays were out of the question. Eventually an unsatisfactory arrangement was reached, the Austrians being given a few days start on the climb. This gave Tichy his first try, but with the Swiss preparing their route as he did.

With no time for the healing of his frost-bitten hands and no time to wait for Pasang's return with supplies the Austrians started up again. They climbed up to their old Camp III below the ice cliffs and excavated a snow cave in case the wind increased again. In the cave Heuberger practised his injection skills on Tichy, hoping to reduce the final frostbite damage, while Jochler and the Sherpas re-established Camp IV. On their return they discovered that the Swiss had placed their own fixed rope on the ice fall – the race had become serious. The next day Pasang reached the cave, grey with the fatigue of a long, fast climb. The team, including Tichy despite his inability to use his hands, now climbed towards Camp IV. To their relief the vicious wind had cleared loose snow from the mountain leaving a hard snow base that made cramponing easy. They moved Camp IV a little higher – to about 6,980m (22,900ft) – but fearing a change in the weather and the Swiss, who could not be far behind, they decided to attempt a long climb for the summit rather than establishing another camp. The plan was for Jochler and Pasang to make the attempt, but late in the evening Tichy decided to join them. The three left camp at 6am, finding the snow still perfect for rapid movement. Despite being 1,220m (4,000ft) from the summit they arrived just below it at 3pm. Pasang Dawa Lama, who was leading at the time, stopped and the three, arm in arm, walked up on to the vast snow dome top – large enough to accommodate ball games – that is the culmination of the huge summit plateau. It was the first post-monsoon ascent of an 8,000er and the first by such a small team.

Pasang Dawa Lama's climb was remarkable: in three days he had climbed from 4,250m (14,000ft) to the summit. On the descent it became clear why: Pasang had bartered a bride in Lukla, agreeing with her father that there would be no price for her (bridegrooms pay compensation to the father for the loss of a daughter in Nepal) if he climbed Cho Oyu, but would pay 1,000 rupees, a vast sum, if he failed. The final chapter of

High on the classic route

Tichy's book deals with Pasang's wedding. Tichy later maintained that for several weeks on their return from the peak the whole team, Austrians and Sherpas alike, were 'either tipsy or completely plastered'. This sustained re-hydration also helped his frostbite injuries which were less serious than he had feared. Ironically in view of the race they had precipitated, the Swiss attempt on Cho Oyu failed, Lambert and Mde Kogan being defeated by high winds at about 7,500m (24,600ft).

Later Ascents

Pasang Dawa Lama climbed Cho Oyu again in 1958, this time as sirdar of an Indian expedition, making the second ascent with Sonam Gyatso. This expedition resulted in the first death on the mountain, Maj ND Jayal, the first Director of the Himalayan Mountaineering Institute in Darjeeling (an organisation set up by Nehru to capitalise on Tenzing's fame after Everest: Tenzing coveted the directorship but was made Chief Instructor, an appointment he resented) dying of pulmonary oedema low on the mountain.

In 1959 an International Woman's Expedition (French, British, Belgium, Swiss and Nepalese) led by Mde Claude Kogan attempted to repeat the original route. Kogan, the Belgian climber Claudine van der Stratten and Sherpa Ang Norbu established Camp IV at 7,100m (23,300ft) but were then pinned down by a storm. In trying to reach them two Sherpas (Wangdi and Chhowang) were hit by an avalanche. Wangdi managed to dig himself out, but was unable to reach his colleague. Subsequently another avalanche destroyed Camp IV killing the three inhabitants. There were further deaths five years later during an expedition which has a much-disputed claim to Cho Oyu's third ascent. The German Fritz Stammberger claimed to have reached the summit alone on 25 April 1964, but the Sherpa Phu Dorje claims to have been with him. The 'summit' photographs were almost certainly not taken at the top, nor at the time Stammberger claims to have reached it. Two other team members, after failing in their

Snow picked up by high winds obscure the view of the classic route

summit attempt reached the top camp exhausted and unable to descend. A rescue attempt found one dead, the other dying on the descent.

For more than a decade Cho Oyu remained undisturbed, but then in 1978 two Austrians (Furtner and Koblmüller), visiting the region on a trekking permit, claimed to have climbed a new route on the south-east face. This unsanctioned

ascent was discounted by many, but not by the Nepalese who banned the pair for several years. Only in 1981, 17 years after the disputed third ascent was a team granted a permit to attempt the peak again, a Nepalese/Japanese team attempting (and failing) on the east face and, subsequently, on the south ridge. The following year an attempt to complete a legitimate ascent of the south-east face ended when Reinhard Karl, one of Germany's foremost climbers (the first German to climb Everest) was killed by an avalanche.

In 1983, having failed in a bid to climb Cho Oyu in winter via the south-east face (in December 1982), Reinhold Messner successfully completed a part-new route on the south-west side reaching the summit with Hans Kammerlander and Michl Dacher. The trio climbed the peak in alpine style, reaching the

Dawn light catches the neighbouring frontier peak of Cho Aui (7,352m/24,121ft); view is to the south west from about 7,600m (25,000ft) on Cho Oyu

top on 5 May after three bivouacs. They were back at Base Camp on 7 May, five days after leaving it. Cho Oyu was Messner's tenth 8,000er. Messner's line was repeated in 1984 by the Czechs Vera Komarkova and Margita Dina Sterbova making the first women's ascent. 1984 also saw a failed attempt to climb the east ridge by a semi-commercial team and a post-monsoon attempt on the south-east buttress, a Yugoslavian team reaching 7,600m (24,900ft) on the latter. This route involved 1,400m (4,600ft) of climbing on a pillar of rock at an average angle of 60°. The team – all Slovenes, a fact which is much more important in today's Balkans than it was at the time – overcame all the difficulties, but were then defeated by winds gusting to 130km/h (80mph). The route was completed on February 1985, a Polish team claiming not only its first winter ascent, but the first winter ascent of Cho Oyu, the first ever winter first ascent of an 8,000er, if a sentence can be allowed to have so many 'firsts' in it. The summit was reached by Maciej Berbeka and Maciej Pawlikowski, then by Zygmunt Heinrich and Jerzy Kukuczka. Kukuczka was successfully claiming his eighth 8,000er and finally admitting that he was in

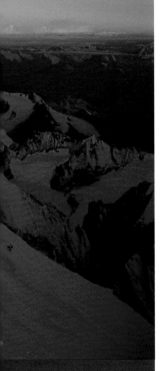

a race with Messner for first man to climb all 14 peaks. However, Kukuczka had no interest in repeating the easy lines to claim the prize, wanting to complete either new routes or first winter ascents. This, and the fact that Messner was already a couple of peaks ahead having begun his campaign almost a decade earlier (he had climbed five before Kukuczka's first), meant Kukuczka's challenge was never very realistic, though at one stage he had climbed eleven peaks to Messner's 12.

Later in 1985 there were several more ascents, including one by a Chinese team. They followed the original route, reversing the trespass of Tichy's team by climbing into Nepal. In December of the same year the second winter ascent was accomplished alpine style by two Czechs (Jaromir Stejskal and Dusan Becik) from an American-Canadian-Czech team, the first alpine style winter ascent of an 8,000er. A new route was established in 1986, a Polish team climbing the lower section of the south-west buttress, joining the normal route at about 7,750m (25,400ft). An international team climbed a variation of this route soon after, Peter Habeler and Marcel Rüedi being the first of seven climbers to reach the summit.

Over subsequent years Cho Oyu became popular with climbers seeking high altitude experience, its reputation as the 'easiest' 8,000er being firmly established by the mid-1980s. It was also an early candidate for fully commercial expeditions, one led by the Austrian Marcus Schmuck climbing a partially new route from the Tibetan side in 1987. Not all the hazards met by climbers were weather or mountain-based however, members of American and Chilean teams which followed the original route, and therefore crossed into Tibet, having their equipment, passports and permits confiscated.

In February 1988 Fernando Garrido climbed the original route solo, the first winter solo of an 8,000er. Despite the mountain being (relatively) easy, Garrido's climb was a remarkable achievement, the Spaniard braving high winds, temperatures down to minus 40°C and being forced to bivouac on his descent. Equally remarkable was Frenchman Marc Batard's ascent with the Sherpa Sungdare in the early September 1988, the pair reaching the summit in 18 hours from Base Camp despite having to break trail throughout the climb, theirs being the first post-monsoon ascent. On the same expedition Bruno Gouvy on snowboard, Véronique Périllat on monoski and Michel Vincent and Eric Decamp on skis descended from summit to base camp. At the same time Bruno Cormier paraglided down, the first descent from such a height without the aid of people to help him open the canopy. Cormier had next planned to parachute on to the summit of Everest and snowboard down to base camp. He was killed before this ambitious, not to say unlikely, scheme could be put into action.

Climbers at around 7,500m (24,600ft) on the classic route

Soon after the ski descents a Yugoslavian team climbed a new and very hard route on the north face, while seven teams were successful on the original route. In the final stages of the climb the Yugoslavs split into two teams, some taking a direct route to the top, the others traversing on to the original route. Iztok Tomazin, who made the direct climb, climbed down the original route, thus making the first traverse. Another first, one

Cho Oyu from the north in evening light

of more dubious merit, occurred in the winter of 89/90 when two teams given permits for the south-east face ended up fighting each other over priority on the route.

Post-monsoon in 1990 the Swiss pair Erhard Loretan and Jean Troillet, together with the Pole Wojciech Kurtyka, climbed a new route on the south-west face, to the right of the Polish buttress. Starting at 6pm they climbed though the night reaching a point 100m below the summit by the following night. They bivouaced, then continued to the summit at first light and descended the original route, a masterpiece of sustained climbing. The following year, also post-monsoon, a Russian/Ukrainian team succeeded in climbing the east ridge, the 'last great problem' which had resisted several attempts. Five members of a 20 strong party reached the top on 20 October 1991, the sixth member of the summit party stopping when he became concerned over his frostbitten fingers. After his colleagues rejoined him he was unfortunately killed by rockfall.

In February 1993 the peak was climbed by a Spanish team which included one Argentinian and the Swiss woman Marianne Chapuisat. The team used neither Sherpas nor bottled oxygen, Chapuisat claiming the first winter female ascent of any 8,000er. Also in 1993 the south-west buttress, first attempted and partially climbed in 1986, was climbed by an Italian/Polish/Portugeuse team approaching from the north. They found the route easier than they had anticipated. The team, which included Krzysztof Wielicki, then went on to climb Shisha Pangma.

A sign of the times was a winter ascent of the original route in January 1994 by a team organised by advertising in the climbing press. Two reached the top, but the teams also suffered two deaths. Later in 1994, while most climbers were attempting the normal route there were two fine climbs on the south-west face. Two Japanese women, Taeko Nagao and Yuka Endo, climbed the Loretan/Kurtyka/Troillet 1990 route alpine-style in four days, while at the same time Yasushi Yamanoi soloed a route to the left in two days. Less fortunate were two Serbian climbers who crossed the Nangpa La into Tibet to climb the W ridge. Chinese officials attempted to arrest them, but they climbed rapidly upwards. The Serbians failed to reached the top and were arrested when they descended. The standard practice on the mountain was now to buy a Nepalese permit, approach from Kathmandu, which virtually allows a drive to base camp, then to cross the border into Tibet to climb the easiest route. But from June 1994 the Chinese stationed an official at Nangpa La and charged $2,000 per climber for the border crossing. The first teams to arrive declined to pay, but many later climbers did.

In 1995 Ang Rita summitted for the fourth time (at that time he had also climbed Everest nine times – now ten – Dhaulagiri four times and Kangchenjunga once). The same year the New Zealand guide Guy Cotter was arrested in Lhasa after sending a fax in which he said he had heard a bomb explode and seen speeding army vehicles. He was held in prison for several days, then forced to confess to his 'crime' and deported to Nepal. This may have been the most spectacular aspect of a Cho Oyu expedition of the year, but the undoubted highlight was the ascent by the Briton Norman Croucher who, as a teenager had both legs amputated below the knee by a train after an accident on a railway line. Croucher climbs with artificial legs, his ascent being the first ascent of an 8,000er by so disabled a climber. On the descent he was forced to bivouac, his disability understandably slowing his progress, but was able to do so in his rucsac by removing his lower limbs!

The summit was reached in eleven hours from base camp in 1996 by the New Zealander Russell Brice: he was back in base camp within 24 hours. Then, in the post-monsoon season of the same year, a Spanish/Austrian team climbed a new route along the north-north-west ridge from the Palung La, the Spaniard Oscar Cadiach and the Austrian Sebastian Ruckensteiner climbing in alpine style and reaching the summit on 28 September. Another new route was climbed in 1997 when the Russian Georgi Kotov and the American Bill Pierson, a client climber on a commercial expedition, who climbed a line close to that of Cadiach and Ruckensteiner.

Cho Oyu is now firmly established as the favourite mountain for commercial expedition clients wanting to add an 8,000er to their list of achievements. Only Everest has received more ascents, but interestingly Cho Oyu has had more climbers reach its summit, the multiple ascents of Everest by many climbers distorting the true picture. It would be interesting to speculate how many of these ascents have been by climbers who reach the edge of the huge summit plateau and turn around, not wishing to spend the long time necessary to reach the true summit which is just a few metres higher. It is rumoured that there are those among the aspirants for all 14 8,000ers who have done exactly that. The test, apparently, is to look for the Everest massif: if you cannot see it then you have not reached the top. Of course if the weather is bad …

Last light on the final slopes of Cho Oyu I. The classic route heads up the centre of the this face to reach a wide summit plateau

'**The shattered granite offered plenty of holds and, no doubt due to the force and frequency of the wind, there was astonishingly little snow or verglas.**'

LIONEL TERRAY

makalu 8,463m

makalu

Makalu was Peak XIII of the Indian Survey, the survey suggesting, in 1884, that its name was Khamba Lung. This seems to have derived from the local area being called Khamba, though the valley to the north of the peak was called Kama Lung (the valley of the River Kama).

Some have suggested that Makalu derives from Kama Lung, the first word having its syllabus transposed. This is a very unconvincing argument and it is far more likely to derive from the Sanskrit Maha Kala, meaning 'great weather' from the mountain's isolated and dominant position in an area renowned for its winds. The Hindu god Shiva, the destroyer, is associated with extremes of weather and the mountain may have been named in deference to him. Interestingly Maha Kala (with an exact or very similar spelling) is Tibetan for 'great black' which is an excellent description of the huge rock pyramid after it has been scoured clean of snow by the wind.

Exploration

The peak was seen and photographed by Howard-Bury's 1921 Everest reconnaissance which explored the Kama Valley and the Kangshung Glacier, heading south from Kharta in Tibet. Wanting to see into Nepal Howard-Bury climbed from the Kangshung on to the ridge below Pethangtse, reaching a height which he estimated at 6,550m (21,500ft). As Pethangtse is only a little over 6,700m (22,000ft) this seems unlikely, more recent research suggesting Howard-Bury probably did not quite reach 6,000m (20,000ft). Nonetheless he had a good view of Makalu's north face (the route of the final part of the first ascent) and glimpsed the west face. In 1933 the Houston flight obtained good photographs of the south and west faces. The west face was also photographed in 1951 and 1952 by Eric Shipton's Everest reconnaissance and Cho Oyu expeditions. In 1952 Shipton, Hillary, Lowe and Evans followed the Barun Glacier to the base of Pethangtse getting a close up view of the west face.

The French has negotiated permission for an attempt on Makalu from Tibet as early as 1934 but the Tibetans had changed their minds before any significant planning was underway. When the British climbed Everest in 1953 the French, who had permission for an attempt in 1954, again turned their attention to the peak. To their surprise and dismay they discovered that Nepal had already given permits to two other groups, one American, the other a New Zealand team under Ed (by then Sir Edmund) Hillary. The French therefore applied for permission for 1955, but also accepted an offer to reconnoitre the peak post-monsoon in 1954.

The Americans – a ten-man group from the Californian Sierra Club led by Dr William Siri and including Dr William Unsoeld who later made the first ascent of Everest's west ridge – arrived on the Barun Glacier in early April. They prospected the south-east and north-

Camp III on the south-east ridge, Californian 1954 Expedition. Baruntse (7,220m/23,688ft) beyond

west ridges, favouring the former along which they placed several camps, but bad weather prevented them from getting above 7,150m (23,460ft). The New Zealand team arrived later, but without Hillary who had broken several ribs during the rescue of another team member from a crevasse. The team explored the northern Barun Glacier towards Pethangtse and also climbed towards the Makalu La (the col between the main summit and Makalu II – also known as Kangchungtse). On this latter climb Hillary, now back with his team, became suddenly, and seriously, ill, the whole team being required to organise his evacuation.

When the French arrived in September, therefore, Makalu was only marginally better explored than it had been pre-war. The French team reached the Makalu La and climbed both Kangchungtse (7,640m/25,066ft) and Chomo Lonzo, both offering a good view of the north face. The climb of Chomo Lonzo, a 7,790m (25,558ft) peak, was a notable achievement, particularly as it was climbed in the teeth of a gale with temperatures down to minus 35°C. In his autobiography Lionel Terray, who made the climb with Jean Couzy, claims it was one of his toughest, most intense, yet memorable and wonderful days, and certainly gives the impression that Chomo Lonzo was climbed for the fun of it rather than as a viewpoint. Nevertheless, the post-monsoon expedition identified the route which would be taken on the first ascent.

First Ascent

As with the post-monsoon team of 1954, the spring 1955 French team was led by Jean Franco. Jean Couzy and Lionel Terray, veterans of Annapurna as well as the 1954 trip, were joined by Jean Bouvier, Serge Coupé, Pierre Leroux. Guido Magnone (who, with Terray, had

MAKALU: ASCENT ROUTES

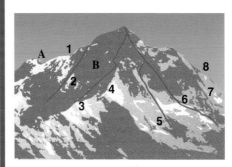

From West

From South-east

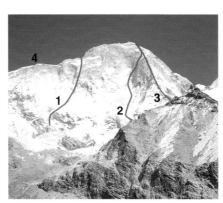

West Face

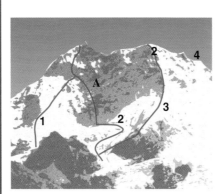

From South

From Makalu La

From West
A *Makalu Col*
B *West face*
1 *NW Ridge, Kukuczka (1981)*
2 *Polish/Brazilian (1982)*
3 *Russians (1997)*
4 *West Ridge/Pillar, French (1971)*
5 *Yugoslavians (1975)*
6 *Beghin (1989)*
7 *South Pillar, Czech (1976)*
8 *SE Ridge, Japanese (1970)*

From South-east
A *South Face*
1 *SE Ridge, Japanese (1970)*
2 *E Ridge, Japanese (1995)*

West Face
1 *Polish/Brazilian (1982)*
2 *Russians (1997)*
3 *West Pillar, French (1971)*
4 *NW Ridge, Kukuczka solo (1981)*

From South
1 *Yugoslavians (1975)*
2 *Beghin (1989)*
3 *S Pillar, Czechs (1976)*
4 *SE Ridge, Japanese (1970)*

From Makalu La
1 *First ascent, French; 'classic' route (1955)*
2 *NW Ridge, Kukuczka solo (1981)*

climbed Fitzroy in Patagonia in 1952, heralding an advance in difficulty for routes on remote peaks, and had also been in the team which climbed the west face of the Dru) and André Vialatte. André Lapras was the team doctor and two geologists, Pierre Bordet and Michel Latreille, accompanied the expedition. The team had no less than 23 Sherpas under sirdar Gyalzen Norbu and a Gurkha soldier, Kindjock Tsering, who acted as a high-altitude porter. The team's equipment showed a step change from that of previous expeditions to the great peaks. Though the base layers were knitted jersey rather than man-made fibre, the one-piece down suits (weighing 800g/1¾lb) were very similar to modern suits, though they needed to be covered with a windproof nylon shell. The French also had improved oxygen sets, based on the British Everest design, but lighter. The vast number of oxygen bottles they took allowed them to use supplementary oxygen from low on the mountain and at high flow rates, and to sleep on bottled gas too, facts which doubtless contributed to the final outcome. The weather also played its part. Though the early stages of the climb were pushed through in indifferent weather, the days of the summit attempts were near perfect, cloudless and almost

still. Snow conditions were equally good, with hard, but cramponable snow, rather than the deep stuff which requires arduous trail-making, or bare ice.

The route to the base of the Makalu La was straightforward, but was much harder to the col. Using, in part, ropes they had placed in 1954 the French fixed ropes all the way to the col where they set Camp V. The ropes helped the Sherpas, several carries with large teams establishing a well-equipped camp at the base of the north-west ridge. The ridge was not attempted, a rising traverse being made across the north face to a last camp, Camp VI, at 7,800m (25,600ft). From it, at 7am on 15 May Terray and Couzy set out. They crossed relatively easy ground to the base of a spur which led up to the east ridge. The spur, which had looked formidable from a distance, was straightforward, the pair reaching the summit at about 11am, having taken only four hours over the mountain's final 660m (2,150ft). The summit was amazing, three almost symmetrical ridges (east, south and north-west) meeting at a pencil-sharp point which could be covered by the palm of a climber's hand and on which a man could sit, but barely stand. (As an aside, the map of the peak, its ridges and the route in Franco's book of the expedition places the summit at the wrong place, at the east end of a short north-south route running ridge: it is at the west end of this – the east – ridge.)

On the following day (16 May) Franco, Magnone and sirdar Gyalzen Norbu repeated the climb, also arriving before noon, and on next day (17 May) Bouvier, Coupé, Leroux and Vialatte reached the summit, again before noon. It was the first time that an entire climbing had reached the summit of an 8,000m peak.

After the climb both Terray and Franco noted the anti-climax they felt at the success. Terray stated that 'victory must be bought at a price of suffering and effort, and the clemency of the weather combined with the progress of technique had sold us this one too cheaply for us to appreciate it at its true value'. Similarly, Franco thought that 'in our hearts we felt a little bit let down. Given the perfection of our tools and the continuity of our good luck, one might even have wished for a slightly tougher adversary'. These seem remarkable sentiments. True, the French had great good fortune with the weather – no wind on the hard climb to Makalu La and perfect conditions on each of the three summit climbs: Franco notes that the knife-sharp summit ridge would have been a much stiffer test if it had carried 0.5m (1½ft) of fresh snow or a significant cornice – good equipment, a small army of Sherpas and almost no sickness among the team members (in part due to the abundant use of bottle oxygen from quite low on the peak). But they also had a strong team and excellent organisation, and they had, after all, climbed the fifth highest mountain in the world, virtually at their first attempt. It seems almost as if, after the trauma of Annapurna, with Herzog and Lachenal barely recovered from their injuries, the team were suffering from the guilt that survivors often experience after major disasters. They had wanted to succeed, but were embarrassed by the ease of the success.

Later Ascents

In 1961 Ed Hillary returned to Makalu on an expedition which, starting in the summer of 1960, had, as objectives, a thorough exploration of the Mingbo region, a search for the yeti and a bottled gas-free ascent of the world's fifth highest peak. The expedition climbed Ama Dablam in March 1961, their permit for Makalu being immediately withdrawn by the Nepalese who claimed the climb was illegal. Hillary spent time in Kathmandu arguing (successful) his case and this may have been the reason why, on climbing to Camp III on Makalu on his return, he suffered a stroke and had to be evacuated. The expedition continued, reaching the Makalu La and establishing a top camp at 8,100m (26,600ft). From here Peter Mulgrew, Dr Tom Nevison and the Sherpa Annullu started for the top. Just 110m (360ft) from it Mulgrew suffered a pulmonary embolism necessitating instant evacuation. Lower on the mountain, with Annullu seeking help, Nevison and Mulgrew were forced to bivouac. As Nevison dug a snow cave he contracted pulmonary oedema, The expedition's second doctor – Michael Ward, who had been

The complex south-east ridge of Makalu

on the British Everest team – fell on his way to render help and contracted pneumonia as a complication to his injuries. The retreat now turned to a near rout, Mulgrew eventually being air-lifted to Kathmandu: he subsequently lost both feet and several fingers to frostbite and had other, serious, complications. So bad were his injuries that his name became a by-word for suffering back in New Zealand. In his book on the climb Mulgrew recalls a stranger, not realising who he was, commiserating with him on his injuries and ending by saying '… it could be worse – look at the rough time that bloke Mulgrew had'.

The rarely-seen Tibetan north-east face of Makalu above the Sakyetang Glacier

117

Not until 1970 was the mountain climbed again. In that year a massive Japanese expedition – 20 climbers, 32 Sherpas and over 400 porters – pushed a route up the long south-east ridge. The 'Black Gendarme', the hardest section of the ridge was climbed, but then bypassed on the west face for ease of load carrying. The first attempt on the summit failed in a

On Chamlang a climber looks north east towards Makalu

snowstorm at about 8,380m (27,500ft), the two climbers being forced to bivouac, but returning safely to camp. The second attempt by Yuichi Ozaki and Hajime Tanaka did reach the summit, but required 17 hours of climbing, the pair continuing to the top after their bottled oxygen had been exhausted. They descended safely by moonlight.

The next ascent, in 1971, pioneered another new route to the top, a French team led by Robert Paragot climbing the west ridge which separates the west and south faces. The ridge is more usually called the west pillar after the near vertical section of rock from 7,350m (24,100ft) to 7,700m (25,250ft). This section required climbing of Grade V+ and A2, very hard at sea level, but an advance in difficulty for an altitude of 7,500m (24,600ft). The weather added to the problems, spring 1971 being the worst of the century with heavy snow, very low temperatures and winds of over 150km/h (almost 100mph). Much of the lead climbing was done by Yannick Seigneur and Bernard Mellet, and it was they, using bottled oxygen from the top of the pillar, who reached the summit after two other summit attempts had failed and the third member of their own party had retreated from about 8,300m (27,200ft). For the time, just a year after the ascent of the south face of Annapurna, this was a remarkable climb, one which has not received the credit it deserves.

Over the next four years there were a series of failures on Makalu's south face by strong teams from Austria (a team which included Reinhold Messner), Czechoslovakia (that team reaching over 8,000m/26,247ft) and Yugoslavia. Finally, post-monsoon in 1975 a Yugoslavian team under Ales Kunaver (who had led the earlier attempt) was successful, seven climbers reaching the summit over a five day period in early October. All the summiteers used supplementary oxygen, though one was forced to abandon his set when it failed well below the top. In 1976 the Czechs also returned and completed their south face line, climbing the south-west buttress to the right of the

Yugoslav route. At the same time a Spanish team was attempting the south-east ridge. The teams decided to combine, with the intention of climbing up the Czech line and down the Spanish. The first summit attempt failed in dreadful weather, but the second succeeded, Milan Krissak, Michal Orolin and Karel Schubert being joined by the Spaniard Jorge Camprubi. Orolin retreated when his oxygen set failed, the other three summitting. On the descent they were caught by a storm. The exhausted Schubert insisted on bivouacing, the other two struggling down. Schubert was never seen again.

In 1977 a British/American/Yugoslav team attempted a

Arial view from the north west shows little Kngchungtse, the Makalu La and the north west ridge and face. Chomo Lonzo on the left (7,790m/25,558ft), is actually in Tibet

Sherpa and bottled oxygen free ascent of the west face. The expedition ended after a series of disasters which, because no one was seriously harmed, seem almost comic: there were illnesses and injuries due to rockfalls, one (unoccupied) camp was destroyed by an avalanche and another by fire when a stove blew up. Without having reached 7,000m (22,950ft) the team retreated. A planned traverse of the peak in 1978 (up the south-east ridge and down the original route) also failed, though the reasons were more to do with the logistics of the climb than bad luck, but seven members of the international team summitted. One of these was Kurt Diemberger who, at 46, was climbing his first 8,000er since his first ascents of Broad Peak and Dhaulagiri. One of the seven, the Sherpa Ang Chappal, became the first man to summit without bottled oxygen.

The French west pillar route was repeated in 1980 by a four man

Alpenglow lights the south face and south-east ridge

Rob Hall approaching the summit

Attempts to complete the first winter ascent were resumed in 1984/85, a Japanese team failing at 7,520m (24,670ft) and Reinhold Messner and Hans Kammerlander reaching a point just above the Makalu La. In September 1986 Messner and Kammerlander returned with Fritz Mutschlechner and completed the original route. This was Messner's thirteenth 8,000er completed at his fourth attempt on the mountain. Two days before Messner's team summitted Krzysztof Wielicki reached the top along a variant of the French west pillar route. Wielicki had been a member of a Polish expedition, but had been asked by Marcel Ruedi to join him in a two-man alpine style ascent. Concerned that he had not acclimatised, and that Reudi's arrival by helicopter implied that he, too, was not properly acclimatised, Wielicki only agreed with reluctance, stressing that at the first sign of trouble the pair should descend. Wielicki took Diamox and performed beyond his wildest hopes. He pulled ahead of Reudi and summitted alone. On his descent he met Reudi who was climbing slowly, but insisted on continuing, despite the fact that it would mean a bivouac. The next day Wielicki saw Reudi descending from the summit as he made his own way down, but later Messner and his colleagues found Reudi sitting in the snow, dead.

American team climbing without oxygen and in alpine style, John Roskelley reaching the summit alone, the others having stopped for a variety of reasons. In December of the same year an attempted winter ascent of the south-east ridge, an ambitious climb, failed. The next year, climbing post-monsoon, Wojciech Kurtyka, Jerzy Kukuczka and Alex McIntyre failed in an attempt on a new line on the west face, Kukuczka then climbing the north-west ridge solo and without supplementary oxygen in four days. This first true solo (several climbers had climbed the final section of the mountain alone previously) was Kukuczka's third ascent of an 8,000er. In May 1982 a Korean team climbing a variant of the south-east ridge route found the small wooden toy which Kukuczka had placed in a crack just below the top. The Anglo-Polish line on the west face was also completed in 1982 by a Polish-Brazilian team, Andrzej Czok soloing to the top, the final section of climbing being along Kukuczka's north-west ridge route.

In 1984, during an attempt at a new route on the east face of Makalu, which failed less than 100m (330ft) from the top, Jean Affanassieff, Doug Scott and Steve Sustad found the body of Karel Schubert in his final bivouac, a sobering experience which may have influenced the decision to retreat down the difficult ascent route rather than continuing to the top and descending the easier original line.

Makalu seen in the early morning by climbers starting towards the summit of Everest up the south-east ridge

In 1988 Marc Batard soloed the west pillar and descended the original route, completing the first traverse. With two Sherpas Batard had fixed rope to 7,750m (25,400ft) and then descended. Then, leaving an equipment dump in the evening of 26 April he climbed to the summit, reaching it at 9.45am on 27th, a fine achievement. Equally noteworthy was Pierre Beghin's virtual solo in the post-monsoon period of 1989. With three friends Beghin climbed a new route on the south face to a height of 7,200m (23,600ft). From a camp at that height Beghin continued alone, climbing up to reach the Yugoslav route which he followed, with two bivouacs, to the summit. He descended the original route, but was avalanched, the snow slide leaving him unharmed within a short distance of the camp of a Catalan expedition. The next day he was avalanched again, but was once more unharmed and continued safely to the base of the peak.

1990 saw the first female ascent of Makalu, the American

Alan Hinkes on the summit

face when he was struck by stonefall and forced to retreat from a height of 7,300m (24,000ft), but in spring 1997 a Russian team succeeded in adding a new route to the face. The 'true' west face route, a line directly up the headwall, would involve very hard rock climbing at very high altitude but is dangerous, being swept by stonefall from the upper headwall. The Russians did not take that line, favouring one to the left of the west pillar which offered some shelter from the stonefall. Nonetheless it was a hard route – one of the hardest to date on the great peaks and a notable achievement – difficulties only easing when the top of the west pillar route was reached – at 8,000m (26,250ft) – by a rising traverse. Above 7,300m (24,000ft) the climb was alpine-style by a team of six, but at 8,200m (26,900ft) Salavat Habibulin, who had done much of the leading and as a result was exhausted, was forced to stop. Alexei Bolotov, Igor Bugachevski, Yuri Ermachek, Dmitri Pavlenko and Nikolai Zhilin continued to the summit, reaching it on 24 May. When they returned they found Habibulin had died. On the descent Bugachevski was struck by stonefall and killed.

The true west face route – which has been attempted by several teams though no one has reached higher than 7,300m (24,000ft) – remains to be climbed: it is arguably the latest 'last great problem' of the 8,000ers and as such is sure to be climbed early in the next century. Makalu is also the only Nepalese 8,000er without a winter ascent, another target climb for the next millenium (assuming, wrongly if pedantic truth is sought, that this will begin on 1 January 2000). Makalu is a beautiful, elegant mountain, but it is also a dangerous peak, second only to Annapurna (of the Nepalese peaks – both are less dangerous than K2) in the death rate of climbers descending from the summit, a fact that is likely to limit the interest of commercial teams for a while.

Kitty Calhoun Grissom reaching the top with John Schutt, the two being members of a small team which made an alpine ascent of the French west pillar route. In 1994 an attempt to climb the peak directly from Makalu La by the Russian Anatoli Boukreev and the Bolivian Bernardo Guarachi failed 30m (100ft) from the top. Later Boukreev and Neil Beidleman completed the route in a continuous push, starting at 6.30pm on 13 May and reaching the top at 4.30pm on 15 May. The following year a Japanese team climbed a new route on the north-east side of the peak. Starting in Tibet the route follows the east ridge, a 10km (6¼ mile) ridge beginning at just 3,920m (12,850ft) where they set their base camp. The team climbed the southern face of the ridge to reach the north-west ridge and the original route which they then followed to the top. Eight Japanese reached the summit in two teams of four on 21 and 22 May.

Post monsoon in 1996 the Japanese Yasushi Yamanoi failed in his ambitious attempt to solo a new route on the west

Difficult ground on Makalu's classic route from Makalu La

'Above 23,000 feet the climber quickly loses weight and grows weak. He is like a sick man, always tired. To turn over in bed, to reach for a boot or a box of matches, brings an attack of breathlessness; every exertion calls for an effort'

CHARLES EVANS

kangchenjunga 8,586m

kangchenjunga

Kangchenjunga, Peak IX of the Indian survey, is the most easterly of the 8,000m peaks, standing on the border between Nepal and Sikkim. From almost any direction the peak looks like a vast tent, the massif being created by four ridges radiating virtually on the cardinal points from the summit.

Kangchenjunga, Peak IX of the Indian survey, is the most easterly of the 8,000m peaks, standing on the border between Nepal and Sikkim. From almost any direction the peak looks like a vast tent, the massif being created by four ridges radiating virtually on the cardinal points from the summit. Strung out along these ridges (which do not meet at the main summit, the east ridge meeting the north-south ridge at the south summit) are a series of tops, the ridges being saw-toothed rather than declining steadily in height. There are, therefore, a number of subsidiary summits, three (at least) over 8,000m (26,247ft): the south summit – occasionally called Kangchenjunga II – was given a unique designation (Peak VIII) by the Indian survey. The central (between the south and main tops) and west summits are both over 8,400m (27,560ft), the west (Yalung Kang) having been the specific object of several expeditions. Some have suggested that Yalung Kang should be added to the list of 8,000ers, but this is unlikely, the peak being insufficiently distinct to be realistically termed a separate mountain.

Kangchenjunga's name is something of a mystery. One Sanskrit scholar claimed it derived from Kancan Jangha, golden thigh, though quite why this should have been is a mystery as there is no physical resemblance (to colour or body part, unless aided by strange, evening light and a vivid imagination), or any obvious legend associated with the area. Most experts now agree a Tibetan origin, deriving from Kang-chen-dzo-nga which would be pronounced (more or less) as Kangchenjunga. One 19th century explorer claimed the name was given to a local Sikkim god who rode a white lion and waved a banner, believing that the lion was the peak, the banner the clouds or snow plume at the summit. The god was believed to live on the summit and early climbers on the peak were asked not to go to the very top to avoid annoying him, causing him to unleash his fury on the locals. This was scrupulously observed by early climbers, but it seems that summiteers have for several years been ignoring the custom. The story of the god is both delightful and plausible, but the actual meaning of the Tibetan words is 'snow-big-treasury-five' which would make the peak the Five Treasures of the Great Snow.

But to what does the five refer? Five summits can be picked out, but more (or less) can just as easily be counted. Some have suggested that the 'five' refers to glaciers, but ten glaciers radiate from the Kangchenjunga massif and it is not easy to unambiguously define any group of just five. The name remains an enigma.

Exploration

In 1848/49 the British botanist Joseph Hooker made two long – and, for the time, remarkable – journeys in Sikkim, travelling to within a few kilometres of Kangchenjunga and sketching it. On his return south from the second trip, accompanied by a Dr. Campbell, an official from Darjeeling, the two men were arrested by the Sikkimese. As Sikkim had become a British protectorate in the wake of Sir David Ochterlony's defeat of a Gurkha army in the Kathmandu valley in March 1816 (which ended the Nepalese war) the British were outraged, the event precipitating the annexing of the southern part of Sikkim by the East India Company. With order, of a sort, restored, travel to the eastern and southern sides of Kangchenjunga became straightforward again. Between 1852 and the end of the century there were at least ten explorations of northern Sikkim,

George Band on the day of the first ascent, crossing slabby rocks about 120m (390ft) below the summit

The north-west flank of Kangchenjunga is seen over the upper reaches of the Kangchenjunga glacier from high above Pangpema. North Col far left, Yalung Lang (Kangchenjunga West) and Kambachen on the right

George Band about 60m (200ft) below the summit on the west ridge during the first ascent. In the background is Yalung Kang, Kangchenjunga's west peak

the area being thoroughly mapped. In 1883 the first true climbing expedition was active in the area, William Graham and his Swiss guides (Josef Imboden on the first trip, Ulrich Kaufmann and Emile Boss on the second) making several first ascents, including the disputed climb of Kabru. Then, in 1899 Douglas Freshfield and a small team including the Italian mountain photographer Vittorio Sella made a complete circuit of the Kangchenjunga massif, involving a few days trek through 'closed' eastern Nepal. Freshfield's book (accurately, if unromantically, called Round Kangchenjunga) illustrated with Sella's photographs not only inspired others, but gave a detailed break-down of the possible routes to the main summit.

Perhaps inspired by Freshfield's book, though he would almost certainly never have admitted such a thing, Aleister Crowley arrived in Sikkim in August 1905 determined to climb the mountain. With the diabolist were Dr. Jacot-Guillarmod who, like Crowley, had been on Eckenstein's 1902 K2 trip, two other Swiss climbers, Alexis Pache and Charles Reymond, an Italian hotelier from Darjeeling called de Righi the team had somehow managed to collect along the way, and a number of porters. The party approached the south-western side of the mountain along the Yalung Glacier, eventually establishing a high camp at about 6,250m (20,500ft). From it Pache explored up to about 6,400m (21,000ft) perhaps a little higher. Faced with the inevitability of defeat – the party was neither experienced enough nor large enough for a serious try – there

was now an argument about what to do next. Crowley had insisted on early morning climbs to reduce the likelihood of avalanches, a sensible precaution, but one to which Guillarmod in particular took exception. Guillarmod now decided to descend from the top camp in the afternoon. Crowley was opposed, claiming later that he should have broken the doctor's leg with his ice axe so as to save his life, but Guillarmod, Pache, de Righi and three porters attached themselves to a single rope and started out. Guillarmod led with de Righi behind him, then the porters, the experienced Pache bringing up the rear. The ill-equipped porters (Crowley did not supply them with boots, apparently claiming to have invoked dark forces to protect them while they walking barefoot in snow) slipped continuously, Pache holding them, but eventually, on a traverse, he was unable to stop another slide. All six men fell, their frantic attempts to stop precipitating an avalanche which buried all but Guillarmod and de Righi. Their shouts for help brought Reymond to the scene, but Crowley declined to help. He was drinking tea and writing a newspaper article and, in any event, was, as he said in the article – which appeared on 11 September 1905 – 'not over-anxious in the circumstances ... to render help. A mountain accident of this sort is one of the things for which I have no sympathy whatever'. Crowley descended past the accident site the next day on his way back to Darjeeling: it took two more days to free the four bodies from the snow. The three porters were buried in a crevasse, Pache beneath a rock cairn which was marked (Pache's Grave) on later maps and on the route diagram of Charles Evans' book of the first ascent.

There were further visits to the area both before and after the 1914–18 War, though none could be classed as an attempt on the peak. In 1921 Alexander Kellas photographed Kangchenjunga before his trip to Everest (during which he died), but not until 1929 was there a further attempt to climb it. That year there were two, the first a clandestine attempt by an American, Edgar Francis Farmer, a young man of limited experience and boundless enthusiasm. Having left his porters on the Yalung Glacier he was last seen climbing towards the Talung Saddle, a col on the south ridge.

Farmer disappeared in May. In August a strong German expedition under Paul Bauer arrived on the other side of the mountain, choosing to attack the eastern side from the Zemu

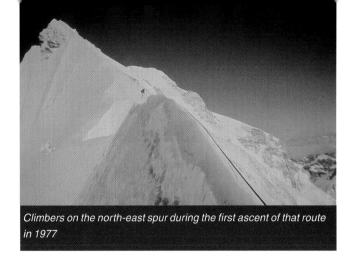
Climbers on the north-east spur during the first ascent of that route in 1977

The north-east spur. This line, which can only be approached from Sikkim, was attempted several times in the 1930s, but not climbed until 1977 when an Indian team completed the route and made the second ascent of the main summit

Glacier and to climb post-monsoon. After a failed attempt to force a route towards the Zemu Gap, the low point on the south-south-east ridge, the team turned their attention to the north-east spur. The climbing was hard and the weather poor, but the Germans doggedly pursued their line, using a series of snow caves as camps high on the spur where tents could not be pitched. By 3 October they had reached about 7,400m (24,300ft) by which time, they judged, they were above the major difficulties. But a five-day storm then kept the team camp-bound. When the weather improved the climbers retreated safely, but a lot of equipment was lost, buried in or swept away by the snow, or discarded by the climbers in an effort to speed up a descent through deep snow. The loss of equipment forced the team to abandon any further attempt.

Strangely, in view of the years Kangchenjunga had been ignored by climbers, two expeditions had sought permission for 1929, the second, under Prof Gunther Dyhrenfurth being offered 1930 as a compensation for losing out to Bauer. Dyhrenfurth, German-born but later a Swiss national, led an international team which included the German Uli Wieland and the Austrian Erwin Schneider (both later involved in the tragic Nanga Parbat expedition of 1934), and the Briton Frank Smythe. Before the trip Dyhrenfurth was contacted by Francis Farmer's mother who, in dreams, had seen her son held captive in the monastery of Detsenroba (occasionally called Dachenrol or Decherol) in the Yalung valley, a vision apparently backed by various clairvoyants. She wanted Dyhrenfurth to visit the monastery, but her hope of seeing her son again was forlorn – Detsenroba was ruinous.

Not wanting to follow in Bauer's crampon marks Dyhrenfurth asked for, and astonishingly, was granted permission for a limited excursion into Nepal. His team followed the Kangchenjunga Glacier to the peak's north-west quadrant and at first attempted a route on to the north ridge. This was abandoned at about 6,100m (20,000ft) when a section of ice cliff collapsed, sweeping away Erwin Scneider and Chettan, a porter, but miraculously leaving three other climbers and

KANGCHENJUNGA: ASCENT ROUTES

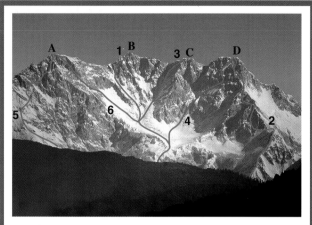

Above South-west Face
A *Yalung Kang* **B** *Main Summit*
C *Central Summit* **D** *South Summit*
1 *First ascent/'classic' route, British (1955)*
2 *South Ridge to S Summit, Prezelj/*
Stremfelj (1991) **3** *Polish to Central*

Summit (1978) **4** *Polish to South Summit*
(1978) **5** *Japanese to Yalung Kang (1973)*
6 *Austro-Germans to Yalung Kang (1975)*
The full traverse of the skyline ridge
(including all four summits) was
accomplished by a Russian team (1989)

Above North-west Face
A *Main Summit* **B** *Yalung Kang*
1 *NE Spur, Indians (1977)* **2** *Messner/*
Mutschlechner/Ang Dorje (1982)

3 *Japanese (1980)* **4** *British (1979)*
5 *Germans (1983) not to summit*
Variations of these routes have also been
climbed

eleven more porters unscathed. Schneider escaped injury, but Chettan was killed. The team then attempted the north-west spur, aiming to join it beyond Kangbachen, the peak to the west of Yalung Kang. Hard climbing and poor snow and ice conditions limited progress and this attempt, too, was abandoned. The team then concentrated on lower peaks, making ascents of several, including Jonsong.

Post-monsoon in 1931 Paul Bauer returned, this time with a team of eleven – he had nine in 1929 – determined to complete the ascent of the north-east spur. The attempt was overwhelmed by problems – a Sherpa and a porter died of sickness, another Sherpa and one of the German climbers died in a fall, several climbers, including Bauer, went down with illnesses which forced their withdrawal, and the weather was bad. Despite this the team climbed a little higher than their 1929 high point before retreating.

Bauer came back to the area in 1936, but Kangchenjunga was not the intention of his team, which made an attempt on the Twins peak, set where the north ridge divides. It is possible that Bauer was interested in assessing the north ridge as an ascent route, but heavy monsoon snow defeated the team while they were still relatively low. The following year another German team also failed on Twins, while a small British team, including John Hunt, later the leader of the successful British Everest expedition, and his wife, failed to reach the col (the North Col) on the north ridge (between the main summit and the Twins peak) from the Twins Glacier, retreating in the face of rockfalls and difficulties which were too great for the size of the party. Then in 1939 a New Zealand team was given permission for an attempt in 1940: war broke out and the attempt was cancelled.

After the war, the independence granted to India and the decline of British influence caused Sikkim to close its borders, hopeful that a secretive neutrality would allow it to escape the attention of its huge southern and northern neighbours. The attempt was successful for a quarter-century, but in 1975 India, increasingly concerned about Chinese intentions and the relative ease of crossing the Sikkim Himalaya annexed the country.

The loss of a route through Sikkim, together with Nepal's opening of its borders necessitated an enthusiasm for exploring Kangchenjunga's western and southern flanks. In 1953 the Britons John Kempe and Gilmour Lewis explored the Upper Yalung glacier and had a good view of the south-west face. What they saw persuaded the British to send a larger reconnaissance team in 1954 comprising Kempe, Lewis and four others. The team reported that the upper face was clearly climbable and that for the approach to it there were two possibilities, one along the 1905 team's route (past Pache's

Grave), the other by way of a rib now called Kempe's Buttress. A third option via Talung Cwm was dismissed. The success of the 1954 reconnaissance persuaded the British to send a full strength team in 1955: although officially termed a reconnaissance, it was clear from the outset that the organisers hoped for greater things.

First Ascent

The 1955 British expedition was led by Charles Evans, a surgeon, who had been Hunt's deputy on the successful 1953 Everest team (when he had reached the south summit). It comprised George Band, who had also been on Everest in 1953, Joe Brown, Dr John Clegg, the team doctor, the New Zealander Norman Hardie, John Jackson, Tom McKinnon, Neil Mather and Tony Streather. The Sherpa team was led by Dawa Tenzing who had been Evans' personal Sherpa on Everest in 1953. (As a short digression, Evans' book of the expedition – an analytical, unromantic read, what one might perhaps expect from a surgeon – notes an incident on the walk when the breakfasting team were surrounded by curious Nepalese villagers. Anxious to avoid them getting too close, the Sherpas waved the villagers back explaining 'Gently there, not too close, crowding makes them restless and difficult', a rather interesting – and refreshing – change from the standard 'sahibs having trouble with the locals' tale.)

The team followed the Yalung Glacier to the foot of the south-west face, exploring the Kempe's Buttress and Pache's Grave options and choosing the latter. They decided on a route which climbed to a dip in a prominent rock spur (the Western Buttress), then through a valley filled by the upper section of an icefall, that joined the Yalung Glacier, to reach the Great Shelf,

On the north-west face during the first ascent in 1979

a flat/low-angled snow basin beneath the horseshoe-shaped rock wall that forms the summit structure of Yalung Kang and the main summit. From this basin a broad snow slope, The Gangway, leads up to the west ridge. However, the ridge itself was pinnacled and potentially difficult, and it was hoped a route existed on the upper south-west face, bypassing these difficulties.

The route was pushed out in reasonable weather and though heavily crevassed it was relatively safe from the continuous stream of avalanches which fell from high on the face. From Camp III in the upper icefall the route to, and up to the back wall of, the Great Shelf to where Camp V was established, was made by climbers using closed circuit oxygen equipment. This was just a test, however, the rest of the climbers, including the summiteers, using open circuit sets.

From Camp V Evans and Mather led up, Evans clearly anxious about whether The Gangway would be avalanche prone or its snow too rotten to climb: it was perfect and a Camp (Camp VI) was established half-way up at about 8,200m (26,900ft). Here Band and Brown, who had been following the lead pair and two Sherpas, stayed using bottled oxygen to aid their sleep. Back at Camp V Evans received a weather forecast stating that the monsoon would arrive in five days. In the

Doug Scott photographs Peter Boardman climbing the last few steps to Joe Tasker and the summit during the first ascent of the north-west face

expedition book Evans refers to Band and Brown as the first summit-ridge pair, perhaps concerned that the difficulties of the headwall would be so severe they would not have the time to complete the climb. With the monsoon approaching fast he must have had his fingers firmly crossed.

Band and Brown left camp at 8.15am and continued up The Gangway. From lower on the mountain the team had spotted a ledged ramp leading across the headwall to the west ridge, reaching it above the pinnacles. The first attempt to reach this was too low, losing 1½ hours as the pair were forced to backtrack. They chose correctly the second time, following the ramp, which was straightforward, but exposed, to the ridge where they rested and enjoyed a magnificent view. The ridge was also straightforward until a rock tower barred the way. Brown, an expert rock climber who had revolutionised British rock climbing and advanced the top level of difficulty, climbed this on his trademark handjams – the pair had removed their crampons on the ramp and so preferred the rock to a detour on steep snow – and was astonished to discover that he was virtually at the summit, the rock tower ending just a few metres below a snow hump. It was 2.45pm, just 15 minutes from the pair's self-imposed deadline for reaching the top. The summit had been reached ten days after the French ascent of Makalu. As promised, in deference to the local belief that the summit was the home of a god, the pair did not set foot on the actual summit, a shallow snow dome on which a small crowd could congregate. The lack of footprints in the summit snows led Charles Evans to call the expedition book Kangchenjunga: The

Untrodden Peak and has persuaded many to agree with George Band's view that it was better that the summit was left unsullied. Later ascents of the peak also left the summit untrodden at first, but at some stage the promise was broken and the peak is no longer untrodden.

At about 3pm Band and Brown began their descent, reaching Camp VI in darkness at 7pm. The camp was already occupied by Hardie and Streather who, on 26 May, repeated the climb, bypassing the final rock tower by following a snow ramp which lead to the south ridge which they then followed to the summit, reaching it at 12.15pm. They were back in Camp VI by 5pm. The expedition then retreated without incident though on the day of the second summit climb a Sherpa, Pemi Dorje, died at Base Camp, probably from pneumonia: he had become exhausted on an earlier carry up the mountain and had never recovered.

Later Ascents

In 1973 a Japanese expedition climbed Yalung Kang, following the British 1953 route at first, then branching off to follow the south-west ridge. Yutaka Ageta and Takeo Matsuda reached the summit, but were forced to bivouac on the way down. The next day Matsuda fell, probably struck by a falling rock, Ageta being rescued by his team mates. Yalung Kang was climbed again in 1975 by an Austro-German team, following the British route to the Great Shelf then a couloir up the peak's south face. The main summit was not reached again until 1977. That year an Indian Army expedition approached the mountain through Sikkim and followed Paul Bauer's 1930s line along the north-east spur to its junction with the north ridge, and then climbed the north ridge to the top. At 3pm on 31 May Major Prem Chand and the Sherpa Nima Dorje stood on the summit.

The following year the south summit (Kangchenjunga II) was reached by a Polish team which, initially, followed the British route to the Great Shelf. The

Looking down on the North Col during the first ascent of the north-west face route

Poles also climbed the highest and second highest tops of the triple-peaked central summit, a Spanish Yalung Kang expedition which joined forces with them climbing the third top. In the aftermath of these climbs the Polish and Spanish expedition leaders were banned from

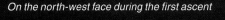
On the north-west face during the first ascent

Battling through jet-stream winds on the upper slopes during the first ascent

Nepal for four years, as each had climbed peaks for which they did not have permission. The Poles were unfortunate – they had always wanted to climb the south summit, but as the Nepalese official who dealt with their application only had the main summit on his list that was written into their permission. The Poles accepted this, not realising the potential implications. The Spaniards had no such excuse – they just did not fancy their peak, and compounded their 'crime' by bypassing Kathmandu on their return so as not to have to face the wrath of officialdom.

In 1979 the main summit was climbed again in fine style. Though Messner and Habeler had climbed Gasherbrum I in alpine style in 1975, then Everest without bottled oxygen in 1978, and Messner had soloed Nanga Parbat, also in 1978, no lightweight, bottled gas-free ascent had yet been made on any of the 'big three peaks'. In early April 1979, after several years persuading the Nepalese to allow an attempt from the west, the Britons Peter Boardman, Doug Scott and Joe Tasker, with Frenchman Georges Bettembourg (who had been on the disputed alpine-style Broad Peak climb in 1978) established a base camp below Kangchenjunga's north-west face, the face

which had defeated Dyhrenfurth's team in 1930. From it a difficult route up the face to the North Col was climbed, three camps being used. A fourth camp was established in a snow cave on the north ridge at 7,440m (24,400ft). A first attempt by Bettembourg, Boardman and Scott (a sick Tasker having retreated) failed in winds estimated at over 140km/h (90mph). A second attempt by Boardman, Scott and the recovered Tasker (Bettembourg not trusting the weather) left the Camp IV snow cave on 15 May, bivouacing that night on the ridge. On 16 May they crossed the north-west face to reach the west ridge close to the line of the first ascent, following that route (the Hardie/Streather variant) to the top, which was reached at 5pm. The trio returned to their bivouac and were safely off the mountain by 19 May. Though not a true alpine style ascent this third ascent of Kangchenjunga was a superb climb.

In 1980 a larger Japanese team, climbing in similar style to the British forced a route up the centre of the north-west face. From a high camp two lightweight summit attempts were made, the first putting four Japanese and a Sherpa on the summit, the second, three days later, also being successful, with two further Japanese and two more Sherpas reaching the top. The Japanese summit climbs were on 14 and 17 May: on 15 May a German climber and two Sherpas from an expedition led by Dr KM Herrligkoffer reached the top along the first ascent route. The following year another Japanese team climbed the main peak, putting five climbers and a Sherpa on the summit, and, in a co-ordinated climb, also placed five climbers on the top of Yalung Kung. The intended traverse between the two was not attempted as it was thought to be more difficult than had been supposed. Later in the year the French pair Jean-Jacques Ricouard and Michel Parmentier repeated the original route in the first post-monsoon ascent. Sadly Ricouard was killed on the descent.

In 1982 Reinhold Messner, Friedl Mutschlechner and the Sherpa Ang Dorje climbed another new route on the north-west face, climbing up to reach the north ridge close to the north col and following the ridge to the top. This was Messner's seventh 8,000er, but not without incident. Messner believes he picked up an amoebic infection on the march in to the peak and was ill during the early part of the climb. He recovered sufficiently to make the summit climb, but during a nightmare descent in a blizzard driven by winds which eventually shredded their tents and intense cold he began to shake and hallucinate. With Mutschlechner frostbitten and Messner seriously ill, the pair escaped only by an effort of will. Messner

was later diagnosed as suffering from an amoebic abscess on his liver.

Pre-monsoon in 1983 the Austrian Georg Bachler soloed the original route from the top camp of the Austrian expedition, but in the post-monsoon period Pierre Beghin completed the first authentic solo by way of the same route. Beghin camped at 6,250m (20,500ft) and 7,700m (25,250ft), reaching the summit on 17 October and descending to 7,200m (23,600ft) on the same day. A Swiss expedition which climbed the north face shortly after found Beghin's altimeter and a note tied to an old oxygen bottle (Beghin climbed without bottled gas) at the summit. In October 1984 Roger Marshall, the British-Canadian

The north-west flank of Kangchenjunga from a camp site at Pangpema

Kangchenjunga from Khesewa Bhanjyang in eastern Nepal

vast team (62 men in total) and ten years after their first ascent of the north-east spur they repeated the climb. This time, however, the summiteers – three rather than two as in 1977 – died on the descent, a prayer flag they had left on the summit being found by the second summit team. On that second attempt, on 31 May, the exact tenth anniversary of their first climb, three more team members reached the top: one of these also died descending. The Indian army had the monopoly of attempts from Sikkim, a fact proved by a non-army Indian team being forced to climb from Nepal in 1988. Their attempt on the north-west face failed, but the Austrian Peter Habeler, once Messner's climbing partner, was successful on a variant of the British north ridge route, climbing alpine style with American Carlos Buhler and Martin Zabeleta of Spain. The following year a huge Soviet team (32 climbers plus 17 Sherpas) succeeded in traversing the four summits (Yalung Kang, main, central and south). In fact separate teams

climber repeated Beghin's solo. The same year, and as a complete contrast to these solo climbs, a vast Japanese expedition (22 climbers plus 31 Sherpas) attempted to climb and traverse the massif's four summits. The south, central and main summits were reached, the main summit by two parties, but Yalung Kang was not climbed.

In spring 1985 a Yugoslavian team made the first ascent of the north face of Yalung Kung (the summit team was Borut Bergant and Tomo Cesen, who was later to solo Jannu and then to claim an ascent of Lhotse's south face), then, in 1986 the main peak was climbed in winter for the first time via the original route by a Polish team, Jerzy Kukuczka and Krzysztof Wielicki reaching the summit on 11 January. It was Kukuczka's tenth 8,000er and his third in winter. Wielicki was also now well on his way to climbing all 14 peaks. Sadly this excellent achievement was marred by the death of Andrzej Czok from oedema. His death echoed that of the American Chris Chandler who had died in January 1985 during a winter attempt on Yalung Kang's north face with his wife Cherie Bremer-Kemp.

The Indian Army returned to the mountain in 1987 with a

The eastern side of Kangchenjunga from the Goecha La in Sikkim

did the traverse in both directions and established new, and very hard, routes to the main and south tops. Given four peaks and 49 climbers a total of almost 200 men-summits was possible and almost half this number was actually achieved, a remarkable record.

By 1991 the peak had still not had an ascent by a woman, and the long south ridge – the border between Nepal and Sikkim – had not been climbed: it was one of the 'last great problems' of the 8,000ers. In that year there were tragedy and success on these outstanding issues. A combined Slovenian/Polish team repeated the original route, two climbers reaching the top with bottled oxygen, but on a subsequent attempt Joze Rozman and Marija Frantar, with just one oxygen bottle between them, reached a point just 150m (less than 500ft) from the top. It was then 4pm and in a radio call to base they said they were cold but that though Ms Frantar was partially snow-blind, she wished to continue despite Rozman's reluctance. Ignoring advice to

The south-west flank of Kangchenjunga is seen up the deep valley of the Yalung Glacier. The main summit is flanked by Yalung Kang and Kangchenjunga South

descend the pair continued up, but at 7pm, night having fallen, reported that they were hopelessly lost. Their bodies were later found near the base of the headwall. In contrast a Slovenian pair, from the same expedition, Marko Prezelj and Andrej Stremfelj succeeded in climbing the south ridge. The pair climbed grade VI, A2 rock and 65°–90° ice to a bivouac at 6,200m (20,350ft) then easier ground to a second bivouac at 7,250m (23,800ft). They were then forced on to the south-west face, but resisted the temptation to traverse to the Great Shelf, climbing up to a third bivouac at 7,600m (24,900ft). The next day they climbed only 300m (1,000ft), bivouacing again at 7,900m (25,900ft) before climbing up through deep snow to join the Soviet route at about 8,100m (26,600ft). They then used the Soviet fixed ropes to move quicker, gaining the south summit. The pair then descended the Polish route to the Great Shelf where the rest of the Slovenian team was attempting the original route. Many observers believe this to be the finest ever alpine-style ascent of the an 8,000er and have even compared it with the Kurtyka/Shauer route on Gasherbrum IV's west face which, though climbed in 1985, is still thought by many to be the finest high-altitude alpine-style ascent to date. The rest of the pair's Polish-Slovenian team succeeded in climbing both the main and central summits.

In 1992 Wanda Rutkiewicz, arguably the leading female high altitude climber of the era with eight 8,000ers to her credit, attempted Kangchenjunga again, having failed to make the summit in 1991. On 12 May her companion Carlos Carsolio, who was climbing faster, summitted and met her still climbing up at 8,250m (27,100ft). He tried to persuade her to go down but she said she would bivouac and continue to the summit the next day. A storm broke during the night and she was never seen again.

There was further tragedy on Kangchenjunga in 1995, a tragedy probably precipitated by the race to be the third person to claim ascents of the 14 8,000ers. The post-monsoon season saw the Swiss Erhard Loretan, who had climbed the other 13 peaks, and Frenchman Benôit Chamoux, who had climbed 12 as well as Shisha Pangma's central summit (Chamoux was claiming this as his thirteenth 8,000er: his ascent of Cho Oyu was also disputed as he and his companions had only reached the edge of the summit plateau) at the base of the mountain. Loretan and his usual partner Jean Troillet, the Italian Sergio Martini (who had climbed ten 8,000ers), Chamoux, Pierre Royer (who was filming Chamoux's fourteenth climb) and three Sherpas (carrying Royer's filming gear as well as other equipment) left together along the normal route, but the Swiss and Martini rapidly drew away from the French and their Sherpas. During a rest period one of the Sherpas

Sunrise over Kangchenjunga from south-south-east on Tiger Hill, Darjeeling

overbalanced and fell to his death. The other two Sherpas descended to him but Chamoux and Royer declined to help. Instead they continued slowly, with Royer now carrying his own film equipment, making frequent radio calls to a French media circus gathered at the mountain's base.

The Swiss ignored the British route above the Great Shelf, continuing up the Gangway to the col between Yalung Kang and the main summit. Sergio Martini, convinced the ridge from the col was too difficult waited for them to return. When they did not he descended. Loretan and Troillet reached the summit at 2.35pm on 5 October and met Chamoux and Royer at 4pm on their descent. At 4.30pm Royer radioed base that he was too tired to continue and was descending, but that Chamoux would continue alone. Chamoux reached the col and bivouaced, radioing at 8am on 6 October that he was continuing up. He was

not heard from again and neither he nor Royer were seen again. In an unpleasant aftermath the Sherpas refused to search for either climber as they had refused to help their fallen comrade and some saw Chamoux's death as his own fault brought on by poor acclimatisation before the climb in his haste to beat Loretan. The events soured what should have been a good reception to Loretan's achievement: at 36 he was the youngest of the three to have completed the 14 8,000ers.

Not until 1998 was Kangchenjunga climbed by a woman (assuming, of course, that Wanda Rutkiewicz failed to make the summit, which seems highly probable). That year Briton Ginette Harrison, a member of a team led by her American husband Gary Pfisterer, climbed a variant of the British route on the north-west face (which had been pioneered by a German team in 1989). Harrison did not use bottled oxygen. In addition to being the first female ascent, Harrison completed the set for female climbers, Kangchenjunga having been the only 8,000er not to have had a female ascent. While the Anglo-American team was on the mountain a Japanese team was also on the same face. Five climbers reached the top, but two died during the descent and the other three were badly frostbitten. Also in 1998 the Italian Fausto de Stefani climbed Kangchenjunga by the normal route and claimed to be the sixth climber to have completed the 14 peak grand slam. However, de Stefani's claimed ascent of Lhotse remains controversial. He admitted not reaching the summit because of high winds which threatened to blow him and his partner (Sergio Martini) off the rotten snow of the final cornice. But a South Korean who climbed Lhotse shortly after claimed the Italian tracks stopped at least 150m from the top.

Of the 14 8,000ers, only Annapurna and Lhotse have had fewer ascents than Kangchenjunga, a tribute to its formidable size and difficulty. It is also a dangerous mountain, one in twenty of those reaching the summit dying during the descent and the peak claiming a victim for every four climbers who reach the top. But as with K2, despite these grim statistics the lure of the world's third highest mountain and its vast faces will continue to attract the world's leading climbers. If travel to Sikkim becomes acceptable in the next millennium it is likely that teams will soon be heading for the east and south-east faces.

South-east face of Kangchenjunga (South) is seen over the upper reaches of the Talung Glacier in Sikkim. The South Ridge, left, was climbed by the Slovenians in 1991

manaslu 8,163m

'Was I lost ? ...
Visibility had by
now dropped to
about ten metres:
there was no
longer any hope
of getting bearings
from distinctive
rock or ice features.
Panic seized me.
I believed I was
simply following a
straight line, but
what if I was going
round in circles?'

REINHOLD MESSNER

Manaslu – the accent is on the second syllable: Man-as-loo rather than mana-sloo – was Peak XXX of the Indian Survey and was at first called Kutang I, a name derived from it being the highest peak in the local district of Kutang.

However, as tang is Tibetan for a flat area the name could be from the virtually flat summit plateau, a distinctive feature of the peak when received from the Larkya La, a high pass to the north which would have been crossed by Tibetan traders to reach the valley of the Dudh Khola. The present name is Sanskrit in origin, deriving from manasa meaning the spirit or soul: Manaslu is the mountain of the spirit. The villagers of Sama, a Nepalese village at the north-eastern foot of the peak, refer to it as Kambung, the name of a local god who is believed to reside on the summit, a belief which had serious consequences for an early Japan reconnaissance of the mountain.

Exploration

In 1950, while the French were on Annapurna, a small team under the British explorer/climber Bill Tilman set up camp at Thonje, a village set where the Dudh Khola meets the Marshandi river. From there the team explored the upper Dudh Khola, photographing the western and northern sides

Manaslu's true summit and the sharp East Pinnacle (7,895/25,902ft) are seen from the north east

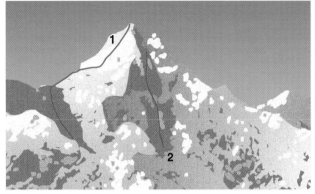

Above South Face
1 *Austrians (1972)*

Below From North-east
A *East Ridge*

B *East Summit (Pinnacle)*
C *Main Summit*
1 *Hajer/Kukuczka (1986)*
2 *First ascent/standard route, Japanese (1956)*

Above From South-east
1 *Polish (1984)*
2 *Kazakh attempt (1990)*

Below From North
1 *Japanese (1971)*
2 *French (1981)*

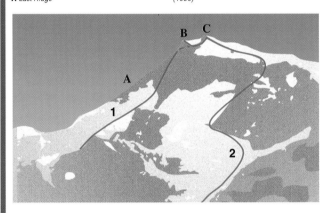

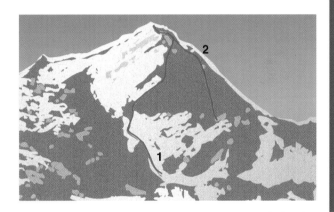

of Manaslu. Tilman knew that his team was not strong enough for a serious attempt on the peak and felt that both the sides he explored offered little chance of success, so turned his attention westward, making an attempt to climb Annapurna IV. When this attempt failed, less than 200m (about 650ft) from the top, the team spent time exploring southern approaches to Manaslu and Himalchuli, the peak to the south-east.

Two years later a small Japanese team arrived intent on exploring all sides of the peak prior to a full-scale attempt in 1953. The team explored the eastern and western sides of the peak, crossing the Larkya La. From Sama they pushed up the east ridge to a height of about 5,250m (17,200ft). From the ridge and later from the Larkya La they identified a feasible route, following the Manaslu Glacier to the peak's North Col then climbing on to the summit plateau. From the Dudh Khola valley they agreed with Tilman's assessment that the western side of the peak was a formidable challenge.

In 1953 the Japanese returned, this time with a full team (13 climbers plus two scientists) and the intention of climbing of the peak. From Sama they ascended to the edge of the Manaslu Glacier, then placed a series of closely spaced camps on a route over the Naike and North Cols (the Naike Col lies north-east of the North Col and stands between the Manaslu and Larkya Glaciers). From the North Col camp (Camp VIII) – which was connected by a telephone cable strung out across the mountain all the way down to Base Camp – an attempt was made on the summit, but was driven back by bad weather. The weather prevented any further attempt for two weeks, but then a new camp (Camp IX) was established at 7,500m (24,600ft) and a further attempt launched. This failed at about 7,750m (25,400ft) when the climbers realised just how far they were from the summit. Today's climber would have continued, but in 1953, early days on the great peaks, especially for individuals without bottled oxygen or the benefits of modern equipment, the idea of an evening arrival at the summit and a night descent or bivouac was beyond the comprehension of most climbers, even though Hermann Buhl had completed just such a climb solo the year before on Nanga Parbat.

In the spring of 1954 the Japanese were back, but on this occasion they faced a threat more difficult to overcome than bad weather and technically difficult climbing. At Sama they were met by an angry mob who claimed that the '53 climb had upset the god who lived on the mountain, his anger being shown in a year of appalling weather and an avalanche of

Gyaltsen on the summit, 9 May 1956

unheard of size and direction which had destroyed the local gompa (monastery), one that had stood for 300 years, killing three monks. There had also been epidemics of smallpox and other diseases. The villagers were unwilling to endure more suffering just so the foreigners could amuse themselves on the mountain and were willing, if necessary, to use physical violence if angry shouting was not sufficient to halt the Japanese progress. To prove the point they

Imanishi and Gyaltsen returning from the summit; Muraki and Pemba Sundar go up to meet them

armed themselves with clubs, stones and knives. The Japanese wisely withdrew (one legend has it that several climbers withdrew trouserless, the villagers adding a touch of humiliation to emphasise their point), contenting themselves with an abortive attempt on Ganesh Himal and an exploration of the eastern approaches to Himalchuli.

On their return to Kathmandu the Japanese sought an assurance from the Nepalese government that if they returned to Manaslu at some later date they would not face further intimidation. When they received it they applied for permission for 1955. Unfortunately the Nepalese agreement was sent by sea rather than air mail and did not arrive in Japan until late February 1955, too late to organise a spring expedition. The Japanese therefore sent a delegation to Kathmandu to re-negotiate permissions for the post-monsoon 1955 and spring 1956. They received further assurances on the Sama situation, but to test the validity of these a three-man team visited the area in autumn 1955. There was no problem at Sama, the three climbing to the site of the 1953 base camp and from there exploring alternative approaches to the summit plateau. Despite the team being so small they climbed to the edge of the plateau, at about 7,500m (24,600ft).

First Ascent

On 11 March 1956 another Japanese expedition left Kathmandu for Manaslu. It was led by Yuko Maki, a 62 year-old former president of the Japanese Alpine Club and well-known to European climbers for his first ascent of the Eiger's Mittellegi ridge, with Fritz Amatter, Samuel Brawand and Fritz Steuri, in 1921. His team comprised Sonosuke Chitani, Minoru Higeta, Toshio Imanishi, Kiichiro Kato, Yuichi Matsuda, Junjiro Muraki, Katsuro Ohara, Hiroyoshi Otsuka, Dr. Hirokichi Tatsunuma, Dr. Atsushi Tokunaga (the official expedition doctor though Tatsunuma was also a medical doctor) and Takayoshi Yoda, the expedition photographer. The team was supported by 20 Sherpas under sirdar Gyalzen Norbu. Several members of the team had been on the expeditions of 1953 and 1954. The Japanese used tents with bamboo frames, a more reasonable alternative to metal than at first appears, bamboo being lighter than steel (though more

The summit of Manaslu as seen from Camp II

Bedouin keffiychs or Samurai helmets. With the long sides folded across their shoulders towards their chests the expedition pictures make the climbers look as though they are auditioning for parts as radiation workers in a sci-fi B movie.

Despite assurances, there was some hostility at Sama, but a Nepalese government official rapidly calmed things and the Japanese were allowed to continue. The route followed in 1953 was taken again, but this time fewer camps were used and the summit plateau was approached by a route that stayed south of the North Col, shortening the overall distance. Having established and stocked a camp (Camp IV) to the east of the col by late April, the team used it as an advanced base. The summit plateau was then approached via a broad snow field the Japanese called the Snow Apron. Camp V was placed at the foot of the Apron, Camp VI (at 7,800m/26,000ft) on the plateau edge almost due west of the Pinnacle, the prominent tower of dark rock which lies north-east of the true summit. Imanishi's account of the climb notes that at this stage conversations over the radio with lower camps became heated and 'strong words were exchanged'. He does not elaborate, but the marked difference between this comment and the overly polite tone of the rest of the account suggests a real confrontation. Presumably the lead climbers were concerned over the lack of

brittle than the aluminium-based alloys and carbon fibre of modern tents). They took open-circuit oxygen sets, but for sleeping used 'oxygen candles'. These used potassium chlorate which, with manganese oxide and iron oxide catalysts, undergo an exothermic reaction, the by-product of which is gaseous oxygen. The candles weighed 3.5kg (almost 8lb) but in exchange for this heavy carrying load released 4–5l (about 1 gallon) of oxygen per minute for up to 1½ hours while at the same time producing enough heat to boil water for several mugs. The problem with the candles seems obvious, the oxygen produced dispersing throughout the tent and leaking outside, though at Camp V before their summit climb Imanishi and Gyalzen were fed oxygen by tubes from the next door tent where Dr Tatsunuma spent the night collecting the liberated oxygen and changing candles. However, in the last camp (Camp VI) both summit parties used bottled gas for sleeping before their climbs. As protection against the sun the Japanese wore loose fitting, shoulder-length head covers, looking like

The North Peak of Manaslu viewed from Camp V

progress on the route when the weather became fine, not wishing to squander what might be a narrow weather window.

Camp VI was established on 8 May and the next day Imanishi and Gyalzen Norbu set off for the summit at 8am on a beautiful and virtually windless, though cold, day. The climb up the relatively gently plateau was straightforward, the pair making for the highest snow point which they reached after less than 4 hours climbing. However, on reaching it they discovered that the true summit was a shattered rock tower a short distance away. This they soon climbed reaching the true summit at 12.30pm. The tower's top could accommodate three or four men, but was narrow, leaving little room for photography, Imanishi's dramatic summit

Manaslu with its south-west face is seen from due west near Chame in the Marsyandi gorges

Camp V below the Snow Apron and the East Pinnacle during the first successful expedition

shot of Gyalzen being taken from the nearby snow top. Having already climbed Makalu with the French in 1955 Gyalzen Norbu became the first man to climb two 8,000ers. The pair stayed at the summit for 1½ hours, then climbed down, passing Camp VI to spend the night at Camp V.

The next day Higeta and Kato climbed to Camp VI and on 11 May – another beautiful and windless day – repeated the climb. Utilising the steps cut by the first pair on their descent the two reached the summit in only 3 hours. They filmed the summit with a 16mm movie camera, but unfortunately then dropped it, complete with film, down the south face. Within six days of the second summit climb the expedition had cleared the peak.

Later Ascents

In 1964 a small Dutch expedition climbed Manaslu North Peak (7,157m/23,480ft), the peak between the North and Naike Cols, but the main summit was not attempted again until 1971 when two teams arrived. A Japanese team was to attempt a route from the north-west side – the side deemed unlikely to offer a reasonable route by Tilman and the early Japanese reconnaissances – while a Korean team attempted to repeat the original route. The Koreans were unsuccessful, calling off their attempt when Kim Ki Sup, brother of team leader Kim Ho Sup, was killed by a fall into a crevasse at 7,600m (24,950ft), but the Japanese succeeded in climbing a very difficult route up the north-west face. The team, led by Akira Takahashi, forced a route up the face to the west-north-west ridge in appalling weather (1971 was the worst weather in recorded Nepalese history) where they were confronted with a 250m (800ft) rock step which they called Kasa-Iwa, Umbrella Rock. This part-overhanging cliff at over 7,000m (23,000ft) took four weeks to climb, involving very hard free climbing and some artificial pitches. To service the camp (Camp IV) above it the Japanese set up an aerial ropeway as the cliff was too difficult for laden climbers. The Japanese then discovered that the ridge had a continuous series of difficult, overhanging rock steps. It was now early May and anxious to avoid too much loss of time the team descended from the ridge and forced a route up a difficult ice face to the south, route involving more artificial climbing. Eventually Camp V was set up at the edge of the summit plateau. From it, on 5 May, Kazuharu Kohara and Motoyoshi Tanaka set off at 5am. The summit was 2.5km (1½ miles) away and almost 800m (2,600ft) above, and the plateau was covered in 1m (3ft) of soft snow. Despite this they reached the top at 12.15pm, a phenomenal achievement. From just below the final rock tower the pair retrieved a piton hammered in by Toshio Imanishi, presenting it to Yuko Maki when they returned to Tokyo. The north-west face route was a major advance in difficulty on an 8,000er peak and was accomplished just a year after the British Annapurna south face climb and has never received the international acclaim it deserves, in part, perhaps, because the absence of an English-language book on the route meant it failed to reach the wider audience the British route commanded.

In 1972 the Koreans returned to Manaslu, again attempting to repeat the original route. Kim Ho Sup was once more leader. The team established Camp IA at about 6,500m (21,300ft) and on the night of 10-11 April it was occupied by 5 Koreans, a Japanese climber and 12 Sherpas. Sometime during the night the camp was overwhelmed by an avalanche, 4 Koreans, the Japanese and 10 Sherpas being killed. The remaining Korean, Kim Ye Sup, another brother of the leader, and two Sherpas were left on the surface by the avalanche, having been swept over 750m (2,500ft) down the mountain. As these survivors were trying to organise themselves another avalanche swept them down a further 300m (1,000ft). Again, miraculously, though badly injured, the three survived. The 15 deaths represent one of the worst-ever accidents in the Himalaya.

The storm which precipitated the avalanche on the northern side of the peak also pinned down members of a Tyrolean expedition on the south side. The Tyroleans, led by Wolfgang Nairz were climbing Manaslu's south face, a huge face split by a valley – called Butterfly Valley by the climbers – at about half height. The climbing on the lower face, a 600m

A close-up picture of Manaslu's formidable south-west face, first climbed by a Tyrolean team in 1972

(2,000ft) rock buttress, was as hard as any on the great peaks at that time, requiring fixed ropes and ladders for load carrying. Above the buttress the upper face was avoided by a rising traverse leftwards to the edge of the summit plateau. There a camp (Camp IV) was placed and from it on 25 April, Franz Jäger and Reinhold Messner set off for the summit. The pair had about 2.5km (1½ miles) to cover and 750m (2,500ft) to climb to reach the summit, but conditions were excellent. However, after some hours Jäger decided to return to camp, concerned that to continue would entail a bivouac. Messner continued alone and climbing without bottled oxygen reached the summit at 2pm: Manaslu was his second 8,000er.

During Messner's descent a storm blew up and he was soon engaged in a life-or-death struggle against wind and cold. With visibility down to 10m (30ft or so) he despaired of finding the tent, but could hear occasional shouts from Jäger who, he assumed, was trying to guide him to it. When, hypothermic and exhausted, he finally found the tent he discovered that Jäger was not there, though two other team-mates, Horst Fankhauser and Andi Schlick, were. Fankhauser and Schlick went out to look for Jäger whose shouts could still be heard. They became disorientated and, unable to regain the tent, were forced to dig a snow cave. During the night Schlick left the cave, whether to look for the tent or Jäger will never be known: Fankhauser did not see him again. The morning dawned bright, but the plateau was covered in 2m (6ft) of fresh snow and despite several hours search by Fankhauser and Messner no trace of Jäger or Schlick was found.

The original route was repeated in 1973 by a small German expedition, a Japanese team reconnoitring the east ridge at the same time. The following year a Japanese Ladies expedition also repeated the original route. On 3 May Mieko

Mori, Naoko Nakaseko and Masako Uchida, together with the Sherpa Jangbu, reached the summit, the first female ascent and the first ascent of an 8,000er by an exclusively female team. Sadly Teiko Suzuki died during a second, failed summit attempt. In 1975 a Spanish team repeated the original route, finding the body of either Jäger or Schlick on the summit plateau. The next year the Koreans tried again, the team led by Kim Jung Sup, another brother of Kim Ho Sup. Two climbers, one of them the leader, were seriously injured by falling ice and had to be air-lifted to Kathmandu, and a summit bid failed at about 7,850m (25,750ft). The Koreans, and the Kim family in particular, could be forgiven for feeling that Manaslu was engaged in a dreadful vendetta against them. Finally, in 1980 a Korean team successfully repeated the original route.

In spring 1981 a commercial expedition led by the German Hans von Kaenel placed 15 men on the summit, an Austrian pair, Josef Hillinger and Peter Wörgötter, skiing down from a point about 30m (100ft) below the summit to Camp I over a two day period. Later in the year a four-person French expedition climbed a hard line up Manaslu's west face. The face is over 3,000m (almost 11,000ft) high and included one 1,000m (3,300ft) section of 70° ice and glazed rocks. The face reaches the summit plateau at the same point as the Tyrolean south face traverse. The summit climbers, Pierre Beghin and Bernard Muller bivouaced at the edge of the plateau, continuing to the summit the next day, 7 October, and returning to the bivouac. They were the first to climb the peak in the post-monsoon period. A few days after the French climb a Japanese team completed the original route, three men reaching the summit.

In the post-monsoon period of 1983 a Korean, Huh Young-Ho soloed the peak from 7,200m (23,600ft) having been accompanied by a Sherpa to that height. His presence on the summit was confirmed by a German team who were astonished to meet him there after they had climbed the south face. The Germans had earlier abandoned an attempt on the south ridge. An Austrian attempt on the east ridge also failed. During the winter of 1983/84 a Polish team succeeded in climbing the Tyrolean route on the south side of the mountain,

Manaslu's East Pinnacle catches the dawn light. View to the south west from the Burui Gandaki Valley near Sama Gompa

completing the first winter ascent of Manaslu. The summit was reached on 12 January 1984 by Maciej Berbeka and Ryszard Gajewski, climbing without bottled oxygen. In spring 1984 a small Yugoslavian team climbed the south face in semi-alpine style, while in the autumn a Polish team added another new route on the south side, climbing the south ridge/south-east face. The team first climbed to the Pungen La (between Manaslu and Peak 29) then climbed the left side of the ridge. They were forced on to the south-east face, but regained the ridge, climbing it to the top. The summit was reached in late October by Aleksander Lwow and Krzysztof Wielicki.

In December 1985 a Japanese team made the second winter ascent of the peak following the original line. On the summit they found a (so far unclaimed) cigarette case and lighter which they believed had been left by the first ascent party. The following year a four man team – the Poles Artur Hajzer, Jerzy Kukuczka and Wojciech Kurtyka and the Mexican Carlos Carsolio – tried the east ridge, but were forced to abandon it due to bad weather and dangerous conditions. It was now early November and Kurtyka left the peak, but the other three climbed a new route on the north-east face. After the three had made the first ascent of the East Summit Carsolio was forced to abandon the climb due to frostbite, but Hajzer and Kukuczka continued to the summit. Manaslu was Kukuczka's twelfth 8,000er and while he was on the mountain he heard, by radio, that Messner had climbed Makalu and then, 20 days later, Lhotse, becoming the first man to climb all 14 8,000ers. From his own account of his climbs it is clear that Kukuczka was disappointed to have lost the race, even though he had never been likely to win it given his own strict rules (new route or first winter ascent). He noted after the news about Makalu that as Messner 'goes up the 8,000ers by the normal route as a rule, and is an excellent alpinist ... he would be extremely unlucky not to achieve his aim.' Messner's success on Lhotse proved him right. After Kukuczka's completion of the grand slam Messner sent him a message saying 'You are not second. You are great.' A cynic might argue that there is no better way of reminding someone that they are second than by making a point of telling them that they are not, but Kukuczka was impressed enough to use the message as a 'foreword' in his own book.

The pace of exploration on Manaslu now began to slow, though there were still recognisable 'last great problems'. A Kazakh team abandoned an attempt on the east face in autumn 1990 when three very experienced high altitude climbers died in a fall and an attempt at a winter solo of the south face by Frenchman Eric Monier also failed when be realised that his perceived climbing companion (a 100,000

The north face of Manaslu from near the Larkya La

year old woman) was probably an hallucination and that retreat might therefore be advisable. Clearly a companion of any age or sex would have invalidated a solo climb.

Following the failure of the Kazakh team in 1990 the east face was also the objective of a Ukrainian team in 1991. They, too, failed, but three members succeeded in climbing the south face alpine style. The trio then descended the original route, completing the first traverse of the peak. Manaslu was climbed in winter for the third time in 1995, then on 12 May 1996, the Mexican Carlos Carsolio became the fourth (and at 33 the youngest) to summit the 14 8,000ers when he finally climbed Manaslu having come so close in 1986 with Jerzy Kukuczka and Artur Hajzer.

In 1997, the South Korean Park Young-Seok, who had already climbed five 8,000ers in the previous six months, failed in winter attempt on Manaslu. There was further failure in 1998 for the Japanese husband and wife team of Yasushi Yamanoi and Teako Nagao during their post-monsoon attempt on the north-west face. Despite these failures Manaslu remains one of the most climbed of the Nepalese 8,000ers: only Everest, Cho Oyu and Dhaulagiri having had more ascents. As a contrast it is one of the most dangerous, over 50 climbers having died in their attempts on the peak. Though obviously distorted by the 15 deaths in the dreadful 1972 accident, Manaslu deserves its reputation as a dangerous mountain, the huge summit plateau being no place to be if bad weather envelops the peak.

lhotse 8,516m

"The névé was as tough as sheer ice, and we were determined not to take a single risk in such an exposed position. I cut a row of steps, which necessitated hundreds of strokes of my ice-axe. Just below the crest of the ridge I hacked out a large stance in the snow-cap and leaned my head against the face of the mountain in an effort to recover from my exertions."

ERNST REISS

Lhotse

Lhotse was E1 of the Indian Survey, but appears to have had no local name either in Tibet or Nepal when Charles Howard-Bury's Everest reconnaissance team advanced along the Kama Valley and the northern edge of the Kangshung Glacier in August 1921.

In the absence of an alternative, Howard-Bury christened it Lho-tse, south peak in Tibetan as it lay to the south of Everest, separated from it by the South Col. Because of the name's Tibetan derivation it has stuck.

Exploration

Despite being the fourth highest mountain in the world, Lhotse's closeness to its mighty neighbour meant that it was ignored by early climbers, though the view from the Kangshung side would have dissuaded anyone tempted to try: the east/north-east face is formidable, while the east ridge appears as a coxcomb, a long, high array of ice-glazed rock towers. The ridge has a number of subsidiary summits, that at the eastern end, Lhotse Shar (shar = east), about 1km (⅔mile) from the main summit rising to 8,398m (27,553ft). Between Shar and the main summit there are two central summits, one about 25m (80ft) lower, the other about 25m higher than Shar. As with Yalung Kang (Kangchenjunga's west peak) it has been suggested that Lhotse Shar is an independent peak, but here again the low point on the east ridge is barely 200m (600–650ft) below the main summit, insufficient for the classification of an independent peak in most people's eyes, though in no way reducing the appeal of Lhotse Shar as an objective.

Other than the south face (though this was observed by Tilman during his reconnaissance of the Solo Khumbu area with Charles Houston and party in 1950 and again by Shipton's reconnaissance in 1951) the approaches to Lhotse were explored as a prelude to expeditions to Everest. The Swiss and British Everest expeditions of 1952 and 1953 identified, in passing, that the west face of Lhotse was climbable by way of a narrow couloir which cuts through the rocky face to a point on the summit ridge close to the top. The north ridge, rising from the

Fritz Luchsinger on the summit after the first ascent in 1955

The west face of Lhotse. The Lhotse-Nuptse ridge runs towards the camera; to the right of the main summit is Lhotse Shar

South Col, was obviously a much more difficult climb, barred by a series of steep rock towers which would need to be turned. Those expeditions would also have noticed the difficulties of an attempt along the west (Nuptse) ridge, that ridge also being a narrow sawtooth.

When, in 1955, the first attempt was made on the peak it is not therefore surprising that it was made by way of the Khumbu Icefall, the Western Cwm and the west face. The team was led by the American Norman Dyhrenfurth – son of Prof Gunther Dyhrenfurth – and included both Swiss and American members, as well as Erwin Schneider, a member of the 1934 Nanga Parbat expedition. Climbing post-monsoon, the team established camps through the icefall and Western Cwm, and up to the west face (the Lhotse Face of Everest expeditions) placing the last (Camp V) at about 7,600m (24,900ft). (As an aside, during this trip Schneider and Bruno Spirig skied down the Khumbu Icefall – with two short intervals – an unheralded event which preceded the famed Japanese success by 16 years.) From Camp V, on 16 October Ernst Senn, Arthur Spöhel and two Sherpas continued towards the summit. Spöhel and the Sherpas stopped after about three hours, but Senn continued, reaching the start of the couloir which splits the face, at about 8,100m (26,600ft), before his bottled oxygen ran out. He then retreated to Camp V, but was unable to follow the others down to Camp IV. A storm now marooned Senn at Camp V for five nights though he survived the experience unscathed. A second summit attempt got no higher than Camp V, defeated by another vicious storm.

First Ascent

In 1956 the Swiss returned to Nepal intent upon making the second ascent of Everest, but also with permission to attempt Lhotse. The team was led by Albert Eggler and comprised Wolfgang Diehl, Hans Grimm, Hansrudolf von Gunten, Dr Eduard Leuthold, the expedition doctor, Fritz Luchsinger, Jürg Marmet, Fritz Müller, Ernst Reiss (who had been on the Swiss Everest expedition in Autumn 1952), Adolf Reist and Ernst Schmied. They were supported by a team of 22 Sherpas under sirdar Pasang Dawa Lama (who had climbed Cho Oyu with Jochler and Tichy). When Pasang fell ill at Base Camp Dawa Tenzing took over as sirdar.

While, to the west, the Japanese were forging their route up Manaslu the Swiss team followed the, by now, well-known route through the Khumbu Icefall and along the Western Cwm.

Lhotse (left), Lhotse Shar (centre, and looking the higher of the two summits) and Everest (right, beyond the ridge line) from near the head of the Barun Glacier

The weather was good and by early May they were further up the mountain than the British had been at the same time in 1953. At that time they decided that an attack on both peaks was feasible – though they had permission for both they had waited until they were on the mountain before making a final decision – and that the strongest pair on the day Camp VI was established near the South Col would make an attempt on Lhotse, the rest of the team continuing to build up for attempts on Everest. But now the weather turned bad, pinning the team down for several days. When it cleared, despite the delay the same plan was put into action.

Camp VI was placed close to the top of the Geneva Spur at about 8,000m (26,250ft) and a cable hoist was installed to drag supplies to it. On 17 May Fritz Luchsinger – who had made a remarkable recovery from serious illness early in the trip – and Ernst Reiss moved up to occupy the camp. They left it at 9am the next morning, but lost an hour soon after when Luchsinger's oxygen mask froze. Luckily they had a spare and,

Lhotse's huge south face dwarfs the tiny Island Peak immediately below from the Amphu Lapcha Pass

replacing the malfunctioning one, climbed on. It took them an hour to reach the base of the couloir. This rose at 40°–50°, but the firm snow allowed steady climbing. The couloir was about 5m (16ft) wide and defined by smooth rock ribs. At about half height a rock step almost closed the couloir, but a narrow 60° ice groove allowed it to be bypassed. Eventually the couloir ended at the razor-sharp summit ridge. Rock towers rose on both sides, that on the left being higher. The pair climbed a heavily corniced ridge, then a vertical rock pitch to arrive at a sharp crest, too narrow to stand on, so narrow that they had to hang their rucsacs from ice axes driven into a snow cap so that they could take photographs. It was 2.45pm on 18 May 1956, nine days after the Japanese ascent of Manaslu. The pair stayed 45 minutes on top, discarding their empty oxygen sets before descending. The descent needed great care, but they were back in Camp VI by 6.15pm, taking less than three hours from the top.

Approaching the summit

Five days after the Lhotse ascent the Swiss team placed two men on Everest's summit, then two more on the next day. The team then retreated from the mountain without incident: the double climb had been a magnificent achievement. Albert Eggler's book on the expedition, Gipfel über den Wolken (Summits above the Clouds) when translated into English was called The Everest-Lhotse Adventure. Though apparently mundane in comparison to the more romantic original, the change did capture the spirit of the expedition – for once, it could be argued, something had been gained in the translation.

Later Ascents

With the main summit climbed, attention passed, briefly, to Lhotse Shar. In 1965 a Japanese team attempted a route up the south-east ridge (the ridge which, beyond a high pass, rises to Island Peak, one of Nepal's most popular trekking peaks). The Japanese established a series of camps up the avalanche-free, but very difficult ridge, but a fall seriously injured one of the team, his evacuation from the mountain taking time and energy. It was over a month before a final camp (Camp V at about 7,300m/23,950ft) was occupied. The camp was almost certainly too low, but a two-man team made a summit attempt, failing at

The classic route up Lhotse's west face from the Western Cwm

just over 8,000m (26,250ft) when it became clear that they had insufficient time to overcome the technical difficulties of the ridge. In 1970 an Austrian team led by Siegfried Aeberli attempted the same ridge. Following a similar

The south face seen from the Imja Khola Khumbu

line to the Japanese they established a top camp (Camp IV) at 7,620m (25,000ft) and from it Sepp Mayerl and Rolf Walter set out on 12 May. Climbing with oxygen sets, but without using the bottled gas at first, they reached the Japanese high point quite quickly. They then turned on their bottled gas for the final difficult section, reaching the summit just after noon. The top was even more knife-edged than the main summit, the men having to sit astride it as standing was too precarious. A second summit attempt the next day failed when the oxygen set of one of the two climbers stopped working.

With the principal summits climbed and the traverse from Lhotse Shar to the main summit looking futuristic, attention now shifted to the stupendous south face, a 3,300m (over 10,000ft) wall of steep (sometimes vertical, even overhanging, and averaging about 55°) rock and ice. The first attempt was in 1973 by a Japanese team led by Ryochei Uchida. The team made little progress on the south ridge (at the left edge of the face) before the danger from avalanches persuaded them to transfer to the west ridge. On that they reached about 7,300m (23,950ft) before

ey in the

Ed Viesturs on the classic (west face) route

LHOTSE: ASCENT ROUTES

Above West Face
A *Lhotse*
B *Nuptse*
C *Lhotse Face*
1 *First ascent/'classic' route, Swiss (1956)*

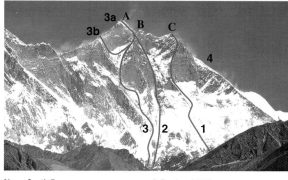

Above South Face
A *Main Summit*
B *Middle Summit*
C *Lhotse Shar*
1 *Czech route to Lhotse Shar (1989). The dotted line represents the route taken by Kukuczka and Pawlowski to the summit ridge of the main summit where Kukuczka fell to his death*

2 *Russians (1990)*
3 *Yugoslavians (1981), but not to summit on either 3a or 3b*
3a *Cesen (1990), following variant of Yugoslavian line on lower face*
4 *SE Ridge of Lhotse Shar, Austrians (1970)*

abandoning the attempt. The following year a Polish team attempted a winter ascent of the original route to the main summit, reaching a height of 8,230m (27,000ft) before cold forced them to abandon, one team member dying of exposure. Before any further attempt could be made the Poles discovered that their permit ended on 31 December and had to retreat.

In 1975 an Italian expedition led by Ricardo Cassin, the legendary pre-war climber (who had made the first ascents of the Walker Spur on the Grandes Jorasses, the north-east face of Piz Badile and the north face of the Lavaredo's Cima Ovest) camped below the south face. The team was very strong, including Alessandro Gogna, Ignazio Piussi and Reinhold

Messner (a Tyrolean, but from the Italian Tyrol). This team, too, found a direct route up the face too dangerous and attempted a leftward traverse towards the Lhotse-Nuptse ridge. The Italians had reached about 7,400m (24,300ft) when avalanches destroyed both their base and top camps, injuring – though not seriously – four men. The attempt was then abandoned. A Japanese team trying the same line in 1976 climbed a little higher but were also forced to abandon by the avalanche danger.

When in 1977, the main summit of Lhotse was finally, after 21 years, reached again it was by an Austro-German team led by Dr. Gerhard Schmatz following the original route. The second ascent was made on 8 May by Johann von Känel, Hermann Warth and the Sherpa Urkien. Two more teams reached the summit – a total of ten summiteers in the three attempts – Michl Dacher completing the first ascent without supplementary oxygen. Sadly, on the third summit climb Max Lutz was killed while descending. The original route was repeated twice in 1979, an Austrian team climbing it in the spring and a Polish team making the first post-monsoon ascent of the peak in October. One of the Poles was Jerzy Kukuczka making his first ascent of an 8,000er.

In 1980 Frenchmen Nicholas Jaegar arrived at the base of the south face with Nicholas Bérardini and Georges Bettembourg apparently with the audacious plan of not only soloing it, but then continuing down to the South Col and climbing Everest. His attempt on the face was soon abandoned because of the avalanche threat and he decided to solo Lhotse Shar and then follow the east ridge to the main summit. He was last seen at a height of about 8,000m (26,250ft) on the south-east ridge. Six days of bad weather then hid the mountain from view. Jaeger's final bivouac was found during a failed attempt to climb Shar in 1983.

A Yugoslav team took up the challenge of the south face in 1981. The team's first camp was a snow cave, the whole area being so constantly swept by avalanches that tents would have been destroyed. The weather was atrocious, with snow daily from noon onwards and descending teams invariably caught in powder snow avalanches. Camp III was placed below a 300m (1,000ft) overhang from which, on one occasion, a vast rock fall hurtled down the route. Thankfully no one was injured. Following further difficult and dangerous climbing the Yugoslav's established Camp V in the U-shaped snow field below the summit headwall. This camp was so vulnerable to avalanches that it was eventually abandoned for one higher on a spur to the east. The final decision to move the camp followed an incident where a tent was so inundated with snow that it was effectively sealed from the outside so that when the climbers began to cook the stove flame exhausted the oxygen and one man fell unconscious. The whole route to the new top camp was fixed with ropes and from it two attempts were made on the headwall, both failing in bad weather. A third attempt was then made, traversing across the snow basin and climbing towards the west ridge. Continuous difficulties finally forced the two climbers – Francek Kenez and Vanja Matijevic – to abandon the attempt, though they did succeed in reaching the ridge. The two finally regained Camp IV 25 hours after starting their climb. It is estimated that the highest point reached was over 8,300m (27,200ft), no more than 200m (650ft) below the top. It had been a remarkable, sensational attempt: the south face had

been climbed, though on the strict rules of Himalayan climbing total success could not be claimed as the summit was not reached.

In the spring of 1984 a Czech team pushed a route up the south face to the right of the Yugoslav line, reaching the summit of Lhotse Shar. The route followed a distinct rock buttress which gave very hard, but relatively avalanche-free, climbing. As with the Yugoslav route, fixed ropes were necessary because of the bad weather and prolonged climb (the Czechs took 51 days over their climb, the Yugoslavs had taken over 60). On 20 May four men left the top camp. Three gave up because of wind and cold but Zoltan Demján continued to the summit. On the next day three more of the team summitted. Post-monsoon in 1985 a Polish team attempted to follow the Czech

line with the intention of bearing west towards the top so as to reach the main summit, but abandoned the attempt when a climber died in a fall.

In the post-monsoon season of 1986, just a week or so after their ascent of Makalu, Reinhold Messner and Hans Kammerlander, together with Friedl Mutschlechner, arrived at Everest base camp for an attempt on Lhotse. Messner had already tried to climb the peak twice in 1975 as part of the Italian south face expedition and in 1980 with one Sherpa. This time his team attached themselves to a commercial Everest expedition, using that party's equipment to reach the Lhotse Face. Here Mutschlechner retreated with toothache, Messner and Kammerlander following the original route to the summit which they reached on 16 October. It was Messner's final climb

of an 8,000er: he had not only climbed all 14, but four to them twice, and all of them without supplementary oxygen, a landmark in Himalayan climbing. Though several of his ascents followed 'normal' routes – while Jerzy Kukuczka, the second man to complete the set, climbed new lines or made first winter ascents on all but one peak – Messner's achievements cannot be underestimated. His ascent of Gasherbrum I with Habeler opened a new era in climbing on the great peaks, while the same pair's bottled gas-free ascent of Everest was an equivalent landmark. Together with his first solo of an 8,000er and solo of Everest when the mountain was free of other climbers these climbs represent a phenomenal CV in climbing on the world's highest mountains.

In the years following Messner grand slam the south face

remained an elusive goal. An international team climbed the face to the summit ridge in the autumn of 1987, but the final 200m (650ft) to the top eluded them as it had the Yugoslavs in 1981. One member of the team was killed in an avalanche. The next year Krzysztof Wielicki (wearing a special part-metal corset following a serious back injury after a fall earlier in the year, an injury which reduced his height by over 1cm (½in), and which made the descent agonising) soloed the original route on the west face from about 7,300m (24,000ft) on 31 December to achieve the first winter ascent. It was not a true solo as the mountain had been prepared to his top camp as part of a Belgian Everest-Lhotse winter expedition, but was still a remarkable climb, Wielicki climbing the final 1,200m (3,950ft) in just 9½ hours. The following year, in attempting

Everest looms above Lhotse's south face in this view from Ama Dablam's north ridge

On the south face

to complete the Polish line on the south face, Jerzy Kukuczka and Ryszard Pawlowski, members of an International team, bivouaced at 8,300m (27,200ft), just below the summit ridge. On 24 October Kukuczka climbed on to the ridge, but then fell, probably when a cornice broke. He had fixed a runner and this held, but the 6mm rope – bought cheap in Kathmandu – broke and he fell 3,000m (10,000ft) to the base of the face. The shocked Pawlowski made his way down safely. Kukuczka was a remarkable climber, seemingly immune to suffering and with an insatiable appetite for high altitude climbing. He had climbed all of the 14 8,000ers either by new routes or in winter, all bar one – Lhotse. Success on the south face would have completed the series.

In 1989 French climbers Marc Batard and Christophe Profit each failed in winter solo bids to climb the south face, but the following year the Slovenian Tomo Cesen soloed a line similar to the Polish route, completing the climb by a direct route on the final headwall. Cesen was a phenomenon. In the winter of 1986 he soloed the Eiger, Grandes Jorasses and Matterhorn north faces in a week and had made other extreme solo climbs and some very fast solos of very hard routes. In the Himalaya he summitted during the first ascent of Yalung Kang's north face in 1985 and then in April 1989 he soloed the north face of Jannu, a 2,800m (9,200ft) face which he climbed in 23

hours. On Lhotse in April 1990 he started climbing at 5am on 22nd, on a route to the left of the Yugoslavian 1981 line. He bivouaced at 7,500m (24,600ft) when the sun hit the wall (so avoiding rock falls). His second bivouac was at 8,200m (26,900ft) and from it he reached the summit at 2.20pm on 24th. The final headwall was very hard, Cesen needing three hours to climb one 60m (200ft) section using pitons. Cesen retreated down the same line to about 7,800m (25,600ft), then used the pitons of the Yugslavian route – the ropes having gone – to speed his abseils. He bivouaced at 7,300m (24,000ft) and reached base camp on 25 April.

But then, in autumn 1990 a Soviet team climbed a direct line up the south face using 'old-fashioned' siege tactics and claimed a first ascent, discounting Cesen's claimed solo, adding something new to a whispering campaign that had grown, particularly in France, about the Slovenian's route. Cesen had no photographs to support his claim and the climbing world was soon divided on the issue though, significantly, several who had tried the face backed him. Later the Russians modified their view (they maintained they had been misquoted originally) claiming that Cesen was unlikely to have reached the main summit because of the difficulties of the final ridge, but that he had probably climbed the face, reaching the top of a lower pinnacle. The debate deflected attention from the Soviet climb which was an extraordinary achievement by a team of, mainly, young, inexperienced – but very good – climbers. The summit was reached on 16 October by Sergei

Bershov and Vladimir Karatajev. Supplementary oxygen was used, but the pair reached the top at 7pm long after it had run out. Karatajev later lost almost all his fingers and toes as a result of frostbite. It is unfortunate that the controversy over Cesen's ascent has detracted from a real appreciation of the Soviet climb which many consider to be the hardest route to the top of an 8,000er.

In 1992 Wally Berg and Scott Fischer climbed Lhotse by the normal route and concluded that Cesen had too. His description of the summit agreed with what they saw and they also saw the old orange oxygen bottle he described. They thought it possible he did not climb the last 8m (25ft) to the top as it was an unstable snow cone on which they felt insecure even though they were roped. In 1994 Carlos Carsolio climbed the normal route in under 24 hours on 13 May (having also summitted Cho Oyu on 25 April). He added to the Cesen controversy by noting that part of the Western Cwm was visible from the summit: Cesen had claimed to have looked into the Cwm, a fact seized on by his detractors as others who had definitely reached the summit claimed the Cwm was not visible. Further fuel was added to the Cesen fire in 1996 when photographs of the east ridge taken by other climbers who had summitted that year were published. Cesen claimed to have climbed the ridge on its southern side as that side was much easier, but the photos appeared to show that the northern side was more straightforward. It is also claimed that Reinhold Messner, who had championed Cesen's cause has now changed his opinion on the climb. The debate rumbles on and, in the nature of arguments about solo ascents unsupported by photographic or other evidence, is unlikely to be satisfactorily resolved.

Unfortunately the debate shrouded some very good climbs on Lhotse. In 1994 Erhard Loretan and Jean Troillet also climbed the normal route, but their intended traverse to Lhotse Shar was defeated by bad weather. Then on 10 May 1996 Chantal Mauduit summitted, the first female ascent. However even this climb proved controversial: a Sherpa who had rescued her from near the summit of Everest in 1995 when she was attempting a bottled oxygen free ascent is said to have approached her after her Lhotse climb and said, very simply, 'You lie'.

There was further controversy in 1997 following the claimed ascent by Italians Sergio Martini and Fausto De Stefani. Each had a good reason for wanting to climb Lhotse, Martini then needing only Everest to complete the 14 8,000ers (he subsequently climbed it in 1999), De Stefani needing only Kangchenjunga (which he subsequently climbed in 1998). The pair were honest in admitting that they had not reached the actual summit, claiming the high wind at the top made climbing the final ridge, its cornice of rotten snow, too dangerous. Since it was known that in poor weather the true summit of Lhotse could be difficult to locate the climbing world accepted the ascent. Later however, a South Korean climber, Park Young-Seok (who had climbed five 8,000ers in six months and then failed in a winter bid on Manaslu which would have made it six) reached the true summit and claimed that the Italians' tracks stopped a full 150m (500ft) from the top, rather too far for a minor case of mistaken identity. As De Stefani and Martini are both claimants of the grand slam this debate too is set to run.

The good news in 1998 – the mountain seeming to attract more than its share of bad – was a real climb, a post-monsoon attempt to traverse from Lhotse Shar to the main summit. A Russian team climbed Shar, but were unable to continue because weather and snow conditions were too poor. This traverse, which would include an ascent of Lhotse Middle, the highest unclimbed 'summit' in the world, remains one of the mountain's last great problems. Though Lhotse will always be a poor relative to its huge cousin – it has had fewer ascents than any 8,000er other than Annapurna – the south face, west ridge and Shar-main peak traverse will ensure that it retains the attention of the world's best climbers.

A close up view of Lhotse's formidable south face

gasherbrum II 8,035m

'He started climbing, while I belayed him from my stance attached to two ice screws. Gradually he moved up. I heard him swearing. There was nowhere to bang in a piton. I watched him struggle, trying once, twice, his calves trembling with the effort ...'

JERZY KUKUCZKA watches Wojciech Kurtyka on the south-east spur

The Gasherbrum group are a series of peaks on a gigantic horseshoe ridge which encloses the South Gasherbrum Glacier. On the eastern side of the glacier is Gasherbrum I, separated by the Gasherbrum La from the pyramidal peaks of Gasherbrum II and III.

To the north-west of these twin peaks another high pass separates them from the trapezoidal Gasherbrum IV. South from here are peaks V and VI, each separated by ridge saddles. In the original classification of the Karakoram peaks Gasherbrum I was K5, Gasherbrum II being K4. The name is from the Balti (a Tibetan dialect) rgasha brum, beautiful mountain (though Dyhrenfurth claimed that he was once told the name meant 'shining wall'). What seems less in doubt than the derivation of the name is that it was originally applied to Gasherbrum IV, the most visible of the peaks. Whether 'beautiful mountain' or 'shining wall' is chosen, the name is appropriate, Gasherbrum IV's elegant shape and sun-catching pale limestone living up to either.

Exploration

The Gasherbrum group lies at the upper end of Baltoro Glacier, close enough to K2 to have shared the early explorations associated with the higher peak. Conway's trip of 1892 saw (and gave the alternative name to) Gasherbrum I, while the Abruzzi expedition of 1909 saw and photographed Gasherbrum I, II and III from what is now called the Sella Pass.

In 1934 the International Himalayan Expedition under Gunther Dyhrenfurth reached the junction of the Abruzzi and South Gasherbrum Glaciers and continued along the latter to the base of Gasherbrum II. From the base Dyhrenfurth could see two obvious lines of ascent to the terrace-like snow-field at the base of the final summit pyramid and was so convinced that from there straightforward climbing would

Larch, Moravec and Willenpart after their summit climb

reach the top that he was tempted to try. Only concerns over the abilities of his Balti porters to establish and support the necessary camps prevented him from doing so.

First Ascent

In 1956 the Austrian Himalayan Society organised an expedition to the Karakoram under Fritz Moravec, the intention being to reconnoitre Gasherbrum II and, if possible, to climb it. In addition to Moravec the expedition included Dr Erich Gattinger, a geologist, Sepp Larch, Hans Ratay, Richard Reinagl, Heinrich Roiss, Dr Georg Weiler, the team doctor, and Hans Willenpart, supported by Cpt Qasim Ali Shah, Hayat Ali Sha and a team of Balti porters. The expedition established a Base Camp near the junction of the Abruzzi and South Gasherbrum Glaciers and Camp I at the base of the south-west spur of the peak. Dyhrenfurth's 1934 reconnaissance had suggested that the easterly of the two spurs (the south spur) rising to the terrace snow-field was the more promising, but the Austrians favoured the other. At its base they found a safe campsite, but after being forced to retreat to Base Camp by a ten-day storm the Austrians discovered that their safe camp had been engulfed by a huge avalanche. Despite two days of digging through debris that was up to 10m (over 30ft) deep they were forced to accept that all their equipment had been lost. Moravec was now forced into an agonising decision – should he abandon the expedition or attempt a rapid ascent with a minimum of camps and support. He decided on the latter.

Ratay and Roiss climbed the ice ridge at the edge of the spur and

Climbers slog up the initial section of the long south-west ridge. The summit, still some 1,500m (5,000ft) above, is seen on the right

established Camp II at 6,700m (22,000ft). Larch and Reinagl then continued up to a shoulder on the spur where they established Camp III at 7,150m (23,500ft). Moravec now hoped to establish a final camp on the terrace snow-field, but the Balti porters were not capable of carrying loads up the spur. As a consequence on 6 July, just four days after abandoning their digging at Camp I, Moravec, Larch and Willenpart left Camp III carrying huge loads, but climbing without bottled oxygen. On dangerous, unstable snow they climbed unroped, as a slip by any one of them could not have been held by the others, and as night fell they reached the terrace. There they were able to find a sheltered spot for a bivouac beneath the cliffs of the summit pyramid's south-east face. They estimated their height at 7,500m (24,600ft). After a bitterly cold night and a meagre

breakfast the three set off along the rising terrace, staying close to the foot of the south-east face. By 9am they had reached the east ridge and could turn along it. Despite deep snow and a final short rock band the ridge was straightforward and at 11.30am on 7 July the three reached the summit, where two man-sized rock pinnacles were set on a small snow dome. The weather was perfect, so warm that the summiteers were able to take off their anoraks and bask in the sun. They built a cairn into which Moravec pushed a film canister with details of their ascent in German and English and an Austrian flag: later sumitteers have not mentioned either the cairn or the pinnacles. After an hour the Austrians descended, the descent being without incident. Perhaps because Gasherbrum II is now seen as one of the easiest 8,000ers this first ascent has tended to be ignored by the climbing press, yet it represented an advance in the history of climbing on the great peaks: never before had an 8,000er been climbed by a team which deliberately chose to bivouac during the ascent. The tactic pointed the way forward, though it was almost three decades before the technique became common practice.

Later Ascents

In 1975, 19 years after the first ascent, a French expedition arrived at the base of Gasherbrum II. The French climbed the south spur – that suggested by Dyhrenfurth – to the terrace snow-field, then followed the east ridge, as taken by the Austrians, to the summit. The French intended to establish a Camp III at the top of the spur, but the two lead climbers, Marc Batard and Yannick Seigneur, continued past the intended site and, realising that the ridge climb was straightforward, erected a small tent at a higher level from which they reached the top –

making the second ascent – by 9am the following day. On their way down they met a second pair, Louis Audobert and Bernard Villaret near the tent site. Based on their experience Batard and Seigneur advised stopping at the tent and making an early start. Consequently Audobert and Villaret stopped, making their summit bid at 3am on the next day. By now the weather had deteriorated and eventually Villaret was forced to abandon the attempt in the face of biting cold and high winds. Audobert continued to a point only some 50m (160ft) from the top where he, too, was forced to turn around. Back at the tent the pair waited out the storm for a whole day. When conditions did not improve Audobert decided to descend, but was unable to persuade Villaret to accompany him. After many hours in temperatures estimated at -40°C or lower, with fierce winds and deep snow, Audobert reached Camp II utterly exhausted. Villaret was not seen again.

The day after Batard and Seigneur reached the summit

High camp on the south-east shoulder of Gasherbrum II. Beyond is the north-western flank of Gasherbrum I

two Polish teams arrived at the base of Gasherbrum II. One was female, led by Wanda Rutkiewicz, and was planning to climb Gasherbrum III, while the other was a male team intent on climbing Gasherbrum II. However, at the time of the arrival of the Poles the men had not been given permission to climb the higher peak and so the two teams combined to attempt Gasherbrum III.

The Poles followed the Austrian (first-ascent) route on the south-west spur, establishing a camp (Camp III) at 7,350m (24,100ft). Permission was now, belatedly, granted for an attempt on Gasherbrum II. On 1 August three men and two women climbed to the col between II and III. The three men felt that the west ridge of Gasherbrum II was too loose to attempt and so traversed around to the north-west face which

160

Climbing the classic route on Gasherbrum II

Messner, who was climbing his eighth 8,000er. The same year the French couple Maurice and Liliane Barrard reached the summit. The flurry of activity was due, in large part, to Gasherbrum II rapidly acquiring a reputation as the easiest 8,000er. The French team which included Christine Janin had very limited experience: neither of the men had been higher than Mont Blanc and Janin had almost no climbing experience at all, though she later completed the Seven Summits. Other ascents – alpine style in three days and semi-solo by the Austrian Joseph (Pepo) Trattner – and rumours of illegal ascents persuaded a number of teams to the peak. But the dangers of high altitude climbing should never be underestimated: in 1982 Gasherbrum II claimed three more victims. The body of one of these, the Austrian Norbert Wolf,

they climbed to the summit, completing the third ascent of the peak and establishing the third route to the summit. The women failed in an attempt to climb Gasherbrum III, but two days later a mixed team, 2 men and 2 women, completed the climb. At that time Gasherbrum III was the highest unclimbed mountain in the world. It is also the highest to have had a first ascent by a woman. Halina Krüger-Syrokomska and Anna Okopinska then repeated the original route to the top of Gasherbrum II. Theirs was the first female ascent and the first female ascent of an 8,000m peak without supplementary oxygen.

Over subsequent years Gasherbrum II was climbed many times along the route of the original ascent. In 1981 the French climbers Eric Beaud, Phillippe Grenier and Christine Janin, and the Pakistani Sher Khan climbed the route alpine style in five days. The following year Sher Khan climbed the peak again, this time in the company of Nazir Sabir and Reinhold

Gasherbrum II from Base Camp. To the left is Gasherbrum III

GASHERBRUM II: ASCENT ROUTES

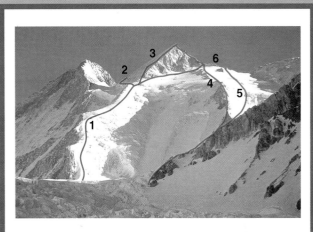

Above South-east Face
1 *First ascent (1956); the 'classic' route*
2 *NW Face, Polish (1975)*
3 *WSW Face, Carsolio (1995)*
4 *French (1975)*
5 *Dutch (1988)*
6 *East Ridge, Kukuczka/Kurtyka (1983)*

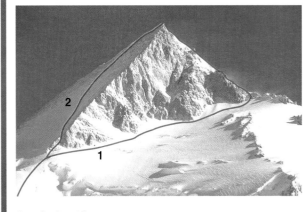

Above South-east Face
1 *First ascent (1956); the 'classic' route*
2 *WSW Face, Carsolio (1995)*

As climbers approach the top of a ridge the view of the high Karakoram peaks opens out

was found by Messner, Khan and Sabir, who attempted a burial. There was a subsequent furore over Messner's willingness to 'climb over bodies' in his pursuit of 8,000m peaks. The comments were both a sign of the times and the result of the jaundiced view of Messner's achievements by some climbers. In later years it has became common practice to camp among bodies on Everest's South Col and the difficulties (some would say impossibility) of retrieving bodies from high altitude have become better understood. As Messner himself has noted, when he climbed Gasherbrum II again in 1984 he found Wolf's body still visible, and at least a dozen other teams had climbed past it in the intervening years. On a happier note, Maurice and Liliane Barrard summitted in 1982, the first husband and wife team, and were accompanied by Liliane's brother for the, to date, only ever ascent of an 8,000er by a brother and sister team.

In 1983 the Poles Jerzy Kukuczka and Wojciech Kurtyka (the pair calling themselves the Alex McIntyre Memorial Expedition) made an alpine ascent of the long, undulating east ridge in three days. The pair descended the original route, thus completing the first traverse of the peak. Gasherbrum II was Kukuczka's fifth 8,000er. The two Poles subsequently climbed

In deep shadow on the classic line

A large team of climbers heads up across a lower section of the classic route

Climber leaving Camp II on the classic route

Gasherbrum I. In 1984 an equally remarkable traverse was achieved by Hans Kammerlander and Reinhold Messner who climbed Gasherbrum II via the original route, then descended south-eastwards before climbing Gasherbrum I.

The following year the peak almost became a circus, Frenchman Pierre Gevaux jumping from the summit beneath a specially designed parachute and Jean-Marc Boivin, another Frenchman, hang-gliding from the top. Boivin climbed the peak on 8 July carrying his 17kg (37½lb) glider. It was too windy to fly, so he descended. Then, on 14 July he climbed the peak again – in 16 hours from base camp – spent four hours digging the glider out of the snow and flew back to base in 20 minutes. Both Gevaux and Boivin established world height records. In the same year the French pair Thierry Renard and Pierre Mure-Ravaud climbed the peak with the intention that Renard should make a ski descent. Mure-Ravaud was unwell and descended with other summiteers, but Michel Metzger accompanied Renard. Renard claimed the descent was a 'solo descent, extreme ski', Metzger viewing the claim with disdain on the grounds that two men do not constitute a solo and the skiing was hardly extreme.

In 1986 an early commercial expedition placed three members on the summit. Several other teams were also successful, Sher Khan making his third ascent of the peak as a member of one of them, but the dangers of even an easy 8,000er were again emphasised, a Spaniard dying of oedema in a high camp. The following year, prior to making a successful ascent, Jeff Little and Lydia Brady claimed to have had the highest recorded sex on

At sunrise the shadow of Gasherbrum II approaches the sunlit pinnacle of Masherbrum

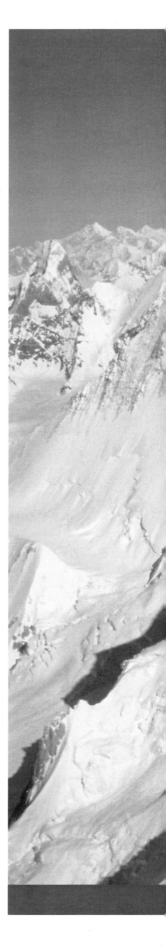

land at about 7,800m (around 26,000ft). There may, of course, be good reasons why other teams have not broadcast an improvement in this particular height record. In 1988 Henri Albet and Pascal Hittinger, together with Michel Buscail and two Balti porters, climbed the original route to the summit from where Albet snowboarded down, Hittinger using a monoski from a point 10m (33ft) below the top. On the second day of descent Albet fell and was killed: Hittinger immediately abandoned his attempt. One day after Albet and Hittinger reached the top four men from a small Dutch team climbed a variant of the French 1975 route.

The increase in commercial traffic on the peak, and the perceived paucity of available lines, dissuaded many of the top climbers from attempting the peak, though there was (and always will be) a steady stream of climbers intent on completing all the 14 8,000ers and some seeking a Karakoram challenge. In 1995 Carlos Carsolio proved the 'no-new-line'

rule by exception, breaking away from the normal route to climb diagonally across the west-south-west face to reach the west ridge, which he followed to the top. The following year the Karakoram challenge was taken up by Frenchman Jean-Christophe Lafaille. Lafaille soloed Gasherbrum II and then Gasherbrum I in a four day climb (see Chapter on Gasherbrum I for fuller details). In 1997 the Russian Anatoli Boukreev, well-known for his involvement in the 1996 Everest tragedy, climbed the peak in 12 hours, although his climb was assisted by ropes fixed by commercial expeditions. The following year an attempt to climb Gasherbrum II from the Chinese side failed due to high winds which threatened to blow the team off the peak. An ascent from that side remains the peak's outstanding problem.

Gasherbrum II is now firmly established as the easiest of the Karakoram's 8,000ers and one of the easiest of all. For some the walk-in along the Baltoro Glacier, with its view of K2, are an advantage, an experience to be savoured, adding to the attraction of the peak. For others, intent only on reaching the summit of an 8,000er the much easier approach to Cho Oyu (and Shisha Pangma now that commercial trips to Tibet have become routine) and its extra metres make that the preferred peak. Only Cho Oyu (and Everest of course) have had more ascents than Gasherbrum II, a situation that is unlikely to change unless politics intervene.

The Chinese – eastern – flank of Gasherbrum II – a sight few Western climbers have seen

View to the north west from high on Gasherbrum I. Left to right, Gasherbrum IV, Gasherbrum III, Gasherbrum II

broad peak 8,047m

"I linked arms with him. He understood immediately what I meant ... At last we were on top ... All I could say was 'Fritz – fantastic'."

MARCUS SCHMUCK TO FRITZ WINTERSTELLAR on reaching the summit on the first ascent

broad peak

Broad Peak was not assigned a peak number in the original Karakoram survey, being hidden from the surveyor's view, and was named by Martin Conway during his expedition of 1892.

Broad Peak was not assigned a peak number in the original Karakoram survey, being hidden from the surveyor's view, and was named by Martin Conway during his expedition of 1892. Catching sight of the massif that defines the eastern side of the valley of the Godwin-Austen Glacier, filling the space between the Sella Pass and the Palchan La/Gasherbrum group, Conway noted 'a fine breadth of mountain splendour … a huge Breithorn, as it were, filling the space between K2 and the hidden Gasherbrum'. Conway therefore not only named the peak but was the first to note the similarity of the triple-summitted massif to the alpine peak which forms a section of the back wall of the Zermatt valley. Since that time grateful writers have frequently referred to Broad Peak as the 'Breithorn of the Karakoram'.

Although Broad Peak is now the accepted name both in Pakistan and internationally, efforts have been made to discover an earlier local one. In the absence of any credible candidate, a name was invented by translating Broad Peak into Balti, the local Tibetan dialect. The resulting name is P'alchan Ri or P'alchan Kangri, but the curious 'stop' between the first letter and the second syllable has led to the mis-spelling Phalchan which, in turn, has led to the spelling Falchan. This is very wrong as there is no 'f' sound in Tibetan. Around the time of the peak's first ascent the Pakistani authorities claimed that P'alchan Ri was indeed a name known by the local people: it is, for instance, used by Ardito Desio in his book on the first ascent of K2 (though interestingly the summit climbers, when quoted in that book, use Broad Peak). Was this discovery politically motivated, a result of half-a-century of translation of Conway's name, or a real name? Whatever the truth, it is unlikely that the mountain will now ever be called anything other than Broad Peak, a name descriptive not only of the massif, but of the summit structure of both the main and central peaks.

The central peak rises above the 8,000m-contour but, unlike Yalung Kang and Lhotse Shar, has few advocates for its inclusion as a separate peak, despite having a better – but still hardly adequate – claim than the other two. If the snow in the col between the main and central peaks, accumulated in the

Three of Broad Peak's four summits – North, Central and Main – can be seen in this evening view from the north west

Marcus Schmuck on the summit after the first ascent. Behind him is K2 while the long ridge from the forepeak curves away to his left

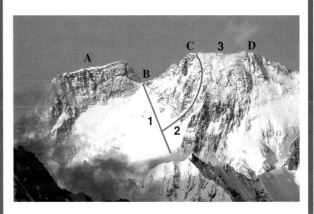

Above From West
A *Broad Peak Central*
B *Broad Col*
C *Forepeak*
D *Main Summit*
1 *Standard route*
2 *Carsolio (1994)*
3 *Long summit ridge. The length of the ridge explains why some climbers, arriving*

at the forepeak, believe they are on the summit, or decide against extending their climb to the main summit. The Kukuczka/Kurtyka (1984) climb followed the skyline ridge from the left. The Polish (1975) route to Broad Peak Central followed the standard route to Broad Col, then the skyline ridge

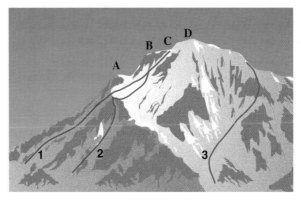

Above From South-west
A *Broad Peak North*
B *Broad Peak Central*
C *Broad Col*
D *Main Summit*
1 *Standard route*
2 *Carsolio (1994)*
3 *Attempts on SSE Spur/South Ridge (1997)*

tight hollow over thousands of years, were to melt, Broad Peak central would qualify as a fifteenth 8,000m peak. Melting might occur if global warming continues. The effect of local glacial and snowfield retreat can be seen in photographs of the summit ridge (between the fore peak and the main summit) taken during the first ascent and more recently. There is a clear reduction in snow cover. It has even been suggested that if the reduction continues, at some point the fore peak might actually overtop the main summit, a fact which would be welcomed by those climbers whose ascentshave finished at the fore peak.

Exploration

After Conway's naming, the mountain's position, on the approach to K2 from Concordia, meant that Broad Peak was well observed on all explorations of the area – by Eckenstein and Abruzzi for instance – and by early expeditions to the higher peak. It was also studied by Gunther Dyhrenfurth's 1934 International Himalayan Expedition to Gasherbrum I. Despite these early sightings, it was not until 1954 that an expedition to Broad Peak was mounted and even then it was only as a second choice. Dr Karl-Maria Herrligkoffer had intended his Austro-German expedition to attempt K2, but finding the Italians had already received permission switched objectives to Gasherbrum I, proposing an audacious approach along the Siachen Glacier. Business commitments delayed Herrligkoffer in Germany and rather than either allowing the expedition to proceed without him or delaying until 1955, he proposed an autumn ascent, eventually arriving in Askole in late September. At that time he was also given permission to attempt Broad Peak and rather than risk difficulties with porters on the Siachen approach he chose the more accessible mountain, taking the familiar route to Concordia.

Herrligkoffer took the view that the obvious ascent route – following the western spur to a snowfield close to the col between the main and central summits, a route proposed by Dyhrenfurth during his 1934 Gasherbrum reconnaissance – would be too difficult for the Balti porters and so chose a longer, less steep route on the eastern side of the south-west ridge. Dyhrenfurth had dismissed this route as too avalanche prone for safety and so it proved, one section – a 300m (1,000ft) couloir – being nicknamed the Kanonenrohr – gun barrel – by

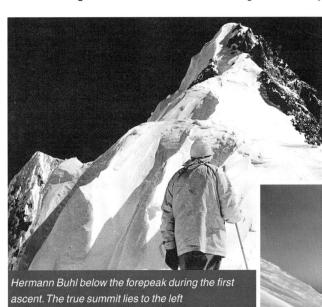

Hermann Buhl below the forepeak during the first ascent. The true summit lies to the left

Hermann Buhl on the summit during the first ascent

the climbers. Despite the avalanche dangers and accidents to three members, all of whom escaped major incidents with minor injuries, the team reached about 6,900m (22,650ft) before winter's early storms forced them to abandon the climb.

First Ascent

In 1957, Hermann Buhl, the lone hero of Nanga Parbat, decided to return to the Karakoram and to try to climb an 8,000er with a small, lightweight expedition. As on Nanga Parbat he intended to dispense with bottled oxygen. When his original team members dropped out he invited Marcus Schmuck to join him. Schmuck wanted to take his normal partner Fritz Wintersteller, and to make up two ropes of two, Hermann Buhl invited the young Kurt Diemberger, after hearing of his ascent of the 'Giant Meringue'. To finance the trip Schmuck persuaded money from the Austrian Alpine Association, of which he was a member, but this was only available on condition that he became the official leader of the expedition. Technically, therefore, Schmuck was the leader, Buhl the climbing leader. In practice the four were a democratic unit.

Buhl's idea was to dispense with porters after Base Camp (at about 5,000m/16,400ft) had been established, using load carrying between camps as a means of acclimatisation. The team arrived at Concordia in May and began work on the west spur – Dyhrenfurth's suggested line – on the 13th. By 21 May they had established and stocked two camps, the first at 5,800m (19,000ft) and the second at 6,400m (21,000ft), intending to use fixed ropes left by Herrligkoffer's 1954 team which they dug out of the ice, as well as some of their own, to establish Camp III. During this work they came across a tin of bacon which the Germans had found in an abandoned Italian camp at K2, and some salami and egg liquor. The meat and drink were still edible despite the curious journey to Broad Peak and the three years high-altitude refrigeration.

Five days of bad weather now pinned the team in Base Camp and not until 28 May did they establish Camp III (6,950m/22,800ft), set at the edge of the snowfield below the col between the main and central peaks. The four abandoned their plan to establish a fourth camp and on 29 May climbed towards the col. Deep snow slowed their progress and it was mid-afternoon before they reached the col, at 7,800m (25,600ft). Believing that the top was the culmination of the ridge above them they continued up, despite the late hour. At 6pm Diemberger and Wintersteller, climbing ahead of Buhl and Schmuck, reached the ridge top, but could then see that the true summit, though only 15–20m (50–60ft) higher, was at least an hour away along a ridge which fell slightly then rose again. As it was too late for a summit bid, reluctantly the four returned to Camp III, reaching it at 9.30pm. Next day they descended to Base Camp in order to rest until their next attempt.

On 8 June they returned to Camp III and at 3.30am the next morning set off for the col again. The weather was good, but the cold intense and Buhl and Diemberger, who took a different line to that of Schmuck and Wintersteller, one that was in shadow for longer, were slowed by fierce pains in Buhl's right foot, the one from which he had lost joints on two toes after his Nanga Parbat climb. Consequently the two reached the col as Schmuck and Wintersteller were leaving it, and then had to wait an hour for Buhl to recover. Not until 2.30pm did Buhl and Diemberger start up the final ridge. Eventually Buhl, exhausted

The first British woman on an 8,000m peak: Julie Tullis on Broad Peak, 1984

Later Ascents

In 1975 a Polish team climbed Broad Peak's central summit, a team of six setting out for the summit on 28 July. The route was as for the 1957 climb to the col between the tops, then along the central summit's final ridge. The col was reached in late afternoon and one of the six retreated to the top camp from it. The remaining five climbed on, overcoming two major obstacles to reach a final rock step. Here three men remained while Kazimierz Glazek and Janusz Kulis climbed on, reaching the top at 7.30pm. During the descent the weather worsened, forcing the climbers to move on to the north-east face to avoid a violent blizzard. There, Bohdan Nowaczyk, the last man on an abseil, was killed when the rope anchor failed. Without a rope the four survivors were forced to bivouac. The next morning a search failed to find their companion or the rope and they tied slings together to form a makeshift line. The appalling weather made the descent painfully slow and another bivouac was inevitable. While searching for a suitable spot Andrzej Sikorski slipped, knocking Marek Kesicki and summiteer Kulis off. Only Kulis survived the fall, he and Glazek eventually making camp. Both were frostbitten, Kulis subsequently losing most of his toes.

In 1976 a small French team led by Yannick Seigneur attempted to repeat the original route to the main summit, but failed, and it was not until 1977, 20 years after the first ascent that Broad Peak was climbed again, a large Japanese team following the original route. On 8 August Kazuhisa Noro, Takashi Ozaki and Yoshiyuki Tsuji reached the summit. In 1978 Yannick Seigneur returned and, climbing with Georges Bettembourg, claimed to have repeated the original route in true alpine style, though he reached the summit alone when Bettembourg stopped. However, Bettembourg claims that Seigneur only reached the foresummit, not the true summit, a claim Seigneur denied strenuously despite having admitted only reaching the col between the fore and main summits in an article on the climb.

Subsequent undisputed ascents all took the original line, with minor variations, including that in 1982 of Sher Khan, Reinhold Messner and Nazir Sabir. Broad Peak was Messner's ninth 8,000er (and his third 8,000er of 1982) and was accomplished nine days after the trio had climbed Gasherbrum II. On their way up Messner's team – who climbed the peak alpine style in four days – met Jerzy Kukuczka and Wojciech Kurtyka on their way down. The Poles had completed a similar alpine-style climb of Broad Peak the day before, but were anxious that news of their climb should be kept secret as they were climbing illegally. The pair were on a K2 expedition with permission to acclimatise on neighbouring peaks. They (rightly

by the pain in his foot was forced to stop, but generously allowed Diemberger to climb on alone. Schmuck and Wintersteller reached the true summit at 5.05pm, Diemberger joined them as they were about to leave the summit. The summit was a triangular snow slope backed by a huge cornice which Schmuck and Wintersteller had avoided, but which Diemberger climbed on to in order to take more extensive photographs, a bold, but somewhat risky venture.

On their descent Schmuck and Wintersteller met Buhl on the ridge top, the subsidiary summit, to which he had climbed with difficulty. They told him he would need at least another hour to reach the top and hurried on down. By the time Diemberger had reached the bottom of the dip between the two tops he could see Buhl advancing along the ridge. Diemberger claims their meeting was wordless, Buhl not stopping but climbing slowly towards the top, another monumental display of willpower. Diemberger turned and followed him, the pair reaching the top at about 7pm. Hermann Buhl became the second man to climb two 8,000ers (after Sherpa Gyalzen Norbu) and, if the marginally time lapse between the other three and himself is ignored, the first to be involved in two first ascents. Gyalzen Norbu was on the first ascent of Manaslu, but climbed Makalu the day after its first ascent. Buhl shares with Diemberger (who later climbed Dhaulagiri) the record of two 8,000er first ascents. After watching the setting sun lighting up the surrounding peaks Buhl and Diemberger left the summit, descending to Camp III in the dark.

The four men descended to Base Camp safely, but the expedition was not to have a happy ending: 18 days later while descending Chogolisa's final ridge after their summit attempt had been halted by bad weather Buhl and Diemberger had to feel their way in near zero visibility. Hermann Buhl strayed too close to the edge of a cornice: it collapsed and the greatest mountaineer of the era – one of the greatest of all time – fell to his death.

On the south ridge during a failed attempt in 1997

before Diemberger's return to the top the Poles Kukuczka and Kurtyka also climbed it for the second time. They began by climbing the North Summit (the 7,600m/24,950ft – third peak of the Karakoram Breithorn – theirs was the first ascent) then climbed over the central summit (making the second ascent, and finding evidence of the Polish 1975 climb on the descent to the col before the main summit) and on to the main summit. This phenomenal climb took just four days. Even quicker was the ascent of Krzysztof Wielicki, a member of a Polish team repeating the original route. He left base camp just after midnight on 14 July and climbing by the light of a full moon reached Camp I at 4am, Camp II at 8am and the col between the central and main summits at 2pm. He was at the top by 4pm (one hour after three other members of the same expedition who had started from the top camp) having completed a 3,150m (10,300ft) climb in 13 hours climbing time. He was back at base camp by 10.30pm, a total time of 22 hours 10 minutes. First solo seems an inadequate description for such a remarkable climb – and there are, of course, those who doubt that 'solo' can be applied to a climb on a prepared mountain, especially as Wielicki rested and took refreshments at the Polish camps. Wielicki's 24-hour climb – the first ascent of an 8,000er in one day – was repeated in 1986 by Benôit Chamoux, then in 1987 Norbert Joos made a 'true' solo reaching the summit on 29 May, the earliest date a Karakoram 8,000er had been climbed.

In March 1988, having failed in a bid to make the first winter ascent of K2, a Polish team transferred its attention to Broad Peak. On 3 March Maciej Berbeka and Aleksander Lwow left base camp and climbed alpine-style through deep snow in intense cold. From a camp at 7,700m (25,250ft) Berbeka continued alone when Lwow was exhausted. He reached what he thought was the top at 6pm on 6 March in appalling weather and was forced to bivouac at 7,900m (25,900ft) on the way down. Though both Berbeka and Lwow suffered frostbite, they reached base camp safely and without permanent injury. Later, when he saw a photograph of the summit area Berbeka acknowledged that because of the bad weather he had not realised he had only reached the foresummit. Technically, therefore, Broad Peak had not been climbed in winter.

1992 saw the first ascent of a Broad Peak summit from the Chinese (east) side, a Spanish team (including one Italian and the Austrian Kurt Diemberger) climbing a hard line to Broad Peak Central which included 70° ice and short vertical walls in the lower section and 65°–70° couloirs higher up. The summit climbers – Spaniards Oscar Cadiach, Enric Dalmau and Lluis Ráfols, and the Italian Alberto Soncini – left Camp III, at 7,350m (24,100ft) and climbed all day, bivouacing with little equipment

as later events showed) considered it unlikely that the Pakistani authorities would consider an ascent of Broad Peak to fall within that definition. The year after Messner and Kukuczka's ascents the trend for alpine-style ascents of Broad Peak continued. Two Polish women, Anna Czerwinska and Krystyna Palmowska, made the first female ascent – and a major contribution to the history of Himalayan climbing with the first wholly female ascent of an 8,000er. On 30 June, after a semi-alpine ascent with two camps, Czerwinska reached the col between the fore and main summits, Palmowska continuing to the main summit alone. Pure alpine-style ascents were also made by Andy Parkin and Al Rouse, Jean Afanassieff and Roger Baxter-Jones, Doug Scott and Steve Sustad, though the success of these teams was tempered by the death of Pete Thexton from oedema during an attempt with Greg Child.

1984 was a memorable year, Kurt Diemberger returning to the mountain. On 18 July, 27 years and 39 days after he had reached the summit with Hermann Buhl he stood there again, this time with Briton Julie Tullis. Despite being avalanched on their descent the pair made it safely off the peak. The day

at 8,000m (26,247ft), just a few metres from the top. At first light they summitted and returned safely to camp.

On his way to becoming the fourth climber to complete the set of all 14 8,000ers, in 1994 the Mexican Carlos Carsolio soloed a new route to the right of the original route, climbing over Pt6230. His third bivouac was below the headwall to the foresummit at the junction with the original route, where Camp III is usually placed. Bad weather then forced him to retreat. Later he climbed the original route to Camp III (the route had been prepared by other expeditions to the peak) and his earlier bivouac site. Here his stove exploded burning down his tent and removing his moustache. Undeterred by either loss he climbed the headwall directly to the foresummit, then followed the original route to the top. He reached the summit as night fell and returned to Camp III where he was helped by a Basque expedition. Also in 1994 Hans Kammerlander climbed the peak, his ninth 8,000er. As with Wielicki on Shisha Pangma, Kammerlander was fed up with climbers reaching the foresummit and claiming an ascent. He therefore left a piece of red and purple rope attached to a ski pole on the summit and asked climbers what they had seen there: in 1994 seven reached the real top, a further six the foresummit only. One of the true summiteers was the Swede Göran Kropp who soloed the peak in 18¼ hours.

The next year three Japanese climbers repeated the Polish route over the north, central and main summits, the only three of the 28 summiteers who did not follow the original route, taking seven days from base camp to base camp.

To date there are just four routes on the mountain (if the route to the Central summit from the Chinese side of the mountain is included), a small number for such a massive, in every sense, peak (attempts to add a fifth along the south-south-east spur to the south ridge, in 1997, firstly by the Basque Iñurrategi brothers and then by a two-man team, Briton Rick Allen and Australian Andrew

Lock, failed). It might be expected that, overshadowed by its near neighbour K2 and more difficult than the equally close Gasherbrum II expeditions to Broad Peak would be limited. Yet the aura of the peak being Hermann Buhl's last great climb has maintained a steady stream of climbers, almost exclusively following the original route and many deciding not to risk the long traverse from the foresummit to the main summit. Of the 14 peaks only Gasherbrum II has had more summit climbers.

Sunrise on the classic route

gasherbrum I 8,068m

'In the viewfinder of the camera I could hardly make out Peter at all. His dark figure merged with the black background of the sky. Only when he moved a few steps could I see his feet in the snow.'

REINHOLD MESSNER films Peter Habeler
reaching the summit of Gasherbrum I

Gasherbrum I was K5 in the first Karakoram survey, but was named Hidden Peak by Conway during his 1892 expedition because it only came into view as he climbed the Upper Baltoro Glacier towards the west ridge of Golden Throne (Baltoro Kangri).

Gasherbrum I was K5 in the first Karakoram survey, but was named Hidden Peak by Conway during his 1892 expedition because it only came into view as he climbed the Upper Baltoro Glacier towards the west ridge of Golden Throne (Baltoro Kangri). However, before Conway named the peak it had already been referred to by its 'correct' name, the Alpine Journal of August 1888 noting the name Gusher-Brum which, it reported, Col Godwin-Austen had been told meant 'Sunset Peak'. As noted in the chapter on Gasherbrum II it is now widely believed that the origin of the name is the Balti rgasha brum, beautiful mountain, though it should be noted that Gasherbrum IV, the peak usually claimed to be the origin of the name, catches the evening light.

Hidden Peak was the accepted name for the peak until very recent times – the account of the first ascent uses the name, as does Messner in his book on the second ascent. But with the trend away from the use of western names for Himalayan peaks Gasherbrum I is now preferred.

Exploration

The early exploration of the Gasherbrum peaks is one shared with the other Baltoro peaks and is considered in more detail in the chapter on K2. Conway's expedition photographed the peak as well as naming it, and it was photographed again by Vittorio Sella during the Duke of the Abruzzi's reconnaissance trip of 1909. Further photographs, and mapping of the Abruzzi Glacier from which the South Gasherbrum Glacier heads north into the cirque of Gasherbrum peaks, were also obtained in 1929 by the Italian expedition of the Duke of Spoleto. Some of the Spoleto team also explored the Urdok Glacier, viewing Gasherbrum I from the east.

In 1934 Gunther Dyhrenfurth's International Himalayan Expedition (a curious venture which included actors and actresses as well as climbers, the former making a film which helped pay for the trip) carried out a more thorough exploration of the peak from the South Gasherbrum Glacier. Dyhrenfurth's team concluded that the only possibility of climbing it was from the south, either by the south spur which falls from a point on the south-east ridge (which links Gasherbrum I to Urdok I) or along another southerly spur to the east (a spur which later became known as the IHE Spur). Dyhrenfurth thought the latter the easiest, because although it offered a longer route to the top, the lower section of the IHE Spur was much less steep than the south spur and so easier for load carrying. Each of the spurs ends at a gentle snow plateau/basin below the south-east ridge. From the plateau the final summit (south-east) ridge appeared to offer little difficulty. Two of Dyhrenfurth's team, the German Hans Ertl and the Swiss André Roch, attempted the IHE Spur, fortunately reaching a height of only about 6,200m (20,350ft) when, on 6 July, they were caught in a violent storm. The two climbers were still 7 or 8 km (5

Gasherbrum I from the west near Advanced Base Camp on the South Gasherbrum Glacier. The icefall leads to the hidden Upper Gasherbrum Cwm and the Gasherbrum La

miles) from the summit, but were able to retreat safely: on Nanga Parbat, to the south, the same protracted storm was killing Merkl, Welzenbach and Wieland. When the storm eventually cleared Dyhrenfurth's team had neither the time nor the resources to make a further attempt on the mountain.

Two years later Gasherbrum I was attempted in earnest by a French team under Henri de Ségogne. The team included Pierre Allain, the greatest French climber of the time, and several other very experienced alpinists, as well as 35 Sherpas brought from Darjeeling. The French chose to attack the south spur rather than the IHE route and in poor weather established a series of camps, the final one (Camp V) at 6,800m (22,300ft). The intention now was to place one more camp near a subsidiary summit which the French called Hidden Sud (7,069m/23,192ft). Though still horizontally some distance from the summit the French believed that they would then have then been above the major difficulties and in a position to make a summit attempt. But at the crucial moment a storm broke. For 10 days it snowed unceasingly making not only further progress impossible, but an orderly retreat hazardous: at one point two Sherpas retreating from Camp III to Camp II were caught in a powder snow avalanche and carried 550m (1,800ft) down the mountain. The pair 'passed Camp II like meteors' and were lucky to escape uninjured. After the epic of the retreat the French were understandably reluctant to return to the peak and the attempt was abandoned.

First Ascent

In 1958, realising that they were running out of opportunities to climb an 8,000er, the American Alpine Club sponsored an expedition to Gasherbrum I. It was led by Nick Clinch and comprised Dick Irvin, Andy Kauffman, Tom McCormack, Dr Tom Nevison, the expedition doctor, Gil Roberts, Pete Schoening, the man who had held the fall on K2 during the retreat which ended in the tragic death of Art Gilkey, and Bob Swift. The team was completed by two Pakistani army officers, Mohammed Akram and Tash Rizvi who were in charge of the six Balti porters used for high altitude carries. The Americans used English, French and Swiss equipment almost exclusively – how things change, within a relatively short time many innovations in climbing equipment were being exported to Europe. The team also used English suppliers for much of their food: Bob Swift noted early on that there was a great deal of tinned oxtail and tinned ox tongue. As he was no lover of either he wondered often why it was that the English seemed capable of only breeding bovines with no middle sections. Swift's personal account of the walk-in is also refreshingly truthful. The Baltoro is often claimed to offer the world's finest trek, its sides

GASHERBRUM I: ASCENT ROUTES

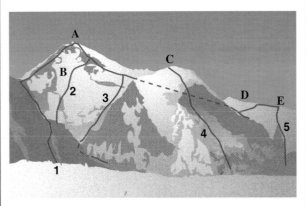

Above Looking North-east from Base Camp on the Abruzzi Glacier
A Gasherbrum I **B** SW Face
C Hidden Sud **D** Urdok I
E Spur Peak

1 SW Ridge, Yugoslavians (1977); complete ridge Japanese (1990)
2 Kukuczka/Kurtyka (1983)
3 Spanish (1983)
4 Hidden Sud to first ascent, French (1980)
5 First ascent (1958), via Spur Peak

Above North-west Face
1 Germans (1982)
2 Swiss (1983)
3 Messner/Habeler (1975)
4 Italians (1985)
5 Japanese Couloir (1986)
Main routes shown only; many variations, particularly of now-standard Japanese Couloir route

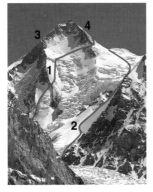

Above South-west Face
1 Kukuczka/Kurtyka (1983)
2 Spanish (1983)
3 SW Ridge. Climbed in part by the Yugoslavians (1977) and fully by the Japanese (1990)
4 SE Ridge. Followed on the first ascent by the Americans (1958), and by the French (1980) and Spanish (1983) on their routes

marked by an array of majestic peaks, but it can also be a nightmare. Swift notes 'June 3rd was misery' a sentence which sums up the effect of the sun on the ice, turning it into deep slush. He is also barely restrained about the difficulties with the Balti porters, though the best comment on this is from Schoening's account. He notes that one day's demand that the porters start walking at 10.30 in the morning was accepted, though the Americans did not know this until 10.29.

The Americans attacked the IHE spur (which they called the Roch Arête after André Roch) using fixed ropes to help load carrying to Camp IV at the edge of the snow plateau below the south-east ridge. On the plateau the climbers had to contend with waist-deep snow and wished they had skis. The snow slowed progress and when, on 4 July, Clinch, Kauffman, Nevison, Schoening and Swift climbed up to establish Camp V, despite using oxygen they could only reach a point at about 7,150m (23,500ft), over 150m (500ft) lower, but more importantly 800m horizontally, from the col below the south summit where they had hoped to place it. That night Kauffman

Nevison, Swift and Clinch leave Camp V during the first ascent

and Schoening remained in Camp V while the other three descended. The pair breathed oxygen not from masks, but from an open-pipe system which bled it into the space near their heads – a real incentive not to turn over during the night.

The next day the two set out at 5am using makeshift snowshoes formed by stamping their crampons through the plywood sides of food boxes and breathing oxygen, now through proper masks. The day was clear and sunny, but bitterly cold, slowing progress. When the slope steepened the box/snowshoes were abandoned, but they had been invaluable, allowing a relatively rapid rate of climb. In fact, when they changed to their second bottle of supplementary oxygen Kauffman and Schoening were able to increase the flow rate. On the final ridge the wind picked up, but the climbing was straightforward. At 3pm on 5 July they reached the summit, a broad snow dome. From it they announced their success to their team-mates at the lower camps using mirrors.

It had been planned that there would be one, perhaps two, further summit attempts, but none of the rest of the team felt fit enough to try, and the mountain was abandoned.

Later Ascents

It was 17 years before a climbing team returned to Gasherbrum I, a delay due to Pakistan government's refusal to open the area to foreigners rather than any lack of enthusiasm on the part of climbers. In the year the Karakoram was re-opened, 1975, two expeditions arrived at the mountain base, one a German team led by Hans Schell, the other the two-man team of Peter Habeler (from the Austrian Tyrol), and Reinhold Messner (an Italian Tyrolean). Since his involvement with big expeditions to Nanga Parbat, Manaslu and, more recently, Lhotse's south face, Messner had been wanting to try an 8,000er in alpine style, both as a reaction to the discipline of the big expeditions and to try to return to a purer style of climbing. His book on the Gasherbrum I expedition refers several times to the four-man team which climbed Broad Peak: Messner clearly saw such small expeditions as the way forward in Himalayan climbing, and saw Hermann Buhl as a father figure of the pure style.

Camp II during the first ascent. In the background are Chogolisa and Masherbrum

Schell had permission to climb Baltoro Kangri, but wrote to Habeler asking to be allowed on to their Gasherbrum I permit. At first Messner was pleased – Schell offered to pay for the permit and money was tight – but eventually was opposed to the idea. He was, in part, annoyed by Schell's assumption of agreement and lack of contact in Pakistan, but was also concerned that critics would seize on the fact that there was another party on the mountain to denigrate his and Habeler's climb. In the event, Schell's party climbed the IHE spur and so were an entire mountain away from Habeler and Messner.

The Tyroleans arrived in Pakistan with 200kg (440lb) of

Andy Kauffman on the summit after the first ascent

equipment compared to the 2 tonnes used by the Broad Peak team. On the first day of the climb proper Habeler and Messner carried rucsacs weighing 13kgs. On the second (summit) day they carried no sacs at all. Following the South Gasherbrum Glacier the pair bivouaced at 5,900m (19,350ft) below the mountain's north-west face. On 9 August they climbed the face, comparing it, in steepness and difficulty to the Matterhorn's north face. They bivouaced close to a distinct shoulder at 7,100m (23,300ft), then, on 10 August, starting at 8am, climbed the ridge between the north and north-west faces reaching the summit at 12.30pm, well before their self-imposed deadline of 3pm. Gasherbrum I was Messner's third 8,000er. The pair returned to their second bivouac site, but that night the weather, which had been near perfect, changed and violent winds almost destroyed their tent. Despite the storm they successfully downclimbed the north-west face on 11 August, being met by the Polish Gasherbrum II/III expedition who congratulated them on their step-change in the standard of Himalayan climbing. This was undoubtedly true. After the era of first ascents, and then the quest for hard routes – Annapurna's south face, Nanga Parbat's Rupal Face – the logical development was for smaller teams climbing in alpine style. Ultimately the two would be put together – two man teams on hard routes – and taken to its logical conclusion – solo ascents of hard routes. In his book on the climb Messner admits to the dangers in the approach – on a big expedition you have some chance of rescue by your team-mates – but claimed that the rewards justify the risk. Messner also claimed that the ascent

had given him 'an answer to the question of mankind's fundamental existence' and that he now saw himself 'in a new relationship with the world'. Though such cod philosophy gave his critics something else to chew on, there was no denying the magnitude of the achievement and that it really did open a new era in the history of Himalayan climbing.

Ironically, on the day after Habeler and Messner made the second ascent of Gasherbrum I, Schell's team climbing in the 'old-fashioned' style made the third, Robert Schauer, Schell himself and Herbert Zefferer following the original route to the top.

Over the next few years there were four further ascents of Gasherbrum I, three of them by new routes. In 1977 an eight-man Yugoslavian team climbed the south-west/west ridges): Andrej Stremfelj and Nejc Zaplotnik reached the summit, but Drago Bergar disappeared during a solo repetition of the climb. In 1980, the French pair Maurice Barrard and Georges Norbaud completed the French 1936 route over 'Hidden Sud'. To cross the snow plateau which had caused the Americans so much trouble the French used skis. Though purely alpine, the French ascent was also a feat of endurance: after climbing the south peak they were forced back to base by bad weather and in all spent over four weeks on the mountain. In 1981 a large Japanese expedition repeated the original route using oxygen on the summit climb, then in 1982 a German expedition led by Günther Stürm climbed a new route on the north-west face to the left (north) of the Habeler-Messner line. Stürm reached the top together with Michl Dacher and Sigi Hupfauer. At the same time a French team repeated the original route. The summit was reached by five climbers, one of them, Marie-Jose Valencot, making the first female ascent. Sylvain Saudan then skied from the summit to base camp, the first full ski descent of an 8,000er, though Manaslu had been substantially skied the previous year.

In 1983 the Polish Alex McIntyre Memorial Expedition comprising Jerzy Kukuczka and Wojciech Kurtyka, having already climbed a new route on Gasherbrum II climbed Gasherbrum I via the south-west face. The climb required three bivouacs, though two nights were spent at the second site as two attempts to climb the final headwall failed necessitating a traverse right on to a south-easterly spur. During the successful summit bid the Poles found one of Kurtyka's crampons dropped the day before on the abortive attempt on the headwall. While the Poles were completing their new routes on Gasherbrum I and II a Swiss team was attempting the two Gasherbrum peaks and Broad Peak, Erhard Loretan and Marcel Reudi completed a partially new route on the north-west face (joining the 1982 German line higher up), the climb being repeated by their colleagues Pierre Morand and Jean-Claude Sonnenwyl the following day. Also in 1983 all the members of a Spanish team under Javier Escartin reached the summit by a partially new route, following the south-west ridge of Hidden Sud, then continuing along the French line.

The following year Hans Kammerlander and Reinhold Messner traversed Gasherbrum I and II, the first traverse of two 8,000ers, and one accomplished with no route preparation or equipment caches. The pair climbed Gasherbrum II, then descended to Gasherbrum La and from there climbed the north-west face by a variant of the Habeler/Messner route before descending to the base of the north-west face which they climbed by a variant of the 1982 German route before descending to the South Gasherbrum Glacier.

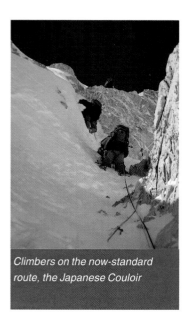

Climbers on the now-standard route, the Japanese Couloir

1985 saw further new routes, the relatively easy-angled faces of the mountain allowing many variations. The Italian 'Quota 8,000' team, set up to climb all 14 8,000ers, completed two new routes on the north-west face, while the French pair of Eric Escoffier and Benôit Chamoux climbed a variant of the 1982 German line. The pair had previously climbed Gasherbrum II together, but Chamoux set off earlier than Escoffier on Gasherbrum I, bivouacing at nightfall. He was caught by Escoffier who started early the following day. Escoffier climbed the peak in 21 hours from the pair's base to the top and back. Their route was repeated

From a high camp a trail leads off to the base of the Japanese Couloir

a short while later by Gianpiero Di Federico the leader of an Italian team attempting the peak – the first solo ascent.

In 1986, during a period of renewed tension with India over Kashmir, Pakistan established a military camp on the Abruzzi Glacier on the southern side of the mountain and banned all expeditions from that area. The ban is still in place, the easy-angled south side of the peak remaining off limits. The original being unavailable, expeditions were now forced to find an alternative 'normal route' for ascents. This was rapidly provided by the Japanese Kiyoshi Wakutsu and Osamu Shimizu who, the same year, climbed a couloir which threaded its way up the north face above the Gasherbrum La. The Japanese Couloir is now the standard route on the peak. But the Japanese success was not shared by all the teams on the peak, a Swiss expedition attempting the north ridge direct from Gasherbrum La failing a heartbreaking 20m (65ft) from the top, stopped by winds which threatened to blow them off the mountain.

After the years of new route activity the peak received fewer ascents in the late 1980s, a combination of military activity between rival Indian and Pakistani forces, bad weather and avalanches keeping teams at bay. A notable attempt to climb the peak during this difficult period was that of a Japanese team who approached along the Sagan Glacier to the north. Bad weather and snow conditions halted the attempt at about 6,100m (20,000ft). In 1990 Wanda Rutkiewicz and Ewa Pankiewicz climbed yet another new line on the north-west face, and a Japanese team climbed the south-west ridge from its base, a new route as the 1977 Yugoslav route joined the ridge at a higher level. The climb involved a lot of fixed rope, a fact which allowed two teams to follow the line in the days after the Japanese had withdrawn. The 1990s saw many further ascents of the peak, chiefly by commercial expeditions. The closeness of Gasherbrum I to Gasherbrum II, a very popular peak with commercial expeditions, meant that many offered clients the choice of either (or even the chance of both) for a shared walk-in and consequent reduction in organisational requirements. There were still innovations though. In 1995 after ascents by a Slovenian team Marko Car, on a snowboard, and Iztok Tomazin, on conventional skis, skied down the Japanese Couloir, going from the summit to Camp II on the first day and on down to base camp the following day. The next year Frenchman Jean-Christophe Lafaille soloed Gasherbrum II and then Gasherbrum I in a four day climb. Lafaille was part of a large party attempting Gasherbrum II and left their Camp 1 at 5,900m (19,350ft) on the evening of 27 July. He reached the summit of Gasherbrum II at 9.10am on 28 July, then descended to a bivouac camp and was back in Camp 1 by the morning of 29 July. At 11pm he climbed Gasherbrum I by a route to the right

High on the Japanese Couloir route

of the Habeler/Messner line. He set up a bivouac at 7,450m (24,450ft) on 30 July, but bad weather forced him down to Camp 3 of other expeditions on the mountain. However, at 11pm he started up again and reached the summit on the morning of 31 July and was back in Camp 1 later the same day.

In 1997 Pakistan issued numerous permits for the Gasherbrum peaks, ostensibly to celebrate the country's Golden Jubilee of Pakistan. The effect was chaotic, with over 150 climbers crammed into the base camp area. Many believe that only perfect climbing weather prevented serious problems. Yet regardless of this number of summit aspirants only K2 of the Karakoram 8,000ers has had fewer summit climbers than Gasherbrum I. Despite the large number of routes on the peak, and the fact that there are still obvious lines – such as the north-east face – the (relative) ease of nearby Gasherbrum II is likely to ensure this remains the case for many years.

> 'And then – there it was ... simply beyond words, mighty, unbelievably beautiful – Dhaulagiri.'

KURT DIEMBERGER

dhaulagiri 8,167m

dhaulagiri

Peak XLII of the Indian survey is named from the Sanskrit dhavala giri, meaning white mountain. It is often, and correctly, said that travellers to the Himalaya, when asking the name of a prominent peak, were told it was dhaulagiri. It seems that when needing a name quickly, the local people chose an obvious one: most Himalayan peaks are, after all, substantially white.

eak XLII of the Indian survey is named from the Sanskrit dhavala giri, white mountain. It is often, and rightly, said that foreign travellers to the Himalaya when asking the name of a prominent peak were told it was dhaulagiri, the locals not wanting to disappoint the man paying their wages and so, when needing a name quickly, choosing an obvious one: most Himalayan peaks are, after all, substantially white. But it is worth noting that to the east of Dhaulagiri are the Nilgiri peaks (nilgiri = blue mountain) and that the vast bulk of Dhaulagiri really is a mountain of purest white, a glowing, dazzling white when viewed from the south in the light of morning sun. This may have been even truer in the past as lately there has been a loss of ice from some Himalayan peaks (another product of global warming?). The surprise,

perhaps, is that the imposing Dhaulagiri has as mundane a name as white mountain and has not been incorporated into a local legend or named for one of the pantheon of Hindu deities.

Exploration

Dhaulagiri was known from the early 1800s when Lt Webb made the measurements for which he was ridiculed, showing that the peak was 2,000m (6,600ft) higher than Chimborazo which was then considered the world's highest mountain. Though there were occasional sightings of the peak later – Lt James Herbert also surveyed it at the time of his advance into Nepal during the Nepalese War, confirming Webb's height – it was not until 1949 that the first photographs of the peak were brought back to Europe. They were obtained by Dr Arnold

The south face of Dhaulagiri is seen from the south east on the superb viewpoint of Poon Hill (3,194m/10,480ft) above the Ghorapani La

Heim, a Swiss scientist, who flew close to the peak, at an altitude of about 4,500m (14,800ft) during one of the earliest explorations of newly open Nepal.

The following year Dhaulagiri was one of the two potential targets for the French expedition under Maurice Herzog. The need to locate the mountain because of the poo quality of available maps meant that the French did not get very close to Dhaulagiri, but what they saw appalled them. Lionel Terray, one of the greatest French climbers of any era, claimed that the mountain would never be climbed and all those who saw it believed it was unclimbable from the northern or southern sides. Later, and hardly surprisingly, the history of climbing being full of those who have had to eat their words after seeing a team climb their 'unclimbable' route, Terray suggested to Max Eiselin (who led the first successful team) that the north-east ridge looked the most reasonable route. This assessment at least was prophetic, Eiselin's team following that ridge.

In 1952 a small British team carrying out botanical research on behalf of the British Museum made a more thorough exploration of the northern side of Dhaulagiri than time had allowed the French. They collected a good deal of information which was probably of value to a Swiss team which arrived in Nepal in 1953 with the intention of reconnoitring the north side and, if possible, climbing the peak. The Swiss, a seven-strong team led by Bernard Lauterburg, approached the peak along the Mayangdi Glacier which flows westwards from the northern side. The approach, particularly along the valley of Mayangdi Khola which required the team to hack their way through otherwise impenetrable jungle, was exhausting, but eventually a Base Camp was set up at the foot of the north face. Straightforward climbing on a rocky spur allowed progress to a height of about 5,900m (19,350ft), but the face above steepened sharply. A top camp (Camp V) was eventually placed at 6,500m (21,300ft) close to the base of a prominent feature of the face which the climbers called the Pear. Above this, it was hoped, they would be able to reach the west ridge, following it more easily to the summit. On 29 May Peter Braun and Ruedi Schatz, together with three load-carrying Sherpas, attacked the Pear. At the top of the feature the three Sherpas were sent down (one of them slipping on the way causing the three to fall 500m/1,600ft – a fall which they survived uninjured) while Braun and Schatz continued using oxygen. They reached about 7,600m (24,900ft), but guessed that it would take a further four hours to reach the ridge. With no way of assessing how long it might then take to reach the summit they retreated. The expedition then carried out valuable exploration work, reaching the north-east col and crossing the French and Dambush Passes to reach Tukuche.

DHAULAGIRI: ASCENT ROUTES

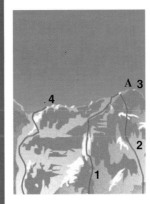

Above West Face
A Summit
1 Kazakh (1991)
2 Czech (1985) but not to summit
3 SW Pillar (Czech/Italian/Russian 1988)
4 Czech route (1984)

Above North Face
1 First ascent (standard) route
2 UK/Russian (1993)
3 The Pear Japanese (1982)

Above From Poon Hill
1 Polish/Canadian (1986) but only to Japanese South Buttress route
2 Humar (1999) but not to summit
3 Slovenians (1981) but only to SE Ridge
4 SE Ridge Japanese (1978); approach was from the far side
5 South Buttress Japanese (1978)

Above East Face
1 SE Ridge, Japanese (1978)
2 East Face, Ghilini/Kurtyka/MacIntyre/ Wilczynski (1980)
3 East Face, Slovenians (1986) but not to summit
4 NE Ridge, first ascent/'classic' route

DHAULAGIRI 185

In 1954 the first ever Argentinian team to one of the great peaks arrived below the north face. It was led by Francisco Ibañez, who had been the liaison officer on the French expedition to Fitzroy. The team of eleven established a base camp very early in the season and followed the Swiss 1953 route. High on the face where the Swiss had been unable to find level ground for a satisfactory camp the Argentinians used dynamite to blast a platform for their Camp VI – a dubious activity (though not the last debatable incident on an 8,000er)

Ernst Forrer at 8,000m during the first ascent

– a procedure which took three days. The Argentinians then climbed the Pear and set up Camp VII at about 7,500m (24,600ft). From it on 1 June four men, Alfredo Magnani, Austrian-born Gerhard Watzl and the Sherpas Pasang Dawa Lama and Ang Nyima, set out for the top. They reached the west ridge, but it turned out to be more difficult than they had hoped, unclimbable pinnacles

Diemberger, Schelbert, Nawang Dorje and Nima Dorje on the summit after the first ascent

forcing them to traverse on to the vast south face. Not until 5pm could they move back on to the ridge. They now bivouaced in a snow cave at over 7,900m (25,900ft) content that the way to the summit was straightforward, requiring no more than three hours climbing. But that night a violent storm broke and instead of the projected summit climb they were forced to battle down

to Camp VII where they found Ibañez waiting for them. Ibañez was severely frostbitten and could only make it down to Camp VI. The others, though also frostbitten and exhausted, continued down. It was five days before Ibañez could be rescued, his condition now so bad that he had to be placed in a makeshift stretcher and lowered down the mountain. On the march out, with echoes of the appalling journey of Herzog and Lachenal from Annapurna, Ibañez lost fingers and toes and then parts of his left foot. But there was to be no happy outcome: he died in hospital at Kathmandu.

In 1955 a German-Swiss team led by Martin Meier (who, with Rudolf Peters had first climbed the Croz Spur on the north face of the Grandes Jorasses) again attempted the north face route. The team was termed the 'Vegetarian (or Bircher-Müesli) Himalayan Expedition' as a requirement of their chief sponsor was that the climbers would have a meat-free diet. The team reached only 7,350m (24,100ft) on the Pear route, though this lack of success had less to do with diet than the lack of experience and expertise of the climbers (Toni Hiebeler had withdrawn from the expedition at an early stage concerned over just this) and the general disorganisation of the attempt.

The following year the Argentines returned, but they fared little better, the early arrival of the monsoon forcing them to abandon at a height only just above that achieved in 1955.

In 1958 the Swiss came back, this time led by Werner Stäuble. Again the Pear route was chosen, but after establishing a camp at 7,350m (24,100ft) an attempt to place a higher camp was thwarted by a violent storm. During this Max Eiselin and Sherpa Pasang Sona, marooned in the snow cave that formed Camp IV, were sealed into the cave by an avalanche. Their frantic attempt to dig themselves out were almost ended by their consuming the cave's remaining oxygen. Only on the point of black-out were they able to struggle free. Later Eiselin and his friend, the team doctor Georg Hajdukiewicz, observed the peak at length and became convinced that the best route to the summit was along the north-east ridge from the north-east col. Eiselin applied for permission to return in 1959, but this had already been given to the Austrian Fritz Moravec, the leader of the successful Gasherbrum II expedition. Eiselin therefore secured permission for 1960, but graciously told Moravec of his view that the expeditions to date had been going the wrong way.

The Austrian team did indeed make an attempt on the north-east ridge and initially made very good progress, Camp IV being established at 6,500m (21,300ft) as early as 24 April. Unfortunately the team was then struck a double blow. On 29 April Heinrich Roiss fell down a crevasse near Camp II. His disappearance was not noticed for a couple of hours and when he was eventually found it was too late: though he was still alive when he was dragged out he was in a very poor state and died during the night. At the same time bad weather destroyed the top camps, keeping the team low on the mountain. When the attempt could resume late in May a top camp was established at 7,400m (24,300ft) and from it Karl Prein and Sherpa Pasang Dawa Lama made several attempts to reach the top. They did not get beyond 7,800m (25,600ft), each time defeated by violent winds and bitter cold.

First Ascent

In 1960 Max Eiselin led an expedition which, though predominantly Swiss, was almost international in its make up.

Seen to the west from the pilgrim village of Muktinath, the sun sets behind Dhaulagiri

In addition to Eiselin, Ernst Forrer, Albin Schelbert, Michel Vaucher and Hugo Weber were Swiss, as was Jean-Jacques Roussi though he was then resident in Nepal. Kurt Diemberger was Austrian and Peter Diener German, while the team doctor Georg Hajdukiewicz and his assistant Adam Skoczylas were Poles. The final member was Norman Dyhrenfurth, the American (but Swiss-born) son of the Swiss-American Günter

On the north face during the Anglo-Russian ascent in 1993

Oskar Dyhrenfurth, who was to make a film of the expedition. The climbers were supported by a team of seven Sherpas under sirdar Ang Dawa (though he was demoted during the expedition for a combination of laziness and over-enthusiasm in eating the best of the expedition's food). The reason there were so few Sherpas was that the expedition was supported by a Pilatus-Porter glacier plane (painted red and yellow and christened 'Yeti') whose pilot and co-pilot/mechanic Ernst Saxer and Emil Wick became critical members of the team.

The plane was to be used to fly equipment and climbers to the north-east col, though an early acclimatisation camp was first set up on the Dambush Pass. The pass is at 5,200m (17,050ft), a world-record height for a plane landing. The north-east col is at 5,700m (18,700ft) and when landings were made there it (obviously) set a new world record. The use of the plane allowed the team to avoid a tedious walk-in and any possible disputes with porters, but the rapid height gain (from Pokhara to 5,200m in about an hour) caused all the climbers and Sherpas problems with altitude sickness. The plane was also not without its problems. Having successfully flown from Switzerland to Pokhara and made numerous flights to Dambush and the Col, it blew a cylinder forcing an emergency landing at Pokhara from which the pilots escaped unscathed. A replacement engine was obtained in a very fast time, but the plane later crashed on the Dambush Pass. Again the pilots escaped unharmed. This time the plane could not be salvaged, though by then all necessary supplies had been air-lifted to the Col. However, some expedition members and some supplies had to arrive the conventional way, on foot along the Mayangdi Glacier.

Max Eiselin's book of the expedition is a curious read. After a long chapter on the flight to Nepal (on which he was a passenger) there are longer ones on the early flights to Dambush and the Col, the engine failure and the crash. Only in the last few pages is the climbing of the mountain mentioned, by which time the team has already reached 7,800m (25,600ft). The first ascent of Dhaulagiri was, the reader gathers, merely a sideshow in the 'Yeti' story. When Yeti crashed Eiselin's concern was not how the mountain could be climbed without it, but how soon a replacement plane could arrive. To gain any real understanding of the difficulties of the north-east ridge it is necessary to read the accounts of the climbers, published elsewhere.

Early on it was discovered that the oxygen cylinders which had been supplied were useless, being virtually empty (for no apparent reason) and so if Dhaulagiri was to be climbed it must

Rob Hall and Veikka Gustafsson high on the classic north-east ridge route, the Annapurna Himal in the distance

The east and south-east ridge of Dhaulagiri and the notorious East Dhaulagiri Glacier are seen from above Larjung in the Kali Gandaki Valley

be without supplementary oxygen. The early arrivals on the Col – Diemberger, Diener, Forrer, Schelbert and several Sherpas – forced the route upwards, though one of their earliest tasks was to stamp out a runway for Yeti when its skis sank in soft snow. The take-off along this makeshift runway was a do-or-die effort by Ernst Saxer flying alone: fail to take-off and he and the plane would disappear into a crevasse; make insufficient height in time and he would crash into seracs. Take-off was successful and represented the most courageous act of the trip.

Using fixed ropes left by the Austrians in 1959, the 1960 team established a series of camps, the top one, Camp V, at 7,450m (25,450ft) being in place by early May, proving the usefulness of Yeti in moving supplies. From the camp a summit attempt was made on 4 May, but this failed at 7,800m (25,600ft) – at the point where the south-east and north-east ridges meet – because of the usual midday break in the weather. It was clear that another camp would be needed before an attempt with any hope of success could be made. But then a storm forced a temporary halt to progress.

When the second attempt was made the attitude of the climbers showed clearly that a new era in Himalayan climbing

had begun. Gone was the altruism of the Annapurna and other early 1950s teams when success for the team was (usually) more important than that of the individual. Some summit fever had always been present, of course, better hidden or better controlled, but now it was rampant. On the north-east col Eiselin's plan for a steady push up the mountain was ignored, particularly by Kurt Diemberger (whose view of these events appears on pp.221–2 of *Summits and Secrets*). His view, according to the leader's account, was that on Broad Peak he had done all the hard work but been beaten to the summit and it was not going to happen again. Diemberger therefore climbed from the col to Camp IV in one day, together with Forrer, Schelbert and two Sherpas. The team doctor was appalled by the risks of this rapid climb, but Eiselin, faced with this minor mutiny, merely said 'oh well, it was all a question of tactics'.

The next day, with Peter Diener having joined in as well, there were nine climbers at Camp V and, in essence, no one below them on the mountain in support. Roussi, Vaucher and Weber who had already spent a night of acclimatisation there, seemed to have been of the view that they deserved first go or, failing that, then the nine could survive one night huddled together. A row broke out and after that night the three descended. This was, with hindsight, a good decision as Vaucher became ill before the three had reached Camp IV and they were forced to take him down to the col. Back at Camp V the remaining six men now climbed on carrying one two-man tent. This was pitched at 7,800 (25,600ft) and occupied, the six, unable to lie down properly, taking up various, uncomfortable positions. In the middle of the night, Diemberger – who appears in some accounts to have been responsible for the row at Camp V – and Forrer asked Sherpa Nima Dorje, who was at the entrance of the tent, to make some tea. But Nima Dorje, who had already done that earlier, took his sleeping bag and mat and went outside, spending the night in the open. The next day, 13 May, was cold but clear and windless, a perfect summit day. The six men started on three ropes. Forrer and Sherpa Nima Dorje first, then Diemberger and Sherpa Nawang Dorje, and Diener and

Schelbert last. Later Diener and Schelbert unroped as Schelbert was moving much quicker. After starting out at 8am the top was reached at 12.30, 4½ hours for about 370m (1,200ft) of climbing including one passage of Grade IV. Although the climbing world might not differentiate between the six men, it is clear from the accounts that they did: Diemberger and Schelbert reached the rocky summit (big enough for all six to stand at the same height, but merely the highest bump on a long ridge whose undulations would confuse later climbers) first and were followed almost immediately by Nawang Dorje, then Forrer and Nima Dorje, and finally Diener. After an hour the six descended. Ten days later the climb was repeated by Vaucher and Weber starting from Camp V. Diemberger thus became, with Buhl (and, technically, Gyalzen Norbu who climbed Manaslu and was in the second team to climb Makalu on the successful French expedition), the only man to be first to the top of two 8,000ers.

Alpenglow on Dhaulagiri, seen from Poon Hill. In the foreground is the mist-filled Kali Gandaki Valley

The Swiss seemed to have had little difficulty in recognising the highest point though later summiteers seemed to have been less successful. Following several incidents in which climbers were accused of not reaching the true summit but a lower point on the long summit ridge a pole was placed on the top in 1998. Unfortunately this was placed on the very point (the lower one) which had caused the original confusion and merely added to the problems.

Later Ascents

Nine years after the first ascent an American team attempted to climb Dhaulagiri's south-east ridge, approaching from the East Dhaulagiri Glacier which is very broken and avalanche prone. On 28 April while a team of six Americans and two Sherpas were bridging a huge crevasse to allow further progress an avalanche engulfed them. Only Lou Reichardt survived.

In 1970 the mountain was climbed for the second time, a Japanese team following the original route and Tetsuji Kawada and Sherpa Lhakpa Tenzing reaching the summit on 20 October, achieving the first post-monsoon ascent. The Japanese used supplementary oxygen, a few full cylinders being left on the mountain and used in 1971 by the American Tom Bech and his wife who were looking for a safer way to reach the south-east ridge team than the 'suicidal' east glacier. Using Bech's photographs, an American team arrived in the spring of 1973 to attempt the south-east ridge by climbing to it from the north-east col. The ridge was successfully reached, but proved to be narrow and difficult. Realising they had neither the time nor resources to climb it the Americans transferred their attention to the original route. On 12 May, climbing without bottled oxygen, Lou Reichardt, the sole survivor of the 1970 tragedy, reached the top with John Roskelley and Sherpa Nawang Samden.

Dhaulagiri's reputation as one of the most difficult 8,000ers, and the number of obvious, but hard, lines now meant that expeditions were an annual event. In 1975 a Japanese team made a first attempt at the south buttress at the left end of the awesome south face but abandoned the attempt when an avalanche killed two team members, two Sherpas and a local porter. (This buttress is sometimes called the south-east pillar, a confusing name as it is on the west side of the south face and is actually a buttress on the south-west ridge. It is, however, to the east of the buttress on the west face, climbed in 1988, which is usually called the south-west pillar.) The following year an Italian team attempted the north-west ridge, but failed and repeated the original line instead, two men reaching the top. Then in spring 1977 Peter Habeler and Reinhold Messner led an international team in an attempt at a direct route on the south face. The extreme avalanche risk forced them to abandon the attempt. In the autumn of the same year the Japanese again failed on the south buttress, but were finally successful in the spring of 1978, Toshiaki Kobayashi and Tatsuji Shigeno reaching the summit on 10 May . Four more team members repeated the climb on the following day. Sadly one team member died of oedema after a bad fall. Post-monsoon the same year a Japanese team climbed the south-east ridge from the East Dhaulagiri Glacier, completing the American line. Six men reached the top, but three of the team were killed in an avalanche and another in a fall.

In 1980 the Poles Wojciech Kurtyka and Ludwick Wilczynski, Briton Alex McIntyre and Frenchman René Ghilini climbed the east face in an alpine-style ascent in atrocious weather. Having reached the north-east ridge they retreated down it (using the fixed ropes of a Swiss 20-year anniversary

Dhaulagiri and its south-east ridge rise steeply over the deep Kali Gandaki Valley in this view from east-north-east near Tukuche

spring 1982 Lutgaerde Vivijs, climbing with a Belgian team on the original route, made the first female ascent of Dhaulagiri. The expedition put seven people on the summit, one of whom, Sherpa Ang Rita, was making his fourth ascent. In the post-monsoon season of the same year a Japanese team finally climbed the Pear route, the summit team of Kozu Komatsu, Yasuhira Saito and Noburu Yamada using bottled oxygen for sleeping at the top camp and also for the climb along the west ridge. Later the same year a Japanese (Hokkaido University) expedition made the first winter ascent of the peak (and the first winter ascent of any 8,000er). The summit was reached on 13 December by Akio Koizumi and Sherpa Wangdu. Climbing with oxygen on the original route the pair began their summit climb from a snow hole bivouac at 7,930m (26,000ft). Their oxygen sets ran out before the top, making the last section and the descent a real trial. Under the strict rules of winter climbing the team's arrival in October and early work on the route in November meant that the climb was technically an autumn/winter ascent, but that seems to be splitting hairs unnecessarily.

Post-monsoon 1984 saw two significant climbs, a 20-man Czech team climbing the west face (rivalling Nanga Parbat's Rupal Face as the highest mountain wall in the world) after an epic, 60-day climb. Karel Jakes, Jan Simon and Jaromir Stejskal reached the top, but Simon, who had climbed ahead of the others, and descended first, was killed on the descent. He had retrieved a summit flag left by the French pair Pierre Beghin and Jean Noel-Roche who climbed the Japanese buttress on the south face alpine style. During the 1984/85 winter a Polish team made the first official winter ascent of the peak following the original route. The summit pair was Andrzej Czok and Jerzy Kukuczka (it was the latter's seventh 8,000er).

team), but then returned 10 days later to climb that route to their high point, continuing to the summit. The Swiss team was also successful, 14 climbers reaching the top including Fritz Luchsinger (then 59 years old) who had been in the first team to climb Lhotse, and Sherpa Ang Rita who reached the summit twice, on 13 May and again on 19 May. In 1981 the Japanese climber Hironobu Kamuro made a solo ascent of the original route, though he was supported as far as the north-east col and assisted on the route by ropes fixed, and a tent left, by an earlier, successful Anglo-Canadian expedition. Nevertheless, the climb, with four bivouacs on the ascent and two on the descent, was a considerable achievement.

In October 1981 the south face was climbed alpine style by a Yugoslav team of six following a route at the right side to the south-east ridge. The climb took 16 days, including nine bivouacs on the ascent and five days on the descent, involved hard climbing on rock and ice at never less than 50°. This magnificent achievement of endurance and climbing ability was unfortunately not capped by the team reaching the summit. The descent also had its moment of pure farce. Without food, fuel and tents the team stumbled on a Japanese south-east ridge camp, their joy being shortlived as a stove exploded when they attempted to light it leaving them fuel-less again. In

In the spring of 1985 Hans Kammerlander and Reinhold Messner also followed the original route. Dhaulagiri was Messner's twelfth 8,000er, climbed just three weeks after his ascent of Annapurna. Later the same year a Czech team climbed a very hard new route on the west face in alpine style. But having reached the south-west ridge (and, therefore, explored ground) they were stopped by violent winds. Later in the year, on 8 December the Swiss Erhard Loretan, Jean Troillet and Pierre-Alain Steiner climbed the Anglo-French-Polish route in 19 hours of night/day climbing, then sat out a second night, reaching the summit the following day, a remarkable achievement.

Post monsoon in 1986 a Polish team (which included two Canadians) had a similar experience to the 1985 Czech team, climbing a very hard new line on the south face as far as the 1978 Japanese route, but being unable to continue because of bad weather. The same year a Slovenian team climbed a new line on the east face, but were also unable to reach the summit. Two years later a Czech/Italian/Russian team completed an alpine style ascent of the south-west pillar (on the west face, to the right of the Czech 1985 line, a line that had been previously attempted by a French team in 1980) which involved pitches of grade VI+ and A2 on the huge (450m/1,500ft) headwall at 7,000m (23,000ft).

Winter sunset over Dhaulagiri from near Muktinath, on the Mustang border

Dhaulagiri's summit rises beyond outlying Jirbang (6,062m/19,888ft) in this view from the south west up the Myagdi Khola near Dharapani

The pace of exploration now, perhaps inevitably, slowed, but phenomenal climbs were still accomplished. In spring 1990, climbing as a member of an international team, Krzysztof Wielicki soloed the original route on 24 April, then on 9/10 May soloed a new route on the east face to the right of the Anglo/Polish/French 1981 route. Having reached the north-east ridge Wielicki did not bother to summit again, descending the line of his earlier ascent. The following year a Kazakh team pushed a new route up the west face, claiming that with long sections at 80° it was even harder than their line on Lhotse's south face. Ten of the eleven men team reached the top. Then, in 1993, a seven-man team (six Russians and the Briton Rick Allen) climbed a very hard direct route up the north face, all seven reaching the summit on 11 May.

In 1994 the Dutchman Bart Vos failed in a winter solo bid having spent a total of 36 days either in Base Camp or above. He returned to the peak in the spring of 1995, but finding too many people on the original route, soloed a line on the east face similar to the Anglo-French-Polish route, reaching the north-east ridge at about 7,400m (24,300ft). He was unfortunately forced to retreat from a point about 50m (160ft) from the top, but returned in the autumn of 1996 and soloed another new line on the east face (similar to that of 1994) claiming to have reached the summit on 17 October, thought this claim is doubted by many experts. Also in 1996 the French climber André Georges soloed Dhaulagiri, finding the body of Albrecht Hammann who had been a member of a 1995 multi-national team on the summit. Eleven days later Georges soloed Annapurna. Two years later the leading female climber Chantal Mauduit and her Sherpa Ang Tsering died in their camp at

6,500m (21,300ft) apparently of asphyxiation after snowfall had built up on the tent (though Mauduit had head injuries, possibly from falling ice hitting the tent). Mauduit had climbed 6 8,000ers, more than any other living female climber at the time. Ironically, post-monsoon in 1999 British climber Ginette Harrison, the new claimant to the title of most 8,000ers by a living female climber was killed in an avalanche on Dhaulagiri. The post-monsoon season had been notable for its snowfall and, therefore, avalanches – Alex Lowe was killed in another on Shisha Pangma – leading many to wonder whether global warming was affecting Himalayan weather and, if so, what the longer term consequences might be for high altitude climbing.

The tragedy slightly overshadowed a phenomenal climb by the Slovene Tomz Humar. In October he attacked the centre of the formidable south face solo, quickly reaching a height of 6,800m (22,300ft). There he was stopped by a rock wall which he had little chance of soloing at speed. He therefore traversed to the south-east ridge and climbed that to about 7,700m (25,250ft) where he traversed back onto the face. He continued up the face to reach the ridge again and followed it to the north-east ridge. At that point he abandoned any thoughts of a summit attempt ('I know I will die') and climbed down the standard route. During his descent, on 24 October, he found the body of Ginette Harrison. It is rumoured that when Humar returned to Europe he was met at the airport by Reinhold Messner. If true this would have been a fitting gesture; the man whose achievements had (arguably) dominated the first 50 years of 8,000m climbing, greeting and congratulating the man whose climb had set the seal on those years and laid down a marker for the next generation.

By the end of the century Dhaulagiri had had more ascents than any peak other then Everest and the 'easy' 8,000ers Cho Oyu and Gasherbrum II, a fact apparently at odds with its reputation as a difficult peak. It seems that the combination of challenging hard faces and ridges, which will continue to attract the top climbers, and a relatively straightforward normal route, together with the peak's imposing beauty make it irresistible.

The great pyramid of Dhaulagiri from Muktinath

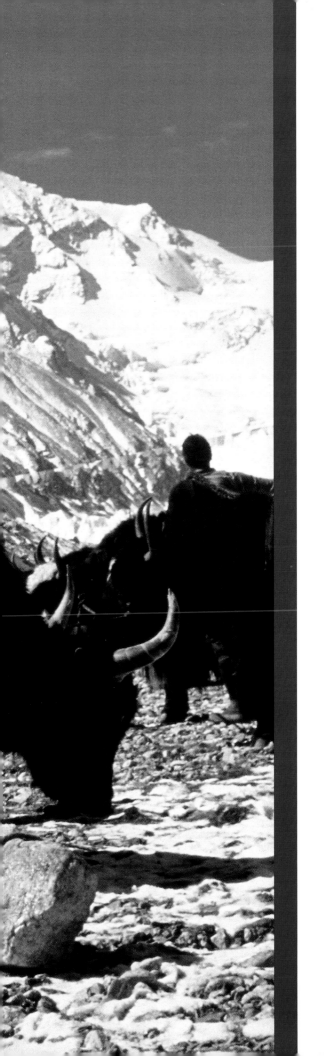

'The ridge grew increasingly narrow and sharp. The north side was powdery and steep, impractical and dangerous to traverse; the south side was steeper, vanishing immediately into a jumble of rock and sugary ice ...'

ALEX MACINTYRE on the summit ridge

shisha pangma 8,046m

shisha pangma

Peak XXIII of the Indian Survey was for many years known by the Sanskrit name Gosainthan which translates as Place of the Saint. The existence of a Sanskrit name for a peak which rises from the Tibetan plateau was, and is, something of a mystery, but is assumed to originate from the mountain's proximity to Gosainkund, a holy lake of the Hindus which lies across the border in Nepal.

The existence of a Sanskrit name for a peak which rises from the Tibetan plateau was, and is, something of a mystery, but is assumed to originate from the mountain's proximity to Gosainkund, a holy lake of the Hindus which lies across the border in Nepal. Legend has it that Shiva rammed his trident into the ground near the pass between the Helambu and Langtang valleys, the holes filling to form the sacred lakes. Gosainkund is the scene of an annual pilgrimage by the Nepalese in August (at the height of the monsoon, a trying time for such a journey) when a ritual bath in its cold waters cleanses the body and soul. It is said that water from the lake is fed by an underground channel to the ponds of the Kumbeshwar Temple in Patan (across the Bagmati River from Kathmandu), some Nepalese choosing to take their ritual bath there rather than endure the long trek to Gosainkund.

The Tibetan name for the peak is Shisha Pangma, meaning the mountain crest above the grassy plain, a very descriptive, if somewhat mundane, name. After the Chinese

occupation of Tibet (or liberation depending upon which version of history you favour) the new rulers tried to impose the apparently arbitrary name of Kaosengtsan Feng on the peak. When this failed they returned to the Tibetan name, but created a Sino-Tibetan version, Xixabangma which, they claimed, meant 'bad weather', presumably because of the weather systems attracted to the remote, solitary peak. In deference to the Chinese, who, after all, issue permits for the peak and for Everest's north side, this version is now frequently seen in the mountaineering literature.

Exploration

The exploration of Shisha Pangma has a relatively short history. In 1921 it was seen from a distance of about 45km (30 miles) by members of the British Everest reconnaissance, probably the first Europeans to view it. All subsequent visitors to this southern part of the Tibetan plateau, including later British Everest expeditions, would also have seen the peak.

In 1945 Shisha Pangma was sketched by Peter Aufschnaiter and Heinrich Harrer during their journey in Tibet after escaping from the Dehra Dun prisoner-of-war camp in which they had been interred in 1939. Then, in 1949, the British climber Bill Tilman led a small team (including Tenzing Norgay) into the Langtang Himal approaching to within 20km (12½ miles) of Shisha Pangma's west face. The following year the peak was photographed from the south-west by Dr Toni Hagen, a Swiss geologist, during an aerial survey of the Langtang and in 1951 was photographed from the east by Peter Aufschnaiter who approached to within about 10km (6 miles). In 1952 Hagen took more photographs of the peak when exploring the Langtang Himal on foot.

In 1961, with Shisha Pangma the only unclimbed 8,000er, the Chinese took an interest in the peak making a reconnaissance from the north. This first trip seems only to have concerned itself with approaches to the mountain, the first climbers to visit Shisha Pangma arriving in 1963. This party

The successful team on the summit of Shisha Pangma

studied the north side in detail, watched the weather patterns closely and made some tentative climbs, reaching a height of 7,160m (23,500ft).

First Ascent

The Chinese returned in 1964 with an expedition numbering over 200 – climbers, scientists and porters – far too many to list by name even if all the names were known.

All the climbers had spent the previous winter in a fitness camp enjoying (or enduring) a regime which involved finger pull-ups and push-ups, forced marches, underwater swimming and much else besides, the camp's message being 'more sweat in training, less pain in climbing'.

The Chinese built a track for wheeled vehicles to a height of 5,900m (19,400ft) where, to keep the vast expedition happy, a small town was built, complete with cinema. The peak was approached along the Shisha Pangma Glacier, which flows from the north face. Three camps were established on it before the team climbed onto the north ridge. They traversed the western side of a peaked section of the ridge placing Camp IV near the col between this section and the main summit. Two more camps were placed on the ridge, from the last of which (Camp VI at 7,700m/25,250ft) ten climbers set out on 2 May climbing as three roped parties and apparently without using supplementary oxygen. There was one slight mishap, Wang Fu-chou (one of the three Chinese climbers to make the first ascent of Everest from the north in 1960: this is the usual western spelling of his name, the preferred Chinese version being Wang Fuzhou) slipping on bare ice and falling 20m (65ft) before being held by his colleagues. Finally, after 4½ hours of climbing the ten men – the Chinese Chen San, Cheng Tianliang, Wang Fuzhou, Wu Zongyue, Xu Jing (the team leader) and Zhang Junyan, and the Tibetans Doje, Mima Zaxi, Sodnam Doje and Yungden – reached the small pointed summit and took their turns in standing on it: Shisha Pangma's summit is a pyramidal snowy point on the mountain's long east-west ridge.

In the immediate aftermath of the climb many western climbers were sceptical of the Chinese claim. The 1960 Everest claim, with its night arrival at the summit and bust of Chairman Mao apparently installed there, and its lack of photographs invited such scepticism and the Shisha Pangma climb followed the same pattern. Again there was a claim that a bust of Mao had been carried to the summit and the summit photographs showed no background – just climbers against a blue sky: were they on top of Shisha Pangma or in a lay-by outside Beijing? But there were photographs taken from the top and later climbs showed that these had indeed been taken either on or very

SHISHA PANGMA: ASCENT ROUTES

Above From South
A *NW Face*
1 *Chinese, 1964, the 'classic' route*

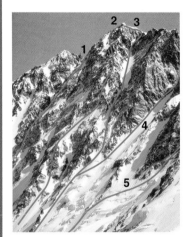

Left South-west Face
1 *Polish/Swiss (1990)*
2 *Slovenian, Kosjek/Stremfelj (1989)*
3 *British (1982)*
4 *Wielicki solo (1993)*
5 *Slovenian, Bence/Groselj (1989)*

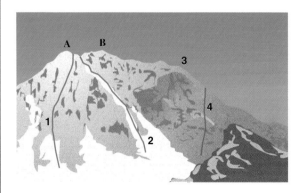

Above NW Face
A *Central Summit; the Main Summit lies behind and to the left of the Central Summit*
B *West Summit*

1 *'Esprit d'Equipe' (1990) but only to Central Summit*
2 *Hinkes/Untch (1987)*
3 *West Ridge, Polish (1987)*
4 *Lafaille (1994) but only to West Summit*

Shisha Pangma is seen from the north east above the usual Base Camp on the Tibetan plateau. Phola Gangchen (7,716m/25,315ft) rises left

close to the summit. Even then there were some who claimed, with little justification, that the Chinese had not reached the true summit but a lower point on the long ridge. Given later controversies over climbers claiming ascents of the peak when they have reached the central rather than the main summit this was understandable: those who stand on the central summit discover that a climb along a narrow, occasionally heavily corniced and dangerous, ridge is required to reach a summit just a couple of metres higher. This ridge can take several hours

to negotiate, though some have found it straightforward and climbed it quickly. However, today few doubt the veracity of the Chinese claim to have climbed to the main summit.

Later Ascents

After the Chinese climb the mountain was left alone for 16 years. Then, in 1980, the Chinese opened Tibet to foreign mountaineers. The Japanese went to Everest and a German team co-led by Manfred Abellin and Günther Sturm went to

making the first female ascent of Shisha Pangma in the company of two Chinese porters. Mrs Tabei did not use bottled oxygen. A month later Reinhold Messner and Friedl Mutschlechner also repeated the original climb, with a slight variation towards the summit. Shisha Pangma was Messner's fifth 8,000er. Messner and Mutschlechner had been members of a team which intended a direct route up the north face. When the early onset of the monsoon forced the team to abandon this attempt, the pair, climbing quickly to avoid being swamped by monsoon snow, reached the top in one long day from a bivouac at about 6,800m (22,300ft) during a brief break in the weather.

In 1982 a second route to the summit was climbed, a small British team climbing the 3,300m (10,000ft) south-west face. The ascent was made alpine style by Roger Baxter Jones, Alex McIntyre and Doug Scott with two bivouacs. The lower section of the route was over mixed ground at about 55°, the upper along a couloir of similar steepness reaching easier ground near the summit ridge. The descent was down the less steep south-east ridge and then the south-west face to the east of the ascent line. The following year saw more successes on the original line, but Fritz Luchsinger, a member of the first team to climb Lhotse and who had climbed Dhaulagiri at the age of 59, became Shisha Pangma's first victim at the age of 62, dying of pulmonary oedema.

In 1985, recognition of the relative ease of Shisha Pangma (as an 8,000er) encouraged the first commercial expedition to the peak, a successful Italian venture. At the same time all 12 members of an Austrian/German/Swiss team reached the summit. Post-monsoon in 1987 new routes were climbed on the peak. On 18 September Arthur Hajzer and Jerzy Kukuczka summitted after climbing the west ridge. Kukuczka made a partial ski descent from the top. With this ascent Kukuczka became the second man to complete the 14 8,000ers. His quest had taken nine years and on all but Lhotse he had climbed either a new line or made a first winter ascent. Also on the 18 September an international team of five (including Carlos Carsolio and Wanda Rutkiewicz) reached the top along the original route. As an aside, it is worth noting that the date of this ascent is disputed. Kukuczka claims the 18th in his book, but Wanda Rutkiewicz was adamant that it was on the 19th (though the difference is really only of academic interest). What is not in disputed is that Kukuczka, perhaps overcome by his situation, hung back from the rest as they approached the summit and was the last of the seven to reach it. A few days later the Briton Alan Hinkes and American Steve Untch climbed a new route on the north-west face, taking the central couloir. At the same time as these successes a large British team attempted the east face but decided it was too dangerous and

Shisha Pangma. On 7 May, after following the Chinese route on the north side of the peak, Michl Dacher, Wolfgang Schaffert, Sturm and Fritz Zintl reached the top, the climb being repeated by Sigi Hupfauer and Manfred Sturm five days later. In the post-monsoon period of the same year the peak was climbed again – the first post-monsoon ascent – by an Austrian team, also along the original route.

In 1981 a Japanese Women's expedition repeated the original route, Junko Tabei (the first woman to climb Everest)

instead attempted a climb along the connecting ridge between Pungpa Ri and the main summit. Luke Hughes and Steve Venables were forced to abandon the traverse at about 7,650m (25,100ft) after a miserable bivouac.

A Yugoslav (Slovene) expedition attacked the south-west face in 1989, producing two new routes. Between 17 and 19 October Pavle Kozjek and Andrej Stremfelj climbed the buttress to the left of the British route with two bivouacs,

On the first ascent of the British 1982 south-west face route

In the couloir, British 1982 south-west face route

while between 18 and 20 October Filip Bence and Viktor Groselj climbed a route that followed, for half the distance, the British descent route, reaching the south-east ridge which the pair then followed to the top. The following year, again in the post-monsoon period, the south face gained another new route. Just one week after climbing Cho Oyu, Erhard Loretan, Wojciech Kurtyka and Jean Troillet climbed the central couloir (which had been attempted by a Yugoslav pair in 1989, but not climbed after one of them contracted pneumonia). The couloir varied from 45°–50° and gave straightforward climbing. Starting during the evening of 2 October and carrying no bivouac gear the trio climbed to the summit ridge. Here Kurtyka rested, the Swiss reaching the central summit at 10am. They then descended, regaining base camp less than 24 hours after starting out. Kurtyka reached the central summit at 4pm, bivouaced during a 'pleasantly warm' night and descended next morning. Another new route was climbed in 1990 when an international team climbed the 'Esprit d'Equipe' Couloir on the north-west face (to the left of the Hinkes/Untsch route). The team – which included Hinkes, Benoît Chamoux and

After the miserable bivouac during the attempt on the Pungpa Ri to Shisha Pangma ridge

Pierre Royer reached the central summit but did not continue to the main summit.

In 1993 a Polish team, having succeeded on Cho Oyu's south-west buttress climbed the 1989 Slovene route alpine style. At the same time, one member of the team, Krzysztof Wielicki, soloed the 50° couloir to the right of the 1982 Scott route. After the climb Wielicki, who was climbing his tenth 8,000er, made an impassioned attack on people who climbed only the central summit, or those who climbed to the edge of the Cho Oyu plateau, and claimed the summit. These are not the tops he stated and should not be claimed. The problems of true summiteers were shown again in 1994 when only two climbers (one in spring, one post-monsoon) reached the main summit though many others reached the central summit. Frenchman Christophe Lafaille soloed the central summit but found it too windy to continue to the main top. Two days later he soloed a new route on the right side of the north face, reaching the west ridge and west summit. On this occasion he did not have sufficient time to continue to the main summit. The same year an attempted ski and snowboard descent failed when the skiers failed on the ascent at 7,990m (26,200ft) in the Hinkes/Untch north face route. Mark Newcomb skied down from this point.

In 1995 Erhard Loretan soloed the original route, starting at 5.30am from base camp (at 5,800m/19,000ft) and reaching the central summit at 11.30am the next day. He continued to the main summit, reaching it at about noon. Loretan was one of only three summiteers in 1995 to reach the main top. A new route was also added to the south-west face by a Spanish team. Reaching the top in thick fog they were dismayed to discover when it lifted that they were east of the main summit. There was deep snow on the ridge and they were too tired to contend with it and so descended. Then, having been somewhat shunted into the background as an easy 8,000er the mountain became headline news again in 1999 when the American Alex Lowe, widely believed to be the finest mountaineer of the time (a title he modestly eschewed) was killed on Shisha Pangma together with David Bridges. The pair were part of a team hoping to achieve the first American ski descent of an 8,000er.

With Shisha Pangma now firmly established as one of the easiest 8,000ers, and having the extra attraction of being in Tibet, the number of commercial expeditions has increased and the number of summit climbers – even allowing for the difficulty of deciding whether those who reach the central summit should be allowed to claim a 'real' ascent – is increasing. It is likely that it will soon lie fourth behind Everest, Cho Oyu and Gasherbrum II in total number. As with all the great peaks, the huge bulk of the mountain allows scope for many new routes and as the millennium closes Shisha Pangma still awaits a winter ascent.

List of Ascent Data For All 14 8,000ers

These data have been collected with the assistance of Elizabeth Hawley (the eight Nepalese peaks), Jan Kielkowski (the five Pakistani peaks and Shisha Pangma) and Xavier Eguskitza (the tables below). The early data on each peak is accurate, but the data for later years is more difficult to obtain. This is, in part, due to the climbing world as a whole being less interested in ascents of the standard routes on the peaks, so that the data is less assiduously collected at source, and the problems caused by disputed ascent claims. The latter are particularly problematic on peaks with more than one summit – the forepeak on Broad Peak, the central summit on Shisha Pangma – the lower being 'easier' to attain, or where reaching the true summit lies beyond some more easily attained point – for instance on Cho Oyu, where the true summit lies across a broad plateau. The advent of commercial expeditions to the 8000ers has added to the difficulty of collecting true ascent data as there are now many more climbers on the peaks, and there is an understandable enthusiasm for claiming a true ascent in order to justify the expenditure of time and money. Nor is this effect confined to the 'amateur' end of the market, the 'race' for the attainment of all 14 peaks and the 'hardest high-altitude climb in the world' leading to its own disputed claims because of the pressure to perform for sponsors and public opinion.

Total ascents of the 8000ers to 31/12/99

	Number of Climbers	Repetitions	Number of Ascents	Number of Ascents by Women
Cho Oyu	998	92	1,090	82 (79 women)
Everest	874	299	1,173	55 (52)
Gasherbrum II	456	12	468	43
Dhaulagiri	290	8	298	11
Broad Peak	212 (*1)	5	217	9
Manaslu	189	1	190	6
Nanga Parbat	184	2	186	9
Shisha Pangma	165 (*2)	2	167	7
K2	163	1	164	5
Gasherbrum I	161	3	164	6
Makalu	156	0	156	5
Kangchenjunga	146	7	153	1
Lhotse	128	1	129	3
Annapurna	106	3	109	5
Totals	(2,768*3)	436	4,664	247 (by a total of 170 women)

Note that apart from Cho Oyu and Everest there have been no repetitions by women.

*1 Main summit only, a further 107 climbers have reached the forepeak.
*2 Main summit only, a further 434 climbers have reached the Central summit.
*3 These data mean that 2,768 climbers have stood on the top of at least one 8000er.

Climbers with one or more 8000er ascents to 31/12/99

The number of peaks does not include personal repetitions of a particular mountain

Number of Peaks	Number of Climbers		Number of Peaks	Number of Climbers
14	6 (Messner, Kukuczka, Loretan, Carsolio, Wielicki, Oiarzabal)		7	4
			6	21
13	2 (De Stefani, Martini)		5	26
12	0		4	64
11	1 (Kammerlander)		3	150
10	13		2	408
9	7		1	2,060
8	6			

Deaths on 8000ers to 31/12/99

	Individual ascents	Deaths on descent	% of summiteers dying on descent	Total no. of deaths
K2	164	22 (*1)	13.4	49
Annapurna	109	8	7.3	55
Makalu	156	8	5.1	19
Kangchenjunga	153	7	4.6	38
Everest	1,173	40 (*2)	3.4	165
Broad Peak	218	4	1.8	18
Gasherbrum I	164	3	1.8	17
Dhaulagiri	298	5	1.7	53
Nanga Parbat	186	3	1.6	61
Manaslu	190	3	1.6	51
Lhotse	129	2	1.6	8
Shisha Pangma	167	2	1.2	19
Gasherbrum II	468	3	0.6	15
Cho Oyu	1,090	5	0.5	23
Totals	4,664	115		591

Note that deaths on Everest, K2, Kangchenjunga and Nanga Parbat include those which occurred on expeditions prior to 1950.

Deaths on descent are usually through exhaustion and falls, rarely as a result of avalanches: K2 is by far the most dangerous mountains in this regard. Deaths on ascents are often as a result of avalanches. Annapurna and Manaslu in modern times, as well as Nanga Parbat prior to 1950 are the most dangerous in this regard.

*1 Does not include the three Ukrainian climbers who died on 10 or 11/7/94. Two were found at a bivouac at 8,400m, the other had fallen, probably from around the same height. It is assumed they died while descending rather than ascending, but it is not known if they had reached the summit.
*2 Not including Mick Burke (26/9/75) and Pasang Temba (13/10/88) who probably reached the summit and died on the descent.

Annapurna ascent data

All climbs by first ascent route (North Face) except where stated.

3/6/50 M Herzog (France), L Lachenal (France); **20/5/70** H Day (Britain), G Owens (Britain); 27/5/70 D Whillans (Britain), D Haston (Britain) S Face; **13/10/77** M van Rijswick (Holland), Sonam Wolang Sherpa (Nepal); **15/10/78** I Miller (f) (US), V Komarkova (f) (US), Mingma Tshering Sherpa (Nepal), Chewang Rinzing Sherpa (Nepal); 30/4/78 Y Morin † (France), H Sigayret (France); **8/5/79** S Tanake (Japan), Pema Sherpa (Nepal); **1/5/80** G Harder (W Germany), K Staltmayr (W Germany), Ang Dorje Sherpa (Nepal); 3/5/80 K Schrag (W Germany), W Broeg (W Germany), Maila Pemba Shepa (Nepal), Ang Tsangi Shepa (Nepal); **19/10/81** K Aota (Japan), Y Yanagisawa (Japan) S Face; **4/5/82** W Bürkli † (Switzerland), T Hägler (Switzerland), Dawa Tenzing Sherpa (Nepal), W Wörgötter (Austria); **24/10/84** N Joos (Switzerland), E Loretan (Switzerland), E Ridge ascent, descent; **24/4/85** H Kammerlander (Italy), R Messner (Italy), NW Face; **21/9/86** A Giambisi (Italy), S Martini (Italy), F De Stefani (Italy); **3/2/87** A Hajzer (Poland), J Kukuczka (Poland); 8/10/87 R López (Spain), J M Maixe (Spain); 11/10/87 J C Gómez (Spain), F J Perez (Spain), Kaji Sherpa (Nepal); 20/12/87 T Kobyashi † (Japan), Y Saito † (Japan), T Saegusa (Japan), N Yamada (Japan) S Face, British (1970) route variant; **10/5/88** S Boyer (US), B Chamoux (France), N Campredon (France), S Dorotei (Italy), J Rakoncaj (Czech) S Face, British (1970) route variant; 2/10/88 J Martis (Czech), J Nezerka (Czech) NW Face; 3/10/88 P Aldai (Spain), J F Azcona (Spain); **28/10/89** L Ianakiev (Bulgaria), P Panayotov (Bulgaria), O Stoykov † (Bulgaria); **5/10/90** G Gazzola (Italy) (claim disputed); 20–1/10/90 G Denamur † (Belgium) S Face, British (1970) route; **21/10/91** B Stefko (Poland), K Wielicki (Poland) S Face, British (1970) route; 22/10/91 R Pawlowski (Poland), W Rutkiewicz (f) (Poland), R Schleypen (Germany), S Face, British (1970) route; 23/10/91 I Baeyens (f) (Belgium), M Sprutta (Poland), G Velez (Portugal) S Face, British (1970) route; 24/10/91 S Arsentiev (USSR), N Cherny (USSR); 26/10/91 V Bashkirov (USSR), S Isaev (USSR), V Obichok (USSR), N Petrov (USSR) S Face, British (1970) route; **26/4/93** Akbu (Tibet), Bianba Zaxi (Tibet), Rena (Tibet), Cering Doje (Tibet); **10/10/94** Park Jung-Hun (S Korea), Dawa Sherpa (Nepal), Ang Dawa Tamang (Nepal), Mingma Tamang (Nepal) S Face, British (1970) route variant; **29/4/95** C Carsolio (Mexico), D Karnicar (Slovenia), A Karnicar (Slovenia); 6/5/95 T Humar (Slovenia); **3/5/96** Kim Hun-Sang (S Korea), Park Young-Seok (S Korea), Kaji Sherpa (Nepal), Gyalzen Sherpa (Nepal); 15/5/96 A Georges (Switzerland); 20/10/96 A Marciniak (Poland), V Terzeoul (Ukraine) NW Ridge; 20/10/96 S Bershov (Ukraine), I Svergun (Ukraine), S Kovalev (Ukraine) S Face, British (1970) route variant; **3/5/98** Han Wang-Yong (S Korea), Ang Dawa Tamang (Nepal) (2nd), Phurba Tamang (Nepal), Arjun Tamang (Nepal), Kami Dorje (Dorchi) Sherpa (Nepal); **29/4/99** F Latorre (Spain), J Oiarzabal (Spain), J Vallejo (Spain), Um Hong-Gil (S Korea), Park Chang-Soo (S Korea), Ji Hyun-Ok † (f) (S Korea), Ang Dawa Tamang (Nepal) (3rd), Kami Dorje Sherpa † (Nepal) (2nd)

First ascents of subsidiary summits
East Summit: 29/4/74 JM Anglada (Spain), E Civis (Spain), J Pons (Spain) N Ridge. Middle Summit: 3/10/80 U Boening (Germany), L Greissl (Germany), H Oberrauch (Germany), to the E of the Dutch Rib

Everest ascent data

This list includes all climbers who have claimed they reached the summit, although there are doubts whether a few of them actually did. The questioned ascents are noted against the relevant ascent. The numbering is not necessarily the order in which climbers reached the summit, even amongst those within the same summit party. Some climbers have been to the top more than once, so the total number of mountaineers atop Everest is not indicated by the number assigned to the last person on the list. Although a person may have scaled Everest ten times, it is still counted as a single person.
All climbs by the first ascent route (Western Cwm, South Col, South-east Ridge) except where stated.

29/5/53 1 Edmund Hillary (NZ), 2 Tenzing Norgay (India); **23/5/56** 3 Jürg Marmet, 4 Ernst Schmied (Switzerland); 24/5/56 5 Adolf Reist, 6 Hansrudolf von Gunten (Switzerland); **25/5/60** 7 Wang Fu-chou (China), 8 Gonpa (China), 9 Chu Yin-hua (claim disputed) (China) N Col to N Ridge, 1st ascent from Tibetan side; **1/5/63** 10 Jim Whittaker (US), 11 Nawang Gombu Sherpa (India); 22/5/63 12 Lute Jerstad (US), 13 Barry Bishop (US); 22/5/63 14 Willi Unsoeld (US), 15 Tom Hornbein (US) W Ridge from Cwm up; SE Ridge to S Col down 1st ascent of W Ridge, 1st traverse of Everest; **20/5/65** 16 AS Cheema (India), 17 Nawang Gombu Sherpa (India) (2nd; first person to climb Everest twice); 22/5/65 18 Sonam Gyatso (India), 19 Sonam Wangyal (India); 24/5/65 20 CP Vohra (India), 21 Ang Kami Sherpa (India); 29/5/65 22 HPS Ahluwalia (India), 23 HCS Rawat, (India), 24 Phu Dorje Sherpa (Nepal); **11/5/70** 25 Teruo Matsuura (Japan), 26 Naomi Uemura (Japan); 12/5/70 27 Katsutoshi Hirabayashi (Japan), 28 Chotare Sherpa (Nepal); **5/5/73** 29 Rinaldo Carrel (Italy), 30 Mirko Minuzzo (Italy), 31 Lhakpa Tenzing Sherpa (Nepal), 32 Shambu Tamang (Nepal); 7/5/73 33 Fabrizio Innamorati (Italy), 34 Virginio Epis (Italy), 35 Claudio Benedetti (Italy), 36 Sonam Gyalgen Sherpa (Nepal); 26/10/73 37 Yasuo Kato (Japan), 38 Hisashi Ishiguro (Japan) First autumn ascent; **16/5/75** 39 Junko Tabei (f) (Japan) First woman to summit, 40 Ang Tshering Sherpa (Nepal); 27/5/75 41 Phantog (f) (China), 42 Sodnam Norbu (China), 43 Lotse (China), 44 Hou Sheng-fu (China), 45 Samdrub (China), 46 Darphuntso (China), 47 Kunga Pasang (China), 48 Tsering Tobgyal (China), 49 Ngapo Khyen (China) N Col to

(f) female climber
† died on descent

N Ridge; 24/9/75 50 Dougal Haston (UK), 51 Doug Scott (UK) SW Face First ascent of SW Face; 26/9/75 52 Peter Boardman (UK), 53 Pertemba Sherpa (Nepal) SW Face; **16/5/76** 54 John (Brummy) Stokes (UK), 55 Michael (Bronco) Lane (UK) Summit claim by Stokes and Lane is disputed; 8/10/76 56 Chris Chandler (US), 57 Bob Cormack (US); **15/9/77** 58 Ko Sang-Don (S Korea), 59 Pemba Nurbu Sherpa (Nepal); **3/5/78** 60 Wolfgang Nairz (Austria), 61 Robert Schauer (Austria), 62 Horst Bergmann (Austria), 63 Ang Phu Sherpa (Nepal); 8/5/78 64 Reinhold Messner (Italy), 65 Peter Habeler (Austria) Messner, Habeler first to summit without use of bottled oxygen; 11/5/78 66 Oswald Oelz (Austria), 67 Reinhard Karl (W Germany); 14/5/78 68 Franz Oppurg (Austria) 1st to top solo from last camp; 14/10/78 69 Hubert Hillmaier (W Germany), 70 Josef Mack (W Germany), 71 Hans Engl (W Germany) (used no oxygen); 16/10/78 72 Siegfried Hupfauer (W Germany), 73 Wilhelm Klimek (W Germany), 74 Robert Allenbach (Switzerland), 75 Wanda Rutkiewicz (f) (Poland), 76 Ang Kami Sherpa (Nepal) (not the same man as 21), 77 Ang Dorje Sherpa (Nepal) (used no oxygen), 78 Mingma Nuru Sherpa (Nepal) (used no oxygen); 17/10/78 79 Georg Ritter (W Germany), 80 Bernd Kullmann (W Germany); 15/10/78 81 Jean Afanassief (France), 82 Nicolas Jaeger (France), 83 Pierre Mazeaud (France), 84 Kurt Diemberger (Austria); **13/5/79** 85 Jernej Zaplotnik (Yugoslavia), 86 Andrej Stremfelj (Yugoslavia) W Ridge from S (from Lho La) First people to reach summit via entire length of W Ridge; 15/5/79 87 Stipe Bozic (Yugoslavia), 88 Stane Belak (Yugoslavia), 89 Ang Phu Sherpa † (Nepal) (2nd) First person to climb Everest via two routes. W Ridge; 1/10/79 90 Gerhard Schmatz (W Germany), 91 Hermann Warth (W Germany), 92 Hans Von Kaenel (Switzerland), 93 Pertemba Sherpa (Nepal) (2nd), 94 Lhakpa Gyalu (Gyalzen) Sherpa (Nepal); 2/10/79 95 Tilman Fischbach (W Germany), 96 Günther Kaempfe (W Germany), 97 Hannelore Schmatz † (f) (W Germany) (first woman to die on Everest), 98 Ray Genet † (US), 99 Nick Banks (NZ), 100 Sungdare Sherpa (Nepal), 101 Ang Phurba Sherpa (Nepal), 102 Ang Jambu Sherpa (Nepal); **17/2/80** 103 Leszek Cichy (Poland), 104 Krzysztof Wielicki (Poland) First winter ascentof any 8,000er; 3/5/80 105 Yasuo Kato (Japan) N Col to N Ridge (2nd) First person to climb north and south sides; 1st non-Sherpa to climb Everest twice; 10/5/80 106 Takashi Ozaki (Japan), 107 Tsuneo Shigehiro (Japan) N Face First ascent of N Face; 14/5/80 108 Martin Zabaleta (Spain), 109 Pasang Temba Sherpa (Nepal); 19/5/80 110 Andrzej Czok (Poland), 111 Jerzy Kukuczka (Poland) S Pillar to S Summit, SE Ridge First ascent of S Pillar; 1st time two new routes climbed in same season (and same month); 20/8/80 112 Reinhold Messner (Italy) (2nd) N Col to N Ridge to N Face. First completely solo ascent; used no oxygen; first person to climb twice with no oxygen; first summer ascent; **21/10/81** 113 Chris Kopczynski (US), 114 Sungdare Sherpa (Nepal) (2nd) S Pillar to SE Ridge; 24/10/81 115 Chris Pizzo (US), 116 Yung Tenzing Sherpa (Nepal), 117 Peter Hackett (US) S Pillar to SE Ridge; **4/5/82** 118 Vladimir Balyberdin (USSR), 119 Eduard Myslovsky (USSR), 120 Sergei Bershov (USSR), 121 Mikhail Turkevitch (USSR) Rib on SW Face to W Ridge; 5/5/82 122 Valentin Ivanov (USSR), 123 Sergei Efimov (USSR) Rib on SW Face to W Ridge; 8/5/82 124 Valeri Krichtchaty (USSR), 125 Kazbek Valiev (USSR) Rib on SW Face to W Ridge; 9/5/82 126 Valery Khomutov (USSR), 127 Vladimir Puchkov (USSR), 128 Yuri Golodov (USSR) Rib on SW Face to W Ridge; 5/10/82 129 Laurie Skreslet (Canada), 130 Sungdare Sherpa (Nepal) (3rd; first person to summit three times), 131 Lhakpa Dorje Sherpa (Nepal); 7/10/82 132 Pat Morrow (Canada), 133 Lhakpa Tshering Sherpa (Nepal), 134 Pema Dorje Sherpa (Nepal); 27/12/82 135 Yasuo Kato † (Japan) (3rd) first person to climb in three different seasons; **7/5/83** 136 Gerry Roach (US), 137 David Breashears (US), 138 Peter Jamieson (US), 139 Larry Nielson (US) (used no oxygen), 140 Ang Rita Sherpa (Nepal) (used no oxygen); 14/5/83 141 Gary Neptune (US), 142 Jim States (US), 143 Lhakpa Dorje Sherpa (Nepal) (not same man as no 131); 8/10/83 144 Louis Reichardt (US), 145 Carlos Buhler (US), 146 Kim Momb (US) E Face to SE Ridge, first ascent of E Face; 9/10/83 147 Dan Reid (US), 148 George Lowe (US), 149 Jay Cassell (US) E Face to SE Ridge; 8/10/83 150 Shomi Suzuki (Japan), 151 Haruichi Kawamura (Japan) S Pillar to SE Ridge, whole team used no oxygen; 8/10/83 152 Haruyuki Endo (Japan), 153 Hiroshi Yoshino † (Japan), 154 Hironobu Kamuro † (Japan), whole team used no oxygen; 16/12/83 155 Takashi Ozaki (Japan) (2nd), 156 Noboru Yamada (Japan), 157 Kazunari Murakami (Japan), 158 Nawang Yonden Sherpa (Nepal); **20/4/84** 159 Hristo Prodanov † (Bulgaria) (used no oxygen) W Ridge from S; 8/5/84 160 Ivan Valtchev (Bulgaria), 161 Metodi Savov (Bulgaria) W Ridge up, SE Ridge to S Col down, 1st traverse via completely different routes; 9/5/84 162 Kiril Doskov (Bulgaria), 163 Nikolay Petkov (Bulgaria) W Ridge up, SE Ridge to S Col down; 9/5/84 164 Phu Dorjee (India); 23/5/84 165 Bachendri Pal (f) (India), 166 Dorjee Lhatoo (India), 167 Sonam Palzor Sarapa (India) 168 Ang Dorje Sherpa (Nepal) (2nd, used no oxygen); 3/10/84 169 Tim Macartney-Snape (Australia) (used no oxygen), 170 Greg Mortimer (Australia) (used no oxygen) N Face; 8/10/84 171 Bart Vos (Holland) (claim disputed); 15/10/84 172 Zoltan Demjan (Czech) (used no oxygen), 173 Jozef Psotka † (Czech) (used no oxygen), 174 Ang Rita Sherpa (Nepal) (2nd, used no oxygen) S Pillar to SE Ridge up, SE Ridge to S Col down; 20/10/84 175 Phil Ershler (US) N Col to N Face to Gt Couloir; **21/4/85** 176 Chris Bonington (UK), 177 Odd Eliassen (Norway), 178 Bjorn Myrer-Lund (Norway), 179 Pertemba Sherpa (Nepal) (3rd), 180 Ang Lhakpa Sherpa (Nepal), 181 Dawa Norbu Sherpa (Nepal); 29/4/85 182 Arne Naess (Norway), 183 Stein Aasheim (Norway), 184 Ralph Hoibakk (Norway), 185 Havard Nesheim (Norway), 186 Sungdare Sherpa (Nepal) (4th; 1st person to climb 4 times), 187 Ang Rita Sherpa (Nepal) (3rd, used no oxygen), 188 Chowang Rinzing Sherpa (Nepal), 189 Pema Dorje Sherpa (Nepal) (2nd); 30/4/85 190 Richard Bass (US) (aged 55, oldest summiter so far), 191 David Breashears (US) (2nd), 192 Ang Phurba Sherpa (Nepal) (not the same man as no 101 or 337); 28/8/85 193 Oscar Cadiach (Spain), 194 Antoni Sors (Spain), 195 Carles Valles (Spain), 196 Shambu Tamang (Nepal) (2nd), 197 Ang Karma Sherpa (Nepal), 198 Narayan Shrestha (Nepal) N Col to N Ridge; 30/10/85 199 Noboru Yamada (Japan) (2nd, used no oxygen), 200 Kuniaki Yagihara (Japan), 201 Hideji Nazuka (Japan), 202 Etsuo Akutsu (Japan), 203 Satoshi Kimoto (Japan), 204 Mitsuyoshi Sato (Japan), 205 Teruo Saegusa (Japan); **20/5/86** 206 Dwayne Congdon (Canada), 207 Sharon Wood (f) (Canada) W Ridge from N; 30/8/86 208 Erhard Loretan (Switzerland), 209 Jean Troillet (Switzerland) N Face; neither man used oxygen in swift alpine-style climb; **22/12/87** 210 Heo Young-Ho (S

Korea), 211 Ang Rita Sherpa (Nepal) (4th, used no oxygen, first winter ascent without oxygen); **5/5/88** 212 Noboru Yamada (Japan) (3rd), 213 Lhakpa Nuru Sherpa (aka Ang Lhakpa) (Nepal), 214 Cerni Doji (China) N Col to N Ridge up, SE Ridge down; first N-S traverse; 5/5/88 215 Ang Phurba Sherpa (Thami) (Nepal) (2nd; not the same man as nos 101 and 337), 216 Da Cering (China), 217 Ringen Pungco (China) SE Ridge up, N Ridge-N Col down; first S-N traverse; 5/5/88 218 Susumu Nakamura (Japan), 219 Syoji Nakamura (Japan), 220 Teruo Saegusa (Japan) (2nd), 221 Munehiko Yamamoto (Japan), 222 Li Zhixin (China), 223 Lhakpa Sona Sherpa (Nepal) N Col to N Ridge; 10/5/88 224 Sungdare Sherpa (Nepal) (5th; first person to climb 5 times), 225 Padma Bahadur Tamang (Nepal); 12/5/88 226 Stephen Venables (UK) (used no oxygen), E Face to SE Ridge; 25/5/88 227 Paul Bayne (Australia), 228 Patrick Cullinan (Australia); 28/5/88 229 John Muir (Australia); 26/9/88 230 Jean Pierre Frachon (France), 231 Jean-Marc Boivin (France) (by parapente from summit to CII, 6,400m), 232 Gerard Vionnet-Fuasset (France), 233 Michel Metzger (France) (used no oxygen), 234 Andre Georges (France), 235 Pasang Tshering Sherpa (Nepal), 236 Sonam Tshering Sherpa (Nepal), 237 Ajiwa Sherpa (Nepal); 26/9/88 S 238 Kim Chang-Sun (S Korea), 239 Um Hong-Gil (S Korea), 240 Pema Dorje Sherpa (Nepal) (3rd) S Pillar to SE Ridge; 29/9/88 241 Jang Bong-Wan (S Korea), 242 Chang Byoung-Ho (S Korea), 243 Chung Seung-Kwon (S Korea) S Pillar to SE Ridge; 2/10/88 244 Nam Sun-Woo (S Korea) S Pillar to SE Ridge; 26/9/88 245 Marc Batard (France) (used no oxygen); fastest ascent to date; 29/9/88 246 Stacy Allison (f) (US), 247 Pasang Gyalzen Sherpa (Nepal); 2/10/88 248 Peggy Luce (f) (US), 249 Geoffrey Tabin (US), 250 Nima Tashi Sherpa (Nepal), 251 Phu Dorje Sherpa (Nepal), 252 Dawa Tshering Sherpa (Nepal); 13/10/88 253 Serge Koenig (France), 254 Lhakpa Sonam Sherpa † (Nepal); 14/10/88 255 Nil Bohigas (Spain), 256 Lluis Giner (Spain), 257 Jeronimo López (Spain), 258 Ang Rita Sherpa (Nepal) (5th, used no oxygen), 259 Nima Rita Sherpa (Nepal) (used no oxygen); 14/10/88 260 Lydia Bradey (f) (NZ) (used no oxygen, 1st woman to top without it) (claim disputed); 17/10/88 261 Jozef Just † (Czech) (used no oxygen) SW Face; **10/5/89** 262 Stipe Bozic (2nd) (Yugoslavia), 263 Viktor Groselj (Yugoslavia) , 264 Dimitar Ilievski † (Yugoslavia), 265 Ajiwa Sherpa (Nepal) (2nd), 266 Sonam Tshering Sherpa (Nepal) (2nd, used no oxygen); 16/5/89 267 Ricardo Torres (Mexico), 268 Phu Dorje Sherpa † (Nepal) (2nd), 269 Ang Dannu Sherpa (Nepal); 24/5/89 270 Adrian Burgess (UK), 271 Sona Dendu Sherpa (Nepal), 272 Lhakpa Nuru Sherpa (Nepal) (2nd), 273 Roddy Mackenzie (Australia); 24/5/89 274 Eugeniusz Chrobak † (Poland), 275 Andrej Marciniak (Poland) W Ridge from S via Khumbutse; 13/10/89 276 Toichiro Mitani (Japan), 277 Tchiring Thebe Lama (Nepal), 278 Chuldin Dorje Sherpa (Nepal) 279 Hiroshi Ohnishi (Japan),280 Atsushi Yamamoto (Japan); 13/10/89 281 Cho Kwang-Je (S Korea) S Pillar to SE Ridge; 13/10/89 282 Carlos Carsolio (Mexico) (used no oxygen); 23/10/89 283 Chung Sang-Yong (S Korea), 284 Nima Rita Sherpa (Nepal) (2nd), 285 Nuru Jangbu Sherpa (Nepal) W Ridge from S; **23/4/90** 286 Ang Rita Sherpa (Nepal) (6th; first person to climb 6 times, used no oxygen), 287 Pasang Norbu Sherpa (Nepal), 288 Ang Kami Sherpa (Nepal) (2nd), 289 Top Bahadur Khatri (Nepal); 7/5/90 290 Robert Link (US), 291 Steve Gall (US), 292 Sergei Arsentiev (USSR) (used no oxygen), 293 Grigory Lunjakov (USSR) (used no oxygen), 294 Daqimi (Tibet), 295 Jiabu (Tibet) N Col to N Ridge; 8/5/90 296 Edmund Viesturs (US) (used no oxygen), 297 Mistislav Gorbenko (USSR), 298 Andrei Tselinschev (USSR) (used no oxygen) N Col to N Ridge; 9/5/90 299 Ian Wade (US), 300 Daqiong (Tibet), 301 Luoze (Tibet), 302 Rena (Tibet), 303 Gui San (f) (China) N Col to N Ridge; 10/5/90 304 Ekaterina Ivanova (f) (USSR), 305 Anatoly Mochnikov (USSR) (used no oxygen), 306 Alexander Tokarev (USSR) (used no oxygen), 307 Ervand Illyinsky (USSR), 308 Mark Tucker (US), 309 Wangjia (Tibet) N Col to N Ridge; 10/5/90 310 Peter Athans (US), 311 Glenn Porzak (US), 312 Ang Jangbu Sherpa (Nepal), 313 Nima Tashi Sherpa (Nepal) (2nd), 314 Brent Manning (US), 315 Dana Coffield (US), 316 Michael Browning (US), 317 Dawa Nuru Sherpa (Nepal); 11/5/90 318 Andrew Lapkass (US); 10/5/90 319 Peter Hillary (NZ); 1st son of any summiteer to summit himself; 320 Rob Hall (NZ), 321 Gary Ball (NZ), 322 Apa Sherpa (Nepal), 323 Rudy Van Snick (Belgium); 11/5/90 324 Mikael Reutersward (Sweden), 325 Oskar Kihlborg (Sweden); 11/5/90 326 Tim Macartney-Snape (Australia) (2nd, used no oxygen); 1st person to go on foot from sea level to summit; 4/10/90 327 Alex Lowe (US), 328 Dan Culver (Canada); 5/10/90 329 Ang Temba Sherpa (Nepal), 330 Hooman Aprin (US); 331 Phinzo Sherpa (Nepal) 7/10/90; 332 Catherine Gibson (f) (US), 333 Aleksei Krasnokutsky (USSR) Gibson and Krasnokutsky 2nd married couple to top together; 4/10/90 334 Yves Salino (France); 7/10/90 335 Jean Noel Roche (France), 336 Bertrand Roche (France), 337 Nima Dorje Sherpa (Nepal), 338 Ang Phurba Sherpa (Nepal) (not same man as nos 101 and 192/215), 339 Denis Pivot (France), 340 Alain Desez (France), 341 Rene De Bos (Holland) Roches first father and son to top together; Bertrand Roche (age 17) youngest non-Nepalese to top; 5/10/90 342 Nawang Thile Sherpa (Nepal), 343 Sona Dendu Sherpa (Nepal) (2nd), 344 Erik Decamp (France), 345 Marc Batard (France) (2nd, used no oxygen), 346 Christine Janin (f) (France), 347 Pascal Tournaire (France); 6/10/90 348 Babu Tshering Sherpa (Nepal); 6/10/90 349 Pok Jin-Young (S Korea), 350 Kim Jae-Soo (S Korea), 351 Park Chang-Woo (S Korea), 352 Dawa Sange Sherpa (Nepal), 353 Pemba Dorje Sherpa (Nepal); 7/10/90 354 Lhakpa Rita Sherpa (Nepal), 355 Andrej Stremfelj (2nd), 356 Marija Stremfelj (f) (Yugosalvia) Stremfeljs first married couple to top together, 357 Janez Jeglic (Yugoslavia); **8/5/91** 358 Ang Temba Sherpa (Nepal), 359 Sona Dendu Sherpa (Nepal) (3rd), 360 Apa Sherpa (Nepal) (2nd); 8/5/91 361 Peter Athans (US) (2nd); 15/5/91 362 Mark Richey (US), 363 Yves LaForest (Canada), 364 Richard Wilcox (US), 365 Barry Rugo (US); 15/5/91 366 Eric Simonson (US), 367 Bob Sloezen (US), 368 Lhakpa Dorje Sherpa (Nepal) (2nd), 369 Ang Dawa Sherpa (Nepal), 370 George Dunn (US), 371 Andy Politz (US) N Col to N Ridge to N Face; 17/5/91 372 Mike Perry (NZ) N Col to N Ridge to N Face; 21/5/91 373 Mark Whetu (NZ), 374 Brent Okita (US) N Col to N Ridge to N Face; 24/5/91 375 Greg Wilson (US) N Col to N Ridge to N Face; 15/5/91 376 Edmund Viesturs (US) (2nd); 15/5/91 377 Mingma Norbu Sherpa (Nepal), 378 Gyalbu Sherpa (Nepal), 379 Lars Cronlund (Sweden) N Face (Hornbein and Japanese Couloirs); 17/5/91 380 Battista Bonali (Italy) (used no oxygen), 381 Leopold Sulovsky (Czech Rep) (used no oxygen) N Face (Great Couloir); 22/5/91 382 Babu Tshering (Ang Babu) Sherpa (Nepal) (2nd), 383 Chuldin Temba Sherpa (Nepal) N Col to N Ridge; 27/5/91

384 Muneo Nukita (Japan), 385 Nima Dorje Sherpa (Nepal) (2nd), 386 Phinzo Norbu Sherpa (Nepal) (not same man as 331), 387 Junichi Futagami † (Japan) N Col to N Ridge to N Face; 6/10/91 388 Jose Antonio Garces (Spain), 389 Francisco Jose Perez (Spain), 390 Antonio Ubieto (Spain), 391 Rafael Vidaurre (Spain); 7/10/91 392 Vladimir Balyberdin (USSR) (2nd, used no oxygen), 393 Anatoli Boukreev (Kazakhstan) (used no oxygen); 10/10/91 394 Roman Giutachvili (USSR), 395 Dan Mazur (US); **10/5/92** 396 Prem Singh (India), 397 Sunil Dutt Sharma (India), 398 Kanhayalal Pokhriyal (India); 12/5/92 399 Lobsang Sherpa (India), 400 Santosh Yadav (f) (India), 401 Sange Sherpa (India), 402 Wangchuk Sherpa (Nepal), 403 Mohan Singh Gunjal (India); 12/5/92 404 Ned Gillette (US), 405 Doron Erel (Israel), 406 Yick Kai Cham (Hong Kong), 407 Gary Ball (NZ) (2nd), 408 Douglas Mantle (US), 409 Rob Hall (NZ) (2nd), 410 Randall Danta (US), 411 Guy Cotter (NZ), 412 Sonam Tshering Sherpa (Nepal) (3rd), 413 Ang Dorje Sherpa (Nepal) (not same man as no 77 and 168), 414 Tashi Tshering Sherpa (Nepal), 415 Apa Sherpa (Nepal) (3rd), 416 Ang Dawa Sherpa (Nepal) (2nd), 417 Ingrid Baeyens (f) (Belgium); 12/5/92 418 Ronald Naar (Holland), 419 Edmond Oefner (Holland), 420 Nima Temba Sherpa (Nepal), 421 Dawa Tashi Sherpa (Nepal); 12/5/92 422 Alexander Gerasimov (Russia), 423 Andrei Volkov (Russia), 424 Ilia Sabelnikov (Russia), 425 Ivan Dusharin (Russia); 14/5/92 426 Sergei Penzov (Russia), 427 Vladimir Zakharov (Russia), 428 Evgueni Vinogradski (Russia), 429 Fedor Konyukhov (Russia); 12/5/92 430 Skip Horner (US), 431 Louis Bowen (US), 432 Vernon Tejas (US), 433 Dawa Temba Sherpa (Nepal), 434 Ang Gyalzen Sherpa (Nepal); 15/5/92 435 Lhakpa Rita Sherpa (Nepal) (2nd), 436 Peter Athans (US) (3rd), 437 Keith Kerr (UK), 438 Todd Burleson (US), 439 Hugh Morton (US), 440 Man Bahadur Tamang ('Gopal') (Nepal), 441 Dorje Sherpa (Nepal); 15/5/92 442 Christian Garcia-Huidobro (Chile), 443 Rodrigo Jordan (Chile), 444 Juan Sebastian Montes (Chile) E Face to; 15/5/92 445 Francisco Gan (Spain), 446 Alfonson Juez (Spain), 447 Ramon Portilla (Spain), 448 Lhakpa Nuru Sherpa (Nepal), 449 Pemba Norbu Sherpa (Nepal) S Pillar to SE Ridge; 15/5/92 450 Mauricio Purto (Chile), 451 Ang Rita Sherpa (Nepal) (7th, used no oxygen), 452 Ang Phuri Sherpa (Nepal); 15/5/92 453 Jonathan Pratt (UK); 25/9/92 454 Pitxi Eguillor (Spain), 455 Patxi Fernandez (Spain), 456 Alberto Iñurrategi (Spain), 457 Felix Iñurrategi (Spain); Iñurrategis first brothers to top together, they used no oxygen; 1/10/92 458 Josu Bereziartua (Spain); 3/10/92 459 Juan Tomas (Spain), 460 Mikel Reparaz (Spain), 461 Pedro Tous (Spain); 28/9/92 462 Giuseppe Petigaz (Italy), 463 Lorenzo Mazzoleni (Italy), 464 Mario Panzeri (Italy) (used no oxygen), 465 Pierre Royer (France), 466 Lhakpa Nuru Sherpa (Nepal) (2nd); 29/9/92 467 Benoit Chamoux (France), 468 Oswald Santin (Italy); 30/9/92 469 Abele Blanc (Italy), 470 Giampietro Verza (Italy); 1/10/92 471 Eugene Berger (Luxembourg); 4/10/92 472 Ralf Dujmovits (Germany), 473 Sonam Tshering Sherpa (Nepal) (4th); 7/10/92 474 Michel Vincent (France); 9/10/92 475 Scott Darsney (US); 9/10/92 476 'Poncho' de la Parra (Mexico), 477 Wally Berg (US), 478 Augusto Ortega Peru, 479 Kaji Sherpa (Nepal), 480 Apa Sherpa (Nepal) (4th); 9/10/92 481 Philippe Grenier (France), 482 Michel Pelle (France), 483 Thierry Defrance (France), 484 Alain Roussey (France), 485 Pierre Aubertin (France); **13/4/93** 486 Heo Young-Ho (S Korea) (2nd), 487 Ngati Sherpa (Nepal) N Col to N Ridge up, SE Ridge to S Col down; 22/4/93 488 Dawa Tashi Sherpa (Nepal) (2nd), 489 Pasang Lhamu Sherpa † (f) (Nepal), 490 Pemba Nuru Sherpa (Pemba Norbu) (Nepal) (2nd), 491 Sonam Tshering Sherpa † (Nepal) (5th), 492 Lhakpa Nuru Sherpa (Nepal) (3rd), 493 Nawang Thile Sherpa (Nepal) (2nd); 5/5/93 494 Ji Mi (China), 495 Jia Chuo (China), 496 Kai Zhong (China), 497 Pu Bu (China), 498 Wang Yong Feng (China), 499 Wu Chin Hsiung (Taiwan) N Col to N Ridge; 10/5/93 500 Alex Lowe (US) (2nd), 501 John Helenek (US), 502 John Dufficy (US), 503 Wally Berg (US) (2nd), 504 Michael Sutton (Canada), 505 Apa Sherpa (Nepal) (5th), 506 Dawa Nuru Sherpa (Nepal) (2nd), 507 Chuldin Temba Sherpa (Nepal) (2nd) S Col to SE Ridge; 10/5/93 508 Kim Soon-Joo (f) (S Korea), 509 Ji Hyun-Ok (f) (S Korea), 510 Choi Oh-Soon (f) (S Korea), 511 Ang Dawa Sherpa (Nepal) (3rd), 512 Ang Tshering Sherpa (Nepal), 513 Sona Dendu Sherpa (Nepal) (4th), 514 Rinzin Sherpa (Nepal); 10/5/93 515 Michael Groom (Australia) (used no oxygen), 516 Lobsang Tshering Bhutia † (India); 10/5/93 517 Harry Taylor (UK) (used no oxygen during ascent); 17/5/93 518 Rebecca Stephens (f) (UK), 519 Ang Pasang Sherpa (Nepal), 520 Kami Tshering Sherpa (Nepal); 10/5/93 521 Dicky Dolma (f) (India), 522 Santosh Yadav (f) (India) (2nd; first woman to climb twice), 523 Kunga Bhutia (f) (India), 524 Baldev Kunwer (India), 525 Ongda Chhiring Sherpa (Nepal), 526 Na Temba Sherpa (Nepal), 527 Kusang Dorjee Sherpa (India), 528 Dorje Sherpa (Nepal) (2nd); 16/5/93 529 Radha Devi Thakur (f) (India), 530 Rajiv Sharma (India), 531 Deepu Sharma (f) (India), 532 Savita Martolia (f) (India), 533 Nima Norbu Dolma (India), 534 Suman Kutiyal (f) (India), 535 Nima Dorje Sherpa (Nepal) (3rd), 536 Tenzing Sherpa (Nepal), 537 Lobsang Jangbu Sherpa (Nepal), 538 Nga Temba Sherpa (Nepal); 10/5/93 539 Mary (Dolly) Lefever (f) (US), 540 Mark Selland (US), 541 Charles Armatys (US), 542 Pemba Temba Sherpa (Nepal), 543 Moti Lal Gurung (Nepal), 544 Michael Sinclair (US) 16/5/93, 545 Mark Rabold (US), 546 Phinzo Sherpa (Nepal) (2nd), 547 Dorje Sherpa (Nepal), 548 Durga Tamang (Nepal); 10/5/93 549 Veikka Gustafsson (Finland), 550 Jan Arnold (f) (NZ), 551 Rob Hall (NZ) (3rd), 552 Jonathan Gluckman (NZ), 553 Ang Chumbi Sherpa (Nepal), 554 Ang Dorje Sherpa (Nepal) (2nd), 555 Norbu (Nuru) Sherpa (Nepal); 10/5/93 556 Vladas Vitkauskas (Lithuania); 10/5/93 557 Alexei Mouravlev (Russia); 15/5/93 558 Vladimir Janochkine (Russia); 16/5/93 559 Vladimir Bashkirov (Russia) (used no oxygen); 17/5/93 560 Vladimir Koroteev (Russia); 16/5/93 561 Josep Pujante (Spain), 562 Ang Phurba Sherpa (Nepal) (3rd); 17/5/93 563 Oscar Cadiach (Spain) (2nd, used no oxygen); 16/5/93 564 Joxe Maria Onate (Spain), 565 Alberto Cerain (Spain), 566 Jose Ramon Aguirre (Spain), 567 Jangbu Sherpa (Nepal), 568 Ang Rita Sherpa (Nepal) (8th, used no oxygen); 16/5/93 569 Jan Harris (US), 570 Keith Brown (US); 16/5/93 571 Park Young-Seok (S Korea), 572 An Jin-Seob † (S Korea), 573 Kim Tae-Kon (S Korea), 574 Kazi Sherpa (Nepal) (2nd); 27/5/93 575 Dawson Stelfox (Ireland/UK) N Col to N Ridge; 6/10/93 576 Park Hyun-Jae (S Korea), 577 Panuru Sherpa (Nepal) N Col to N Ridge; 6/10/93 578 Francois Bernard (France), 579 Antoine Cayrol (France), 580 Eric Gramond (France) (used no oxygen), 581 Gyalbu Sherpa (Nepal) (2nd), 582 Dawa Tashi Sherpa (Nepal) (3rd); 9/10/93 583 Alain Esteve (France), 584 Hubert Giot (France) (used no oxygen), 585 Norbu (Nuru) Sherpa (Nepal) (2nd), 586 Nima Gombu Sherpa (Nepal); 7/10/93

587 Juanito Oiarzabal (Spain), 588 Ongda Chhiring Sherpa (Nepal) (2nd) S Pillar; 7/10/93 589 Ginette Harrison (f) (UK), 590 Gary Pfisterer (US) (Spain), 591 Ramon Blanco (Spain) (age 60, oldest summiter so far), 592 Graham Hoyland (UK), 593 Stephen Bell (UK), 594 Scott McIvor (UK), 595 Na Temba Sherpa (Nepal) (2nd), 596 Pasang Kami Sherpa (Nepal), 597 Dorje Sherpa (Nepal) (3rd); 9/10/93 598 Martin Barnicott (UK), 599 David Hempleman-Adams (UK), 600 Lee Nobmann (US), 601 Tenzing Sherpa (Nepal) (2nd), 602 Nga Temba Sherpa (Nepal) (2nd), 603 Lhakpa Gelu Sherpa (Nepal), 604 Ang Pasang Sherpa (Nepal); 9/10/93 605 Maciej Berbeka (Poland), 606 Lhakpa Nuru Sherpa (Nepal) (4th; first person to climb by three different routes) N Col to N Face; 10/10/93 607 Jonathan Tinker (UK), 608 Babu Tshering Sherpa (Nepal) (3rd) N Col to N Face; 18/12/93 609 Hideji Nazuka (Japan) (2nd), 610 Fumiaki Goto (Japan) SW Face; first winter ascent of SW Face; 20/12/93 611 Osamu Tanabe (Japan), 612 Sinsuke Ezuka (Japan) SW Face; 22/12/93 613 Yoshio Ogata (Japan), 614 Ryushi Hoshino (Japan) SW Face; **8/5/94** 615 Kiyohiko Suzuki (Japan) S Pillar; 616 Wataru Atsuta (Japan), 617 Nima Dorje Sherpa (Nepal) (4th), 618 Dawa Tshering Sherpa (Nepal), 619 Na Temba Sherpa (Nepal) (3rd), 620 Lhakpa Nuru Sherpa (Nepal) (5th) S Pillar; 13/5/94 621 Tomiyasu Ishikawa (Japan), 622 Nima Temba Sherpa (Nepal), 623 Dawa Tashi Sherpa (Nepal) (4th), 624 Pasang Tshering Sherpa (Nepal) (2nd) S Pillar; 8/5/94 625 Shih Fang-Fang † (Taiwan) N Col to N Face; 9/5/94 626 Lobsang Jangbu Sherpa (Nepal) (2nd, used no oxygen), 627 Rob Hess (US) (used no oxygen), 628 Scott Fischer (US) (used no oxygen), 629 Brent Bishop (US); 630 Sona Dendu Sherpa (Nepal) (5th); 13/5/94 631 Steven Goryl (US); 9/5/94 632 Ang Dorje Sherpa (Nepal) (3rd), 633 Hall Wendel (US), 634 Helmut Seitzel (Germany), 635 David Keaton (US), 636 Ekke Gundelach (Germany), 637 Rob Hall (NZ) (4th), 638 Ed Viesturs (US) (3rd), 639 Nima Gombu Sherpa (Nepal) (2nd), 640 Norbu (Nuru) Sherpa (Nepal) (3rd), 641 David Taylor (US), 642 Erling Kagge (Norway); 13/5/94 643 Lhakpa Rita Sherpa (Nepal) (3rd), 644 Chuwang Nima Sherpa (Nepal), 645 Man Bahadur Tamang (Nepal) (2nd), 646 Kami Rita Sherpa (Nepal), 647 Dorje Sherpa (Nepal) (4th), 648 Ryszard Pawlowski (Poland), 649 Robert Cedergreen (US), 650 Paul Morrow (US), 651 Peter Athans (US) (4th), 652 Todd Burleson (US) (2nd); 19/5/94 653 David Hahn (US) N Col to N Ridge; 25/5/94 654 Steve Swenson (US) (used no oxygen) N Col to N Ridge; 26/5/94 655 Mark Whetu (NZ) (2nd), 656 Michael Rheinberger † (Australia) N Col to N Ridge; 31/5/94 657 Bob Sloezen (US) (2nd) N Col to N Ridge; 10/10/94 658 Muneo Nukita (Japan) (2nd), 659 Apa Sherpa (Nepal) (6th), 660 Chuwang Nima Sherpa (Nepal) (2nd), 661 Dawa Tshering Sherpa (Nepal); 11/10/94 662 Charlie Hornsby (UK), 663 Roddy Kirkwood (UK), 664 Dorje Sherpa (Nepal) (5th), 665 Dawa Temba Sherpa (Nepal) (2nd); **7/5/95** 666 Lobsang Jangbu Sherpa (Nepal) (3rd, used no oxygen); 11/5/95 667 Kiyoshi Furuno (Japan), 668 Shigeki Imoto (Japan), 669 Dawa Tshering Sherpa (Nepal) (2nd), 670 Pasang Kami Sherpa (Nepal) (2nd), 671 Lhakpa Nuru Sherpa (Karikhola) (Nepal) (6th; with Nima Dorje Sherpa (no672), first person to climb by 4 different routes), 672 Nima Dorje Sherpa (Nepal) (5th; see no 671) NE Ridge; first ascent of NE Ridge; 11/5/95 673 Vladimir Shataev (Russia), 674 Iria Projaev (Russia), 675 Fedor Shuljev (Russia) N Col to N Ridge; 13/5/95 676 Kazbek Khamitsatev (N Ossetia) (Russia), 677 Evgueni Vinogradski (Russia) (2nd), 678 Sergei Bogomolov (Russia), 679 Vladimir Korenkov (Russia), 680 Ang Rita Sherpa (Nepal) (9th, used no oxygen) N Col to N Ridge; 12/5/95 681 Piotr Pustelnik (Poland) N Col to N Ridge; 13/5/95 682 Marco Bianchi (Italy) (used no oxygen), 683 Christian Kuntner (Italy) (used no oxygen) N Col to N Ridge; 12/5/95 684 Ryszard Pawlowski (Poland) (2nd) N Col to N Ridge; 14/5/95 685 Mozart Catao (Brazil), 686 Waldemar Niclevicz (Brazil) N Col to N Ridge; 17/5/95 687 Graham Ratcliffe (UK), 688 Anatoli Boukreev (Kazakhstan) (2nd, used no oxygen), 689 Nikoli Sitnikov (Russia) N Col to N Ridge; 23/5/95 690 Michael Jorgensen (Denmark), 691 Crag Jones (UK) N Col to N Ridge; 12/5/95 692 Cheng Kuo-Chun (Taiwan), 693 Chiang Hsui-Chen (f) (Taiwan), 694 Mingma Tshering Sherpa (Nepal), 695 Lhakpa Dorje Sherpa (Nepal) (used no oxygen), 696 Tenzing Nuru Sherpa (Nepal) N Col to N Ridge; 13/5/95 697 Alison Hargreaves (f) (UK) (first woman to top in unsupported climb, used no oxygen) N Col to N Ridge; 17/5/95 698 Constantin Lacatusu (Romania) N Col to N Ridge; 26/5/95 699 Greg Child (Australia), 700 Karsang Sherpa (Nepal), 701 Lobsang Temba Sherpa (Nepal) N Col to N Ridge; 14/5/95 702 Reinhard Patscheider (Italy) (used no oxygen), 703 Teodors Kirsis (Latvia), 704 Imants Zauls (Latvia) N Col to N Ridge; 14/5/95 705 George Mallory (Australia), 706 Jeffrey Hall (US), 707 Jim Litch (US), 708 Dan Aguillar (US), 709 Kaji Sherpa (Nepal) (3rd), 710 Ongda Chhiring Sherpa (Nepal) (3rd), 711 Wangchu Sherpa (Nepal) N Col to N Ridge; 16/5/95 712 Colin Lynch (US), 713 Jay Budnik (US), 714 Steve Reneker (US), 715 Kurt Wedberg (US), 716 Phinzo Sherpa (Nepal) (3rd), 717 Jangbu Sherpa (Nepal) N Col to N Ridge; 14/5/95 718 Luc Jourjon (France), 719 Babu Tshering Sherpa (Nepal) (4th) N Col to N Ridge; 17/5/95 720 George Kotov (Russia), 721 Ali Nasuh Mahruki (Turkey) N Col to N Ridge; 24/5/95 722 Jeff Shea (US), 723 Lhakpa Gelu Sherpa (Nepal) (2nd), 724 Tshering Dorje Sherpa (Nepal) N Col to N Ridge; 26/5/95 725 Patrick Hache (France), 726 Robert Hempstead (US), 727 Lama Jangbu Sherpa (Nepal), 728 Babu Tshering Sherpa (Nepal) (5th, first person to make 2 ascents in same season) N Col to N Ridge; 27/5/95 729 Michael Smith (UK), 730 Patrick Falvey Ireland, 731 James Allen (Australia) N Col to N Ridge; 14/5/95 732 Josef Hinding (Austria) (used no oxygen) N Col to N Ridge; 15/5/95 733 Brad Bull (US), 734 Tommy Heinrich (Argentina), 735 Apa Sherpa (Nepal) (7th), 736 Arita Sherpa (Nepal), 737 Nima Rita Sherpa (Nepal) (3rd); 16/5/95 738 Tony Tonsing (US), 739 Musal Kazi Tamang (Nepal) N Col to N Ridge; 14/10/95 740 Jo Yong-Il (S Korea), 741 Zangbu Sherpa † (Nepal) N Col to N Ridge; 742 14/10/95 42 Han Wuang-Yong (S Korea), 743 Hong Sung-Taek (S Korea), 744 Tashi Tshering Sherpa (Nepal) (2nd) N Col to N Ridge; 14/10/95 745 Park Jung-Hun (S Korea), 746 Kim Young-Tae (S Korea), 747 Keepa (Kipa) Sherpa (Nepal), 748 Dawa Tamang (Nepal) SW Face; **10/5/96** 749 Anatoli Boukreev (Kazakhstan) (3rd); 750 Neil Beidleman (US), 751 Martin Adams (US), 752 Klev Schoening (US), 753 Charlotte Fox (f) (US), 754 Tim Madsen (US), 755 Sandy Hill Pittman (f) (US), 756 Scott Fischer † (US) (2nd), 757 Lena Nielsen-Gammelgaard (f) (Denmark), 758 Lobsang Jangbu Sherpa (Nepal) (4th, used no oxygen), 759 Nawang Dorje Sherpa (Nepal), 760 Tenzing Sherpa (Nepal) (3rd), 761 Tashi Tshering Sherpa (Nepal) (3rd); 10/5/96 762 Jon Krakauer (US), 763 Andrew Harris † (NZ) (Japan), 764 Michael Groom (Australia) (2nd), 765 Rob Hall † (NZ) (5th), 766 Yasuo

Namba † (f) (Japan), 767 Douglas Hansen † (US), 768 Ang Dorje (Chuldim) Sherpa (Nepal) (4th), 769 Norbu Sherpa (Nepal) (4th); 10/5/96 770 Gau Ming-Ho (Taiwan), 771 Nima Gombu Sherpa (Nepal) (3rd), 772 Mingma Tshering Sherpa (Nepal) (2nd); 10/5/96 773 Tsewang Smanla † (India), 774 Tsewang Paljor † (India), 775 Dorje Morup † (India) (claim disputed) N Col to N Face; 17/5/96 776 Sange Sherpa (India) (2nd), 777 Hira Ram (India), 778 Tashi Ram (India), 779 Nadra Ram (India), 780 Kusang Dorjee Sherpa (India) (2nd) N Col to N Face; 11/5/96 781 Hiroshi Hanada (Japan), 782 Eisuka Shigekawa (Japan), 783 Pasang Tshering Sherpa (Nepal) (3rd), 784 Pasang Kami Sherpa (Nepal) (3rd), 785 Ang Gyalzen Sherpa (Nepal) N Col to N Face; 13/5/96 786 Mamoru Kikuchi (Japan), 787 Hirotaka Sugiyama (Japan), 788 Nima Dorje Sherpa (Nepal) (6th), 789 Chuwang Nima Sherpa (Nepal) (3rd), 790 Dawa Tshering Sherpa (Thami) (Nepal) (2nd) N Col to N Face; 17/5/96 791 Hirotaka Takeyuchi (Japan), 792 Pemba Tshering Sherpa (Nepal), 793 Na Temba Sherpa (Nepal) (4th) N Col to N Face; 21/5/96 794 Koji Yamazaki (Japan) N Col to N Face; 17/5/96 795 Sven Gangdal (Norway), 796 Olav Ulvund (Norway), 797 Dawa Tashi Sherpa (Nepal) (5th), 798 Dawa Tshering Sherpa (Beding) (Nepal) (3rd) N Col to N Face; 18/5/96 799 Morten Rostrup (Norway), 800 Josef Nezerka (Czech Rep), 801 Fausto De Stefani (Italy), 802 Gyalbu Sherpa (Nepal) (3rd) N Col to N Face; 19/5/96 803 Alan Hinkes (UK), 804 Matthew Dickinson (UK), 805 Lhakpa Gelu Sherpa (Nepal) (3rd), 806 Mingma Dorje Sherpa (Nepal), 807 Phur Gyalzen Sherpa (Nepal) N Col to N Face; 20/5/96 808 Petr Kouznetsov (Russia), 809 Valeri Kohanov (Russia), 810 Grigori Semikolenkov (Russia) couloir between N and NE Ridges; 23/5/96 811 Thierry Renard (France), 812 Babu Tshering Sherpa (Nepal) (6th, used no oxygen), 813 Dawa Sherpa (Nepal); 23/5/96 814 Ed Viesturs (US) (4th, used no oxygen), 815 David Breashears (US) (3rd), 816 Robert Schauer (Austria) (2nd), 817 Jamling Tenzing Norgay Sherpa (India) (son of Tenzing Norgay), 818 Araceli Segarra (f) (Spain), 819 Lhkapa Dorje Sherpa (Nepal) (2nd, used no oxygen), 820 Dorje Sherpa (Nepal), 821 Jangbu Sherpa (Nepal) (2nd), 822 Muktu Lhakpa Sherpa (Nepal), 823 Thilen Sherpa (Nepal); 23/5/96 824 Goren Kropp (Sweden) (used no oxygen), 825 Ang Rita Sherpa (Nepal) (10th, used no oxygen) S Pillar to S Col; 23/5/96 826 Jesus Martinez (Spain) (used no oxygen) S Pillar to S Col; 24/5/96 827 Hans Kammaerlander (Italy) (used no oxygen) N Col to N Face; 235 hrs base-summit-base; descended most of route by ski; 24/5/96 828 Yuri Contreras (Mexico), 829 Hector Ponce de Leon (Mexico) N Col to N face; 25/5/96 830 Ian Woodall (S Africa), 831 Cathy O'Dowd (f) (S Africa), 832 Bruce Herrod † (UK), 833 Pemba Tenji Sherpa (Nepal), 834 Ang Dorje Sherpa (Nepal), 835 Lama Jangbu (Nepal) (2nd); 26/9/96 836 Clara Sumarwati (f) (Indonesia) (claim disputed), 837 Kaji Sherpa (Nepal) (4th), 838 Gyalzen Sherpa (Nepal), 839 Ang Gyalzen Sherpa (Nepal) (2nd), 840 Dawa Tshering Sherpa (Nepal) (3rd), 841 Chuwang Nima Sherpa (Nepal) (4th) N Col to N face; 11/10/96 842 Choi Jong-Tai (S Korea), 843 Shin Kwang-Chal (S Korea), 844 Panuru Sherpa (Nepal) (4th), 845 Keepa (Kipa) Sherpa (Nepal) (2nd), 846 Dawa Tamang (Nepal) (2nd); **26/4/97** 847 Apa Sherpa (Nepal) (8th), 848 Anatoli Boukreev (Kazakhstan) (4th), 849 Dawa Nuru Sherpa (Nepal), 850 Vladimir Bashkirov (Russia) (2nd), 851 Asmujiono (Indonesia); 2/5/97 852 Vladimir Frolov (Kazakhstan), 853 Andrej Molotov (Kazakhstan), 854 Sergei Ovsharenko (Kazakhstan), 855 Vladimir Souviga Kazakh (Kazakhstan) (used no oxygen) N Col to N Face; 7/5/97 856 Ivan Plotnikov † (Russia), 857 Nikolai Chevtchenko † (Russia) N Col to N Face; 20/5/97 858 Konstantin Farafonov (Kazakhstan), 859 Sergei Lavrov (Kazakhstan), 860 Dmitri Grekov (Kazakhstan), 861 Dmitri Sobolev (Kazakhstan), 862 Dmitri Mouravev (Kazakhstan), 863 Lyudmila Savina (f) (Kazakhstan) N Col to N Face; 22/5/97 864 Andy Evans (Canada) N Col to N Face; 7/5/97 865 Lee In (S Korea), 866 (Ang) Dawa Tamang (Nepal) (3rd) N Col to N Face; 8/5/97 867 Antoine de Choudens (France) (used no oxygen), 868 Stephane Cagnin (France) N Col to N Face; 20/5/97 869 Doytchin Vassilev (Bulgaria) N Col to N Face; 21/5/97 870 Nikola Kekus (UK), 871 Bjorn Olafsson (Iceland), 872 Hallgrimur Magnusson (Iceland), 873 Einar Stefansson (Iceland), 874 Babu Tshering Sherpa (Nepal) (7th), 875 Dawa Sherpa (Nepal) (2nd); 23/5/97 876 Mark Warham (UK, 877 Eric Blakeley (UK), 878 Hugo Rodriguez (Mexico), 879 Lhakpa Gelu Sherpa (Nepal) (4th), 880 Da Tenzi Sherpa (Nepal); 21/5/97 881 Danuri Sherpa (Nepal); 22/5/97 882 Franc Pepevnik (Slovenia) N Col to N Face; 23/5/97 883 Pavle Kozjek (Slovenia) (used no oxygen) N Col to N Face; 23/5/97 884 David Breashears (US) (4th), 885 Peter Athans (US) (5th), 886 Jangbu Sherpa (Nepal) (3rd), 887 Dorje Sherpa (Nepal) (2nd), 888 Kami Sherpa (Nepal); 23/5/97 889 Jamie Clarke (Canada), 890 Alan Hobson (Canada), 891 Lhakpa Tshering Sherpa (Nepal) (2nd), 892 Gyalbu Sherpa (Nepal) (4th), 893 Tashi Tshering Sherpa (Nepal) (4th), 894 Kami Tshering Sherpa (Nepal) (2nd); 23/5/97 895 Guy Cotter (NZ) (2nd), 896 Ed Viesturs (US) (5th), 897 Tashi Tenzing (Australia) (first grandson of any summiter), 898 Veikka Gustafsson (Finland) (2nd, used no oxygen), 899 David Carter (US), 900 Ang Dorje Sherpa (Nepal) (5th), 901 Mingma Tshering Sherpa (Nepal) (3rd); 23/5/97 902 Mohandas Nagapan (Malaysia), 903 Magendran Munisamy (Malaysia), 904 Na Temba Sherpa (Nepal) (5th), 905 Dawa Temba Sherpa (Nepal) (3rd), 906 Gyalzen Sherpa (Nepal) (2nd), 907 Ang Phuri Gyalzen Sherpa (Nepal), 908 Fura Dorje Sherpa (Nepal); 23/5/97 909 Andres Delgado Mexico (UK), 910 Tenzing Sherpa (Nepal) (4th); 27/5/97 911 Brigitte Muir (f) (Australia), 912 Kipa Sherpa (Nepal) (3rd), 913 Dorje Sherpa (Nepal) (6th); 24/5/97 914 Alexandre Zelinski (Russia), 915 Sergei Sokolov (Russia) N Col to N Face; 25/5/97 916 Wally Berg (US) (3rd), 917 Kami Rita Sherpa (Nepal) (2nd), 918 Ang Pasang Sherpa (Nepal) (2nd), 919 Pemba Tenji Sherpa (Nepal) (2nd), 920 Mingma Tshering Sherpa (Nepal), 921 Lhakpa Rita Sherpa (Nepal) (4th), 922 Nima Tashi Sherpa (Nepal) (3rd), 923 Tenzing Nuru Sherpa † (Nepal) (2nd); 27/5/97 924 Yuri Contreras (Mexico) (2nd), 925 Ilgvars Pauls (Latvia), 926 Dawa Sona Sherpa (Nepal); 29/5/97 927 Russell Brice (NZ), 928 Richard Price (NZ) N Col to N Face; 29/5/97 929 Daqimi (China) (Tibet), 930 Tenzing Dorje (China), 931 Kai Zhong (China) (2nd) N Col to N Face; **18/5/98** 932 Shoji Abe (Japan), 933 Toshiya Nakajima (Japan), 934 Pasang Kami Sherpa (Nepal) (4th), 935 Na Temba Sherpa (Nepal) (6th), 936 Ang Gyalzen Sherpa (Nepal) (3rd) N Col to N Face; 19/5/98 937 Hitoshi Onodera (Japan), 938 Hiromichi Kamimura (Japan), 939 Chuwang Nima Sherpa (Nepal) (5th), 940 Dawa Tshering Sherpa (Nepal) (4th) N Col to N Face; 18/5/98 941 Surendra Chavan (India), 942 Dawa Tashi Sherpa (Nepal) (6th), 943 Dawa Nuru Sherpa (Nepal) (2nd), 944 Thomting Sherpa (Nepal), 945 Nawang Tenzing Sherpa (Nepal) N Col to N Face; 19/5/98 946

Loveraj Dharmshaktu (India), 947 Phinzo Norbu Sherpa (Nepal) (2nd), 948 Nima Gyalzen Sherpa (Nepal) N Col to N Face; 18/5/98 949 Hidetoshi Kurahashi (Japan), 950 Masaru Sato (Japan), 951 Koichi Nagata (Japan), 952 Hisashi Hashimoto (Japan), 953 Shoji Sakamoto (Japan), 954 Ang Mingma Sherpa (Nepal) N Col to N Face; 20/5/98 955 Toshiaki Yano (Japan), 956 Yoshinori Kawahara (Japan), 957 Gyalzen Sherpa (Nepal) (3rd) N Col to N Face; 22/5/98 958 Kazuyoshi Kondo (Japan), 959 Dawa Sherpa (Nepal) N Col to N Face; 18/5/98 960 Alexei Bolotov (Russia), 961 Valeri Perchine (Russia), 962 Sergei Timofeev (Russia), 963 Yevgeni Vinogradski (Russia) (3rd) N Col to N Face; 21/5/98 964 Anatoly Mochnikov (Russia) (2nd, used no oxygen), 965 Gilles Roman (France); 22/5/98 966 Francys Arsentiev † (f) (US) (used no oxygen), 967 Sergei Arsentiev † (Russia) (2nd, used no oxygen) N Col to N Face; 18/5/98 968 Victor Koulbatchenko (Belorussia), N Col to N Face; 19/5/98 969 Peter Hamor (Slovakia), 970 Vladimir Zboja (Slovakia), 971 Vladimir Plulik Slovakia (used no oxygen) N Col to N Face; 24/5/98 972 Ci Luo (China) N Col to N Face; 19/5/98 973 Noriyuki Muraguchi (Japan), 974 Minoru Sawada (Japan), 975 Mingma Tshering Sherpa (Nepal) (4th), 976 Tshering Dorje Sherpa (Nepal), 977 Pasang Kitar Sherpa (Nepal) N Col to N Face; 19/5/98 978 Radek Jaros (Czech Rep) (used no oxygen), 979 Vladimir Nosek (Czech Rep) (used no oxygen) N Col to N Face; 20/5/98 980 Bob Hoffman (US), 981 Donald Beavon (US), 982 Pasquale Scaturro (US), 983 Charles Demarest (US), 984 Mark Cole (US), 985 Apa Sherpa (Nepal) (9th), 986 Pemba Norbu Sherpa (Nepal), 987 Nima Rita Sherpa (Nepal) (4th), 988 Gyalzen Sherpa (Nepal), 989 Chuldim Nuru Sherpa (Nepal), 990 Ang Pasang Sherpa (Nepal), 991 Arita Sherpa (Nepal) (2nd); 20/5/98 992 Jalal Cheshmeh Ghasabani (Iran); 993 Mohammad Hassan Najarian (Iran), 994 Hamid Reza Olanj (Iran), 995 Mohammad Oraz (Iran), 996 Dawa Tenzi Sherpa (Nepal) (2nd), 997 Chuldim Sherpa (Nepal), 998 Pemba Rinzi Sherpa (Nepal); 20/5/98 999 Jeffery Rhoads (US), 1000 Tashi Tshering Sherpa (Nepal) (5th); 27/5/98 1001 Jeffery Rhoads (US) (2nd; 2 ascents in one week), 1002 Tashi Tshering Sherpa (Nepal) (6th; 2 ascents in one week), 1003 Tom Whittaker (US) (first amputee to summit), 1004 Norbu Sherpa (Nepal) (5th), 1005 Lhakpa Tshering Sherpa (Nepal) (3rd), 1006 Dawa Sona Sherpa (Nepal) (2nd); 20/5/98 1007 Wally Berg (US) (4th) S Col to SE Ridge; 22/5/98 1008 Rustam Radjapov N Col to N Face; 23/5/98 1009 Svetlana Baskakova (f), 1010 Sergei Sokolov (Uzbekistan) (not same man as no 915), 1011 Marat Usaev (Uzbekistan), 1012 Oleg Grigoriev (Uzbekistan), 1013 Angrew Fedorov (Uzbekistan) N Col to N Face; 24/5/98 1014 Aleksei Dokukin (Uzbekistan), 1015 Ilyas Tukhvatullin (Uzbekistan), 1016 Andrew Zaikin (Uzbekistan) N Col to N Face; 25/5/98 1017 Khaniv Balmagambetov (Uzbekistan), 1018 Roman Mats (Uzbekistan) N Col to N Face; 24/5/98 1019 Lama Jangbu Sherpa (Nepal) (3rd), 1020 Lhakpa Gelu Sherpa (Nepal) (5th) N Col to N Face; 25/5/98 1021 Bernardo Guarachi (Bolivia); 25/5/98 1022 Khoo Swee-Chiow (Malaysia), 1023 Siew Cheok-Wai (Malaysia), 1024 Kami Rita Sherpa (Nepal) (3rd), 1025 Dorje Sherpa (Nepal) (3rd), 1026 Fura Dorje Sherpa (Nepal) (2nd), 1027 Nawang Phurba Sherpa (Nepal); 25/5/98 1028 Sundeep Dhillon (UK), 1029 David Walsh (UK) , 1030 Nima Gombu Sherpa (Nepal) (4th), 1031 Kusang Dorje Sherpa (India) (3rd), 1032 Nima Dorje Sherpa (Nepal); 25/5/98 1033 Russell Brice (NZ) (2nd) N Col to N Face; 1034 Sumio Tsuzuki (f) (Japan), 1035 Karsang Sherpa (Nepal) (2nd); 25/5/98 1036 Mark Jennings † (UK), 1037 Nima Wangchu Sherpa (Nepal) N Col to N Face; 25/5/98 1038 Craig John (US), 1039 Dawa Nuru Sherpa (Nepal), 1040 Lhakpa Rita Sherpa (Nepal) N Col to N Face; 27/5/98 1041 Richard Alpert (US), 1042 Robert Sloezen (US) (3rd), 1043 Panuru Sherpa (Nepal) (3rd) N Col to N Face; 26/5/98 1044 Alan Silva (Australia), 1045 Neil Laughton (UK), 1046 Edward Grylls (UK), 1047 Pasang Dawa Sherpa (Nepal), 1048 Pasang Tshering (Pangboche) (Nepal); 26/5/98 1049 Heinz Rockenbauer (Austria) N Col to N Face; 15/10/98 1050 Carlos Pitarch (Spain) (claim disputed); 17/10/98 1051 Kaji Sherpa (Nepal) (5th, used no oxygen in ascent) (claimed fastest ascent if summit claim is true), 1052 Tashi Tshering Sherpa (Nepal) (7th); **5/5/99** 1053 Peter Athans (US) (6th), 1054 William Crouse (US), 1055 Chuwang Nima Sherpa (Nepal) (6th), 1056 Phu Tashi Sherpa (Nepal), 1057 Dorje Sherpa (Nepal) (7th), 1058 Gyalzen Sherpa (Nepal) (4th), 1059 Na Temba Sherpa (Nepal) (7th); 18/5/99 1060 Charles Corfield (UK), 1061 Chuwang Nima Sherpa (Nepal) (7th, 2nd this season), 1062 Nima Tashi Sherpa (Nepal) (4th), 1063 Dawa Sona Sherpa (Nepal) (3rd); 5/5/99 1064 Graham Ratcliffe (UK) (2nd), 1065 Ray Brown (UK), 1066 Elsa Avila (f) (Mexico), 1067 Andrew Lapkass (US) Mexico (2nd, 1068 Pasang Tshering Sherpa (Nepal) (2nd); 13/5/99 1069 Michael Trueman (UK), 1070 Pasang Dawa Sherpa (Nepal) (2nd); 5/5/99 1071 Renata Chlumska (f) (Sweden), 1072 Goren Kropp (Sweden) (2nd), 1073 Mingma Tshering (Nepal) (5th), 1074 Kami Sherpa (Nepal) (2nd), 1075 Ang Chiri (Nepal); 5/5/99 1076 Bernard Voyer (Canada), 1077 Dorje Sherpa (Nepal) (4th) (not same man as no 1057), 1078 Chhongba Nuru Sherpa (Nepal); 6–7/5/99 1079 Babu Tshering Sherpa (Nepal) (8th, stayed at summit for 215 hours, used no oxygen), 1080 Dawa Sherpa (Nepal) 6/5/99 (3rd), 1081 Nima Dorje Sherpa (Nepal) 6/5/99 (2nd); 26/5/99 1082 Thomas Sjogren (Sweden), 1083 Tina Sjogren (f) (Sweden), 1084 Babu Tshering Sherpa (Nepal) (9th; 2nd this season, used no oxygen), 1085 Dawa Sherpa (Nepal) (4th, 2nd this season), 1086 Nima Dorje Sherpa (Nepal) (3rd, 2nd this season), 1087 Dawa Temba Sherpa (Nepal) (4th); 8/5/99 1088 Vasili Kopytko † (Ukraine) (used no oxygen), 1089 Vladislav Terzeoul (Ukraine) (used no oxygen), 1090 Valdimir Gorbach (Ukraine) (used no oxygen) N Col to N Face; 12/5/99 1091 Joby Ogwyn (US), 1092 Tenzing Sherpa (Nepal) (5th), 1093 Nima Gombu Sherpa (Nepal) (5th), 1094 Guillermo Benegas (US); 13/5/99 1095 Augusto Ortega (Peru) (2nd), 1096 Constantine Niarchos (Switzerland), 1097 David Rodney (Canada), 1098 Katja Staartjes (f) (Holland), 1099 Christopher Brown (UK), 1100 Martin Doyle (UK), 1101 Michael Smith (UK) (2nd), 1102 Michael Matthews † (UK), 1103 Lhakpa Gelu Sherpa (Nepal) (6th), 1104 Nima Gyalzen Sherpa (Nepal) (2nd, 1105 Kami Rita Sherpa (Nepal) (4th), 1106 Pasang Kitar Sherpa (Nepal) (2nd), 1107 Tshering Dorje Sherpa (Nepal) (2nd), 1108 Pemba Rinzi Sherpa (Nepal) (2nd), 1109 Dawa Nurbu Sherpa (Nepal); 12/5/99 1110 Lev Sarkisov (Georgia) (oldest summiter, 1 day more than Ramon Blanco, no 591), 1111 Afi Gigani (Georgia), 1112 Bidzina Gujabidze (Georgia), 1113 Benedict Kashakashvili (Georgia), 1114 Chewang Dorje Sherpa (Nepal), 1115 Nawang Tenzing Sherpa (Nepal); 13/5/99 1116 Ken Noguchi (Japan), 1117 Dawa Tshering Sherpa (Nepal) (5th), 1118 Nima Wangchu Sherpa (Nepal) (2nd), 1119 Nawang Wangchu Sherpa

(Nepal), 1120 Krishna Bahadur Tamang (Nepal); 17/5/99 1121 Conrad Anker (US), 1122 David Hahn (US) (2nd) N Col to N face; 18/5/99 1123 Jacek Maselko (Poland), 1124 Tadeusz Kudelski † (Poland), 1125 Ryszard Pawlowski (Poland) (3rd) N Col to N Face; 18/5/99 1126 Joao Garcia (Portugal) (used no oxygen), 1127 Pascal Debrouwer † (Belgium) N Col to N Face; 26/5/99 1128 Gheorghe Dijmarescu (US), 1129 Apa Sherpa (Nepal) (10th) N Col to N Face; 26/5/99 1130 Fred Barth (US), 1131 Nanda Dorje Sherpa (Nepal) N Col to N Face; 26/5/99 1132 Andrei Louchnikov (Russia) N Col to N Face; 26/5/99 1133 Hugo Rodriguez (Mexico) (2nd), 1134 Carlos Guevara Mexico, 1135 Lhakpa Nuru Sherpa (Nepal), 1136 Mingma Chhiri (Tshering) Sherpa (Nepal) (2nd, same man as no 920), 1137 Pemba Sherpa (Nepal); 26/5/99 1138 Merab Khabazi (Georgia), 1139 Irakli Ugulava (Georgia), 1140 Mamuka Tsikhiseli (Georgia), 1141 Man Bahadur Tamang (Nepal) (3rd) N Col to N Face; 26/5/99 1142 Sergio Martini (Italy), 1143 Maria Lago (f) (Spain) (used no oxygen in ascent), 1144 Samdu Sherpa (Nepal) N Col to N Face; 27/5/99 1145 Geoffrey Robb (Australia), 1146 Helge Hengge (f) (Germany), 1147 Kazuhiko Kozuka (Japan), 1148 Karsang Sherpa (Nepal) (3rd), 1149 Lobsang Temba Sherpa (Nepal) (2nd), 1150 Phurba Tashi Sherpa (Nepal) N Col to N face; 27/5/99 1151 Ivan Vallejo (Ecuador) (used no oxygen), 1152 Heber Orona (Argentina) (used no oxygen), 1153 Karla Wheelock (f) (Mexico), 1154 Fura Dorje Sherpa (Nepal) (3rd), 1155 Ari Piela (Finland), 1156 Antti Maniken (Finland) N Col to N Face; 28/5/99 1157 Akbu (Tibet), 1158 Luotze (Tibet) (2nd), 1159 Rena (Tibet) (2nd), 1160 Gui Sang (f) (China) (2nd), 1161 Jiabu (Tibet) (2nd), 1162 Bianba Zaxi (Tibet), 1163 Jiji (f) (China), 1164 Cering Doje (Tibet) (2nd), 1165 La Ba (China), 1166 Tashi Tshering (China) N Col to N Face; 28/5/99 1167 Amar Prakash (India), 1168 Kusang Dorjee Sherpa (India) (4th), 1169 Sange Sherpa (India) (3rd) E Face to SE Ridge, 1168 and 1169 are first from N, S and E; 29/5/99 1170 Cathy O'Dowd (f) (S Africa) (2nd), 1171 Ian Woodall (UK) (2nd), 1172 Lama Jangbu Sherpa (Nepal) (4th), 1173 Pemba Tenjee Sherpa (Nepal) (3rd) N Col to N Face

Nanga Parbat ascent data

All ascents via the 'Kinshofer' route on the Diamir Face at the left (north) end of the face: the first ascent climbed directly to the Bazhin Gap, then followed Buhl's route to the summit, but it is now more usual to traverse right and then to climb directly to the top) unless otherwise stated.

3/7/53 H Buhl (Austria) From Rakhiot Glacier via N Face of Rakhiot Peak, then E Ridge to Silver Saddle, across Silver Plateau and along SE Ridge; **22/6/62** T Kinshofer (Germany), S Löw † (Germany), A Mannhardt (Germany); **27/6/70** G Messner † (Italy), R Messner (Italy) Central Rib of SE (Rupal) Face; 28/6/70 F Kuen (Austria), P Scholz (Austria) Central Rib of SE (Rupal) Face; **11/7/71** I Fiala (Slovakia), M Orolin (Slovakia) Buhl Route; **11/8/76** S Gimpel (Austria), R Schauer (Austria), H Schell (Austria), H Sturm (Austria) S/SW Ridge at left (west) edge of Rupal Face, the 'Schell' route; **9/8/78** R Messner (Italy) (2nd) Right (west) edge of Diamir Face; 23/8/78 W Bauer (Austria), R Streif (Austria), R Wurzer (Austria); 28/8/78 A Imitzer (Austria), A Indrich (Austria); **5/8/81** R Naar (Holland) Schell route variant; 19/8/81 S Fassi (Italy), L Rota (Italy), B Scanabessi (Italy); **10/6/82** N Joos (Switzerland), E Loretan (Switzerland) Schell route; 14/7/82 H Engl (Germany); **17/7/83** E Koblmüller (Germany) Schell route; 31/7/83 N Nakanishi (Japan), M Taniguchi (Japan); 5/8/83 E de Pablo (Spain), JL Zuloaga (Spain); **3/6/84** M Ruedi (Switzerland); 27/6/84 L Barrard (f) (France), M Barrard (France); 7/8/84 O Cadiach (Spain), J Magrinyá (Spain) Schell route; **8/7/85** L de la Ferrière (f) (France), H Hanada (Japan), M Kikuchi (Japan), B Muller (France); 12/7/85 M Dacher (Germany), P Habeler (Austria); 13/7/85 C Carsolio (Mexico), AZ Heinrich (Poland), J Kukuczka (Poland), S Lobodzinski (US) SE Pillar of Rupal Face; 15/7/85 A Czerwinska (f) (Poland), F De Stefani (Italy), M García (Spain), M Gómez (Spain), S Martini (Italy), K Palmowska (f) (Poland), W Rutkiewicz (f) (Poland), R Vidaurre (Spain); **16/8/86** H Lanters (Holland), J Van Hees (Belgium), L Vivijs (f) (Belgium); **5/7/87** G Calcagno (Italy), B Chamoux (France), S Dorotei (Italy), T Vidoni (Italy); 9/8/87 F Alvarez (Spain), P Expósito (Spain), D Hernández (Spain), J Martínez (Spain); 19/8/87 K Matsui (Japan), R Okabayashi (Japan); **13/7/88** H Endo (Japan), Y Endo (f) (Japan); 29/7/88 S Hupfauer (Germany), T Mügge (Germany); 9/8/88 O Gassler (Austria); **13/7/89** E Gundelach (Germany), Atta-ul-Haq (Pakistan), Sher Khan (Pakistan), Mohammad Ullah (Pakistan), Rajab Shah (Pakistan); **1/7/90** H Kammerlander (Italy); 25/7/90 M Sato (Japan), R Portilla (Spain); 31/7/90 M Frantar (f) (Slovenia), J Rozman (Slovenia) Schell route; 11/8/90 P Nicolás (Spain), C Soria (Spain), A Fredborg (Norway); 12/8/90 R Joswig (Germany), P Mezger (Germany) Schell route; 18/8/90 M Todaka (Japan) Schell route; **21/7/91** R Mear (UK), D Walsh (UK); 29/6/92 Park Hee-Taek (S Korea), Song Jea-Deuk (S Korea), Kim Ju-Hyun (S Korea); **4/7/92** J Nezerka (Czech Rep), J Rakoncaj (Czech Rep); 8/7/92 C Häuter (Switzerland); 12/7/92 M Abrego (Spain), A Apellaniz (Spain), J Gozdzik (Poland), P Pustelnik (Poland) M Ruiz de Apodaka (Spain), J Oiarzabal (Spain); **7/7/93** P Barrenetxea (Spain), JL Clavel (Spain); 30/7/93 R Estiú (Spain), J Permanyé (Spain); 16/8/93 Y Mochizuki (Japan); 18/8/93 T Tonchev (Bulgaria); 24/8/93 R Pawlowski (Poland), B Stefko (Poland); 28/8/93 M Konewka (Poland), R Schleypen (Germany); **23/6/94** JR Agraz (Spain), J Castillón (Spain), L Ortiz (Spain); **23/7/95** T Akiyama (Japan), H Sakai (Japan), Y Yabe (Japan) NE Ridge of NE Peak to Silver Saddle then Buhl route; **1/9/96** K Wielicki (Poland); **15/6/97** Akbu (Tibet), Aziz Baig (Pakistan), Bianba Zaxi (Tibet), Cering Doje (Tibet), Jiabu (Tibet), Luoze (Tibet), Mohammad Ullah (Pakistan) (2nd), Rena (Tibet); 7/7/97 M Sawada (Japan); 7–14/7/97 A number of S Koreans from a team led by Yoon Kye-Joong (including Park Jun-Hun); 14/7/97 C Buhler (USA), I Dusharin (Russia); 18/7/97 V Kolisnichenko (Russia), A Volkov (Russia); 18/7/97 3 Japanese from a team led by M Kajiura; 19/7/97 3 Japanese from a team led by M Sawada; 27/7/97 J Bretcha (Spain), J Colet † (Spain), T Comerma (Spain), M Gioroianu (Romania), E Sallent (Spain); 31/7/97 S Bershov (Ukraine), V Terzeoul (Ukraine); **20/7/98** R Benet (Italy), N Meroi (f) (Italy); 21/7/98 A Hinkes (UK), A Lock (Australia), Kang Seong-Gyu (S Korea), Park Young-Seok (S Korea), Ra Kwang-Ju (S Korea), Han Wuang-Young (S

Korea), Rozi Ali (Pakistan); 6/8/98 T Kitamura (Japan); 10/8/98 L Fraga (Spain), JI Gordito (Spain), Y Tanahashi (Japan); **2/7/99** Asad Hassan (Pakistan), A Christensen (Denmark), N Cofman (USA), M Granlien (Denmark), P Guggemos (Germany), D Porsche (Germany), A Tremoulière (France), M Vincent (France); 12/7/99 Ang Dawa Tamang (Nepal), Um Hong-Gil (S Korea); 27/7/99 H Kurahashi (Japan), S Mori (Japan), Y Seino (Japan); 28/7/99 T Ikeda (Japan); 29/7/99 A Iñurrategi (Spain), F Iñurrategi (Spain), K Kondo (Japan), JC Tamayo (Spain)

K2 ascent data

All climbs by first ascent route (Abruzzi Spur) unless otherwise stated.

31/7/54 A Compagnoni (Italy), L Lacedelli (Italy); **8/8/77** S Nakamura (Japan), T Shigehiro (Japan), T Takatsuka (Japan); 9/8/77 Ashraf Aman (Pakistan), M Hiroshima (Japan), M Onodera (Japan), H Yamamoto (Japan); **6/9/78** L Reichardt (USA), J Wickwire (USA) NE Ridge/Abruzzi; 7/9/78 R Ridgeway (USA), J Roskelley (USA) NE Ridge/Abruzzi; **12/7/79** M Dacher (Germany), R Messner (Italy); **7/8/81** E Ohtani (Japan), Nazir Sabir (Pakistan) W Ridge/SW Face; **14/8/82** N Sakashita (Japan), Y Yanagisawa † (Japan), H Yoshino (Japan) N Ridge; 15/8/82 H Kamuro (Japan), H Kawamura (Japan), T Shigeno (Japan), K Takami (Japan) N Ridge; **31/7/83** A Da Polenza (Italy), J Rakoncaj (Czech Rep) N Ridge; 4/8/83 S Martini (Italy), F De Stefani (Italy) N Ridge; **19/6/85** N Joos (Switzerland), M Ruedi (Switzerland); 6/7/85 E Escoffier (France), E Loretan (Switzerland), P Morand (Switzerland), J Troillet (Switzerland); 7/7/85 D Lacroix † (France), S Schaffter (Switzerland); 24/7/85 K Murakami (Japan), N Yamada (Japan), K Yoshida (Japan); **23/6/86** M Abrego (Spain), L Barrard † (f) (France), M Barrard † (France), J Casimiro (Spain), M Parmentier (France), W Rutkiewicz (f) (Poland); 5/7/86 G Calcagno (Italy), B Chamoux (France), S Dorotei (Italy), B Fuster (Switzerland), M Moretti (Italy), J Rakoncaj (Czech Rep) (2nd), T Vidoni (Italy), R Zemp (Switzerland); 8/7/86 J Kukuczka (Poland), T Piotrowski † (Poland) S Face; 3/8/86 Chang Bong-Wan (S Korea), Chang Byong-Ho (S Korea), Kim Chang-Son (S Korea); 3/8/86 P Bozik (Slovakia), P Piasecki (Poland), W Wróz † (Poland) SSW Buttress; 4/8/86 W Bauer (Austria), A Imitzer † (Austria), K Diemberger (Austria), J Tullis † (f) (UK), A Rouse † (UK); **9/8/90** H Imamura (Japan), H Nazuka (Japan) NW Face; 20/8/90 G Child (Australia), G Mortimer (Australia), S Swenson (USA) N Ridge; **15/8/91** P Beghin (France), C Profit (France) W Face/NW Face/ N Ridge; **1/8/92** V Balyberdin (Russia), G Kopieka (Ukraine); 3/8/92 C Mauduit (f) (France), A Nikiforov (Russia); 16/8/92 S Fischer (USA), C Mace (USA), E Viesturs (USA); **13/6/93** S Bozic (Croatia), C Carsolio (Mexico), V Groselj (Slovenia), Z Pozgaj (Slovenia); 23/6/93 G Kropp (Sweden); 7/7/93 D Culver † (Canada), J Haberl (Canada), P Powers (USA); 30/7/93 D Bidner † (Sweden), A Bukreev (Kazakhstan), R Jansen (Denmark), R Joswig † (German), A Lock (Australian), P Mezger † (German); 2/9/93 D Mazur (USA), J Pratt (UK) W Ridge/SW Face; **24/6/94** A Iñurrategi (Spain), F Iñurrategi (Spain), J Oiarzabal (Spain), E de Pablo (Spain), J Tomás (Spain) SSE Spur; 9/7/94 R Hall (NZ); 10/7/94 D Ibragimzade † (Ukraine), A Kharaldin † (Ukraine), A Parkhomenko † (Ukraine) (see text); 23/7/94 R Dujmovits (Germany), M Gorbenko (Ukraine), M Groom (Australia), V Gustafsson (Finland), A Schlönvogt (Germany), V Terzeoul (Ukraine), M Wärthl (Germany); 30/7/94 S de la Cruz (Argentina), JC Tamayo (Spain) N Ridge; 4/8/94 A Apellaniz † (Spain), J San Sebastián (Spain) N Ridge; **17/7/95** A Hinkes (UK), R Naar (Holland), Mehrban Shah (Pakistan), Rajab Shah (Pakistan), H Van der Meulen (Holland); 13/8/95 J Escartin † (Spain), J Olivar † (Spain), L Ortiz † (Spain) SSE Spur; 13/8/95 A Hargreaves † (f) (UK), R Slater † (USA), B Grant † (NZ); **29/7/96** G Maggioni (Italy), L Mazzoleni † (Italy), M Panzeri (Italy), S Panzeri (Italy), M Todaka (Japan); 10/8/96 M Bianchi (Italy), C Kuntner (Italy), K Wielicki (Poland) N Ridge; 12/8/96 K Akasaka (Japan), M Matsubara (Japan), B Murata (Japan), A Shiina (Japan), T Tanigawa (Japan), Y Yoshida (Japan) SSE Spur; 13/8/96 M Alvial (Chile), W Farías (Chile), C Garcia-Huidobro (Chile), M Purcell (Chile) SSE Spur; 14/8/96 H Inaba (Japan), K Nagakubo (Japan), T Sano (Japan), K Takahashi (Japan), H Takeuchi (Japan), A Yamamoto (Japan) SSE Spur; 14/8/96 I Benkin † (Russia), C Buhler (USA), R Pawlowski (Poland), S Penzov (Russia), P Pustelnik (Poland) N Ridge; **19/7/97** K Nakagawa (Japan), M Suzuki (Japan), O Tanabe (Japan) W Ridge/SW Face variant; 28/8/97 Pemba Dorje (Nepal), Gyalbu (Nepal), M Kobayashi (Japan), A Nakajima (Japan), M Takine (Japan), Dawa Tashi (Nepal), Mingma Tshering (Nepal), R Yamada (Japan) W Ridge/SW Face variant

Cho Oyu ascent data

All climbs by first ascent route (West Ridge and West Face) except where stated. In the early years of ascents the route was generally approached from the South (Nepal), but is now more generally approached from the North (Tibet). Note: many Sherpas have the same names and have been identified by their home towns.

19/10/54 H Tichy (Austria), S Jochler, Pasang Dawa Lama (India); **15/5/58** Sonam Gyatso (India), Pasang Dawa Lama (India) (2nd); **25/4/64** F Stammberger (W Germany) (claim disputed); **29/10/78** A Furtner (Austria), E Koblmueller (Austria) SE Face; **10/10/79** M Saleki (Iran) (claim disputed); **?/10/82** H D Sauer (W Germany) (claim disputed); **5/5/83** M Dacher (W Germany), H Kammerlander (Italy), R Messner (Italy); 15/11/83 N Hertkorn (W Germany), R Klingl (W Germany); 17/11/83 R Klingl (W Germany) (2nd); ?/11/83 M Saleki (Iran) (claim disputed); **13/5/84** V Komarkova (f) (US), D Sterbova (f) (Czech.), Ang Rita Sherpa (Thami) (Nepal), Nuru Sherpa (Nepal); 20/9/84 A Llasera (Spain), C Vallès (Spain), Sambhu Tamang (Nepal), Ang Karma Sherpa (Nepal); 21/9/84 J Clemenson (France), J Pons (Spain); **12/2/85** M Berbeka (Poland), Z Heinrich (Poland), J Kukuczka (Poland), M Pawlikowski (Poland) South Ridge; 1/5/85

Renqing Pingcuo (Tibet), Danzeng Tobgyal (Tibet), Da Tobgyal (Tibet), Da Cering (Tibet), Xiao Tobgyal e (Tibet), Wanjia (Tibet), Gaisang (Tibet), Lawang (Tibet), Bianba (Tibet); 15/5/85 J Amezgarai (Spain), M Apodaca (Spain), J Oiarzabal (Spain), I Querejeta (Spain); 15/5/85 J Apellaniz (Spain), X Garaioa (Spain), F Uriarte (Spain); 28/5/85 M Gardzielewski (Poland), J Jezierski (Poland); 3/10/85 M Kitamura (Japan), T Mitani (Japan), N Nakanishi (Japan); 5/12/85 D Becik (Slovakia), J Stejskal (Slovakia); **29/4/86** R Gajewski (Poland), M Pawlikowski (Poland) (2nd) SW Ridge to W Face; 1/5/86 P Konopka (Poland), SW Ridge to W Face; 3/5/86 M Danielak (Poland), A Osika (Poland) SW Ridge to W Face; 5/5/86 P Habeler (Austria), M Reudi (Switzerland) SW Ridge to W Face; 9/5/86 R Schleypen (W Germany), J Smith (US) SW Ridge to W Face; 10/5/86 J Daum (W Germany) SW Ridge to W Face; 11/5/86 B Brakus (Croatia) SW Ridge to W Face; 11/5/86 J Frush (U.S.), D Hambly (UK); 12/5/86 H Vollmer (W Germany) (claim disputed); 16/5/86 M Lorenz (Austria) SW Ridge to W Face; 16/10/86 E Hino (Japan); **29/4/87** M Purto (Chile), Ang Phuri Sherpa (Beni) (Nepal), Ang Rita (Thami) (Nepal) (2nd), I Valle (Chile), F Graf (Switzerland), J Wangeler (Switzerland); 5/5/87 O Gassler (Austria), H Wagner (Austria), P Wörgötter (Austria); 6/5/87 K Wimmer (W Germany); 7/5/87 R Hofer (SWizerland); 8/5/87 R Strouhal (Austria); 9/5/87 P Ganner (Austria), K Hecher (Austria), H Pree (Austria), S Wörgötter (Austria); 12/5/87 B Vos (Holland); 20/9/87 A Hayakawa (Japan), K Kondo (Japan); 21/5/87 Y Okura (Japan), K Takahashi (Japan), T Kato (Japan), E Otani (Japan), Nima Dorje Sherpa (Beding) (Nepal), Ang Dawa Tamang (Nepal); 22/9/87 S Kobayashi (Japan), M Takahashi (f) (Japan), Lhakpa Tenzing Sherpa (Nepal), Ang Phurba Sherpa (Beding) (Nepal), Mingma Tenzing (Thami) (Nepal); 23/9/87 T Renard (France), Ang Rinzee Sherpa (Nepal); 30/9/87 T Karolczak (Poland), A Lwow (Poland); 2/10/87 W Berg (US); **6/2/88** F Garrido (Spain); 30/4/88 D Walsh (UK); 1/5/88 G De Marchi (Italy), F Spazzadeschi (Italy), L Zani (Italy); 2/5/88 O Forno (Italy); 10/5/88 H Engl (W Germany), G Schmatz (W Germany); 11/5/88 S Wörner † (Switzerland); 30/5/88 T Fischbach (W Germany), K Gürtler (Austria), P Konzert (Austria), H Bärnthaler (Austria), W Kuzendorf (W Germany), D Thomann (W Germany); 1/9/88 M Batard (France), Sungdare Sherpa (Nepal); 12/9/88 B Cormier (France), E Decamp (France), R Eynard-Machet (France), B Gouvy (France), V Perillat (f) (France), M Vincent (France), Ang Dorje Sherpa (Chaplung) (Nepal), Da Gombu Sherpa (Nepal); 13/9/88 A Busettini (Italy), E Fergio (Italy); 14/9/88 J Hoeffelman (Belgium), J Sesma (Spain), M Vincent (France) (2nd), Lhakpa Gyalu (Chaunrikarka) (Nepal), Da Gombu Sherpa (Nepal) (2nd); 17/9/88 S Martini (Italy), F De Stefani (Italy); 27/9/88 F Castenuovo (Italy), M Conti (Italy), L Mazzoleni (Italy), M Panzeri (Italy); 16/10/88 P Henschke (Poland); 2/11/88 I Tomazin (Slovenia) N Face ascent, W side descent; 5/11/88 V Groselj (Slovenia), J Rozman (Slovenia) N Face to W side; 6/11/88 T Saegusa (Japan), O Shimizu (Japan), N Yamada (Japan), A Yamamoto (Japan); 8/11/88 R Nadvesnik (Slovenia), M Prezelj (Slovenia) North Face; 9/11/88 B Jereb (Slovenia), R Robas (Slovenia) N Face to W side; **8/4/89** C Buhler (US), M Zabaleta (Spain) SW Ridge to W Face; 2/9/89 Hong Kyung-Pyo (South Korea), Lee Dong-Yeon (South Korea), Wangel Sherpa (Nepal); 17/9/89 A Brugger (Italy), R Zeyen (Luxembourg); 18/9/89 M Casella (Switzerland), P Giuliani (Switzerland), E Rosso (Italy); 19/9/89 M Capelli (Switzerland), C Margna (Switzerland), M Nos King (f) (Spain), M Verge (f) (Spain), Ang Phuri (Beni) (Nepal) (2nd); **27/4/90** H Kato (Japan), Y Tanahashi (Japan), Mingma Tenzing (Thami) (Nepal) (2nd), Pemba Tenjee Sherpa (Nepal); 30/4/90 B Chamoux (France), Y Detry (France), A Hinkes (UK), J Rakoncaj (Czech), M Rossi (Italy), P Royer (France), F Valet (France) (claim disputed); 11/5/90 M Groom (Australia); 19/5/90 G Haerter (Germany), G Lindebner (Austria), R Mueller (Germany), D Porsche (Germany), W Treibel (Germany) (claim disputed); 26/5/90 G Binder (W Germany), P Blank (W Germany), W Funkler (W Germany), B Hochstuhl (W Germany), G Hupfauer (f) (W Germany), S Hupfauer (W Germany), G Kurze (f) (W Germany), H Rössner (W Germany), U Schmitz (W Germany), F Stark (W Germany), J Tschoten (Austria), K Westphal (W Germany), U Zehetleitner (W Germany), K Zöll (W Germany), Nawang Thile Sherpa (Beding) (Nepal); 21/6/90 H Taylor (UK), R Brice (NZ), Dawa Nuru Sherpa (Phortse) (Nepal), Lhakpa Gyalu (Portse) (Nepal); 23/8/90 A Hubert (Belgium), L Lange (Belgium); 20/9/90 W Kurtyka (Poland), E Loretan (Switzerland), J Troillet (Switzerland) S-facing part of SW Face from N; 4/10/90 A Koncz (Hungary), J Straub (Hungary), R Wlasich (Austria); 6/10/90 K Aranguren (Spain), P Eguillor (Spain), P Fernandez (Spain), M Martinez (Spain), J Pujante (Spain), J Tapias (Spain), Ang Phurba Sherpa (Thami) (Nepal); 7/10/90 J Csíkos (Hungary), I Pajor (Hungary), C Tóth (Hungary), L Várkonyi (Hungary), L Vörös (Hungary); 8/10/90 S Nagy (Hungary), S Szendrö (Hungary), I Decsi (Hungary), P Tous (Spain), M Reparaz (Spain); 19/10/90 A Apellaniz (Spain) (2nd), R Portilla (Spain), J San Sebastian (Spain), A Trabado (Spain); **22/4/91** S Beck (Brazil), A Hantz (France), Man Bahadur Gurung (Gorkha) (Nepal), Iman Singh Gurung (Gorkha) (Nepal); 8/5/91 A Beetschen (Switzerland), P Kapsomenakis (Greece), I Konstantinou (Greece), M Rizzi (Switzerland), A Ruiz (Spain), Tirtha Tamang (Nepal), K Tsivelekas (Greece); 9/5/91, E Eder (Austria), W Maier (Germany), F Pantillon (Switzerland), T Pichler (Austria), M Respondek (Germany), N von Schumacher (Switzerland), E Wullschleger (f) (Switzerland), P Wullschleger (Switzerland); 27/5/91 A Albrecht (Germany), H Bauer (Germany), H Conrad (Germany), R Erardi (Italy), O Fangauer (Germany), R Gasser (Italy), G Hofer (f) (Italy), M Kumpf (f) (Germany), J Pallhuber (Italy), K Renzler (Italy), H Tauber (Italy), A Wiedemann (Germany) J Weissenberger (Germany), K Wolfsgruber (f) (Italy); 25/9/91 C Kuntner (Italy), S De Leo (Italy), J Reichen (Switzerland); 26/9/91 W Rutkiewicz (f) (Poland); 28/9/91 Tsindin Temba Sherpa (Nepal), T Ishikawa (Japan), Y Nezu (Japan), B Quetglas (Spain), T Watanbe (f) (Japan), Mingma Norbu Sherpa (Beding) (Nepal), Nima Temba Sherpa (Nepal); 29/9/91 C Armstrong (US), K Groninger (US), K Ikeda (Japan), C Richards (f) (US), Pemba Norbu Sherpa (Nepal), K Young (f) (US), M Mojaev (Russia), E Prilepa (Russia), V Skripko (Russia); 1/10/91 B Dimitrov (Bulgaria), I Dimitrova (f) (Bulgaria); 4/10/91 M Imbert (France), Dawa Dorje Sherpa (Makalu) (Nepal); 5/10/91 M Zalio (France), Kilu Temba Sherpa (Nepal); 20/10/91 S Bogomolov (Russia), V Pershin (Russia), I Plotnikov (Russia), Y Vinogradski (Russia), A Yakovenko (Russia) E Ridge from S; **7/5/92** P Debrouwer (Belgium), G Kropp (Sweden); 8/5/92 L LeBon (f) (Belgium), Danu Sherpa (Nepal), B Ongis (Italy), M Soregaroli (Italy), G Vigani (Italy), M Lutterjohann (Germany); 14/5/92 P Kowalzik (Germany), Musal Kazi Tamang (Nepal); 17/5/92 T Finkbeiner (Germany); 22/5/92 M Schneider (Germany);

4/6/92 P Guggemos (Germany), M Schumacher (Germany); 15/8/92 M Saleki (Iran), S Tsuzuki (f) (Japan); 17/9/92 A Aranzabal (f) (Spain), J Bereziartua (Spain), J Colet (Spain); 20/9/92 J Artetxe (Spain), P Ganuza (f) (Spain), Nam Sun-Woo (S Korea), Kim Young-Tae (S Korea), Mingma Norbu (Beding) (2nd) (Nepal), Nima Dorje (Beding) (2nd) (Nepal); 20/9/92 H Baba (Japan), A Hayasimoto (Japan), K Kondo (Japan), M Taniguchi (Japan), S Tsukamoto (Japan), T Suzuki (Japan), An Young-Jong (N Korea), Nima Sherpa (Taksindu) (Nepal), Mingma Tenzing (Thami) (3rd) (Nepal); 21/9/92 K Kanazawa (Japan), S Kimoto (Japan), Y Sato (f) (Japan), T Yanagihara (Japan), H Yatsuhashi (Japan), Ang Phurba (Thami) (2nd) (Nepal), Dawa Norbu Sherpa (Nepal); 20/9/92 F Airoldi (Italy), P Gugliermina (Italy); 21/9/92 A Cvahte (Slovenia), M Gregorèiè (Slovenia), S Lagoja (Slovenia), F Urh (Slovenia), M Urh (Slovenia); 29/9/92 A Ballano (Spain), J B Jimeno (Spain); **8/2/93** M González (Spain), F Guerra (Spain), M Morales (Spain), M Salazar (Spain); 10/2/93 L Arbués (Spain), M Chapuisat (f) (Switzerland), M A Sánchez (Argentina); 29/4/93 G Seifried (Germany); 2/5/93 Chiang Yung-ta (Taiwan), Tsai Shang-chih (Taiwan), Tenzing Sherpa (Nepal), Ang Kami Lama (Nepal); 4/5/93 Liang Chin-mei (f) (Taiwan), Liu Chi-man (Taiwan), Pasang Lama (Nepal), D Alessio (Argentina), R Mear (UK), E Tryti (Norway), C Giorgis (Italy), V Lauthier (f) (Italy), G Sacco (Italy); 4/5/93 M Fernandez (Argentina) E Ridge/Face (N); 5/5/93 P Stadler (Switzerland), A Würsch (Switzerland); 7/5/93 A Georges (Switzerland); 15/5/93 A Neuhuber (Austria); 16/5/93 P Y Guichard (Switzerland); 16/5/93 M Breuer (Germany), C Gabl (Austria), F Kühnhauser (Germany), R Ratteit (Germany), M Moreni (Switzerland), A Verzaroli (Switzerland); 10/9/93 Choi Byung-Soo (S Korea), Min Kyoung-Tee (S Korea), Um Hong-Gil (S Korea), J A Serrano (Spain); 18/9/93 M Bianchi (Italy), K Wielicki (Poland) W Ridge from N; 21/9/93 F Campos (Spain), B Sabadell (Spain); 24/9/93 J Garcia (Portugal), P Pustelnik (Poland) W Ridge from N; 30/9/93 D Caillat (France), J Cardona (Spain), F Faure (France), J Lafaille (France), J R Lasa (Spain); 8/10/93 T Akiyama (Japan), F Goto (Japan), R Hoshino (Japan), H Nazuka (Japan), Y Ogata (Japan), M Sato (Japan); 11/10/93 S Ezuka (Japan), O Tanabe (Japan), Pasang Tshering (Beding) (Nepal), Lobsang Jangbu Sherpa (Nepal); 12/10/93 T Miyazaki (Japan), T Terada (Japan), K Yagihara (Japan), F Yoshida (f) (Japan), Nawang Sakya (Beding) (Nepal), Dawa Tshering (Beding) (Nepal), Nima Dorje (Beding) (3rd) Mingma Norbu (Beding) (3rd); 8/10/93 J Garcia (Spain), C Pitarch (Spain); 10/10/93 J Elorrieta (Spain), J Gómez (Spain), Y Martin (f) (Spain); 31/10/93 M de la Matta (Spain), C Mauduit (f) (France); **26/1/94** J Garra (Spain), J Magrinyá (Spain); 26/4/94 C Carsolio (Mexico); 29/4/94 F Pedrina (Switzerland); 3/5/94 E Schwarzenlander (Austria); 4/5/94 H Katzenmaier (Germany), W Korber (Germany), H Spindler (Germany), L Protze (Germany), A Ratka (Germany), T Türpe (Germany); 8/5/94 J Delgado (Venezuela), M Duff (UK), C Jones (NZ), N Lindsey (UK), Pasang Gombu (Lokhim) (Nepal); 12/5/94 Z Hruby (Czech Rep), S Silhan (Czech Rep), A Giovanetti (Italy), O Piazza (Italy); 14/5/94 L Kamarad (Czech Rep), B Lodi (Italy); 16/5/94 A Oberbacher (Italy); 20/5/94 H Blatter (Switzerland), N Joos (Switzerland); 23/5/94 Y Yamanoi (Japan) SW Ridge ascent W Ridge/Face down; 25/9/94 Y Endo (f) (Japan), T Nagao (f) (Japan) SW Face; 26/9/94 G Frey (France), R Geoffrey (France), Y Salino (France), Ang Rita (Thami) (3rd) (Nepal), Pasang Jambu Sherpa (Nepal); 27/9/94 Park Young-Seok (S Korea), Ngati Sherpa (Nepal); 28/9/94 Cha Jin-Chol (S Korea), Han Sang-Kook (S Korea), Han Wuang-Yong (S Korea), Panuru Sherpa (Phortse) (Nepal); 29/9/94 T Harada (Japan), S Imoto (Japan), Kunga Sherpa (Rolwaling) (Nepal), Nawang Dorje (Rolwaling); 30/9/94 Akbu (Tibet), Daqimi (Tibet), Daqiong (Tibet), Jaibu (Tibet), Luoze (Tibet), Bianba Zaxi (Tibet), Rena (Tibet), Cering Doje (Tibet), Wangjia (2nd) (Tibet); 2/10/94 F Bibollet (France); 4/10/94 S Sasahara (Japan), H Tabata (Japan), Chhong Ringee (Beding) (Nepal), Lhakpa Gyalu † (2nd) (Chaunrikarka) (Nepal); 6/10/94 J Arnold (f) (NZ), R Hall (NZ), E Viesturs (US); **18/4/95** F Pepevnik (Slovenia); 6/5/95 H Eibl (Germany), B Zedrosser (Austria); 9/5/95 A Delgado (Mexico), H Ponce de Léon (Mexico), P Arvis (France), R Brand (Germany), P Brill (Germany), R Dujmovits (Germany), L Edel (Germany), A Haüsler (Germany), K Hub (Germany), P Hub (f) (Austria), F Prasicek (Austria), J Spescha (Germany), A Vedani (Switzerland), Nawang Thile (Beding) (2nd) (Nepal), H Konishi (Japan), Pembra Tshering (Thamo) (Nepal), M Yamamoto (Japan); 11/5/95 U Blasczyk (Germany), A Kraus (Germany), W Kuch (Germany), C Fox (f) (US), D Hahn (US), M Hutnak (US), Tenzing Phinzo (Phortse) (Nepal); 12/5/95 M Bazillian (US), J Findlay (US), H Macdonald (f) (US), R Sloezen (US); 16/5/95 B Hill (US), W Thompson (US), Dawa Nuru (Phortse) (2nd) (Nepal), A Van Steen (US); 17/5/95 C John (US), M O'Day (US), A Rausch (US); 29/5/95 I Peter (UK), P Walters (Australia), Nima Timba Sherpa (Nepal); 30/5/95 N Croucher (UK), Ang Temba Sherpa (Beding) (Nepal); 1/6/95 W Kleinknecht (Germany), E Resch (Austria); 13/9/95 F Iñurrategi (Spain), A Iñurrategi (Spain), Onchu Lama (Nepal); 25/9/95 H Hashiyada (Japan), J Miyakawa (Japan), T Yamamoto (Japan), Ang Phurba (Beding) (2nd) (Nepal), Dawa Tshering (Beding) (2nd) (Nepal), Nawang Tenzing Sherpa (Nepal), Dawa Tashi Sherpa (Nepal), B Separoviĉ (Croatia), B Puzak (Croatia), Nawang Dorje (Rolwalking) (2nd) (Nepal); 26/9/95 K Ikeda (Japan), Y Ogio (Japan), R Rosenbaum (Australia), Ang Temba Sherpa (2nd) (Nepal), Tendu Sherpa (Nepal), Nawang Sakya Sherpa (2nd) (Nepal); 26/9/95 J Arnold (f) (2nd) (NZ), R Hall (2nd) (NZ), L Harvey (Australia) D Mantle (US), Ang Dorje (Pangboche) (Nepal), Norbu Sherpa (Beding) (Nepal); 27/5/95 S Burnik (Slovenia), D Petrin (Croatia), F Seiler (Germany), J Stiller (Germany); 28/5/95 R Buccela (Italy), A Clavel (Italy), A Stremfelj (Slovenia), M Stremfelj (f) (Slovenia); 29/9/95 K Ito (Japan), J Sawataishi (Japan), Y Ueno (Japan), Pasang Kami Sherpa (Nepal), Ang Gyalzen Sherpa (Nepal), Man Bahadur Gurung (Sitalpati) (Nepal); 1/10/95 M Hatakeyama (Japan), T Tanaka (Japan), Na Temba Sherpa (Nepal), Ang Gyalzen Sherpa (2nd) (Nepal) Kunga (Rowaling) (2nd); 1/10/95 C Jager (France), A Thevenot (France), Kunga (Rowaling) (2nd) (Nepal) J Botella de Maglia (Spain) Gyalbu Sherpa (Nepal); 2/10/95 F Alvárez (Spain), A Gómez (Spain), A Pallarés (Spain), J L Sanz (Spain), Kami Tenzing Sherpa (Kumjung) (Nepal), L Drda (Czech Rep), R Hunter (US), H Magnusson (Iceland), V Mysik (Czech Rep), B Olafsson (Iceland), N Shustrov (Russia), E Stefansson (Iceland), J Tinker (UK) Babu Tshering (Taksindu) (Nepal), Lama Jangbu (Nepal); 3/10/95 O Louka (Czech Rep); 4/10/95 V Yanotchkin (Russia), P Sicouri (Italy), Lhakpa Rita Sherpa (Nepal); 6/10/95 J Kardhordo (Czech Rep), O Srovnal (Czech Rep); 7/10/95 P Athans (US), W Prittie (US), I Woods (S Africa), Lhakpa Rita Sherpa (2nd) (Nepal), Dawa Sherpa (Nepal); 8/10/95 T Hromadka (Czech

Rep); 10/10/95 A Cheze (France); 13/10/95 F Delrieu (f) (Spain), J Desplan (France), Ang Rita (Thami) (4th) (Nepal); **2/5/96** M Schmid (Switzerland), C Zinsli (Switzerland), C Bannwart (Switzerland), C Bitz (Switzerland), S Bonvin (Switzerland), R Laveikis (Latvia), J Osis (Latvia), A Rutkis (Latvia), Jangbu Sherpa (Nepal), Nawang Chokleg (Thami) (Nepal); 3/5/96 J Hermosillo (Mexico); 4/5/96 D Bieri (Switzerland), B Hasler (Switzerland), A Käslin (Switzerland), R Real (f) (Spain), M Boggelmann (Germany), A Heckele (Germany), K Schmidt (Germany), R Stihler (Germany), Nawang Thile (Beding) (3rd) (Nepal), Ongchu Sherpa (Karikhola) (Nepal), H Stockert (Germany), A Buhl (Germany), C J Schulte (Germany); 8/5/96 T Masuda (Japan), H Masunaga (Japan), N Miki (Japan), T Toda (f) (Japan), Tshering Dorje Sherpa (Nepal), Kunga (Rolwaling) (3rd) (Nepal); 9/5/96 T Saito (Japan), S Sato (Japan), M Yamaguchi (f) (Japan), S Yasukawa (Japan), Nima Sherpa (Taksindu) (2nd) (Nepal), Tshering Dorje Sherpa (Nepal) (2nd); 10/5/96 B Pederiva (Italy), (N) Kancha Nuru Sherpa (Khumjung) (Nepal) W Ridge/Face; 13/5/96 J Ellis (US), H Macdonald (f) (2nd) (US), T Richards (US) Dawa Nuru (Phortse) (3rd) (Nepal); 14/5/96 E Leas (US), J Race (US); 15/5/96 D Stefani (Italy), M Tosi (Italy), S Valentini (Italy); 16/5/96 A de Boer (f) (Holland), R Brice (2nd) (NZ), B Hasler (NZ), P Reynal-O'Connor (NZ), A Salek (NZ), M Whetu (NZ); 19/5/96 M Leuprecht (Austria), F Obermüller (Austria); 26/5/96 A Fink (Austria), C Haas (Germany), A Hinterplattner (Austria), P Perlia (Luxembourg); 27/5/96 E Gatt (Austria), S Gatt (Austria), S Greve (f) (Norway), I Gruber (Austria), E Huber (f) (Austria); 20/9/96 R Brice (3rd) (NZ), T Kurai (f) (Japan), J Tabei (f) (Japan), Karsang Sherpa (Nepal); 21/9/96 S Blackmore (UK), H Majima (f) (Japan), Lobsang Temba Sherpa (Nepal), Chuldin Temba Sherpa (Nepal); 23/9/96 Byun Mi-Jung (f) (S Korea), Kim Young-Ki (S Korea), Lee Sang-Bae (S Korea), Park Jung-Hun (S Korea), Nima Sherpa (Taksindu) (3rd) (Nepal), Ang Phurba (Thami No. 2) (Nepal), Chewang Dorje Sherpa (Nepal), V Bashkirov (Russia), A Klimin (Russia), A Kovalchuk (Estonia), B Mednik (Russia), A Paskin (Russia), V Pershin (2nd) (Russia), A Sedov (Russia), B Sedusov (Russia), Y Vinogradski (2nd) (Russia), G Tortladze (Georgia), N Zakharov (Russia), J Berbeka (Poland), A Boukreev (Kazakhstan), M McDermott (UK), Babu Tshering (Taksindu) (2nd) (Nepal); 25/9/96 K Noguchi (Japan), Pasang Tshering (Beding) (2nd) (Nepal); 27/9/96 K Boskoff (US), D Brown (Canada), R Dorr (US), C Feld-Boskoff (f) (US), D Robinson (Canada), L Hall (US), M Pfetzer (US), H Todd (UK), Pemba Dorje Sherpa (Pangboche) (Nepal), Jyamang Bhote (Nepal), P Mahenc (France), Kancha Nuru (Khumjung) (2nd) (Nepal), R Brice (4th) (NZ), S Tsuzuki (W, 2nd) (Japan); 28/9/96 P Morrow (US), Danuru Sherpa (Namche) (Nepal); 28/9/96 O Cadiach (Spain), S Ruckensteiner (Austria) North Ridge; 29/9/96 N Kekus (UK), I Loredo (Mexico), K Wheelock (f) (Mexico), Lhakpa Gelu Sherpa (Nepal), R Boice (US), M Buchan (UK), S French (f) (NZ), S Horner (US), E Viesturs (2nd) (US), Ang Dorje (Pangboche) (2nd) (Nepal), Chuldin Dorje (Khumjung) (Nepal); 1/10/96 A Arnold (Switzerland), B Huc-Dumas (France), M Kittleman (US), I Pauls (Latvia), Babu Tshering (Taksindu) (3rd) (Nepal, Pemba Tshering (Karikhola) (Nepal), Nima Sherpa (Karikhola) (Nepal), M Saul (f) (Canada), H Sovdat (f) (Canada), Nawang Phurba Sherpa (Nepal); 6/10/96 K Farafonov (Kazakhstan), S Gataoulin (Kazakhstan); 9/10/96 L Bečak † (Czech Rep), M Otta (Czech Rep); 10/10/96 M Penalva (Spain), O Ribas (Andorra); 14/10/96 S Gataoulin (2nd) (Kazakhstan), O Malikov (Kazakhstan), Y Moiseev (Kazakhstan); **27/4/97** D Beavon (US), S Bull (US), D Johnck (US), P Scaturro (US), K Tenzing (Khumjumg) (2nd) (Nepal); 28/4/97 C Demarest (US), B Hoffman (US), Pemba Norbu Sherpa (Nepal), Pasang Phutar Sherpa (Nepal); 30/4/97 H Rainer (Austria); 2/5/97 J Inhöger (Austria), H Nikol (Germany), S Allan (UK), J Sparks (US), Dorje Sherpa (Nepal), Lhakpa Gyalzen Sherpa (Nepal), H Rockenbauer (Austria), O Cadiach (2nd) (Spain), N Duró (f) (Andorra), J Tosas (Spain); 3/5/97 H Chlastak (Germany), H Goger (Austria), L Ioffe (Russia), E Lebedeva (f) (Russia), T Zoeva (f) (Russia), E Andueza (Spain), V Izquierdo (Spain), A Navas (Spain); 6/5/97 R Nicco (Italy), V Strba (Slovakia), J Leupold (Germany), M Walter (Germany), G Wiegand (Germany); 7/5/97 S Pasmeny (Canada) F Ziel (US); 8/5/97 T Slama (Czech Rep), W Turek (Austria); 12/5/97 M Mayerhofer (Austria), H Ortner (Austria); 13/5/97 K Braun (US); 14/5/97 H Dolenga (Germany); 15/5/97 F Alldredge (US), R Alpert (US), D Hahn (2nd) (US), T La France (US); 19/5/97 W Kugler (Germany), J Mayer (Germany), A Metzger (Germany), A Teuchert (Germany), Tenzing Phinzo (Phortse) (2nd) (Nepal); 20/5/97 C Arthur (UK), D Spencer (UK), S Stacey (UK), Mingma Dorje Sherpa (Nepal), Pemba Tshering (Karikhola) (Nepal); 19/9/97 Jang Hun-Moo (S Korea), Kim Hong-Sang (S Korea), Oh Jun-Young (S Korea), Park Young-Seok (2nd) (S Korea), Tashi Tshering Sherpa (Nepal); 20/9/97 Jang Kum-Duk (S Korea), P Schmidt (France), C Trommsdorff (France), Nawang Thile (Beding) (4th) (Nepal); 21/5/97 G Kotov (Russia), W Pierson (US) North Ridge; 21/9/97 Kim Seong-Seok (S Korea), Park Heon-Ju (S Korea), Panuru Sherpa (Phortse) (2nd) (Nepal), G Scaccabarozzi (Italy); 22/9/97 M Ellerby (US), Ang Pemba Sherpa (Nepal), M Jesús Lago (f) (Spain), Ongchu (Karikhola) (2nd) (Nepal); 26/9/97 I Beltrán de Lubiano (Spain), G Velez (Portugal), M Kadoya (Japan), K Maeda (Japan), K Tsubosa (f) (Japan), Dawa Dorje (Makalu) (2nd) (Nepal), Man Bahadur Gurung (Sitalpati) (2nd) (Nepal), P Garcés (Spain), J L Gómez (Spain), V Leontyev (Ukraine), V Kopytko (Ukraine), S Kovalev (Ukraine), G Cemmi (Italy), M Perego (Italy); 27/9/97 M Airoldo (Italy), G Harrison (f) (UK), G Pfisterer (US), Pasang Tshering (Pangboche) (Nepal); 28/9/97 D Jewell (NZ), R Koval (Ukraine), V Zboja (Slovakia), A Collins (NZ), G Cotter (NZ), D Hiddleston (NZ), Leung Yick-Nam (Hong Kong) Keith Kerr (UK), Ang Dorje (Pangboche) (3rd) (Nepal), Chuldin Dorje (Khumjung) (2nd) (Nepal), Khoo Swee Chiow (Malaysia), J Lean (Singapore), D Lim (Malaysia), M R Maarof (Malaysia), A Silva (Australia), Kunga (Rolwaling) (4th) (Nepal), Lila Bahadur Gurung (Nepal), M Dunnahoo (US), K Gattone (f) (US), S Greenholz (US), C Horley (US), L Lewis (US), R Link (US), A Mondry (US), J Norton (US), E Simonson (US), Tenzing Phinzo (Phortse) (3rd) (Nepal), Ang Pasang Sherpa (Nepal), A Nasuh Mahruki (Turkey); 30/9/97 A Akinina (f) (Russia), S Krylov (Russia); 3/10/97 V Saunders (UK), Y Contreras (Mexico), S Le Poole (Holland) W Ridge/Face; 13/10/97 E Escoffier (France), A Paret (France), I Singh Gurung (Gorkha) (2nd) (Nepal); 15/10/97 S Mondinelli (Italy), P Paglino (Italy); 6/11/97 J Martínez (Spain); **21/4/98** Three Chinese led by Tang Yuan Xin; 28/4/98 N Pimkin (Russia), D Sergeev (Russia); 1/5/98 F Loubert (Canada), C-A Nadon (Canada); 6/5/98 J Hinding (Austria), R Hofer (Austria), G Kaltenbrunner (f) (Austria), T Prinz (Austria), F Scharmüller (Austria), H Wolf (Austria); 12/5/98 A Poppe (Germany), G Rösner † (Germany); 14/5/98 B Prax (US); 19/5/98 K-D Grohs (Germany),

R Rackl (Germany), Nawang Thile (Beding) (5th) (Nepal), M Della Santa (Italy), S Dotti (Italy), R Pizzagalli (Italy), C Romano (Italy), G Santi (Italy); 20/5/98 G Anders (US), G Bate (UK), P Falvey (Ireland), Nima Sherpa (Karikhola) (2nd) (Nepal), Phenden Sherpa (Nepal), A Wildsmith (UK), M Frankhauser (Austria), B Hirschbichler (f) (Germany), A Huber (Germany), G Simair (Austria), K Koomen-Staartjes (f) (Holland), Nanda Dorje (Khumjung) (Nepal); 21/5/98 M Pearson (UK); 22/5/98 B Friedrich (Germany), T Lämmil (Germany), R Lebek (Germany), R Roozen (Austria), M Staschull (Germany), G Weinberger (Austria), Y De Jong (Holland), S Terwee (Holland), H Van der Meulen (Holland), Chhong Ringee (Beding) (2nd) (Nepal); 23/5/98 K Schmid (Germany), A Blanc (Italy), M Camandona (Italy), W Niclevicz (Brazil), H Gogl (Austria), H Lechner (Austria), J Murg (Austria), P Perlia (2nd) (Luxembourg); 24/5/98 M Mlynarczyk (f) (Germany), Z Mlynarczyk (Germany); 29/5/98 A Smets (Holland); 31/5/98 A Dingemans (Holland), Nawang Chokleg (Thami) (2nd) (Nepal); 1/6/98 P Bergevoet (Holland); 24/9/98 R Tudor Hughes (UK), Sonam Tashi Sherpa (Nepal), Phurba Tashi Sherpa (Nepal), S Fear (f) (Australia), Nima Dorje Tamang (Kerung) (Nepal), M Blanchebarbe (Germany), Mingma Sherpa (Nepal), T Nousiainen (f) (Finland), Chhong Ringee (Beding) (3rd) (Nepal), Nanda Dorje (Khumjung) (2nd) (Nepal), C Lacatusu (Romania); 25/9/98 M Comes (Spain), Tarke Sherpa (Lokhim) (Nepal), K Morooka (Japan), A Jaggi † (Switzerland), Norbu (Beding) (2nd) (Nepal); 26/9/98 M Nukita (Japan), M Taniguchi (Japan), Nima Dorje (Beding) (4th) (Nepal), Mingma Tshering Sherpa (Nepal), Tashi Sherpa (Nepal), T Cowen (US), M Goddard (US) D Lambert (UK), A Lapkass (US), L Medina (f) (US), D Ryan (Ireland), Pasang Tshering (Pangboche) (2nd) (Nepal), R Benedetti (Italy), M Dibona (Italy); 27/9/98 G Ferlan (Yugoslavia), N Gubser (US), D Jacimovič (Yugoslavia), A Mayer (Austria), D Mellor (UK), Pemba Dorje (Pangboche) (2nd) (Nepal), A Gil (Spain), J M Lete (Spain), J R Bacena (Spain), J L Bolado (Spain), A Cinca (Spain), J C Gómez (Spain), S Mingote (Spain); 28/9/98 S Woolums (US), J Robinson (US), B Ousland (Norway), E Urtaran (Spain), J Verdeguer (Spain); 9/10/98 T Riga (Estonia), A Sarapuu (Estonia); 11/10/98 R Plumer (Estonia), M Proos (Estonia), T Sarmet (Estonia), R Dujmovits (2nd) (Germany), R Eberhard (Germany), W Goering (Germany), S Mayr (Germany), H Steger (Germany), S Weiche (Germany), Chuldim Nuru Sherpa (Nepal), Ang Phurba (Beding No. 2) (Nepal), Nawang Thile (Beding) (6th) (Nepal); **13/4/99** J Gangdal (Norway), Tamtin Sherpa (Nepal), Dawa Tshering (Beding) (3rd) (Nepal); 23/4/99 A Delgado (2nd) (Mexico); 25/4/99 M Arbelaez (Colombia), M Barrios (Colombia), F González (Colombia); 26/4/99 A Boll (f) (Switzerland), M Borrmann (Germany); 30/4/99 C Soria (Spain), Sona Dendu Sherpa (Nepal); 1/5/99 M Küng (Switzerland); 3/5/99 A Delgado (3rd) (Mexico), A Ochoa (Mexico); 4/5/99 R Robinson (Canada), S Wyatt (Canada), A Bullard (f) (US), K Hess (f) (US), G Stanley (f) (US); 5/5/99 R Ariano (Colombia), N Cardona (Colombia), J P Ruiz (Colombia); 6/5/99 J Bach (US), J Gauthier (Canada), W Krause (Germany); 7/5/99 O Rieck (Germany), T Türpe (Germany) (2nd), M Abrego (Spain), A López (Spain), Tarke Sherpa (Lokhim) (2nd) (Nepal); 18/5/99 F Luchsinger (Chile), C Prieto (f) (Chile), Pemba Sherpa (Nepal); 19/5/99 T Fritsche (Austria), S Gatt (2nd) (Austria); 20/5/99 C Bäumler (f) (Germany), T Becherer (Germany), M Beuter (Germany), H Bielefeldt (Germany), M Bischoff (Switzerland), F Everts (Germany), M Farenzena (f) (Luxembourg), H Hackl (Germany), E Schmitt (Germany), T Zwahlen (Switzerland), Chuldim Sherpa (Nepal); 22/5/99 J Einwaller (Austria), J Koller (Austria), J Streif (Germany), R Benet (Italy), N Meroi (f) (Italy); 23/5/99 A Abramov (Russia), L Abramova (f) (Russia), N Cherny (Russia), V Elagin (Russia), J Khokhlov (Russia), S Larin (Russia); 25/5/99 T Klösch (Austria), R Knebel (Germany), W Scheidl (Austria), J Schoff (Austria); 26/9/99 Kang Seong-Gyu (S Korea), Kim Sang-Jo (S Korea), Moon Bong-Su (S Korea), Oh Hee-Joon (S Korea), Pemba Pasang Sherpa (Nepal), Pasang Gombu (Lokhim) (2nd) (Nepal), J McGuinness (NZ), I Okanda (f) (Japan), S Sakamoto (Japan), S Takahashi (f) (Japan), Man Bahadur Gurung (3rd) (Nepal); 27/9/99 B Johnson (US), P Kenny (US), C Warner (US), A de Choudens (France), S de Choudens (f) (France), S Juvet (Switzerland), C Mirmand (France), Nawang Thile (Beding) (7th) (Nepal); 28/9/99 J Marmet (France), B Muller (France), K Nagakubo (Japan), K Nakamura (Japan), M Okuda (Japan), T Tanigawa (Japan), A Collet (f) (France), Tarke Sherpa (Lokhim) (3rd) (Nepal), Ang Phurba Sherpa (Lukla) (Nepal), S Vetter (France); 30/9/99 F Oderlep (Slovenia), P Stular (Slovenia); 1/10/99 T Kitamura (Japan), A Lapkass (2nd) (US), J Litch (US), P Pappas (US) D Staples (NZ), K Tucker (US) T Aryama (Japan), Ang Dorje (Pangboche) (4th) (Nepal), Lhakpa Tshering Sherpa (Nepal)

Makalu ascent data

All climbs by first ascent route (NW Cirque, Makalu La and North Face) except where stated.

15/5/55 J Couzy (France), L Terray (France); 16/5/55 J Franco (France), G Magnone (France), Gyalzen Norbu Sherpa (India); 17/5/55 J Bouvier (France), S Coupe (France), P Leroux (France), A Vialatte (France); **23/5/70** H Tanaka (Japan), Y Ozaki (Japan) SE Ridge; **23/5/71** B Mellet (France), Y Seigneur (France) W Pillar; **6/10/75** S Belak (Yugoslavia), M Manfreda (Yugoslavia) S Face ; 8/10/75 J Azman (Yugoslavia), N Zaplotnik S Face; 10/10/75 V Groselj (Yugoslavia), I Kotnik S Face; 11/10/75 J Dovzan (Yugoslavia), S Face; **24/5/76** J Camprubi (Spain) SE Ridge; 24/5/76 K Schubert † (Czech), M Krissak (Czech) SE buttress to SE Ridge; **1/5/78** H Warth (W Germany), Ang Cheppal (Nepal); 10/5/78 H von Kaenel (Zwitzerland) K Landvogt (W Germany) Nga Temba Sherpa (Nepal); 21/5/78 K Diemberger (Austria), Nawang Tenzing Sherpa (Nepal); **15/5/80** J Roskelley (US) W Pillar; **25/4/81** R Schauer (Austria); 15/10/81 J Kukuczka (Poland) W Face to NW Ridge; **20/5/82** Heo Young-Ho (S Korea), Pasang Norbu Sherpa (Nepal) Ang Phurba Sherpa (Nepal) SE Ridge to E Face; 30/9/82 M Ishibashi (Japan), Y Michiwaki (Japan), K Yuda (Japan); 10/10/82 A Czok (Poland) N Face to NW Ridge, between Kukuczka route and W Pillar; **16/5/84** M Abrego (Spain), E de Pablo; 29/9/84 R Nottaris (Switzerland) Kukuczka route; **1/10/85** A Giambisi (Italy) S Martini (Italy), J C de San Sebastian (Spain), F Stedile (Italy), F De Stefani (Italy); **24/9/86** M Ruedi † (Switzerland), K Wielicki (Poland); 26/9/86 H Kammerlander (Italy), R Messner (Italy), F Mutschlenchner

(Italy); **12/5/87** C Pizzo (US), G Porzak (US), Lhakpa Nuru Sherpa (Nepal); 16/5/87 G Neptune (US), Dawa Nuru Sherpa (Nepal), Moti Lal Gurung (Nepal); **27/5/88** M Batard (France) W Pillar ascent NW side descent; 12/10/88 C Carsolio (Mexico); 14/10/88 T Kolakowski † (Poland), T Kopys (Poland); **6/10/89** P Beghin (France) S Face ascent NW side descent; **6/5/90** H Onishi (Japan) Nima Dorje Sherpa (Nepal); 18/5/90 K Calhoun (f) (US) J Schutt (US) W Pillar; 3/10/90 J Angles (Spain), A Bros (Spain), Lhakpa Sherpa (Nepal) Kukuczka route; **24/9/91** C Figueras (Spain), J Permane (Spain), X Robiro (Spain) Kukuczka route; 30/9/91 A Iñurrategi (Spain), F Iñurrategi (Spain), F Uriarte (Spain) Kukuczka route; 2/10/91 M Badiola † (Spain), E Loretan (Switzerland), F Troillet (Switzerland), C Valles (Spain) W Pillar; 5/10/91 Y Futamata (Japan), H Imamura (Japan), Y Okada (Japan), Ang Dorje Sherpa (Nepal); 7/10/91 T Ishizaka † (Japan), T Nagao (f) (Japan); **22/5/93** F Manoni (Italy), S Panzeri (Italy), D Spreafico (Italy), L Sulovsky (Czech Rep), Tirtha Tamang (Nepal), Mingmar Tamang (Nepal); **15/5/94** N Beidleman (US), A Bukreev (Kazakhstan); **5/5/95** B Chamoux (France) P Royer (France) NW side (claim disputed); 8/5/95 M Auricht (Australia), D Hume † (Australia), J Oiarzabal (Spain), B Ruiz de Infante (Spain), J Vallejo (Spain), Um Hong-Gil (S Korea); 9/5/95 A Zerain (Spain); 18/5/95 V Gustafsson (Finland), R Hall (New Zealand), E Viesturs (US); 21/5/95 T Arai (Japan), M Matsubara (Japan), O Tanabe (Japan), A Yamamoto (Japan) E Ridge to NW side; 22/5/95 T Ono (Japan), T Tanigawa (Japan), H Takeuchi (Japan), M Yamamoto (Japan), E Ridge to NW side; 9/10/95 A Collins (UK), D Mazur (US), A Nikiforov (Russia), J Pratt (UK) SE Ridge; **19/5/96** N Kogemiako (Russia), V Koroteev (Russia), I Plotnikov (Russia), G Sokolov (Russia); 23/5/96 V Bashkirov (Russia), S Bogomolov (Russia), V Foigt (Russia), Y Outechev (Russia), V Stalkovski (Russia), A Vegner (Russia); **21/5/97** A Bolotov (Russia), I Bougatshevski † (Russia), Y Ermatchek (Russia), N Jiline (Russia), D Pavlenko (Russia) W Face; **16/5/98** A Alexandrov (Russia), I Aristov (Russia), N Kadoshinikov (Russia); 19/5/98 O Cadiach (Spain), N Duro (f) (Andorra), A Horoaov (Bulgaria), Z Petkov (Bulgaria), J Simunek (Czech Rep), I Valtchev (Bulgaria) D Vassilev (Bulgaria), S Vomackova (f) (Czech Rep), Lahkpa Dorje Sherpa (Nepal); **30/4/99** M Jorgensen † (Denmark) M Stofer (Switzerland); 13/5/99 A Georges (Switzerland) NW side; 16/5/99 M Groom (Australia), D Bridges (US); 22/5/99 G Harrison (f) (UK), H Robertson (Australia); 23/5/99 A Hinkes (UK), Dawa Chiri Sherpa (Nepal); 25/5/99 W Pierson (US)

Kangchenjunga ascent data

All climbs by first ascent route (South-west Face) except where stated.

25/5/55 G Band (UK), J Brown (UK); 26/5/55 N Hardie (NZ), T Streather (UK); **31/5/77** P Chand (India), Nima Dorje Sherpa (Nepal) NE spur to N Ridge; **16/5/79** P Boardman (UK), D Scott (UK), J Tasker (UK) NW Face to N Ridge; **14/5/80** R Fukuda (Japan), S Kawamura, (Japan), N Sakashita (Japan), S Suzuki (Japan), Ang Phurba Sherpa (Nepal) NW Face; 15/5/80 G Ritter (W Germany), Nima Dorje Sherpa (Nepal), Lhakpa Gyalu Sherpa (Nepal); 17/5/80 M Ohmiya (Japan), T Sakano (Japan), Pemba Tshering Sherpa (Nepal), Dawa Norbu Sherpa (Nepal) NW Face; **9/5/81** K Fujikura (Japan), A Hosake (Japan), K Kataoka (Japan), S Suzuki (Japan), N Yamada (Japan), Nima Temba Sherpa (Nepal); 20/5/81 J Psotka (Czech), L Zahoransky (Czech) NW Face; 15/10/81 M Parmentier (France), J Ricouard † (France); **2/5/82** I Menbreaz (Italy), O Squinobal (Italy), Nga Temba Sherpa (Nepal); 6/5/82 R Messner (Italy), F Muschlechner (Italy), Ang Dorje Sherpa (Nepal) NW Face to N Ridge; **28/5/83** G Bachler (Austria); 17/10/83 P Beghin (France); 21/10/83 M Buchez (Switzerland), V May (Switzerland) NW Face; **19/5/84** T Ozake (Japan), Ang Tshering Sherpa (Nepal); 20/5/84 T Mitani (Japan), S Wada (Japan) SW Rib to S Ridge up, down in traverse of 3 summits; 18/10/84 R Marshall (Canada); **11/1/86** J Kukuczka (Poland), K Wielicki (Poland); 24/10/86 J Permane (Spain), Ang Rita Sherpa (Nepal); **25/5/87** F Bhutia † (India), P Dorjee † (India), C Tsering † (Nepal) NE spur to N Ridge; 31/5/87 S Limbu (India), C Singh † (India), B Singh (India), NE spur to N Ridge; 10/10/87 J Coulton (Australia), M Groom (Australia); **2/1/88** Lee Jeong-Chel (S Korea); 3/5/88 C Buhler (US), P Habeler (Austria), M Zabaleta (Spain) N Ridge; 17/10/88 M Unno (Japan), Nima Temba Sherpa (Nepal) (2nd); **9/4/89** V Elagin (USSR), E Kinezky (USSR), V Koroteev (USSR), A Sheinov (USSR); 16/4/89 Z Chalitov (USSR), V Dedy (USSR), A Glushkovsky (USSR), G Lunjakov (USSR), Y Moiseev (USSR), V Suviga (USSR), L Trotschinenko (USSR), K Valiev (USSR); 29/4/89 S Bogomolov (USSR), R Chaibullin (USSR), V Karataev (USSR), M Mozaev (USSR), V Pastuk (USSR); 1/5/89 S Bershov (USSR), A Bukreev (USSR), A Pogorelov (USSR), M Turkevitch (USSR), S Vinogradski (USSR) S Ridge to SW rib up and W Face down; grand traverse from Yalung Kang 30/4; 1/5/89 S Arentiev (USSR), E Kineszky (USSR) (2nd), V Khrichtchaty (USSR), V Suviga (USSR) (2nd); 1/5/89 V Babyberdin (USSR), Z Chalitov (USSR) (2nd), V Elagin (USSR) (2nd), V Karataev (USSR) (2nd), G Lunjakov (USSR) (2nd) SW rib and W Face to S Ridge up, SW down in grand traverse ending at Yalung Kang on 2/5; 3/5/89 N Cherny (USSR), S Efimov (USSR), Ang Babu Sherpa (Nepal); 18/5/89 P Ershler (US), C van Hoy (US), E Viesturs (US) NW Face to N Ridge; 21/5/89 R Link (US), L Nielson (US), G Wilson (US) NW Face to N Ridge; **15/5/90** M Udall (US); **1/5/91** S Bozic (Yugoslavia), V Groselj (Yugoslavia); 24/5/91 H Imamura (Japan), H Nazuka (Japan), R Oda (Japan) NE spur to N Ridge; 5/5/91 K Lal (India), S D Sharma (India), T Smanla (India) N E spur to N Ridge; **12/5/92** C Carsolio (Mexico) NW Face to N Ridge; **23/5/93** V Borko (Ukraine), A Kharaldine (Ukraine), A Serpak (Ukraine), M Sitnik (Ukraine), V Terzeoul (Ukraine) NE spur to N Ridge; 26/5/93 S Perkhomenko (Ukraine), I Zade (Ukraine) NE spur to N Ridge; **23/10/94** V Koulbatchenko (Belarussia); **5/10/95** E Loretan (Switzerland), J Troillet (Switzerland); 14/10/95 A Blanc (Italy), S Martini (Italy); **6/5/96** F Iñurrategi (Spain), A Iñurrategi (Spain), J Oiarzabal (Spain) NW Face; **24/5/97** S McKee (US) NW Face; **9/5/98** Akbu (Tibet), Daqiong (Tibet), Jaibu (Tibet), Luoze (Tibet), Baibo Zaxi (Tibet), Rena (Tibet), Cering Doje (Tibet); 15/5/98 F De Stefani (Italy), Gyalzen Sherpa (Nepal); 15/5/98 K Aksaka † (Japan), K Hirose (Japan), M Okuda (Japan), A Shiina † (Japan), T Tanigawa (Japan)

NW Face; 18/5/98 G Harrison W (UK), T Horvath (US), J Pratt (UK), C Shaw (US) NW Face; 18/5/98 K Auer (Italy), H Kammerlander (Italy); **12/5/99** Park Young-Seok (S Korea), Sherap Jangbu Sherpa (Nepal), Sange Sherpa (Nepal)

First ascents of subsidiary summits
South summit: 19/5/78 E Chrobak (Poland), W Wroz (Poland) W Face. Central Summit: 22/5/78 W Branski (Poland), Z Heinrich (Poland), K Olech (Poland) W Face. West Summit (Yalung Kang): 14/5/73 Y Ageta (Japan), T Matsuda † (Japan) SW Ridge

Manaslu ascent data
All climbs by first ascent route (North-east Face) except where stated.

9/5/56 T Imanishi (Japan), Gyalzen Norbu Sherpa (Nepal); 11/5/56 M Higeta (Japan), K Kato (Japan); **17/5/71** K Kohara (Japan), M Tanaka (Japan) NW Face; **25/4/72** R Messner (Italy) S Face; **22/4/73** S Hupfauer (W Germany), G Schmatz (W Germany), Urkien Tshering Sherpa (Nepal); **4/5/74** M Mori (f) (Japan), N Nakaseko (f) (Japan), Jangbu Sherpa (Nepal), M Uchida (f) (Japan); **26/4/75** G Blazquez (Spain), J López (Spain), Sonam Wolang Sherpa (Nepal); **12/10/76** M J Assadi (Iran), J Kageyama (Japan), Pasang Sherpa (Nepal); **28/4/80** Seo Dong-Hwan (S Korea), Ang Pasang Sherpa (Nepal), Ang Zawa Sherpa (Nepal); **7/5/81** H Von Kaenel (Switzerland), J Mecke (W Germany), Wangchu Sherpa (Nepal); 9/5/81 F Graf (Switzerland), K Horn (W Germany), A Loferer (W Germany), H Müller (Switzerland), H Zabrowski (W Germany); 19/5/81 W Heimbach (W Germany), J Millinger (Austria), R Schleypen (W Germany), Pasang Norbu Sherpa (Nepal), P Weber (Switzerland), P Wörgötter (Austria), S Wörner (Switzerland); 7/10/81 P Beghin (France), B Muller (France) W Face; 12/10/81 T Ozaki (Japan); 14/10/81 M Tomita (Japan), Y Kato (Japan); **10/10/82** L Audobert (France), Nawang Tenzing Sherpa (Nepal); **22/10/83** Heo Young-Ho (S Korea); 22/10/83 G Härter (W Germany), Ang Dorje Sherpa (Nepal), Nima Rita Sherpa (Nepal), H Streibel (W Germany), H Tauber (W Germany), H Wehrs (W Germany) S Face; **12/1/84** M Berbeka (Poland), R Gajewski (Poland) S Face; 30/4/84 E Loretan (Switzerland), M Ruedi (Switzerland); 4/5/84 S Bozic (Yugoslavia), V Groselj (Yugoslavia) S Face; 7/5/84 M Dacher (W Germany), F Zintl (W Germany); 11/5/84 N Joos (Switzerland), W Schaffert (W Germany), R Schaider (W Germany), Ang Cheppal Sherpa (Nepal), Wongel Sherpa (Nepal), G Sturm (W Germany); 20/10/84 A Lwow (Poland), K Wielicki (Poland) S Ridge to SE Face; **1/5/85** Ang Kami Sherpa (Nepal), W Studer (Austria) E Ridge to NE Face; 14/12/85 Y Saito (Japan), N Yamada (Japan); **10/11/86** A Hajzer (Poland), J Kukuczka (Poland) E Ridge; **7/10/87** J Etschmayer (Austria), W Hauser (Austria), Lhakpa Sonam Sherpa (Nepal); **1/5/88** B Fuster (Switzerland), U Huber (f) (Switzerland), R Ott (Switzerland) E Ridge to NE Face; 25/10/88 J Agullo (Spain), Ang Lhakpa Sherpa (Nepal); **9/5/89** B Chamoux (France), P Royer (France) S Face; 10/5/89 S Dorotei (Italy), J Rakoncaj (Czech) S Face; 11/5/89 Y Detry (France), F Valet (France) S Face; 12/5/89 A Hinkes (UK), M Rossi (Italy), Tirtha Tamang (Nepal) S Face; **26/4/90** F De Stefani (Italy); **6/5/91** A Makarov (Russia), V Pastuck (Ukraine), I Svergoun (Ukraine) S Ridge up, down; 25/10/91 H Brantschen (Switzerland), M Ferrari (Switzerland); **28/9/92** M Bianchi (Italy), C Kuntner (Italy), K Wielicki (2nd) (Poland); **2/5/93** J Brunner (Austria), G Flossmann (Austria), J Hinding (Austria), M Leuprecht (Austria); 13/10/93 S Mondinelli (Italy) S Face; 15/10/93 S Inhoeger (Austria); 19/10/93 V Lopatnikov (Russia); 21/10/93 E Ivanova (f) (Russia), I Khmiliar † (Russia); **19/10/94** A Georges (Switzerland), A Salamin (Switzerland); **7/5/95** J Bartock (Germany), S Thomas (Germany), M Zunk † (Germany); 8/12/95 A Baimakhanov (Kazakhstan), A Bukreev (Kazakhstan), S Gataoulin (Kazakhstan), O Malikov (Kazakhstan), J Moiseev (Kazakhstan), D Mouravev (Kazakhstan), D Sololev (Kazakhstan), V Sougiva (Kazakhstan); **3/5/96** Akbu (Tibet), Cering Doje (Tibet), Rena (Tibet), Bianba Zaxi (Tibet); 4/5/96 Daqiong (Tibet), Jaibu (Tibet), Luoze (Tibet), Wangjia (Tibet); 12/5/96 A Carsolio (Mexico), C Carsolio (Mexico); 24/5/96 C Mauduit (f) (France); 27/9/96 R Benedetti (Italy), L Campagna (Italy), T Ishikawa (Japan), S Martini (Italy), Nima Dorje Sherpa (Nepal), Tshering Dorje Sherpa (Nepal); 28/9/96 M Konishi (Japan), Pemba Tshering Sherpa (Nepal), T Sugiyama (Japan), Dhanjeet Tamang (Nepal); 30/9/96 M Mimura (Japan), H Arikawa (Japan); 13/10/96 A Blanc (Italy), A Favre (Italy), P Obert (Italy; 27/9/96 Um Hong-Gil (S Korea), Ngati Sherpa (Nepal); **19/9/97** Santa Bahadur Gurung (Nepal), K Kobler (Switzerland), Nima Tamang (Nepal), I Vallejo (Ecuador); 27/9/97 C Mace (US), A McPherson (UK); 8/10/97 Y Kato (Japan), T Mitani (Japan), Pertemba Sherpa (Nepal), K Takahashi (Japan), T Toyoshima (Japan), A Yamamoto (Japan); 8/10/97 J I Fernandez (Spain), J R Lasa (Spain), J Oiarzabal (Spain), I Querejeta (Spain); 8/10/97 M Rybansky † (Slovakia), P Sperka (Slovakia); 9/10/97 A Harada (Japan), M Hirose (Japan), Y Seki (Japan), Dawa Nuru Sherpa (Nepal), Phurba Tshering Sherpa (Nepal); **6/12/98** Park Young-Seok (S Korea), Kami Dorchi Sherpa (Nepal), Ang Dawa Tamang (Nepal); **22/4/99** V Gustafsson (Finland), A Montalban (Spain), J Noguera (Spain), E Viesturs (US); 29/4/99 G Wiegand (Germany), G Stingl (Germany); 2/5/99 M Walter (Germany), V Tiller (Germany); 5/5/99 R Mittag (Germany), D Ruelker (Germany); 7/5/99 J Alzner (US), E Eriksson (US), M Manarik (Czech Rep), F Ziel (US)

Lhotse ascent data
All climbs by first ascent route (West Face) except where stated

18/5/56 F Luchsinger (Switzerland), E Reiss (Switzerland); **8/5/77** H Warth (W Germany), H Von Kaenel (Switzerland), Urkien Tshering Sherpa (Nepal); 9/5/77

G Sturm (W Germany), P Vogler (W Germany), F Zintl (W Germany); 11/5/77 M Dacher (W Germany), M Lutz † (W Germany), P Wörgötter (Austria), W Wörgötter (Austria); **5/5/79** W Axt (Austria), H Ladreiter (Austria); 10/5/79 I Exnar (Czech refugee in Switzerland), B Klausbruckner (Austria); 4/10/79 A Czok (Poland), Z Heinrich (Poland), J Kukuczka (Poland), J Skorek (Poland); 9/10/79 J Baranek (Poland), A Bilczewski (Poland), S Cholewa (Poland), R Niklas (W Germany); **30/4/81** H Prodanov (Bulgaria); **9/10/83** K Murakami (Japan), T Ozaki (Japan), N Yamada (Japan); 10/10/83 T Kagawa (Japan), T Miyazaki (Japan), Dawa Norbu Sherpa (Nepal); 14/10/83 Pemba Norbu (Nepal), S Suzuki (Japan), K Takahashi (Japan); **4/5/86** M Fukushima (Japan), T Haruki (Japan), Nima Temba Sherpa (Nepal), Nima Dorje Sherpa (Nepal); 14/5/86 A Lwow (Poland), T Karolczak (Poland); 16/10/86 H Kammerlander (Italy), R Messner (Italy); **28/9/88** D Becik (Czech), J Just (Czech); 2/10/88 Chung Ho-Jin (S Korea), Lim Hyung-Chil (S Korea), Park Hee-Dong (S Korea), Park Quay-Don (S Korea); 31/10/88 K Wielicki (Poland); **30/4/89** V Groselj (Yugoslavia); 14/10/89 Heo Young-Ho (S Korea); **24/4/90** T Cesen (summit claim doubted including claim to have soloed) (Yugoslavia) S Face; 13/5/90 W Berg (US), S Fischer (US); 16/10/90 S Bershov (USSR), V Karataev (USSR) S Face; **4/10/93** G Vionnet-Fuasset (France), Nuru Sherpa (Nepal); **9/5/94** O Kihlborg (Sweden), M Reutersward (Sweden); 13/5/94 C Carsolio (Mexico); 16/5/94 R Hall (NZ), E Viesturs (US); 1/10/94 E Loretan (Switzerland), J Troillet (Switzerland); 11/10/94 B Chamoux (France), R Pawlowski (Poland); **6/5/95** M Groom (Australia), V Gustafsson (Finland); 10/5/95 B Bishop (US), K Kerr (UK), Kipa Sherpa (Nepal), Danu (Danuri) Sherpa (Nepal); 27/9/95 A Iñurrategi (Spain), F Iñurrategi (Spain), Onchu Lama (Nepal); 2/10/95 J Oiarzabal (Spain), J Vallejo (Spain); **10/5/96** C Mauduit (f) (France); 22/5/96 S Darsney (US), J Pratt (UK); 23/5/96 D Mazur (US); 17/5/96 A Boukreev (Kazakhstan); **23/5/97** A Hinkes (UK), M K Jorgensen (Denmark); 24/5/97 I Outechev (Russia), N Tchernyi (Russia), S Zuev (Russia); 26/5/97 C Feld-Boskoff (f) (US); 26/5/97 V Babanov (Russia), V Bashkirov † (Russia), S Bogomolov (Russia), A Foigt (Russia), V Koroteev (Russia), V Pershin (Russia), G Sokolov (Russia), S Timofeev (Russia); 26/5/97 A Boukreev (2nd) (Kazakhstan), S Moro (Italy); 27/5/97 A Blanc (Italy); 28/5/97 J C Lafaille (France), M Panzeri (Italy), S Panzeri (Italy); 18/10/97 Han Wang-Yong (S Korea), Park Young-Seok (S Korea), Kaji Sherpa (Nepal); 21/10/97 K Nagaoka (Japan), S Sakamoto (Japan); **17/5/98** A Georges (Switzerland); 18/5/98 A N Mahruki (Turkey); 25/5/98 I Pauls (Latvia), Kami Sherpa (Nepal); 27/5/98 B Bull (US), T Heinrich (Argentina), A Lapkass (US); 13/10/98 Daqiong (Tibet), Bianba Zaxi (Tibet), Cering Doje (Tibet), Rena (Tibet), Luoze (Tibet); **21/4/99** I Ochoa (Spain); 12/5/99 J Simunek (Czech Rep), S Vomackova (f) (Czech Rep), Lhakpa Dorje Sherpa (Nepal); 13/5/99 J Moravek (Czech Rep), Z Hruby (Czech Rep); 22/5/99 M Doya (Japan), Man Bahadur Gurung (Nepal), Phurba Chhiri Sherpa (Nepal)

First ascents of subsidiary summits
East Summit (Lhotse Shar): 12/5/70 J Mayerl (Austria), R Walter (Austria) SE Ridge. Middle Summit: Unclimbed as of 31/12/99

Gasherbrum II ascent data
All climbs via first ascent route (SW Ridge, base of SE Face and E Ridge) except where stated.

7/7/56 S Larch (Austria), F Moravec (Austria), H Willenpart (Austria); **18/6/75** M Batard (France), Y Seigneur (France) S Ridge/E Ridge; 1/8/75 L Cichy (Poland), J Onyszkiewicz (Poland), K Zdzitowiecki (Poland) SW Ridge to col between GII and GII then NW Face; 9/8/75 M Janas (Poland), A Lapinski (Poland), WL Wozniak (Poland); 12/8/75 H Krüger-Syrokomska (f) (Poland), A Okopinska (f) (Poland); **9/8/78** G Brosig (Germany); 9/6/79 C Lucero (Chile), G Oyarzun (Chile); **31/7/79** K Hub (Germany), R Karl (Germany), H Sturm (Austria); 4/8/79 K Diemberger (Austria), Fayyaz Hussain (Pakistan), W Lösch (Austria), H Schell (Austria), A Schwab (Austria), W Weitzenböck (Austria); **2/8/80** P Aymerich (Spain), E Font (Spain), M Fukushima (Japan), K Imada (Japan), H Sato (Japan); **29/6/81** F Neumayer (Austria), G Neumayer (Austria); 3/8/81 R Nottaris (Switzerland), A Trabado (Spain), T Zünd (Switzerland); 6/8/81 E Beaud (France), P Grenier (France), C Janin (f) (France), Sher Khan (Pakistan); **9/6/82** G Markl (Austria), G Kaser (Austria); 10/6/82 M Grüner (Austria), R Renzler (Austria); 11/6/82 J Trattner (Austria); 12/6/82 L Barrard (f) (France), M Barrard (France), A Bontemps (France); 24/7/82 Sher Khan (Pakistan) (2nd), R Messner (Italy), Nazir Sabir (Pakistan); **15/6/83** F Graf (Switzerland), E Loretan (Switzerland), A Meyer (Switzerland), M Ruedi (Switzerland), JC Sonnenwyl (Switzerland), S Wörner (Switzerland); 1/7/83 J Kukuczka (Poland), W Kurtyka (Poland) SE Ridge over Pt 7200 and E Peak then E Ridge; **25/6/84** H Kammerlander (Italy), R Messner (Italy) (2nd); 31/7/84 J Demarolle (France), P Glaizes (France), P Guedu (France), F Maurel (France); 6/8/84 P Bournat (France), W Pasquier (Switzerland); **6/6/85** G Calcagno (Italy), G Scanabessi (Italy), T Vidoni (Italy) S Ridge/E Ridge; 15/6/85 B Chamoux (France), E Escoffier (France) S Ridge/E Ridge; 8/7/85 JM Boivin (France), L Chevallier (France), F Diaféria (France), Abdul 'Little' Karim (Pakistan), M Poincet (France), B Prudhomme (France), G Vionnet-Fuasset (France); 11/7/85 Mohammad Ali (Pakistan), G Casarotto (f) (Italy), R Casarotto (Italy), C Frémont (France), P Gévaux (France), G Hassan (Pakistan), Ibrahim (Pakistan), T Mayer (USA), A Molinaire (France), O Paulin (France), A Re (Italy), M Vincent (France), G Ubaldini (Italy), G Vionnet-Fuasset (France) (2nd); 14/7/85 JM Boivin (France) (2nd); 16/7/85 F Germain (Switzerland), T Kato (Japan); 28/7/85 M Matsumoto (Japan), T Takahashi (Japan); 31/7/85 PO Bergström (Sweden), N Campredon (France), G Flecher (France), L Le Pivain (France), M Metzger (France), P Mure-Ravaud (France), R Pillière (France), T Renard (France), T Sandberg (Sweden), P Weng (Sweden); 2/8/85 M Berquet (France), E Julliard (f) (France), H Sigayret (France); **6/6/86** R Carminati (France), G Chardiny (France), E Guillot (France); 9/7/86 JC del Olmo (Spain), R Vázquez (Spain); 3/8/86 Atta-ul-Haq (Pakistan), Fakhar-ul-Haq

(Pakistan), Abdul Jabbar Bhatti (Pakistan), Sher Khan (Pakistan) (3rd); 4/8/86 B Bisèak (Slovenia), V Groselj (Slovenia), P Kozjek (Slovenia), A Stremfelj (Slovenia); 16/8/86 J Altgelt (Germany), M Fischer (Switzerland), D Siegers (Germany), V Stallbohm (Germany), K Zöll (Germany); **28/6/87** D Heilig (USA), M Miller (USA), P Powers (USA), JP Hefti † (Switzerland), R Thorns (UK), G Hupfauer (f) (Germany), S Hupfauer (Germany); 10/7/87 M Dacher (Germany), G Halliburton (NZ), I Peter (UK), U Schmidt (Germany), D Stewart (UK); 8/8/87 E Berger (Luxembourg), F De Stefani (Italy), M Giordani (Italy), S Martini (Italy); 16/8/87 A Apellaniz (Spain), L Bradey (f) (NZ), J Little (Australia), C McDermott (NZ), J Oiarzabal (Spain); **22/6/88** G Lozat (France), B Muller (France), J Pons (Spain), JP Renaud (France), B Vallet (France); 23/6/88 N Joos (Switzerland), J Pêche (France), D Schaer (Switzerland), D Wellig (Switzerland), P Zehnder (Switzerland); 24/6/88 H Albet † (France), M Buscail (France), P Hittinger (France), Abdul 'Little' Karim (Pakistan) (2nd), Rozi Ali (Pakistan); 25/6/88 R de Bos (Holland), J Jacobse (Holland), H Van der Meulen (Holland), A van Waardenburg (Holland) S Ridge/SE Face to E Ridge; 25/6/88 H Hollwig (Germany), L Klembarova (f) (Slovakia), M Sterbova (f) (Czech Rep), H Wassmann (Germany); 5/7/88 R Borra (Switzerland), R Wellig (Switzerland); 7/8/88 H Sachetat (France); 8/8/88 I Baeyens (f) (Belgium), S Hashimoto (f) (Japan), J van Hees (Belgium), Ibrahim (Pakistan) (2nd), F Kimura (f) (Japan), M Kitagawa (f) (Japan), JM de Robert (France), L Vivijs (f) (Belgium), N Yanagizawa (f) (Japan), M Yasuhara (f) (Japan); 13/8/88 G Gadani (France), S Ravel (France); **30/5/89** C Forster (Switzerland), T Fullin (Switzerland), T Planzer (Switzerland), P Stadler (Switzerland); 12/7/89 R Lampard (f) (UK), W Rutkiewicz (f) (Poland); 13/7/89 X Erro (Spain), JM Goñi (Spain), A Ibarguren † (Spain); **18/7/90** R Lang (Germany); 19/7/90 P Pustelnik (Poland); 26/7/90 H Endo (Japan), Y Endo (f) (Japan), T Suzuki (Japan), O Tanabe (Japan); 30/7/90 L García (Chile), F Luchsinger (Chile), M Purto (Chile); 31/7/90 I Valle (Chile); 1/8/90 V Dewaele (Belgium), R Muys (Belgium); **28/6/91** C Haymoz (Switzerland), P Menu (Switzerland), Ali Mohammad (Pakistan), F Thurlir (Switzerland); 19/7/91 Han Sang-Kuk (S Korea), Kim Chang-Seon (S Korea), Kim Su-Hong (S Korea), You Seok-Jae (S Korea); 20/7/91 Cho Jae-Chul (S Korea), Han Young-Jun (S Korea), Jang Sang-Gi (S Korea), Lee Young-Soon (S Korea), Park Eul-Gyu (S Korea); **18/7/92** G Beggio (Italy), L Cárdenas (Mexico), G Figueroa (Mexico), R González (Mexico), V Lauthier (f) (Italy), J Pracker (Germany), G Schmieder (Germany), A Velázquez (Mexico), H Wittmann (Germany); 20/7/92 S Hasholzner (Germany), R Steffens (Germany); 23/7/92 M Benavent (Spain), G Dinev (Bulgaria), M Miranda (Spain), R Rachev (Bulgaria), JC Recio (Spain); **7/7/93** 3 Koreans from a team of 6 led by Yi Seok-Yang; 8/7/93 2 Koreans from a team of 6 led by Yi Seok-Yang; 21/7/93 R Gocking (USA), T Kieser (USA), C Landon (USA); 22/7/93 R Broshears (USA), C Mace (USA), SA McPherson (UK); 22/7/93 I Ogasawara (Japan), K Ohbayashi (Japan), M Sato (Japan), T Tanigawa (Japan), H Nagakubo (Japan), Y Yoshida (Japan) S Ridge/E Ridge; 28/7/93 L Hall (USA), A Lwow (Poland), P Snopczynski (Poland); 29/7/93 G Fuller jr (USA), C Haugh (USA); 31/7/93 L Bancells (Spain), J Barrachina (Spain), H Konishi (Japan), T Nagao (f) (Japan), A Serra (Spain), M Todaka (Japan), T Tonsing (USA), Y Yamanoi (Japan); 16/8/93 W Angermeier (Germany), P Kowalzik (Germany), M Putz (f) (Germany), H Wohlwent (Liechenstein); **1/8/94** O Banar (Ukraine), R Coffman (USA), BA Evensen (Norway), C Fox (f) (USA), J Giban (USA), T Hargis (USA), S Mordre (Norway), E Tryti (Norway); 2/8/94 J Garrido (Spain), JL Hurtado (Spain), JC Llamas (Spain), P Nicolás (Spain), C Soria (Spain), A Tapiador (Spain); **17/6/95** J Wangeler (Germany), D Porsche (Germany); 4/7/95 E Viesturs (USA); 4/7/95 C Carsolio (Mexico) SW Ridge and WSW Face to W Ridge; 7/7/95 Jawad Pirzada (Pakistan), Ali Raza (Pakistan), Nabi Raza (Pakistan), Mohammad Yousaf (Pakistan); 8/7/95 J Berbeka (Poland); 9/7/95 K Wielicki (Poland); 10/7/95 Akbu (Tibet), Bianba Zaxi (Tibet), Cering Doje (Tibet), Luoze (Tibet); 11/7/95 Daqiong (Tibet), Jiabu (Tibet), Rena (Tibet), Wangjia (Tibet); 16/7/95 M Sprutta (Poland); **24/7/96** V Terzeoul (Ukraine), Choi Byung-Soo (S Korea), Park Mu-Taek (S Korea), Ha Chang-Soo (S Korea); 28/7/96 JC Lafaille (France); 29/7/96 A Hinkes (UK), H Howkins (f) (USA), I Otxoa de Olza (Spain), R Portilla (Spain), JC Tamayo (Spain); **8/7/97** Danawang Dorje (Nepal), F Goto (Japan), Y Ogata (Japan); See Note 1; 10/7/97 R Naghavi (Iran), H Najarian (Iran), HR Owlanj (Iran); 13/7/97 P Egillor (Spain), A Gianotti (USA), E Havlick (USA), M Hernández (f) (Spain), K Knox (f) (USA), G Roach (USA); 14/7/97 Ang Chhiri (Nepal), Ang Gylazen (Nepal), Y Baba (Japan), A Bukreev (Kazakhstan), S Ezuka (Japan), S Iwazaki (Japan), T Miyazaki (Japan), H Nazuka (Japan), Norbu (Nepal), T Tajima (Japan), T Watanuki (Japan); See Note 1; 15/7/97 B Ader (USA), F Barth (USA), T Bradác (Czech Rep), K Gardyna (Poland), L Kamarád (Czech Rep), V Mysik (Czech Rep), G Neptune (USA), P Plsek (Czech Rep), M Reparaz (Spain), C Soles (USA), K Volz (USA), J Zurawski (Poland); 16/7/97 Ang Dorje (Nepal), G Cotter (NZ), D Mantle (USA), Um Hong-Gil (S Korea); 17/7/97 L Drda (Czech Rep), S Falcón (Spain), R Fernández (f) (Spain), Z Hruby (Czech Rep), J Kardhórdó (Czech Rep), C Mauduit (f) (France), J Natkinski (Poland), N Orviz (Spain), M Palacky (Czech Rep), Park Young-Seok (S Korea), together with two female S Koreans, L Pavlik (Czech Rep), Q Ruiz de la Peña (Spain), J Rybicka (Czech Rep), J Smid (Czech Rep), D Zulaski (Poland); 20/7/97 B Batko (f) (Poland), E Margueritte (France/Poland), R Pawlowski (Poland); 21/7/97 J Gozdzik (Poland), J Maselko (Poland), P Pustelnik (Poland) (2nd); **7/7/98** J Martínez (Spain), JA Martínez (Spain); 9/7/98 F Blanco (Spain), R Blanco (Spain), RF Brown (Australian), J Brunner (Austria), F Criado (Spain), J Davies (UK), D Hamilton (UK), A Hinterplattner (Austrian), M Leuprecht (Austria), S McIvor (UK), Ali Raza (Pakistan) (2nd), J Reynders (Belgium), S Stacey (UK), S Thorburn (USA), P Walters (Australia); 22/7/98 P Guggemos (Germany), Jin Hyun-Ok (f) (S Korea), H Rickert (f) (USA), B Zeugswetter (Austria) together with 6 Japanese from the 'Silver Tortoise' team of climbers aged 47–61 led by K Ikeda (including K Ikeda, T Ishikawa, Y Nezu and T Watanabe (f) and two younger Japanese who were filming the expedition) and Rajab Shah (Pakistan), Qurban Mohammad (Pakistan), Hashil Shah (Pakistan), Mehrban Shah (Pakistan) and two other porters; 25/7/98 E Bolda (f) (Austria), B Saxinger (Austria), H Weiss (f) (Austria); 26/7/98 M Gioroianu (Romania), A Gionvanetti (Italy); 29/7/98 F Facchinetti (Italy), J Hancock (USA), E Jensen (USA); 31/7/98 B Zacahry (USA); 5/8/98 Y Anciaux (France), A Delade (f) (France), CP Blondot (France), JF Janvier (France), C Mirmand (France), F Odine (f) (France), E Rambaud (France); 12/8/98 R Larrandaburu (France); **9/7/99** O Cadiach (Spain), S Corta (Spain), N Duró (f) (Andorra), P Garcés (Spain), P Goñi (Spain), D

Hamilton (UK) (2nd), C Jones (NZ), A Lock (Australia), I Ollé (Spain), LM Picabea (Spain), Ali Raza (Pakistan) (3rd), J Reketa (Spain), O Ribas (Andorra), Shakoor Ali (Pakistan), X Zubieta (Spain) 10/7/99 A Blanc (Italy), Cho Hyung-Gyu (S Korea), Choi Byoung-Woo (S Korea), Kim In-Kie (S Korea), C Kuntner (Italy), Lee Sang-Bae (S Korea), W Niclevicz (Brazil); 29/7/99 L Boucher (France), H Ponce de Leon (Mexico), R Real (f) (Spain), W Schmidt (Austria), C Tudela (Spain), F Wolf (Austria), W Zohrer (Austria); 31/7/99 JL Arnald (France), P Melani (France); 3/8/99 H D'Aubarede (France), M Guillemette (f) (France), Mehrban Shah (Pakistan) (2nd); 8/8/99 M Argeles (France), JC Stalla (France); 19/8/99 E Bladé (Spain), C Feld-Boskoff (f) (USA), X González (Spain), S García-Prades (Spain), J Rhoads (USA), G Ritchi (USA)

Note 1: In 1997 the large Japanese Gunma team attempted Broad Peak, Gasherbrum I and Gasherbrum II with supporting Sherpas. The whole team was divided into three groups each of which attempted two of the peaks. The Gasherbrum II groups were:

(and attempting Gasherbrum I = Team A)

H Nazuka (leader), Y Baba, S Ezuka, S Iwazaki and T Miyazaki together with Ang Gyalzen and Ang Chhiri

(and attempting Broad Peak = Team C)

F Goto (leader), R Hoshino, A Nozawai, Y Ogata, T Tajima, T Terada, T Watanuki together with Danawang Dorje and Norbu

On 8 and 14 July these groups are said to have put 11 Japanese and 4 Sherpas on the summit. This number is not consistent with the names quoted, which show 2 Japanese and 1 Sherpa summitting on 8 July, and 7 Japanese and 3 Sherpas on 14 July. It is likely that the names quoted are correct and that only 9 Japanese and 4 Sherpas summitted.

Broad Peak ascent data

All climbs via first ascent route (W Spur to Broad Col, then over forepeak to summit ridge) except where stated. NB Some of the ascents below may only have been to forepeak. Definitive details on summit reached are occasionally hard to obtain.

9/6/57 H Buhl (Austria), K Diemberger (Austria), M Schmuck (Austria), F Wintersteller (Austria); **8/8/77** K Noro (Japan), T Ozaki (Japan), Y Tsuji (Japan); **4/6/78** (Y Seigneur (France), G Bettembourg (France) – Bettembourg did not reach the main summit and claims that Siegneur also failed); **5/8/81** M Hernández (Spain), E Pujol † (Spain); **23/7/82** G Bachler (Austria), R Bärtle (Germany), P Gloggner (Germany), H Kirchberger (Germany), K Lewankowski (Germany), W Lösch (Austria), W Sucher (Austria); 30/7/82 J Kukuczka (Poland), W Kurtyka (Poland); 2/8/82 Sher Khan (Pakistan), R Messner (Italy), Nazir Sabir (Pakistan); **25/6/83** J Afanassieff (France), R Baxter-Jones (UK), A Parkin (UK), A Rouse (UK); 28/6/83 D Scott (UK), S Sustad (USA); 30/6/83 F Graf (Switzerland), E Loretan (Switzerland), K Palmowska (f) (Poland), M Ruedi (Switzerland), S Wörner (Switzerland); 2/7/83 P Morand (Switzerland), JC Sonnenwyl (Switzerland); **26/6/84** M Barrios (Colombia), T Hägler (Switzerland), A Reinhard (Switzerland), L Deuber (Switzerland), R Franzl (Austria); 27/6/84 G Calcagno (Italy), A Enzio (Italy), T Vidoni (Italy); 13/7/84 G Calcagno (Italy) (2nd), K Hub (Germany), R Schleypen (Germany), T Vidoni (Italy) (2nd); 14/7/84 W Fiut (Poland), J Majer (Poland), R Pawlowski (Poland), K Wielicki (Poland), H Zebrowski (Germany); 17/7/84 J Kukuczka (Poland) (2nd), W Kurtyka (Poland) (2nd) (W Ridge of N Peak, then along ridge to Central Peak, down to Broad Col and along first ascent route); 18/7/84 K Diemberger (Austria) (2nd), J Tullis (f) (UK); 8/8/84 R Joswig (Germany), R Schauer (Austria); **31/7/85** Fayyaz Hussain (Pakistan), Zahid Mahmood (Pakistan), Jawad Pirzada (Pakistan); 12/8/85 S Kashu (Japan), R Nishizutsumi (Japan), T Shigehiro (Japan), T Toyama (Japan), J Wada (Japan), M Yamamoto (Japan); **20/6/86** B Chamoux (France) (probably to forepeak only), S Dorotei (Italy), M Giacometti (Italy), M Moretti (Italy); 21/6/86 B Fuster (Switzerland), M Prechtl (Germany), D Wellig (Switzerland), P Wörgötter (Austria), R Zemp (Switzerland); 22/6/86 J Rakoncaj (Czech Rep); 23/6/86 H Koch (Germany), J Labisch (Germany); 7/7/86 S Hölzl (Austria), F Schreinmoser (Austria); 28/7/86 B Biščak (Slovenia), V Groselj (Slovenia); 29/7/86 T Cesen (Slovenia), R Fabjan (Slovenia), T Jamnik (Slovenia), A Stremfelj (Slovenia), M Stremfelj (f) (Slovenia); 30/7/86 P Kozjek (Slovenia); 4/8/86 D Jelinčič (Slovenia), S Karo (Slovenia), M Lenarcic (Slovenia), M Stangelj (Slovenia); 16/8/86 B Agnew (Australian), J Chester (Australian), P Cullinan (Australian), M Dacher (Germany), K Fassnacht (Germany), G Hupfauer (f) (Germany), S Hupfauer (Germany), P Lambert (Australian), T McCullagh (Australian), M Rheinberger (Australian), J Van Gelder (Australian), Z Zaharias (Australian); **29/5/87** N Joos (Switzerland); 7/6/87 B Honegger (Switzerland), E Müller (Switzerland); **27/6/88** S Matsumoto (f) (Japan), K Sakai (Japan), M Sasaki (Japan), K Shimakata (Japan); 1/8/88 C Schranz (Italy); 12/8/88 J Saito (Japan), M Taniguchi (Japan); 9/9/88 L Gómez (Spain), C Vallès (Spain); **12/7/91** K Hayasaka (Japan), I Ogasawara (Japan), M Sato (Japan), T Tanigawa (Japan), T Yawata (Japan); 16/7/91 R Beadle (UK), R Blanco (Spain), A Hinkes (UK); 30/7/91 M Abe (Japan), H Konishi (Japan), T Nagao (f) (Japan), Y Yamanoi (Japan), T Yoshimura (Japan); **2/8/92** D Hambly (UK), S McKee (USA), C Lacatusu (Romania), E Martínez (Spain), P Rodríguez (Spain), A Tapiador (Spain); **6/7/93** M Bianchi (Italy), C Kuntner (Italy); 7/7/93 A Brugger (Italy), S De Leo (Italy), T Heymann (Germany), F De Stefani (Italy); 21/7/93 Sarwar Khan (Pakistan), Rajab Shah (Pakistan), M Tamura (Japan), N Tsuji (Japan); 29/7/93 A Blanc (Italy), S Martini (Italy), Nima Temba (Nepal), Ali Raza (Pakistan); 24/8/93 S Ezuka (Japan), K Mino (Japan), T Nakamura (Japan), O Tanabe (Japan), K Uchida (Japan); **21/6/94** H Kammerlander (Italy); 2/7/94 G Kropp (Sweden); 3/7/94 A Busca (Italy); 9/7/94 C Carsolio (Mexico) (In two stages, going over Pt 6230 then WSW Spur to first ascent route then directly up headwall to forepeak); 10/7/94 E Morin (France); 23/7/94 B Christensen (Denmark), P Ibarbia

(Spain), J Mathorne (Denmark); **12/7/95** M Abrego (Spain), J Casimiro (Spain), Lee Jeong-Hyun (S Korea), J Oiarzabal (Spain), Park Hyun-Jae † (S Korea), Park Sin-Young (S Korea), Um Hong-Gil (S Korea); 20/7/95 T Hattori (Japan), T Kitamura (Japan), M Todaka (Japan) (W Ridge of N Peak, then along ridge to Central Peak, down to Broad Col and along first ascent route); 13/8/95 Ang Dorje II (Nepal), J Alzner (USA), S Ballard (f) (Canada), M Boyle (USA), Dawa Galjen (Nepal), J Ehrlich (Germany), C Feld-Boskoff (f) (USA), S Fischer (USA), P Goldman (USA), R Hess (USA), J Leupold (Germany), Lobsang Jangbu (Nepal), A Lish (USA), I Loredo (Mexico), A McKinlay (Canada), W Soroka (Poland), M Walter (German), F Ziel (USA); 23/7/96 Han Dong-Keun † (S Korea), Yang Jae-Mo † (S Korea); **13/7/97** A Iñurrategi (Spain), F Iñurrategi (Spain); 16/7/97 See Note 1; 19/7/97 J Coburn (USA), B Montoya (USA), M Schneider (Germany), T Tonsing (USA); 20/7/97 See Note 1; 7/8/97 A Lock (Australia); 9/8/97 JC Cirera (Spain); **5/7/98** R Bösch (Switzerland), K Kobler (Switzerland), I Vallejo (Ecuador); (29/7/98 E Escoffier (France), P Bessiéres (France) last seen on the summit ridge); **16/7/99** R Dujmovits (Germany), G Hafele (Austria), Qudrat Ali (Pakistan), J Rozas (Spain), S von Roth (Switzerland); 17/7/99 P Fessler (Austria), E Koblmüller (Austria)

Note 1: In 1997 a large team from the Japanese Gunma Mountaineering Association attempted Broad Peak, Gasherbrum I and Gasherbrum II with supporting Sherpas. The whole team was divided into three groups each of which attempted two of the peaks. The Broad Peak groups were:

(and attempting Gasherbrum I = Team B)

M Sato (leader), M Fukumoto, H Iwazaki, K Nakajima, S Yanase, H Yoshida and F Yoshida (f) together with Dawa Tsering and Arjun Tamang

(and attempting Gasherbrum II = Team C)

F Goto (leader), R Hoshino, A Nozawai, Y Ogata, T Tajima, T Terada and T Watanuki together with Danawang Dorje and Norbu

On 16 July 6 of the 7 Japanese from Team B, together with both Sherpas climbed Broad Peak. On 20 July F Goto and Y Ogata, together with Danawang Dorje, all from Team C, climbed Broad Peak. Other sources indicate that in total 3 Japanese and 2 Sherpas reached the main summit (probably including the three climbers of 20 July), the other 3 Japanese reaching the forepeak.

First ascent of subsidiary summit
Central Summit: 28/7/75 K Glazek (Poland), M Kesicki † (Poland), J Kulis (Poland), B Nowaczyk † (Poland), A Sikorski † (Poland) Main Summit first ascent route to Broad Col, then along the Central Summit's N Ridge

Gasherbrum I ascent data

5/7/58 A Kauffman (USA), P Schoening (USA) Roch Arête (IHE Spur) to SE Ridge; **10/8/75** P Habeler (Austria), R Messner (Italy) NW Face; 11/8/75 R Schauer (Austria), H Schell (Austria), H Zefferer (Germany) First ascent route; **8/7/77** A Stremfelj (Slovenia), N Zaplotnik (Slovenia) W Ridge; **15/7/80** M Barrard (France), G Narbaud (France) Over Hidden Sud to SE Ridge; **3/8/81** H Azuma (Japan), K Shimotori (Japan) First ascent route; **22/7/82** M Dacher (Germany), S Hupfauer (Germany), G Stürm (Germany) NW Face (German variant); 27/7/82 Mohammad Ali (Pakistan), JP Ollagnier (France), S Saudan (Switzerland), D Semblanet (France), MJ Valençot (f) (France) First ascent route; **23/6/83** E Loretan (Switzerland), M Ruedi (Switzerland) NW Face (Swiss variant); 24/6/83 P Morand (Switzerland), JC Sonnenwyl (Switzerland) NW Face (Swiss variant); 23/7/83 J Kukuczka (Poland), W Kurtyka (Poland) SW Face; 22/8/83 V Arnal (Spain), I Cinto (Spain), J Escartín (Spain), J López (Spain), L Ortas (Spain), A Ubieto (Spain) W Ridge of Hidden Sud, then French 1980 route; **28/6/84** H Kammerlander (Italy), R Messner (Italy) (2nd) NW Face (variant of German route); **9/6/85** P Camozzi (Italy), A Da Polenza (Italy) NW Face to the right (south) of Habeler-Messner line, then as Habeler-Messner; 19/6/85 G Calcagno (Italy), T Vidoni (Italy) NW Face (German variant); 22/6/85 B Chamoux (France), E Escoffier (France) NW Face (Swiss variant); 15/7/85 G De Federico (Italy) NW Face (Swiss variant); **2/8/86** O Shimizu (Japan), K Wakutsu (Japan) Japanese Couloir; 3/8/86 A Berthélemy (France), C Janin (f) (France), R Joswig (Germany) NW Face (Swiss variant); 17/8/86 R Lang (Germany) (but only to a point about NW Face 20m below the summit) (German variant); 18/8/86 A Bührer † (Switzerland), K Kölleman (Austria), M Lorenz (Austria), G Schmatz (Germany) NW Face (German variant); **20/6/88** R Gálfy (Slovakia), I Urbanovic (Slovakia) Japanese Couloir; 20/6/88 F Soltes (Slovakia) NW Face (Habeler-Messner); 12/7/89 Tsindi Dorje † (Nepal), H Endo (Japan), Y Endo (f) (Japan) Japanese Couloir; **16/7/90** T Katayama (Japan), E Pankiewicz (f) (Poland), Park Hyeok-Sang (S Korea), Ali Raza (Pakistan), W Rutkiewicz (f) (Poland), R Shah (Pakistan), T Yamane (Japan) Japanese Couloir; 26/7/90 G Derycke (France), A Estève (France), W Ridge; Y Tedeschi (France), Mohammad Ullah (Pakistan), M Yousaf (Pakistan); 29/8/90 P Bergeron (Canada), C Bernier (Canada) W Ridge; **25/8/92** Nazir Sabir (Pakistan), Rajab Shah (Pakistan) (2nd), Mehrban Shah (Pakistan) Japanese Couloir; **7/6/93** H Bumann (Switzerland), N Joos (Switzerland), M Stoller (Switzerland) Japanese Couloir; **3/8/94** S Martini (Italy), S De Leo (Italy), F De Stefani (Italy), G Valle (Italy) Japanese Couloir; 4/8/94 F Lévy (France), JM Meunier (France), J Pratt (UK), M Staehelin (Switzerland) Japanese Couloir; 12/8/94 A Collins (UK), H Inaba (Japan), M Saeki (Japan), M Taniguchi (Japan), D Mazur (USA) Japanese Couloir; **5/7/95** M Car (Slovenia), I Tomazin (Slovenia) Japanese Couloir; 15/7/95 J Berbeka (Poland), C Carsolio (Mexico), E Viesturs (USA), K Wielicki (Poland) Japanese Couloir; 16/7/95 K Lasa (Spain), T Lete (Spain), LM López (Spain) Japanese Couloir; **10/7/96** D Carroll (UK), J Doyle (UK), A Hinkes (UK), A Hughes (UK), S Hunt (NZ), I Otxoa de Olza (Spain), J Tomás (Spain) Japanese Couloir; 11/7/96 M Alvarez † (Spain), A Juez (Spain) Japanese Couloir; 30/7/96 Y Karahashi (Japan), T Kawanabe (Japan), H Masaki (Japan) Japanese Couloir; 31/7/96 JC Lafaille (France) NW

Face (Swiss variant); **7/7/97** Ang Gyalzen (Nepal), Ang Chhiri (Nepal), Y Baba (Japan), S Ezuka (Japan), S Iwazaki (Japan), H Nazuka (Japan), T Miyazaki (Japan) Japanese Couloir See Note 1; 9/7/97 Ali Raza (Pakistan) (2nd), J Åkerstrom (Sweden), J Bermúdez (UK), R Foulquier (UK), D Hamilton (UK), Z Hruby (Czech Rep), Ji Hyun-Ok (f) (S Korea), J Kardhordo (Czech Rep), K Kimura (Japan), V Mysik (Czech Rep), J Oiarzabal (Spain), Park Young-Seok (S Korea), M Ryden (Sweden), S Silhan (Czech Rep), Um Hong-Gil (S Korea) Japanese Couloir; 13/7/97 Han Wuang-Yong (S Korea) Japanese Couloir; 15/7/97 A Giovannetti (Italy), J Gozdzik (Poland), J Maselko (Poland), R Pawlowski (Poland), O Piazza (Italy), P Pustelnik (Poland)Japanese Couloir; 16/7/97 T Kitamura (Japan), H Konishi (Japan), Rozi Ali (Pakistan) Japanese Couloir; **9/7/98** B Christensen (Denmark), J Mathorne (Denmark), M Granlien (Denmark) Japanese Couloir; 10/7/98 D Porsche (Germany) Japanese Couloir; 29/7/98 Y Iwasita (Japanese) Japanese Couloir; 31/7/98 J Martínez (Spain), JA Martínez (Spain) Japanese Couloir; **3/7/99** A Blanc (Italy), C Kuntner (Italy) Japanese Couloir; 17/7/99 P Garcés (Spain), A Lock (Australia) Japanese Couloir; 18/7/99 4 Koreans led by Lee Byong-Chui Japanese Couloir

Note 1: In 1997 a large team from the Japanese Gunma Mountaineering Association attempted Broad Peak, Gasherbrum I and Gasherbrum II with supporting Sherpas. The whole team was divided into three groups each of which attempted two of the peaks. The Gasherbrum I groups were:

(and attempting Broad Peak = Team B)

M Sato (leader), M Fukumoto, H Iwazaki, K Nakajima, S Yanase, H Yoshida and F Yoshida (f) together with Dawa Tsering and Arjun Tamang. No members of this ream summitted on Gasherbrum I.

(and attempting Gasherbrum II = Team A)

H Nazuka (leader), Y Baba, S Ezuka, S Iwazaki and T Miyazaki together with Ang Gyalzen and Ang Chhiri

These groups are said to have put 5 Japanese and 2 Sherpas on the summit. All of these were from Team A on 7 July.

Dhaulagiri ascent data

All climbs by first ascent route (North-east Ridge) except where stated.

13/5/60 K Diemberger (Austria), P Diener (W Germany), E Forrer (Switzerland), A Schelbert (Switzerland), Nawang Dorje Sherpa (Nepal), Nima Dorje Sherpa (Nepal); 23/5/60 M Vaucher (Switzerland), H Weber (Switzerland); **20/10/70** T Kawata (Japan), Lhakpa Tenzing Sherpa (Nepal); **12/5/73** L Reichardt (US), J Roskelley (US), Nawang Samden Sherpa (Nepal); **4/5/76** S Simoni (Italy), G Zortea (Italy); **10/5/78** T Kobayashi (Japan), T Shigeno (Japan) SW Ridge; 11/5/78 Y Kato (Japan), S Shimizu (Japan), Ang Kami Sherpa (Nepal), H Yoshino (Japan) SW Ridge; 19/10/78 A Abe (Japan), T Miyazaki (Japan), H Tani (Japan); 21/10/78 Nawang Yonden Sherpa (Japan), S Suzuki (Japan), N Yamada (Japan) SE Ridge; **12/5/79** I Aldaya (Spain), F J Garayoa (Spain), G Plaza (Spain), J Pons (Spain), Ang Rita Sherpa (Nepal); **13/5/80** H Von Kaenel (Switzerland), F Luchsinger (Switzerland), Ang Rita Sherpa (2nd) (Nepal); 14/5/80 J Buholzer (Switzerland), R Monnerat (Switzerland), H J Mueller (Switzerland), H Zimmermann (Switzerland); 17/5/80 H Bergstaller (Austria), H Eitel (W Germany), F Graf (Switzerland), M Ruedi (Switzerland); 18/5/80 M Ballmann (Switzerland), R Bleiker (Switzerland), Mingma Gyalzen Sherpa (Nepal), Lhakpa Gyalzen Sherpa (Nepal); 19/5/80 S Burkhardt (Switzerland), J Mueller (Switzerland), Ang Rita Sherpa (3rd) (Nepal); 18/5/80 W Kurtyka (Poland), A MacIntyre (UK), R Ghilini (Italy), L Wilczynski (Poland) E Face to NE Ridge; **17/5/81** A Burgess (UK), A Burgess (UK); 2/6/81 H Kamuro (Japan); **5/5/82** P Cornelissen (Belgium), R Van Snick (Belgium), Ang Rita Sherpa (4th) (Nepal); 6/5/82 M Lefever (Belgium), Ang Jangbo Sherpa (Nepal), J Van Hees (Belgium), L Vivijs (f) (Belgium); 17/10/82 T Mitani (Japan), J Tanaka (Japan); 18/10/82 K Komatsu (Japan), Y Saito (Japan), N Yamada (2nd) (Japan) N Face to NW Ridge; 13/12/82 A Koizumi (Japan), Wangchu Sherpa (Nepal); **18/5/83** M Gardzielewski (Poland), J Jezierski (Poland), T Laukajtys (Poland), W Otreba (Poland); 11/11/83 A de Blanchaud (France), M Metzger (France); **4/10/84** P Beghin (France), J N Roche (France) SW Ridge; 23/10/84 K Jakes (Czech), J Simon † (Czech), J Stejskal (Czech) W Face to NW Ridge; 21/1/85 A Czok (Poland), J Kukuczka (Poland); 15/5/85 H Kammerlander (Italy), R Messner (Italy); 8/12/85 E Loretan (Switzerland), P-A Steiner (Switzerland), J Troillet (Switzerland) E Face to NE Ridge; **3/5/86** G Härter (W Germany), J Hirtreiter (W Germany); 5/5/86 W Larcher (Austria), W Odenthal (W Germany), L Pfleging (W Germany); 16/10/87 91 K Calhoun (f) (US), J Culberson (US), C Grissom (US); 2/12/87 M Batard (France), Sungdare Sherpa (Nepal); 4/12/87 M Kregar (Yugoslavia), I Tomazin (Yugoslavia) E Face to NE Ridge; **6/10/88** Z Demjan (Czech), Y Moiseev (USSR), K Valiev (USSR) SW Pillar; 14/11/88 Choi Tea-Sik (S Korea), Da Gombu Sherpa (Nepal), Wangel Sherpa (Nepal); **11/5/89** S Martini (Italy), F De Stefani (Italy); 18/5/89 J Inhoeger (Austria); **24/4/90** K Wielicki (Poland); 11/5/90 I Baeyens (f) (Belgium), R Dujmovits (W Germany); 30/9/90 K Kobler (Switzerland), H Roesti (Switzerland), P Rothlisberger (Switzerland), H Willi (Switzerland); 5/10/90 H Kindle (Liechtenstein), M Morales (Spain), C Pfistner (Switzerland), M Sanchez (Argentina); 6/10/90 S Silhan (Czech), L Sulovsky (Czech); 9/10/90 F Kimura (f) (Japan), Dawa Tshering Sherpa (Nepal), Changba Norbu Sherpa (Nepal), M Yasuhara (f) (Japan); 19/10/90 G Lowe (US); 31/10/90 C Buhler (US), D Makauskas † (USSR), Nuru Sherpa (Nepal); **10/5/91** A Bukreev (USSR), R Chaibullin (USSR), Y Moiseev (2nd) (USSR), V Suviga (USSR), A Tselishev (USSR) W Face; 13/5/91 V Khrichtchaty (USSR), Z Mizambekov (USSR), V Prisjashny (USSR), A Savin (USSR), A Shegai (USSR) W Face; 14/5/91 S Smidt (Denmark); 2/10/91 J Corominas (Spain); 11/10/91 T Nakajima (Japan), Keepa Sherpa (Nepal), K Yokoyama (Japan); **30/4/92** A Guliaev (Russia), V Kohanov (Russia), P Kouznesov (Russia), N Smetanin (Russia), N Zacharov (Russia); **11/5/93** R Allen (UK),

S Bogomolov (Russia), S Efimov (Russia), A Lebedikhim (Russia), Vi Pershin (Russia), I Plotnikov (Russia), B Sedusov (Russia) N Face; 30/5/93 Akbu (Tibet), Daqimi (Tibet), Daqiong (Tibet), Cering Doje (Tibet), Jiabu (Tibet), Luoze (Tibet), Rena (Tibet), Bianba Zaxi (Tibet), Wangjia (Tibet); 6/10/93 B Chamoux (France), M Koseki (Japan), A Nozawai (Japan); 9/10/93 V Gustafsson (Finland); 10/10/93 T Kirsis (Latvia), I Pauls (Latvia), I Zauls (Latvia); 11/10/93 S Sekiya (Japan), Mingma Tshering Sherpa (Nepal), J Vanmarsenille (Belgium), Dorje Sherpa (Nepal); **25/9/94** P-V Amaudruz (Switzerland), M Bianchi (Italy), C Kuntner (Italy); 26/9/94 S Albasini (Switzerland), R Caughron (US), J Garcia (Portugal), J Gozdzik (Poland), P Pustelnik (Poland); 27/9/94 P Boven (Switzerland), N Gex (Switzerland), O Roduit (Switzerland); 27/9/94 Y Ueno (Japan), Man Bahadur Tamang (Nepal), Pa Nima Sherpa (Nepal); 1/10/94 K Ikeda (Japan), T Ishikawa (Japan), M Konishi (Japan), K Netsu (Japan), Nima Dorje Sherpa (Nepal), Nima Temba Sherpa (Nepal), Wangchu Sherpa (Nepal), T Watanabe (f) (Japan); 3/10/94 R Henke (US), B Johnson (US), R Taylor (US); 4/10/94 R Green (US); 11/10/94 G Lebedev (Ukraine), I Svergun (Ukraine); 13/10/94 I Chaplinsky (Ukraine), T Ena (f) (Ukraine), V Gorbach (Ukraine), V Lanko (Ukraine), G Tchekanova † (f); **9/5/95** A Akinia (f) (Russia), D Botchkov (Russia), J Outeshev (Russia), V Solomatov (Russia); 14/5/95 V Bashkirov (Russia), V Khilko (Russia), S Krylov (Russia), E Popov (Russia); 15/5/95 C Carsolio (Mexico); 17/5/95 R Schmid (f) (Switzerland), M Kofler (Switzerland); 19/5/95 U Braschler (Switzerland), G Ennemoser (Austria), A Hammann † (Germany), N Joos (Switzerland); 4/10/95 M Sawada (Japan), Dawa Sherpa (Nepal) (2nd); 6/10/95 Hasta Bahadur Gurung (Nepal), H Tawaraya † (Japan); 6/10/95 K Narusaki (Japan), Pemba Rinzi Sherpa (Nepal), Arjun Tamang (Nepal), K Ueda (Japan); 6/10/95 T Hayashi (Japan), K Kondo (Japan), I Kuwabara (Japan), Pemba Tshering Sherpa (Nepal), Mingma Nuru Sherpa (Nepal), S Takeda (Japan); 8/10/95 A Bukreev (2nd) (Kazakhstan), R Rachev (Bulgaria); 9/10/95 T Tontchev (Bulgaria); 11/10/95 O Gigani (Georgia), B Gujabidze (Georgia); 12/10/95 B Dimitrov (Bulgaria), A Shinkarenko (Belarussia), I Vialenkova (f) (Belarussia); 14/10/95 Z Horozov (Bulgaria), D Vassilev (Bulgaria); 15/10/95 T Fritsche (Austria), R Mattle (Austria); **1/5/96** Um Hong-Gil (S Korea), Ngati Sherpa (Nepal); 5/5/96 A Georges (Switzerland); 17/10/96 B Vos (claim disputed) (Holland) E Face to NE Ridge; 21/10/96 A Mochnikov (Russia); 5/11/96 E Koblmueller (Austria), M Koblmueller (Austria), F Schmollngruber (Austria), H Schuetter (Austria); **27/4/97** Han Wuang-Yong (S Korea), Kim Hun-Sang (S Korea), Park Young-Seok (S Korea), Kaji Sherpa (Nepal); 25/5/97 A Lock (Australia), M Rogerson (Australia), Z Zaharias (Australia); 31/5/97 T Kitamura (Japan), H Konishi (Japan), Gyalzen Sherpa (Japan); 24/9/97 J Martinez (Spain), J A Martinez (Spain), J Rodriguez (Spain); 25/9/97 N Petkov (Bulgaria); **22/5/98** A Iñurrategi (Spain), F Iñurrategi (Spain), J Oiarzabal (Spain); 23/5/98 G Lacen (Slovenia), M Marence (Slovenia); 24/5/98 T Jakofcic (Slovenia), P Meznar (Slovenia); 26/5/98 T Bello (Italy), T Golob (Slovenia), J Meglic (Slovenia), D Polenik (Slovenia), M Vielmo (Italy); 30/9/98 H Kudo (Japan), T Saito (Japan), Y Shimoma (Japan), T Sugiyama (Japan), Pasang Gyalzen Sherpa (Nepal), Man Bahadur Tamang (2nd) (Nepal), Tul Bahadur Tamang (Nepal); **4/5/99** V Gustafsson (2nd) (Finland), E Viesturs (US); 16/10/99 T Strausz (Austria), P Walters (Australia)

Shisha Pangma ascent data

All ascents via the original Chinese line (Shisha Pangma Glacier/E Cwm/N Ridge/NE Face traverse) unless otherwise stated. NB Some of the ascents below may only have been to the Central summit. Definitive details on summit reached are occasionally hard to obtain.

2/5/64 Chen San (China), Cheng Tianliang (China), Doje (Tibet), Mima Zaxi (Tibet), Sodnam Doje (Tibet), Wang Fuzhou (China), Wu Zongyue (China), Xu Jing (China), Yungden (Tibet), Zhang Junyan (China); **7/5/80** M Dacher (Germany), W Schaffert (Germany), G Sturm (Germany), F Zintl (Germany); 12/5/80 S Hupfauer (Germany), M Sturm (Germany); 13/10/80 E Obojes (Austria), E Putz (Austria); **30/4/81** Jiabu (Tibet), Rhinzing Phinzo (Tibet), J Tabei (f) (Japan); 28/5/81 R Messner (Italy), F Mutschlechner (Italy) Chinese route variant; **28/5/82** R Baxter-Jones (UK), A MacIntyre (UK), Central Couloir; D Scott (UK) SW Face; 10/10/82 M Hara (Japan), H Komamiya (Japan), H Konishi (Japan); 12/10/82 T Chiba (Japan), M Ohmiya (Japan), M Tomita (Japan); **29/4/83** U Schum (Germany), J Walter (Germany), M Walter (f) (Germany); 30/9/83 M Browning (USA), C Pizzo (USA), G Porzak (USA); **6/5/84** D Howe (USA), M Jenkins (USA), D Kelley (USA), M Wingert (USA); 8/5/84 S Creer (USA), M Lehner (USA); **10/5/85** O Gassler (Austria), L Schausberger (Austria), P Wörgötter (Austria); 12/5/85 G Heinzel (Austria), B Kendler (Austria), A Vedani (Switzerland), T Schilcher (Austria), H Wagner (Austria), J Wangeler (Switzerland), M Wettstein (Switzerland); 16/5/85 G De Marchi (Italy); 19/5/85 L Karner (Austria), H Schell (Austria), T Schilcher (Austria) (2nd); 14/9/85 O Oelz (Austria), M Ruedi (Switzerland), D Wellig (Switzerland); **20/5/87** M Perry (NZ), M Whetu (NZ); 18/9/87 E Avila (f) (Mexico), C Carsolio (Mexico), R Navarrete (Ecuador), W Rutkiewicz (f) (Poland), R Warecki (Poland) Central Summit traverse (ie Central Summit to Main Summit); 18/9/87 A Hajzer (Poland), J Kukuczka (Poland) W Ridge to Central Summit to Main Summit; 19/9/87 A Hinkes (UK), S Untch (USA) Central Couloir N Face to Central Summit to Main Summit; 1/10/87 S Nagy (Hungary), A Ozsváth (Hungary); 8/10/87 Z Balaton (Hungary), J Csíkos (Hungary), L Várkonyi (Hungary), L Vörös (Hungary); **13/5/88** T Fischbach (Germany), K Gürtler (Austria), P Konzert (Austria) Central Summit traverse; 14/5/88 B Kullmann Germany), A Metzger (Germany), H Og (f) (Germany), K Schuhmann (Germany); 17/5/88 H Bärnthaler (Austria), T Hochholzer (Germany), W Kunzendorf (Germany), J Schütz (Germany), D Thomann (Germany); 5/9/88 P Berhault (France), F De Stefani (Italy), S Martini (Italy); 6/9/88 G Daidola (Italy), D Givois (France), P Negri (Italy); 24/10/88 T Saegusa (Japan), N Yamada (Japan), A Yamamoto (Japan); **16/4/89** K Suzuki (Japan), S Takamura (Japan), Y Tsuji (Japan); 19/10/89 P Kozjek (Slovenia), A Stremfelj (Slovenia) Central Buttress, SW Face; 20/10/89 F Bence (Slovenia), V Groselj (Slovenia) Right side of SW Face to S Ridge; **12/5/90** E Fries (Germany), J Neuhauser (Austria); 13/10/90 P Expósito (Spain), F

Gan (Spain), F Pérez (Spain), R Santaeufemia (Spain), J Martínez † (Spain), MA Vidal (Spain); **20/5/91** O Dörrich (f) (Germany), T Fritsche (Austria), G Härter (Germany), K Hecher (Austria), D Porsche (Germany), H Schnutt (Austria); 8/10/91 Kim Chang-Seon (S Korea), Central Couloir Kim Jae-Soo (S Korea) SW Face; **4/10/93** O Cadiach (Spain), M de la Matta (Spain), Central Couloir C Mauduit (f) (France) SW Face; 6/10/93 M Bianchi (Italy), P Pustelnik (Poland) Central Buttress, SW Face; 7/10/93 K Wielicki (Poland) SW Face between British route (1982) and Slovenia route (1989); **7/5/94** Akbu (Tibet), Bianba Zaxi (Tibet), Cering Doje (Tibet), Daqiong (Tibet), Daqimi (Tibet), Jiabu (Tibet) (2nd), Luoze (Tibet), Rena (Tibet), Wangjia (Tibet) Central Summit traverse; 28/5/94 J Kirschmer (Germany) Central Summit traverse; 4/10/94 N Kekus (UK) Central Summit traverse; **29/4/95** E Loretan (Switzerland) Central Summit traverse; 12/5/95 R Ratteit (Germany) Central Summit traverse; 13/5/95 P Kotronaros (Greece), Sonam (Nepal) Central Summit traverse; **1/5/96** N Joos (Switzerland) Central Summit traverse; 1/5/96 S Sluka † (Slovakia), P Sperka (Slovakia); 21/5/96 B Hasler (Switzerland), C Zinsli (Switzerland); 30/5/96 P Guggemos (Germany), M Schneider (Germany); 11/10/96 J Bereziartua (Spain), A Iñurrategi (Spain), F Iñurrategi (Spain) SW Face (British Route); **24/5/97** P Brill (Germany), R Dujmovits (Germany), K Hub (Germany), A Neuhuber (Austria), G Osterbauer (Austria), F Prasicek (Austria); **6/5/98** S Andres (Italy), C Kuntner (Italy); 14/5/98 A Blanc (Italy), M Comandona (Italy), V Niclevicz (Brazil) Central Summit traverse; 10/10/98 J Oiarzabal (Spain), C Stangl (Austria) Central Couloir SW Face; 11/10/98 I Querejeta (Spain) Central Couloir SW Face

In addition to the multiple ascents of the main summit given above, 14 climbers have made multiple ascents of the central summit. Mingma Norbu (Nepal) has made three ascents of the central summit. A Hinkes (UK), E Loretan (Switzerland) and Cering Doje (Tibet) have also climbed both the main and central summits on separate occasions.

First ascent of subsidiary summit
Central Summit: 29/4/83 G Schmatz (Germany) Main Summit's first ascent route with a final variant to the lower summit. Schmatz had become separated from his companions and was unaware that he was making the first ascent, believing he was climbing the main summit. Only on descent did he discover that he had climbed a different summit.

List of books of the first ascents of the 8,000ers

Annapurna
Annapurna by Maurice Herzog, Jonathan Cape, 1952.
There is also an account of the climb in *Conquistadors of the Useless* by Lionel Terray, Gollancz, 1963

Everest
The Ascent of Everest by John Hunt, Hodder and Stoughton 1953
There are accounts of the expedition and summit climb in Ed Hillarys autobiography *High Adventure* and Tenzings biography *Man of Everest*

Nanga Parbat
Nanga Parbat by Karl M Herrligkoffer, Elek Books, 1954
There is also an account of the expedition and summit climb in *Nanga Parbat Pigrimage* by Hermann Buhl

K2
Ascent of K2 by Ardito Desio Elek Books, 1955

Cho Oyu
Cho Oyu by Herbert Tichy, Methuen, 1957

Makalu
Makalu by Jean Franco, Jonathan Cape, 1957

Kangchenjunga
Kangchenjunga, The Untrodden Peak by Charles Evans

Manaslu
Manaslu 1954–6 by Japanese Alpine Club, The Mainichi Newspapers, 1956

Lhotse
The Everest-Lhotse Adventure by Albert Eggler, George Allen and Unwin, 1957

Gasherbrum II
Weisse Berge – Scwarze Menschen by Fritz Moravec, Österreichischer Bundesverlag, Wien, 1958. Not translated into English

Broad Peak
Broad Peak 8,047m: Meine Bergfahrten mit Hermann Buhl by Marcus Schmuck, Verlag Das Bergland Buch Salzburg/Stuttgart, 1958. Not translated into English. There is also an account of the climb in *Summits and Secrets* by Kurt Diemberger, George Allen and Unwin, 1971

Gasherbrum I
A Walk in the Sky by Nicholas Clinch, The Mountaineers, 1982

Dhaulagiri
The Ascent of Dhaulagiri by Max Eiselin, Oxford University Press, 1961

Shisha Pangma
Limited accounts of the climb can be found in *Mountaineering* in China by Guozi Shuddian, Foreign Language Press, Beijing 1965 and *Footprints on the Peaks: Mountaineering in China* by Zhou Zheng and Liu Zhenkai, Cloudcap, 1995

Picture Credits

All reasonable efforts have been made by the Publisher to trace the copyright holders of the photographs contained in this publication. In the event that a copyright holder of a photograph has not been traced, but comes forward after the publication of this edition, the Publishers will endeavour to rectify the position at the earliest opportunity.

All photographs researched and supplied via Mountain Camera Picture Library. Copyright in the photographs belongs to the following:
Front cover photograph: Doug Scott, Shisha Pangma. Back cover photographs: Doug Scott, Everest; Colin Monteath/Mountain Camera, K2; John Cleare/Mountain Camera, Kangchenjunga; Ian Evans/Mountain Images, Lhotse; John Cleare/Mountain Camera, Makalu; David D Keaton/Mountain Camera, Cho Oyu; John Cleare/Mountain Camera, Dhaulagiri; John Cleare/Mountain Camera, Manaslu; Doug Scott, Nanga Parbat; Darryn Pegram/Hedgehog House, Annapurna; Guy Cotter/Hedgehog House, Gasherbrum I; Doug Scott, Broad Peak; John Cleare/Mountain Camera, Shisha Pangma; Alan Hinkes, Gasherbrum II. Back flap photographs: l Tony Oliver, r Alastair Stevenson/Mountain Camera

The positions of the photographs on each page of the book are indicated as follows: t = top, l = left, c = centre, r = right, b = bottom
Duke of Abruzzi, National Mountain Museum, Turin 19 bc, 88 tl; Rick Allen 172, 188 tl; Peter Aschenbrenner 22 br; Bill Atkinson/Hedgehog House 161 br, 176; Pat Barrett/Hedgehog House 28, 184, 185 br; Fritz Bechtold 22 tl; Chris Bonington 36, 38, 39, 56 tl, 65 tl, 79, 90–91, 98 tl, tr; Brenner 21 br; Joe Brown/Mountain Camera 124, 126; Hermann Buhl 169 tl; John Cleare/Mountain Camera 20 tl, 37, 41, 48 br, 51 cr, 62, 65 tr, 72 tl, 82, 88 br, 89 t, 105 tr, 122, 128 tl, 142 tr, 149 b, 151 tl, tr, 174, 190, 195; Nick Clinch 178 tl, br, 179; Guy Cotter/Hedgehog House 3 br, 5 tl, 7, 50, 51 tl, 146, 160 bl, 163 bc; Henry Day/British Nepalese Army, Annapurna Expedition 26, 29, 30 cl, bl, 32 cr, 32–33, 33 tl, 34, 35 tr, c, 40; Kurt Diemberger Collection 78, 149 tr, 164 bl, 170 l, c, 171 (K2 – The Endless Knot), 186 br, cl (The Kurt Diemberger Omnibus); Grant Dixon/Hedgehog House 45 t, 46 bl, 85 cr, 151 tr; Ian Evans/Mountain Images 4 b, 42, 52, 89 br, 100, 102, 104 tr, 185 tr, 192, 194; John Fowler/Mountain Camera 199 tr, 200; German Himalaya Foundation, Munich 21 tc; Jon and Lindsay Griffin 115 c; Hall and Ball Archive/Hedgehog House 86 c, 90 tr, 103, 120 tl, 151 cl, 154 c, 188 br; David Hamilton 4–5, 9 br, 94 bl, 95, 156, 161 tl, bl, cr, 162 br, 163 t, 164 tl, 180 tc, 181; Bunshow Hattori 87, 91 cr; Karl Herligkoffer 66 bl, c; Alan Hinkes 2 l, br, 9 tl, 12–13, 65 cr, 67, 68 bl, c, 69, 76, 77, 80, 84, 85 tr, 86 tl, 92–93, 94 br, 97 tl, br, 99, 112, 121 tl, br, 139 tl, 143, 150 b, tr, 154 tr, 155, 159, 162 t, 165, 166, 173, 177 cl, cr, 180, 196; T. Imanishi (Mainichi Newspapers) 140 cl, 141 tl; Indian Air Force/Mountain Camera 148 bc; Tadashi Kajiyama/Mountain Camera 66 tl, 70, 71 tr, 72 cr, 73, 74 bl, 75 tl, 81; David D Keaton/Mountain Camera 3 bl, 54–55, 58, 60, 104 tl, 105 cl, 106 bl, tr, 107 bc, tr, 108 tc, b, 109 br, 110, 111; Col. Kumar 127 bl, tr; Louis Lachenal 31; Alex McIntyre 202 c; Helen Mason 14, 15, 18, 19 cl, 65 br; Colin Monteath/Mountain Camera 46 tl, 53, 56 cr, 59 bl, 185 cr, 189, 193; Fritz Moravec 158; Patrick Morrow 13br, 48 tl, 59 tr, 96, 119, 120 c, 132, 135 b, 152–153, 168, 182, 187; Mountain Camera Archive 19; Hugh Van Noorden/Hedgehog House 8, 44, 45 b; Steve Razzetti 11, 30 t, 30–31, 46 cl, 61 cl, 117 tr, 125, 128 cl, 133 tl, bc, 134, 136, 138, 144, 145l; Ernst Reiss 148 cr; RGS 20 br, 21 bl; RGS/The Times 49 tl; Marcus Schmuck 117 b; Doug Scott 25 tl, 61 tr, 64 bl, 71 bl, 75 b, 118 tc, 129 tr, b, 130 bl, 131 cl, tr, 169 tr, 199 cr, 202 bl; Eric Shipton 24 tl, bc; Will Siri 114; Dick Smith/Hedgehog House 118–119; Pip Smith/Hedgehog House 3 tr, 47; Frank Smythe 23; Geoff Spearpoint/Hedgehog House 135 tl; Lionel Terray 116; Herbert Tichy 104 bl; HW Tilman 25 tl; Jon Tinker 46 tr; Stephen Venables 6, 10 tc, b, 57, 203; Takayoshi Yoda (Mainichi Newspapers) 140 bc, 141 br, 142 bl; Zhou Zheng/Liu Zhenkai 198

Captions for the chapter openers are as follows: pp.26–27 This is the still rarely climbed northern flank of Annapurna. Finding a safe route through this jumble of ice and rock is no easy task; pp.42–43 The formidable northern flank of Everest from the Rongbuk Monastery as the first expedition would have seen it; pp.62–63 From this aerial viewpoint high over the Babusar Pass, Nanga Parbat –the westernmost peak of the Himalayan chain – dominates the skyline; pp.82–83 The spectacular first sight of K2 up the Godwin-Austen Glacier from the south near Concordia; pp.100–101 The southern – Nepalese – flank of Cho Oyu walls the head of the long Ngozumpa Glacier; pp.112–113 Among the old moraines near the snout of the Barun Glacier below the south-west face and south-east ridge of Makalu; p.122–123 A classic view of Kangchenjunga – 'the Five Treasures of the Great Snows' – from the south-west on the Milke Danda Ridge. The summits right to left are Kangchenjunga South, Kangchenjunga and Kangchenjunga West (Yalung Kang). On the far left is the formidable peak of Jannu; pp.136–137 Manaslu is seen westwards from Sama Gompa high in the Buri Gandaki valley; pp.146–147 Lhotse towers beyond the South Col where several tents and climbers can be picked out in this interesting view from Everest's south-east ridge; pp.156–157 The distinctive south-west and south-east spurs of Gasherbrum II fall towards the icefall of the South Gasherbrum Glacier; Gasherbrum III (7,952m//26,089ft) is on the left; p.166–167 Expedition porters rest near K2 Base camp below the formidable north eastern flanks of Broad Peak; pp.174–175 Gasherbrum I or 'Hidden Peak' seen from the south-west near Base Camp; pp.182–183 Wreathed in eerie morning mists, the southern flanks of Dhaulagiri are seen from the south-east on the famous viewpoint of Poon Hill; pp.196–197 Baggage yaks at Advanced Base Camp at about 5,640m (18,500ft) among the moraines of the Yabukangala Glacier